The Marrano Phenomenon

The Marrano Phenomenon

Jewish 'Hidden Tradition' and Modernity

Special Issue Editor

Agata Bielik-Robson

MDPI • Basel • Beijing • Wuhan • Barcelona • Belgrade

MDPI

Special Issue Editor
Agata Bielik-Robson
The University of Nottingham
UK

Editorial Office
MDPI
St. Alban-Anlage 66
4052 Basel, Switzerland

This is a reprint of articles from the Special Issue published online in the open access journal *Religions* (ISSN 2077-1444) from 2018 to 2019 (available at: https://www.mdpi.com/journal/religions/special_issues/marrano).

For citation purposes, cite each article independently as indicated on the article page online and as indicated below:

LastName, A.A.; LastName, B.B.; LastName, C.C. Article Title. *Journal Name* **Year**, *Article Number*, Page Range.

ISBN 978-3-03897-904-3 (Pbk)
ISBN 978-3-03897-905-0 (PDF)

This special issue of *Religions* has been supported by the NCN Opus 13 Grant: /The Marrano Phenomenon: The Jewish 'Hidden Tradition' and Modernity/, registered in the OSF system as 2017/25/B/HS2/02901.

Contents

About the Special Issue Editor

Agata Bielik-Robson is a Professor of Jewish Studies at the University of Nottingham and a Professor of Philosophy at the Polish Academy of Sciences. She has published articles in Polish, English, German, French, and Russian on philosophical aspects of psychoanalysis, romantic subjectivity, and the philosophy of religion (especially Judaism and its crossings with modern philosophical thought). Her publications have been included in the following books: The Saving Lie: Harold Bloom and Deconstruction (in English, Northwestern University Press, May 2011); Judaism in Contemporary Thought: Traces and Influence (coedited with Adam Lipszyc, Routledge 2014); Philosophical Marranos: Jewish Cryptotheologies of Late Modernity (Routledge 2014); and Another Finitude: Messianic Vitalism and Philosophy (Bloomsbury 2019).

Preface to "The Marrano Phenomenon"

What we call here the 'Marrano phenomenon' is still a relatively unexplored fact of modern Western culture: the presence of the borderline Jewish identity, which avoids clear-cut cultural and religious attribution, but nevertheless exerts significant influence on modern humanities: philosophy, literature, and art. Our aim, however, is not a historical study of the Marranos (or conversos), i.e., the mostly Spanish and Portuguese Jews of the 15th and 16th century, who were forced to convert to Christianity, but were suspected of retaining their Judaism 'undercover'; such an approach already exists and has been developed within the field of historical research (e.g., Roth 2001; Yerushalmi, 1981). We rather want to apply the 'Marrano metaphor' to explore the fruitful area of mixture and crossover which allowed modern thinkers, writers, and artists of Jewish origin to enter the realm of universal communication—without, at the same time, making them relinquish their Jewishness, which they subsequently developed as a 'hidden tradition'.

The 'Marrano metaphor' was used by Hannah Arendt for the first time, who, in her essay "The Jew as Pariah: A Hidden Tradition", implicitly compared the great European thinkers and writers of Jewish origin to the Marranos who were permitted to enter the realm of universality only on the condition of concealing their particular 'bias':

> When it comes to claiming its own in the field of European arts and letters, the attitude of the Jewish people may best be described as one of reckless magnanimity. With a grand gesture and without a murmur of protest it has calmly allowed the credit for its great writers and artists to go to other peoples, itself receiving in turn the doubtful privilege of being acclaimed father of every notorious swindler and mountebank. True enough, there has been a tendency in recent years to compile long lists of European worthies who might conceivably claim Jewish descent, but such lists are more in the nature of mass graves for the forgotten than of enduring monuments to the remembered and cherished. Useful as they may be for purposes of propaganda (offensive as well as defensive), they have not succeeded in reclaiming for the Jews any single writer of note unless he happened to have written specifically in Hebrew or Yiddish. Those who really did most for the spiritual dignity of their people, who were great enough to transcend the bounds of nationality and to weave the strands of their Jewish genius into the general texture of European life, have been given short shrift and perfunctory recognition [...]. These great figures have been left perforce to the tender mercies of assimilationist propagandists [...]. No one fares worse from this process than those bold spirits who tried to make of the emancipation of the Jews that which it really should have been – an admission of Jews as Jews to the ranks of humanity, rather than a permit to ape the gentiles or an opportunity to play a parvenu. (Arendt 2007, p. 275; my emphasis)

Arendt depicts the 'Marrano' condition of the 'Jewish genius' forced to play the role of a parvenu in mostly negative terms: its 'reckless magnanimity', which gives generously from the sources of Judaic tradition without expecting any recognition in return, meets nothing but doubt, scorn, and suspicion. In result, all that is 'worthy' becomes immediately assimilated by the host tradition, which sees itself as the only universal one—and all that is 'doubtful' falls back on the deficiencies of Jewish particularism. The

'Marrano' emancipation does not allow an admission of 'Jews as Jews'; it only allows for a clandestine game of imitation, which sometimes leaves a secret trace—or signature—to be readable only by those in the same predicament. Yet, although Arendt's diagnosis is bitterly true, it also omits a chance to look at the 'Marrano phenomenon' in a more affirmative way: not just as the condition imposed 'perforce' by the outsiders, but also as a new model of internally assumed subidentity which indeed "transcends the bounds of nationality and weaves the strands of the Jewish genius into the general texture of European life". If Arendt rightly complains that so far, all the 'lists of worthies', enumerating the instances of the 'Jewish genius', managed to reclaim for Jewishness only those who "happened to have written specifically in Hebrew or Yiddish", our project aims to meet this complaint. Thanks to the 'Marrano' methodology of reading the texts of culture as performing 'hidden tradition', the list of those thinkers and writers who can be 'reclaimed for Jewishness' can be significantly expanded. But this is not the only—or even most important—goal. The main purpose of the 'Marrano' project is to offer a new view on modern culture, which can be accessed only via the Marrano perspective: a 'Marrano modernity' which transforms our approach to the problem of universal communication as well as the modern—secret, hidden—life of religious traditions which survive in the process of secularization, although merely in the form of 'traces'.

The Marrano Phenomenon

It is not at all an accident that the first Jewish thinkers who entered the world of modern Western thought were mostly of Marrano origin: not just the radical followers of Sabbatai Zevi, the 17th century 'false Messiah' who proclaimed the messianic revolution and, having converted to Islam and Christianity, left Jewish ghettos of Eastern and Southern Europe to spread the revolutionary news (which eventually led some of them to take active part in the French Revolution); but also such eminent individuals as Uriel da Costa, Isaac la Peyrere, and Baruch Spinoza. The last one of this great philosophical line, Jacques Derrida, openly claimed to be "a sort of marrane of French Catholic culture" (Derrida 1993, p. 170), and this declaration prompted him to articulate this peculiar experience of the 'third language'—to denote a type of thinker, like himself, who will never break through the Joycean 'jew-greek, greek-jew' confusion, but nonetheless will try to turn it to his advantage; that is, not to approach the 'Alexandrian mixture' (ibid.) of idioms as a curse of dispersion and contamination, but as a chance to get out of the circle of a self-enclosed identity, and thus to repeat the liberating gesture of the Sabbatians.

The privileged site of this liberation—of leaving the ghetto of rigid cultural and religious identity—is modern philosophy offering the 'philosophical Marranos' (Bielik-Robson, 2014) an opportunity of 'free thinking': according to Yirmiyahu Yovel, it was precisely Spinoza who embraced this possibility for the first time, thus paving the way for his future imitators (Yovel, 1989). There are many ways to approach the phenomenon of 'Jewish Philosophy', but perhaps the most convincing way focuses on the linguistic aspect of this problem. For the medieval Jewish philosophers, such as Saadia Gaon or Moses Maimonides, thinking according to Aristotle or Plotinus was mostly a matter of appropriation which would leave the essential structure of Jewish thought intact. Yet for these modern thinkers so often already acquainted with the Marrano experience, 'philosophizing' meant a confrontation with a radically foreign linguistic medium, which would issue in a wholly new reflection on the language of philosophy; first of all, putting in doubt its alleged and self-professed universality. Always accused of particularism, the Jewish thinkers started to turn tables and throw the same objection against the Western philosophy which formulated it in the first place.

However, they rarely do it openly under Jewish auspices. Franz Rosenzweig bitterly protested when his ambitious philosophical project, *"The Star of Redemption"*, landed as a 'Jewish book' on the same shelf with other pious and educational Bar Mitsvah presents for young boys. He feared that his effort to create *neues Denken*, 'new thinking', would be thwarted the moment it opened itself defencelessly to the objection of nonuniversality. Walter Benjamin's celebrated image of the puppet and the dwarf, in which the former represents the public philosophical discourse and the latter stands for hidden—'ugly and wizened'—theology, goes even deeper in the 'Marrano' direction by encoding the strategy of deliberate secrecy and ruse; once fully revealed, the Jewish theological message would lose all its conceptual force (Benjamin, 2003). Still later, Max Horkheimer, asked during the interview for the German radio about the shortest possible definition of the Frankfurt School, answered immediately that it was a 'Judaism undercover' (Horkheimer 1985–1996, p. 403). And, finally, this Marrano tendency culminates in Jacques Derrida, where it becomes a secret du Polichinelle, a non-secret secret secretly known by everybody, where the phrase 'but don't tell anyone' (used by Derrida in *Archive Fever*) ironically turns into positive, though still indirect, communication.

New Universalism

Derrida is particularly useful for our analysis, mostly because of his openly declared linguistic promiscuity. By discarding faithfulness to any monolingual tradition, he stands firmly on the post-Babelian grounds of the dispersion of idioms which can approach universality only horizontally: not by assuming a transcendent and superior meta-position, but by engaging in clashes, interchanges, and mixtures. There is, therefore, no such thing as a homogenous universal language. Yet, universality can nonetheless be approached by "marrying the speeches of strangers" (Reznikoff, 2005), which completes the broken whole on the horizontal level without usurping the God-like point of view hovering over the clamour of differences. As Walter Benjamin says in "The Task of the Translator" (the essay which serves Derrida as the canvas of his Babel variations; Benjamin, 1996), the only possible strategy of universalization rests on the awareness of particularity of all languages which then lend themselves to the practices of translation (Übersetzung) and completion (Ergänzung). The universal can only be made out of the patchwork of mutually strange idioms which are forced into 'marriage' by the translator.

Walter Benjamin, also positing himself within the line of philosophical Marranos, shows how the true universality emerges only through the clashes—or 'marriages'—of two or more idioms which at first seem separate, yet soon reveal their insufficiency and their inherent tropism towards 'completion' (Ergänzung). In order to approach universality, therefore, languages must infect one another and leave their traces in the 'language of the other', thus disturbing the illusion of its linguistic purity and autarchy, which, as Benjamin emphasizes, is indeed nothing but illusion from the start. The truly universal language can never be spoken as such, i.e., as one homogenous idiom; neither Greek philosophy nor Christian religion can undo the 'catastrophe' of Babel which resulted in the scattering and particularization of languages. However, the Babel predicament of linguistic dispersion does not need to be interpreted as a curse, at least as long as translation is still possible; though there is no meta-language, which could raise us above the clamor of differences, men are still capable of 'marrying the speeches of strangers' and thus complete the broken whole on the horizontal level. They do not reach universality 'vertically'; i.e., by renouncing or growing out of their particularity; this way was clearly rejected by the parable of the tower of Babel, which was supposed to hover above the plane of human differences. Yet, the temptation to repeat the Babel mistake persists, and the unreflected universality of philosophy, which claims to be a transparent language of every man as animal rationale, or of Pauline Christianity, which claims to know 'neither Jew, nor Greek', but only one general 'God's child', is a good illustration of this persistence. The only way to reach universality is horizontally, never pretending to abandon the realm of particularity; the way leading through a completing translation, making various languages 'clash', 'marry', and 'weave into' one other. This openness towards 'translatability' (Tradierbarkeit) reveals the heterogeneous element present in all languages: their wishful gesturing towards universal communication. In this manner, the Marrano strategy offers an alternative practice of universalization, conceived as an 'after-Babel project' to mend the broken whole from within, horizontally, without assuming the lofty abstract position of a general meta-language, but through the effort of bi- or multilinguality, and also without overstressing the catastrophic nature of the Babelian dispersion of tongues. Dispersion, leading to particularization, is not a curse in itself: on the contrary, by making every idiom and every tradition 'incomplete', it prevents them from assuming an absolutist hegemonic power. This Marrano linguistic messianicity is thus very far from the Pauline 'foundation of universalism' (Badiou, 2003), which attempts to undo the 'Babel catastrophe' by raising the Babel tower again, this time in the form of the 'neither Jew, nor Greek' universal discourse that would later give rise to the philosophical meta-language of the Hegelian 'grand narrative', serving as a blueprint for all modern systems of 'imperial' universalization (Buck-Morss, 2009). The road to universality does not lead through the purification of 'neither–nor', but through 'marriages'; that is, confusions, conjunctions, and contaminations of the Joycean 'jew-greek, greek-jew'; and not through immediate abstractions, which want to distil a purely universal human nature, spirit, or reason; but through collisions of differences, which, far from being an unwelcome disturbance, constitute a healthy life of all particular traditions.

The 'Marrano phenomenon', therefore, is not a negative experience, which would deplore the loss of a fixed religious and cultural identity brutally destroyed by modern revolution. Modernity merely exacerbated the processes of contamination present in all traditions—a universal condition the modern Marranos simply discovered first and in a particularly traumatic manner. Testing the 'Marrano hypothesis' in a positive manner leads the authors of this collection to ponder on the 'new strategy of universalization', which is the first goal of our project. They understand 'the wish to be a Marrano' (Cixous 2007, p. 55) as being synonymous with the desire to universalize one's own message, which, when expressed too openly and idiomatically, immediately becomes accused of particularism and thus is denied access to the proper conversation of mankind. It is a wish, which means that it cannot safely rely on either universal substance ('human nature') or equally universal formal procedures ('human reason'); it is, in a way, only a wish, formulated within one's particular framework of thought, to gesture towards universalization as a task and goal-horizon of one's linguistic practice. As such, the wish—as well as the plea—for the practice of dynamic universalization that would replace the static dualism of abstract universality, on the one hand, and content-full particularity, on the other, is still a valid case in late modern humanities. If the contributors to this volume, therefore, choose the Benjaminian–Derridean tactic of 'the task of the translation', it is because it offers a chance to step beyond this crippling dualism and offer a practice of universalization which is not based on a belief in a ready-made universal essence of human being, but on the conviction that particular traditions are all inherently open to mutual communication. It is not a simply normative position, but also a descriptive one: if cultures should change their archives into 'open access' (Buck-Morss 2009, p. 127), it is because they can, for they already are oriented towards the possibility of translation. This is precisely 'the task of the translation': "The translator must expand and deepen his language by means of the foreign language" (Benjamin 1996, p. 262). When cultures and religions translate into one another, they do not compromise their differences—they, in the spirit of Arendtian 'magnanimity', merely help each other to survive.

The Antinomian Specter

The Marrano 'free thinking' aiming at the freedom of universal communication also has another important dimension, which we want to explore as our second goal: the cryptotheological one. Just as 'the wish to be Marrano' indicates a liberty to cross borders of particular identities, it also expresses a desire to engage in religious thinking which would not be bound or wholly determined by the dogmas of any orthodoxy. More than that, as a truly liberated theological speculation, it often goes against the rigid law of the tradition—and thus becomes antinomian. The fascination with which so many 20th century diasporic Jews approached the 'Marrano theology' as a living hypothesis is mostly indebted to Gershom Scholem's not purely historical work devoted to presenting it as a still actual phenomenon within the Jewish world. Thanks to Scholem, the Marrano idea acquired a rich symbolic potential, linked to the messianic ferment of the Sabbatians, of whom, as Scholem has shown, a large number were Marranos. The most famous of them, Abraham Miguel Cardozo, wrote an entire treatise, "Magen Abraham (The Shield of Abraham)", devoted to the messianic significance of Marranism, in which the seeming vice of secrecy cunningly turns into a virtue of deeper truth. For, says Cardozo, the true faith can only be hidden.

The Marrano rule, therefore, reads: only what is concealed can be an authentic faith; what becomes positively revealed is nothing but an official religion. Hence, the real faith needs to protect its subversive–antinomian character by avoiding open pronouncement and articulation. It was thus mostly due to this Marrano influence that Sabbatai Zwi's conversion to Islam became almost immediately interpreted as an act of free will, demonstrating that only 'hidden faith' can be genuine: inner, unconcerned, and unhindered by official norms and religious institutions. Cardozo believed the Marranos to be the truly chosen people, 'the righteous remnant of a true Israel', destined to save the world and spread the divine message through all the nations by subverting their pagan institutions from within. Sabbatai, therefore, not only followed the way of those reflexive Marranos, but also justified it and showed its deeper spiritual meaning; now, to convert to Christianity or Islam meant to be able to expand the messianic practice of 'lifting the sparks' from the realm of kelipot, the 'broken vessels', and to penetrate the darkest regions of the created world (such as Islam or Roman-Catholic 'Edom'). To choose faith in a hidden way meant a deliberate effort to keep the antinomian impulse opposed to all oppressive laws of this world, both secular and religious, from contamination with a fallen reality; to maintain it in a form of a hovering 'specter', distanced from any direct positive realization. It is precisely here that the 'hidden tradition' loses all persecutory and negative aspects of deficiency and becomes a positive mode of living, believing, and thinking.

Yet, as I have already indicated, the true contemporary champion of the Marrano strategy, cunningly playing with the 'revealment and concealment' of the secret antinomian specter, is Jacques Derrida. Derrida performs his Marrano identification, but, being a 'true' Marrano (which, as Scholem rightly observes, is a paradox in itself), he never—or very rarely—talks about it openly. There are but few instances in his work where he alludes to his 'secret'. In *Archive Fever*, Derrida divulges his Marrano sympathies while referring to Yerushalmi's essay on the photographs of the 'last Marranos' in Portugal made by Frederic Brenner. While watching the portraits of the Portuguese Marranos, Yerushalmi asks: "But are they really the last?", and this question receives a kind of oblique reply from Derrida: no, they are not; this secret tradition will continue. And not only does he assert that he has "always secretly identified" with the Marrano heritage (immediately adding in the joking parenthesis: "but don't tell anyone"), but also drags into this heritage of Jewish secrecy the father of psychoanalysis himself by saying that "this crypto-Judaic history greatly resembles that of psychoanalysis after all" (Derrida 1996, p. 70). Then, on the next few pages, Derrida gives us a brief prolegomenon to any future Marrano strategy, which he identifies with messianicity, "radically distinguished from all messianism" (ibid., p. 72): a universal form of Jewishness which, in distinction to the 'terminable Judaism' of the rabbinic formation, remains interminable:

It can survive Judaism. It can survive it as a heritage, which is to say, in a sense, not without archive, even if this archive should remain without substrate and without actuality [. . .]. This is what would be proper to the 'Jew' and to him alone: not only hope, not only a 'hope for the future,' but 'the anticipation of a specific hope for the future' (ibid., p. 72).

This is what "constitutes Jewishness beyond all Judaism": "To be open toward the future would be to be Jewish, and vice versa [. . .]. In the future, remember to remember the future" (ibid., 74; 76). What therefore counts in the 'archive of Judaism' is the unique index of its imperative to remember (zakhor): it is not past-oriented towards the acts of grounding and legitimating a supposedly distinct 'Jewish identity', but future-oriented, open to a common worldly futurité. 'The wish to be a Marrano' transforms the religious message of the Judaic tradition from within: even if it practices 'Judaism undercover', its thrust is different: universal and messianic.

Method and Synopsis

In the recently started discussion on the paradoxes of the Marrano nonidentitarian subidentity and its relation to modern philosophical 'free thinking', there emerged two basic approaches: the earlier one, proposed by Gershom Scholem, which favors the conjunctive model, and the later one, proposed by Yovel, which prefers the disjunctive approach. According to Scholem, the Marrano subversion of rigid identities consists in being 'and–and': the Marrano religiosity (as presented by Miguel Abraham Cardozo) constitutes an amalgam of Christian and Jewish motives, which cannot be easily dissected into separate ingredients. The 'third language', therefore, turns out to be irreducible to the sum of its parts: the innovation issuing from the Judeo-Christian conflation is not only creative, but also opens a new realm of universalization, in which Jewish and Christian influences comingle without repressing and dominating one another (Maciejko, 2011). According to Yirmiyahu Yovel, on the other hand, who focused mostly on Spinoza as the 'paradigmatic Marrano', the Marrano novelty consists in the disjunctive evasion of 'neither–nor'—neither Jew nor Greek; neither Jewish nor Christian—which not so much creates an abstract universal identity as rather a void of identity: a permanent refusal to become this or that, or to choose one's cultural form of belonging (Yovel, 1989; 2009). And if 'free thinking' needs a space, it is delivered precisely by this very void or the radical emptying of all identitarian logic, which paves way to truly liberated—i.e., uprooted—philosophical reflection. It is, however, possible to combine these two views which seem contradictory only on the surface: in fact, the Marrano subidentity (where the prefix sub- suggests another and more complex level of identification and simultaneously a subversion of simpler models of belonging) uses both strategies, conjunctive and disjunctive, in order to combine heterogeneous influences and, at the same time, gain distance to the cultural totalities from which they derive.

There is, however, yet another approach, formulated by Leo Strauss in his *Persecution and the Art of Writing*, which the authors of this volume tend to avoid, because it focuses only on the negative— persecutory—aspect of the 'Marrano phenomenon'. According to Strauss, writers like Spinoza resorted to secrecy and concealedness primarily because of fear: they avoided the issue of 'coming out' due to the anxiety of persecution, caused by the discrepancy between their radical views and the opinion of the masses, still entrenched in their fixed cultural identities. They were, therefore, forced to convey their messages 'in between the lines' to connect with those in the similar position, capable of immediately recognizing the 'secret message' (Strauss, 1988). And although there is a lot of truth in Strauss' subtle account, it also raises controversial issues of negative 'secrecy' and 'cunning': controversial, because they very easily associate with the typically anti-Semitic accusation, levelled against those Jews who only pretend to be part of the universal Greco-Christian culture, but in reality 'smuggle in' the alien contents of their 'hidden faith'. Our goal is to counteract this negative view of the Marrano, which constitutes a significant part of late modern anti-Semitism, and replace it with a much more positive image: a Marrano whose main motivation is not fear, resentment, and revenge, but a 'magnanimous' (Arendt 2007, p. 275) wish to become universal—without, at the same time, giving up on the cultural difference and heterogeneity. The following thirteen articles present the Marrano phenomenon in modernity, starting with Spinoza and ending with Derrida, with many thinkers (Benjamin, Bloch, Adorno, Arendt, Rosenzweig, Solovyov, Levinas, and Agamben) and writers (James Joyce) in between. This is just a beginning of the project which is far from closed—it should rather be treated as an invitation to rethink the 'Marrano' subidentity as one of the legitimate forms which, in Derrida's words, 'Jewish survival' (Derrida 2002, p. 100) takes in the modern age.

References

Arendt, Hannah. 2007. The Jew as Pariah: A Hidden Tradition. In *Jewish Writings*. Edited by Jerome Kohn and Ron H. Feldman. New York: Schocken Books.

Badiou, Alain. 2003. *Saint Paul: The Foundation of Universalism*. Translated by Ray Brassier. Stanford: Stanford University Press.

Benjamin, Walter. 1996. The Task of the Translator. In *Selected Writings*. Translated by Howard Eiland and
    Michael W. Jennings. Cambridge: Harvard University Press, vol. 1.

Benjamin, Walter. 2003. On the Concept of History. In *Selected Writings*. Translated by Howard Eiland and
    Michael W. Jennings. Cambridge: Harvard University Press, vol. 4.

Bialik, Haim Nachman. 1992. *Revealment and Concealment*. Five Essays. Jerusalem: Ibis Editions.

Bielik-Robson, Agata. 2013. Modernity: The Jewish Perspective. In *New Blackfriars*. No. 1/2013. Oxford: Blackwell.

Bielik-Robson, Agata. 2014. *Jewish Cryptotheologies of Late Modernity*. Philosophical Marranos. London & New York: Routledge.

Buck-Morss, Susan. 2009. *Hegel, Haiti, and Universal History*. Pittsburgh: University of Pittsburgh Press.

Cixous, Helene. 2007. The Stranjew Body. In *Judeities. Questions for Jacques Derrida. Edited by Joseph Cohen and Raphael
    Zagury-Orly*. Translated by Bettina Bergo and Michael B. Smith. New York: Fordham University Press.

Derrida, Jacques. 1978. *Writing and Difference*. Translated by Alan Bass. Chicago: The University of Chicago Press.

Derrida, Jacques. 1993. Circumfession. In *Jacques Derrida, Jacques Derrida and Jeffrey Bennington*. Chicago: University of
    Chicago Press.

Derrida, Jacques. 1996. *Archive Fever. A Freudian Impression*. Translated by Eric Prenowitz. Chicago: The University of
    Chicago Press.

Derrida, Jacques. 2002. *Acts of Religion*. Edited by Gil Anidjar. London: Routledge.

Horkheimer, Max. 1985–1996. Die Sehnsucht nach dem ganz Anderen [Gespräch mit Helmut Gumnior 1970. In
    Gesammelte Schriften in 19 Bände, Max Horkheimer. Frankfurt am Main: Fischer Verlag, vol. 7, pp. 385–404.

Lipszyc, Adam, and Agata Bielik-Robson. 2014. *Judaism in Contemporary Thought: Traces and Influence*. London:
    Routledge.

Maciejko, Paweł. 2011. *Mixed Multitude. Jacob Frank and the Frankist Movement, 1755–1816*. Philadelphia: University of
    Pennsylvania Press.

Mendes-Flohr, Paul. 1991. *Divided Passions. Jewish Intellectuals and the Experience of Modernity*. Detroit: Wayne State
    University Press.

Reznikoff, Charles. 2005. *The Poems of Charles Reznikoff: 1918–1975*. Edited by C. Reznikoff and Jaffrey S. Cooney.
    New Hampshire: Black Sparrow Books.

Roth, Cecil. 2001. A History of the Marranos. Skokie, Illinois: Varda Books.

Scholem, Gershom. 1963a. Die Theologie des Sabbatianismus im Lichte Abraham Cardosos. In *Judaica 1*. Frankfurt am
    Main: Suhrkamp Verlag.

Scholem, Gershom. 1963b. Die Metamorphose des häretischen Messianismus der Sabbatianer in religiösen Nihilismus
    in 18. Jahrhundert. In *Judaica 3*. Studien zur Jüdischen Mystik. Frankfurt am Main: Suhrkamp Verlag.

Scholem, Gershom. 1992. Ursprünge, Widerspruche und Auswirkungen des Sabbatianismus. In Judaica 5.
    Frankfurt am Main: Suhrkamp Verlag.

Scholem, Gershom. 1995a. *The Messianic Idea in Judaism. And Other Essays on Jewish Spirituality*. New York: Schocken
    Books.

Scholem, Gershom. 1995b. Der Nihilismus als religiöses Phänomen. In *Judaica*. Frankfurt am Main: Suhrkamp Verlag,
    vol. 4.

Strauss, Leo. 1988. *Persecution and the Art of Writing*. Chicago: The Chicago University Press.

Yerushalmi, Yosef Hayim. 1981. From Spanish Court to Italian Ghetto. Isaac Cardoso: A Study in Seventeenth-Century
    Marranism and Jewish Apologetics. Seattle, London: University of Washington Press.

Yerushalmi, Yosef Hayim. 1991. *Freud's Moses. Judaism Terminable and Interminable*. New Haven: Yale University Press.

Yerushalmi, Yosef Hayim. 1996. *Zakhor. Jewish History and Jewish Memory*. Seattle & London: University of
    Washington Press.

Yovel, Yirmiyahu. 1989. *Spinoza and Other Heretics. The Marrano of Reason.* Princeton: Princeton University Press.

Yovel, Yirmiyahu. 2009. *The Other Within. The Marranos: Split Identity and Emerging Modernity.* Princeton: Princeton University Press.

Agata Bielik-Robson
Special Issue Editor

religions

MDPI

Article

Marranism as Judaism as Universalism: Reconsidering Spinoza

Daniel H. Weiss

Faculty of Divinity, University of Cambridge, Cambridge CB3 9BS, UK; dhw27@cam.ac.uk

Received: 7 December 2018; Accepted: 3 March 2019; Published: 7 March 2019

check for
updates

Abstract: This essay seeks to reconsider the relation of the universal-rational ethos of Spinoza's thought to the Jewish tradition and culture in which he was raised and socially situated. In particular, I seek to engage with two previous portrayals—specifically, those of Isaac Deutscher and Yirmiyahu Yovel—that present Spinoza's universalism as arising from his break from or transcendence of Judaism, where the latter is cast primarily (along with Christianity) as a historical-particular and therefore non-universal tradition. In seeking a potential source of Spinoza's orientation, Yovel points Marrano culture, as a sub-group that was already alienated from both mainstream Judaism and mainstream Christianity. By contrast, I argue that there are key elements of pre-Spinoza Jewish-rabbinic conceptuality and material culture that already enact a profoundly universalist ethos, specifically in contrast to more parochialist or particularist ethical dynamics prevalent in the culture of Christendom at the time. We will see, furthermore, that the Marrano dynamics that Yovel fruitfully highlights in fact have much in common with dynamics that were already in place in non-Marrano Jewish tradition and culture. As such, we will see that Spinoza's thought can be understood not only as manifesting a Marrano-like dynamic in the context of rational-philosophical discourse, but also as preserving a not dissimilar Jewish-rabbinic dynamic at the same time. This, in turn, will point to new possibilities for tracing this latter dynamic through the subsequent history of modern philosophy and modern Jewish thought.

Keywords: Spinoza; universalism; Marranos; Judaism; rabbinic; exile; ethics; philosophy; reason; Christianity; Christendom

1. Introduction

The present essay seeks to reconsider the relation of the universal-rational ethos of Spinoza's thought to the Jewish tradition and culture in which he was raised and socially situated. In particular, I seek to engage with two previous portrayals—specifically, those of Isaac Deutscher and Yirmiyahu Yovel—that present Spinoza's universalism as arising from his break from or transcendence of Judaism, where the latter is cast primarily (along with Christianity) as a historical-particular and therefore non-universal tradition. In seeking a potential source of Spinoza's orientation, Yovel points to Marrano culture, as a sub-group that was already alienated from both mainstream Judaism and mainstream Christianity. By contrast, I argue that there are key elements of pre-Spinoza Jewish-rabbinic conceptuality and material culture that already enact a profoundly universalist ethos, specifically in contrast to more parochialist or particularist ethical dynamics prevalent in the culture of Christendom at the time. We will see, furthermore, that the Marrano dynamics that Yovel fruitfully highlights, in fact, have much in common with dynamics that were already in place in non-Marrano Jewish tradition and culture.[1] As such, we will see that Spinoza's thought can be understood not only as manifesting a Marrano-like dynamic in the context of rational-philosophical discourse, but also as preserving a not dissimilar Jewish-rabbinic dynamic at the same time. This, in turn, will point to new possibilities for tracing this latter dynamic through the subsequent history of modern philosophy and modern Jewish thought.

While there have been various scholarly attempts in recent decades to identify ways in which Spinoza's thought can be understood in connection with earlier Jewish tradition, most of these studies classify the 'Jewish' elements in Spinoza by drawing links to Maimonides and to medieval Jewish philosophy more broadly, or, conversely, to kabbalistic thought.[2] By contrast, the historical Jewish-rabbinic elements that I seek to highlight, with their focus on aspects of material social structures, constitute a distinctly different type of correlation between Spinoza and Judaism, a type, moreover, which has not received much recognition in scholarship. While Deutscher and Yovel may in certain ways be less representative of contemporary research on Spinoza, their assumptions concerning the non-universalist ethos of previous Jewish tradition may be more widely held; thus, engagement with their portrayal of Spinoza helps to bring these assumptions to the surface in order to call them into question more clearly and directly.

Moreover, the non-association of Spinoza's universalism with the ethos of Judaism may be an assumption of a distinctly more recent provenance: as Willi Goetschel has emphasized, many earlier Jewish voices, from Moses Mendelssohn and Heinrich Heine, to Leo Baeck, Martin Buber, and Margarete Susman, saw important connections between Spinoza's thought and their own assertion of Judaism's universalistic dimensions.[3] However, recent scholarship has echoed and corroborated these positions only infrequently; as such, a more concrete spelling-out of historical, textual, and material dimensions of Jewish culture and thought prior to Spinoza can help to revive and illuminate some of the potential bases for these earlier intuitions.[4]

Methodologically, in arguing for the significance of previous Jewish-rabbinic culture and conceptuality for understanding Spinoza's universalism, I follow an approach similar to the one that Yovel in his argument for a 'Marrano' influence on Spinoza's thought.[5] Specifically, I do not seek to claim that the Jewish-rabbinic dynamics that I highlight constitute the sole historical-explanatory source for Spinoza's universalism; rather, I posit it as one factor alongside other factors, such as his engagement with thinkers such as Hobbes or Descartes. However, because many scholars who have discussed the relation of Spinoza's thought to Jewish tradition have associated the latter primarily with particularity rather than with universalism, it remains an understudied and overlooked factor that deserves greater attention.[6]

Likewise, my argument does not require a claim that Spinoza himself consciously viewed Jewish tradition as a source for his own universalism. Indeed, my argument does not focus on how Spinoza viewed Judaism vis-à-vis universalism, but rather on the ways in which modern scholars have understood the relation between Spinoza's universalism and previous Jewish tradition, that is to say,

---

[1] While in one sense this analysis criticizes Yovel, it also helps to uphold the legitimacy of Yovel's discernment of Marrano-like dynamics in Spinoza's thought, since such dynamics *also* turn out to be similar to 'mainstream' Jewish dynamics. This connection aids in defending Yovel's basic analysis from critics who (insofar as Spinoza himself grew up in an openly Jewish community) discount the likelihood of Marrano influence. For such criticisms, see, e.g., (Nadler 2009, pp. 502–3).

[2] For a good overview of such studies, see (Nadler 2009, pp. 494–98); for an example of a recent collection of essays that generally take such an approach, see (Ravven and Goodman 2002).

[3] See (Goetschel 2013, p. 159), as well as the scholarly references on pp. 254–55.

[4] Goetschel himself, although he does not delve into the details of previous Jewish tradition, presents Spinoza's Jewishness in relation to his universalism in a manner broadly similar to my analysis in the present essay; see (Goetschel 2004, pp. 4–7; Goetschel 2013, pp. 150–51).

[5] (Yovel 1992, pp. 205–8).

[6] By contrast, outside of scholarship on Spinoza, a number of scholars have highlighted ways in which Jewish tradition can and should be understood as containing important universalist elements, intertwined with and not simply despite the historical-particular elements of the tradition, in ways that resonate with the argument that I put forth here. See, for instance, (Levenson 1996; Schwarzschild 1990; Runesson 2000).

on scholarship's *image* of this relationship and of its two component parts. The assumption that the universal elements in Spinoza's thought must be attributed to something *other than* Jewish cultural and theological dynamics prevents a clear understanding of both Judaism and Spinoza's relation to it, and it is this assumption that I seek to challenge. Once this unwarranted assumption has been criticized, and the potential and actual universalism in pre-Spinoza Jewish tradition more recognized, it will be more possible for future scholarship to assess the degree to which Spinoza himself was aware of these connections. To be sure, it may be the case that Spinoza himself did not perceive his own universalism as stemming from the Jewish cultural dynamics that I describe below. Yet, even if Spinoza himself were to have viewed 'Judaism' largely as representing a non-universalist ethos, it may still be possible that the material-cultural and theological dynamics that I highlight played a role in shaping Spinoza's thought, regardless of Spinoza's own awareness or non-awareness thereof. In addition, shedding light on ways in which Spinoza's universalism may have roots in previous Jewish tradition can enable greater insight into underrecognized Jewish cultural dimensions of similar 'universalistic' thinkers, as well as into hitherto underrecognized universalistic dimensions of authors who wrote in a more traditional Jewish idiom.

Finally, my argument likewise does not depend on a claim that previous Jewish tradition is wholly or purely characterized by universalism; rather, there are also various 'particular' or 'particularist' elements in Jewish texts and culture. However, I argue that even when these elements are acknowledged, they can nevertheless be seen as simultaneously sitting alongside significant and practically-enacted universalist elements, without the former undermining or gainsaying the latter. Likewise, when I highlight the universalistic potential of certain aspects of the material conditions of Jewish culture, these material conditions should not be seen as necessarily or automatically giving rise to universalistic thought. Yet, I argue that these conditions can be understood as creating cultural space for a distinctive type of universalism *potentially* to arise, and furthermore, that one can find actualizations of this potential in various streams of pre-Spinoza Jewish thought and theology. Even if not all Jewish individuals actualized this potential in the same ways or to the same degree, the structures and traditions that I highlight make it possible to view the universalism of at least one individual—namely, Spinoza—in relation to these earlier cultural dynamics.

2. Deutscher and Yovel

Deutscher and Yovel both discuss the relation of Spinoza to universalism and to Judaism in similar ways, although, notably, Yovel does not cite or refer to Deutscher's earlier essay at all. Yovel does acknowledge some connections between Spinoza's ideas and previous Jewish tradition, whereas Deutscher provides less attention to such connections. By contrast, Deutscher places a focus on the lack of geographic boundedness in relation to the Jewish social-political situation out of which Spinoza emerged, while Yovel does not highlight this element. Both writers, however, treat Spinoza as drawing upon aspects of his Jewish background and as extrapolating a rational and universal outlook by taking Judaism 'to its logical conclusion'. Yet, in putting forth this portrayal, Deutscher and Yovel appear to be operating with the assumption that Judaism itself is not rational or universal, that these elements emerge specifically in the process of Spinoza's divergence from the particularity of Judaism.

Thus, Deutscher presents Spinoza as an exemplar of the pattern of "[t]he Jewish heretic who transcends Judaism" and as falling within a line of Jewish thinkers who "found Jewry too narrow, too archaic, and too constricting."[7] Here, the breadth and universalism of Spinoza's thought is achieved specifically by transcending the narrowness and particularity of Judaism. Yet, Deutscher emphasizes that Spinoza transcends not only Judaism, but Christianity as well, so that he was "not bound by the dogmas of the Christian churches, Catholic and Protestant, nor by those of the faith in which

---

[7]   (Deutscher 1968, p. 26).

he had been born."[8] While Deutscher sees the roots of Spinoza's notion of a "universal God" as stemming from Jewish tradition, he views Spinoza's resistance to the notion of linking this God to one particular community as generating a tension that ultimately led to Spinoza's break from the Jewish community.[9] Thus, he sees the unfettered universalism of Spinoza's thought, even though it has a connection to Judaism, as ultimately constituting an attitude qualitatively different from that of the Jewish tradition: "Spinoza's ethics were no longer the Jewish ethics, but the ethics of man at large—just as his God was no longer the Jewish God: his God, merged with nature, shed his separate and distinctive divine identity. Yet, in a way, Spinoza's God and ethics were still Jewish, only that his was the Jewish monotheism carried to its logical conclusion and the Jewish universal God thought out to the end; and once he had been thought out to the end, he ceased to be Jewish."[10]

In my discussion below, I will challenge the notion that Spinoza's thought is best understood as 'no longer the Jewish ethics' and that Spinoza's thinking out of Jewish monotheism 'to its logical conclusion' leads to a stance that is best understood as having 'ceased to be Jewish.' Rather, I will argue that there are elements in previous Jewish tradition that can be seen as *already* corresponding to Spinoza's rational-universalistic ethics, such that Spinoza's stance can be understood as resulting not from having 'transcended' Judaism (along with Christianity), but rather from reformulating pre-existing Jewish attitudes and orientations in a philosophical idiom. While this reformulation may differ in certain ways from some elements of earlier Jewish thought, the relation between the two will be shown to be much more complex than the sharper caesura that Deutscher presents.

Deutscher himself points to a key component of Jewish existence in Spinoza's cultural context, although he does not fully draw out its implications for understanding the relation between Jewish conceptuality and Spinoza's universalism.[11] In describing Spinoza and the other 'non-Jewish' Jewish thinkers that he highlights, Deutscher writes:

> Yet I think that in some ways they were very Jewish indeed. They had in themselves something of the quintessence of Jewish life and of the Jewish intellect. They were *a priori* exceptional in that as Jews they dwelt on the borderlines of various civilizations, religions, and national cultures. They were born and brought up on the borderlines of various epochs. Their minds matured where the most diverse cultural influences crossed and fertilized each other. They lived on the margins or in the nooks and crannies of their respective nations. They were each in society and yet not in it, of it and yet not of it. It was this that enabled them to rise in thought above their societies, above their nations, above their times and generations, and to strike out mentally into wide new horizons and far into the future.[12]

In other words, while Deutscher presents Spinoza as living on the borderlines of Jewish and Christian cultures, his statement points to the fact that *Jews in general already* lived at the borderlines of different social groupings. Jews, in their specific situation as the archetypal minority group in Christian Europe, were both part of and not part of the Christian-majority cultures in which they lived. While Deutscher emphasizes the interstitial aspect of borderline-living within a given society, we will see below that this same social situation also corresponds to a type of geographic universalism when considering the ways in which Jewish communities in different counties related to and identified with other Jewish communities, across the national boundaries and borderlines of the specific Christian-majority society in which each community lived.

Like Deutscher, Yovel also presents key aspects of Spinoza's thought, particularly his emphasis on tolerance, as arising from his going beyond both Judaism and Christianity, in relation to "leaving one

---

[8]   (Deutscher 1968, p. 27).
[9]   (Deutscher 1968, p. 28).
[10] (Deutscher 1968, p. 30).
[11] For analysis of ways in which Deutscher's personally conflicted relation to Jewish tradition may have contributed to this lack of drawing-out, see (Farber 2017).
[12] (Deutscher 1968, p. 27).

religious community without joining another."[13] He sees Spinoza, in being part of neither community, as adopting an identity "marked only by his rational powers—a universalist capacity, with no root or affiliation in a particular religious community."[14] In Yovel's presentation, it is the absence of root or affiliation in a particular religious community that makes possible the universalist capacity, with the implication that a true universalist capacity could not be found within Judaism, but only by going beyond it. To be sure, Yovel also states that certain 'Jewish motifs' such as the eternity of Israel, redemption, and covenant with God can be seen as playing a role in Spinoza's thought; but he also emphasizes that they are preserved in a specifically 'secular form', and that the universalism of Spinoza's thought is to be seen as stemming from these transformed 'secular' iterations rather than from their starting 'Jewish' forms.[15] Thus, Yovel states, "For Spinoza ... the universalization of Judaism must result in the rule of reason, that will displace *all* historical religions, those of persecutors and persecuted alike, and will abolish religious persecution altogether by granting equality and tolerance to all (including Jews who wish to remain as such)."[16] Here, Spinoza's thought arises from the universalization *of* Judaism: the transformation that starts from the non-universal stance of Judaism and arrives at the universal stance of reason. This universal orientation conceptually negates the 'historically particular' stance of Judaism, as well as Christianity, even though this conceptual negation is accompanied by a practical tolerance in the envisioned society that allows Jews to practice their historically particular traditions should they choose to continue to do so. Against Yovel's presentation, I will call into question the notion that the 'rational' affirmation of tolerance and opposition to religious persecution should be seen primarily as the result of moving beyond Judaism; rather, Spinoza's rational tolerance can been seen as linked to elements already present in the tradition of Jewish thought itself.

In Yovel's account, a key intermediary category for understanding Spinoza's transition from Judaism to rational universalism is the phenomenon of Marranism.[17] As Jews who had converted to Christianity but continued to preserve a 'hidden' Jewish identity, Marranos were, as outward Christians, distanced from their previous Jewish community, and yet, in upholding an inward existential commitment to Judaism, also remained alienated from the Christian community that they had joined.[18] In this sense, the Marrano orientation prefigured Spinoza's later stance of being distanced (whether by force of excommiunication or by choice) from both the Jewish and the Christian communities. As Yovel argues, the neither/nor position of the Marranos gave rise to a dynamic in which a significant number of them "were led by the confusion of both religions to skepticism and secularism, preferring the life of this world, or even (as happened to some) arriving at a positive rationalist philosophy."[19] Thus, he presents the alienated Marrano stance as containing an internal dynamic leading to rationalism. Without rejecting his analysis of the Marranos, I will argue that Yovel overlooks ways in which Judaism's exilic self-conception can also be seen as displaying a similar dynamic, such that the Jewish stance can itself be viewed as a type of Marranism *avant la lettre*.

Similarly, Yovel links Spinoza's emphasis on tolerance as stemming from a Marrano sensitivity to persecution. Spinoza's "rejection of all forms of fanatic imposition of beliefs" can be seen as stemming from his familial cultural inheritance of the Marrano experience, as Marranos were "the community that suffered most from the Inquisition."[20] Insofar as Spinoza's family background would have attuned him the harms and evils of religious persecution, we can understand his desire to move beyond all forms of religious persecution and philosophically to promote a social structure based upon religious

---

[13] (Yovel 1992, p. 34).

[14] (Yovel 1992, p. 34).

[15] (Yovel 1992, pp. 194–95).

[16] (Yovel 1992, p. 195, italics in the original).

[17] Deutscher also notes a link between Spinoza and the Marranos, but mentions this only briefly (Deutscher 1968, p. 28).

[18] (Yovel 1992, pp. 22–23)

[19] (Yovel 1992, p. 24). For an argument that it makes more sense to view the Marrano phenomenon in terms of both/and rather than in terms of neither/nor, see (Bielik-Robson 2014, p. 8).

[20] (Yovel 1992, p. 32).

tolerance. Likewise, Yovel argues that Spinoza upholds a stance in which truth may be unique, but in which the one who possesses this truth should not seek to impose it on others, but should generally tolerate the erroneous positions that others may hold. This stance entails that "[r]ational wisdom thus becomes esoteric": a person can hold to rational truth without needing to proclaim it to others or insist that all must affirm it.[21] Yovel sees this as reflecting a Marrano orientation, insofar as the Marranos lived among mainstream Christians while keeping their Jewish commitments hidden, accepting a gap between their inner convictions and the dominant practices of the society in which they participated.[22] Again, while Yovel provides insightful analysis into potential connections between Spinoza and the Marrano experience, we will see that he may overlook ways in which these elements of tolerance and hiddenness may also have links to important elements in previous Jewish tradition.

3. Universalism and Jewish Conceptuality

In what follows, I seek to highlight ways in which the rational-universal elements of Spinoza's thought that Deutscher and Yovel associate with a transcendence of Judaism can instead be understood as having deeper roots in previous Jewish conceptuality and experience. To the extent that this analysis is correct, it will call into question the assumption that universalist capacity is to be found only by going beyond every particular-historical religious tradition.[23] Rather, it may be that Spinoza's type of universality can potentially also be identified in some, even if not in all, particular-historical streams of thought. To the extent that this is the case, we can view Spinoza as bringing a type of 'Jewish' rational-universal thought *into* the discourse of Western philosophy, in a context in which this type of rational-universal conceptuality may previously have been more lacking within the Western philosophical tradition. As such, rather than viewing Spinoza as achieving universalism by going beyond the narrowness of Judaism, we can view him as going beyond the narrowness of previous Western thought by bringing a 'Jewish' universalism into the philosophical idiom. We will see that certain types of historical-religious particularity, far from undermining universality, may in fact function as a foundation for the generation of certain types of universality, especially ethical-rational universality.

Let us first consider ways in which the material factors of the pre-Spinoza Jewish geographic-social situation can be understood as challenging certain forms of particularistic conceptuality. As Deutscher points out, Jews in Europe lived at the 'borderlines' of majority-Christian societies, being both part of the society and culture in which they lived, and yet also separate from it. They were thus simultaneously at home and distanced from the place where they lived.[24] For Deutscher, this interstitial stance enabled a simultaneous familiarity with the broader society and a critical distance from it. At the same time, a related aspect of Jewish positionality can be discerned by considering the ways in which a Jewish community in one geographic location maintained a sense of shared identity and connection with Jewish communities in other geographic locations. These bonds of communal connection cut across the boundary lines of the various particular kingdoms and principalities of Europe and beyond, thus rendering Jews existentially positioned as members of a *geographically universal* community.[25]

By contrast, the social situation of Christians in Europe, as the dominant majority group in each country, led to a situation in which Christians were more closely bound with a geographically-particular sense of identity. While in principle Christians were spiritually connected to Christians in other geographic locations, the closer identification of Christians with their 'home country' constituted

---

[21]   (Yovel 1992, p. 31, see also p. 35).

[22]   (Yovel 1992, p. 35).

[23]   For analysis of ways in which later Jewish thinkers, particularly Moses Mendelssohn and Hermann Cohen, seek to present philosophies in which they affirm universalism yet without seeking to 'go beyond' Judaism, and indeed in which they present not only their 'Jewish' universalism, but also Western universalism more generally, as arising precisely from the Jewish tradition and sources, see (Fogel 2019, pp. 41–43); see also (Erlewine 2010; Hess 2002; Goetschel 2004, 2013).

[24]   Cf. (Yerushalmi 1997).

[25]   Cf. (Weiss 2016).

a material factor of existential particularism. That is to say, while Jews may have been simultaneously 'at home and not at home' in the place where they lived, Christians' less-alienated relation to the dominant social structures meant that they were more univocally 'at home' in relation to the place where they lived, and accordingly their sense of identity would have been proportionally more distanced from Christians living in other countries. In this sense, it was the higher degree of Jewish social-material alienation and exclusion from the dominant culture of the specific places where they lived that *enabled* a more materially universalistic sense of community and identity. While such structures of geographic universality are not in themselves sufficient for generating an attitude of ethical or existential universalism (it is still possible to hold to an ethically particularist stance even in such a situation), they nevertheless constitute an important material condition for the formation of the latter.

The potential ethical significance of Jewish geographic universality stands out even more clearly when considered alongside the phenomonenon of warfare, Historically, the elements of international warfare can be seen as playing a strongly significant role in shaping a mindset of ethical particularism—and this factor would have been particularly prominent in the decades leading up to Spinoza's lifetime. To the extent that one country or kingdom, with the approval of political and religious authorities, fights in wars against other countries or kingdoms, and in so doing engages in the physical negation of individuals from those other groups, the subjects or citizens of the first country or kingdom will tend to develop an oppositional sense of communal self-conception—a dynamic that ultimately contributed to the rise of modern nationalism. That is to say, the sense of 'us' (versus 'them') will form in relation to a geographically-bounded structure, and will likewise involve carrying out acts of killing and physical destruction against inhabitants of other locations, while simultaneously rejecting the legitimacy of outwardly-similar acts of killing and physical destruction carried out against one's own group. In structural terms, engaging in warfare and seeking to gain dominance over other countries or kingdoms will go along with a practical-material enactment of a particularist ethic vis-à-vis other groups. Thus, these material structures and practices militate against the development of a properly universal ethic and orientation, wherein one would respect the life and existence of all human beings equally, regardless of national borderlines and boundaries.

By contrast, because Jews were in the position of an excluded minority in the various European countries, and were accordingly more distanced from the material practices of military competition and combat against people in other countries, they were less subject to the ethically particularistic cultural mindset generated by those practices. Moreover, whereas Christians engaged in lethal combat against Christians in other countries, thus undermining the practical weight of the in-principle spiritual universalism among Christians, the exclusion of Jews from the military institutions of Christian-majority society meant that Jews did not engage in physical acts of lethal combat against Jews (or Christians) in other societies.[26] As such, the geographic universalism that characterized Jewish identity functioned not only on a spiritual or theoretical level, but also on a significant material and practical level, marked by the absence of acts of organized physical killing and destruction across geographic boundaries. As one noteworthy cultural-legal manifestation of this orientation, Joseph Karo, in his influential *Shulchan Arukh*, includes (in a list of problematic genres of texts to be avoided by Jews) a prohibition on reading "books of wars" (*sifrei milchamot*), an activity that he presents as prohibited both for the Sabbath and for the weekday.[27] Such military exploits are understood as characteristic of the gentile 'nations of the world', specifically in contrast to Israel's calling to a holy life. Again, while ideological and practical opposition to geographically-particularistic militarism does not in itself automatically give rise to ethical universalism, it nevertheless creates cultural space for the

---

[26] For a twentieth-century literary rendition of this dynamic see (Reisen 1917). English translation: "His Brother's Bullets," translated by Max Rosenfeld, in *"Jewish Life" Anthology*, 1946–1956, Edited by Louis Harap (New York: Jewish Life, 1956), pp. 71–74.

[27] Joseph Karo, *Shulchan Arukh, Orach Chayyim* 307:16. I thank David Pruwer for this reference.

latter to arise, whereas cultural affirmation of geographically-particularistic militarism 'salts the earth' and makes it more difficult for such ethical universalism to germinate.[28]

In addition, even if Jewish communities may often had a level of particularistic 'us versus them' orientation towards the members of the Christian majority in the society in which they lived, in which Jews may more often have acted with more care and concern for members of their own Jewish community than towards members of the Christian community, this dynamic still differed in important ways from the particularistic ethic in which Christians were shaped. First of all, the 'us versus them' orientation of Jews in relation to Christians was also found, in a reversed form, in the orientation of Christians in relation to Jews. And, in material terms, Christians, being in a position of greater power, were more able to physically-materially *enact* ethical particularism in their relation to Jews than Jews were able to do in relation to Christians. Thus, even if both Jewish and Christian *texts* of the time displayed 'particularistic' hostility towards the competing religious group, the power differential meant that Jewish life would have been, in practice, less structurally marked by the physical enactment of material harm or oppression to Christians, in contrast to *vice-versa*. In other words, by refraining from physical acts of warfare, and by refraining from physical oppression of other religious groups, Jewish existence in this historical context can be viewed as characterized (in practical terms, even if not always in textual-conceptual-theoretical terms) by a *significantly universal* ethic. That is to say, Jewish dynamics of thought were less shaped, culturally speaking, by the material need to justify, ideologically or theologically, acts of killing and destruction carried out against 'others'.

Thus, in order for a Christian writer of the time to put forth a truly universal ethic, that writer would need to distance himself or herself from the inherently ethically-particularist social structures of the dominant society. Yet, such a task would carry a greater social-cultural penalty for such a writer, as this writer would functionally be negating key practical values of community of which he or she was a part. By contrast, a Jewish writer would have been more in a position to put forth a universal ethic without having to cease from support of major practices that structurally shaped his or her community. While this universalistic stance would place a writer in tension with the structures of dominant Christian society, the Jewish writer would *already* have been in a position of alienation from these structures, and so putting forth a universalistic stance would not create the same risk of cultural loss. Thus, the position of Jewish alienation from the dominant institutions of Christian society, and the corresponding daily Jewish physical enactment of non-killing and non-warfare, can be seen as forming a material basis for the formulation of a conceptually universalistic ethic. To be sure,

---

[28] For an expression, from an internal Jewish theological perspective, of a related view, see Eliezer Berkovits's statement in his 1943 essay "On the Return to Jewish National Life" (Berkovits 2002, pp. 169–71):

> It has been said in modern times that the world cannot exist half-free and half-slave; far less is it possible to create a state of God in one corner of the earth amidst a world of imperial Caesars and power politics .... Thus we went into exile to bide our time there, to wait, however long it might be, until the time when the establishment of the state of God on earth might be attempted once more .... Might and pomp, national honor and "greatness," imperial majesty and power politics, are conceived in guilt and maintained in guilt. From the beginning of recorded history, collective or national existence has always been bound up with crime. Consequently, taking part in national life meant living in sin; Political transactions became synonymous with iniquity and corruption. There has been no place for us as Jews in international life. Our national history in exile has always been passive. We have had to accept the crumbs which "great civilizations" have graciously thrown out to us.
>
> All this has been unpleasant, but thank God for it. Let us thank God that it was not we who were throwing out these soiled crumbs to others. Let us thank God that we were not the masters but only the pariahs of these great civilizations; that we had no share in their criminal inhumanities. We have often been trampled on, but let us thank God that it was not we who have trampled upon justice, decency, freedom, and human dignity whenever it suited our selfish purposes. Let us be grateful to the exile; it has freed us from the guilt of national existence in a world in which national existence meant guilt. We have been oppressed, but we were not oppressors. We have been killed and slaughtered, but we were not among the killers and slaughterers. We have been hunted from country to country, but there were no fugitives fleeing from their homes because of fear of us .... Not every form of eretz yisrael is worth the trouble, and many a form could be unworthy of Judaism.

some individuals within an oppressed minority group may also respond to such exclusion by adopting a more defensive stance of ethical particularism, and such a stance could also be compatible with the structures of their material conditions. Yet, the dynamics of exclusion from dominant power structures that I have sketched out can simultaneously give rise, in other individuals, to different type of response, opposing and resisting the oppressive imposition of particularist power by willfully upholding a non-particularist ethical stance.

In light of this analysis, we can reconsider Deutscher's assertion that "Spinoza's ethics were no longer the Jewish ethics, but the ethics of man at large." Instead of setting up this contrast, we can instead assert that in important senses, the universalistic aspects of Spinoza's ethics may have a material grounding in social-cultural orientation of the Jewish culture in which Spinoza was raised. This Jewish cultural context involved a basic stance of not engaging in the physical negation of others, regardless of religious or national groupings or borders. This stance would have stood out all the more notably in the context of sixteenth and seventeenth century 'wars of religion', which did involve killing on the basis of geographically and culturally particularist causes. In opposing such forms of ethical particularism, Spinoza can be seen as translating into philosophical terms a Jewish view of such behavior as characteristic of 'the wars of the nations' and as standing in contrast to the true service of God. As such, in practical terms, Jewish ethics can be seen as closely approximating a refusal of ethically particularistic forms of killing, so that, in a significant sense, we can correct Deutscher's statement to: "Spinoza's ethics were the Jewish ethics: the ethics of man at large."

Deutscher's formulation was likely unduly shaped by a focus on certain textual formulations, insofar as Jewish texts often did not express themselves in the explicitly universalistic phrasings that one finds in Spinoza's texts. He may thus have been misled by 'narrow' textual formulations, and may have neglected the ways in which the practical-material forms of Jewish cultural praxis may have provided a basis for Spinoza's formulations of ethical universalism. Moreover, the practical absence of engagement in ethically particularistic warfare and killing was not simply imposed on Jewish communities by force of circumstances, but also had a significant theological and ideological basis in the Jewish textual tradition itself. In rabbinic conceptuality, the community of Israel as a whole was viewed as in a state of exile imposed not simply by more powerful other nations, but by God's divine will and decree. In this condition, the dominant rabbinic theological understanding held, Israel is to accept the situation of subservience to the nations and is not to seek to engage in warfare against them. Thus, if subservience to the nations is willed by God in the present era of exile, then Jewish refraining from engagement in particularistic warfare against other nations is likewise willed by God. Even if on various levels rabbinic texts may provide a basis for Israel to 'dislike' the other nations who oppress them, they are nevertheless to uphold a practice of non-warfare in relation to them, thus establishing a universal ethic as God's present will for Israel. By contrast, while post-Constantinian and medieval Christian traditions generally upheld the prohibition on killing on the level of the individual, they left a much wider scope for killing on the political and collective levels. Thus, while Christian texts may in some cases have displayed more outwardly universal formulations in their discourse, the material praxis of Christian societies corresponded to a more ethically particularistic stance in these regards.

Likewise, on the level of individual ethics, rabbinic law held that Israel is prohibited from engaging in acts of killing against both Jews and non-Jews. While the positive attitude of providing active care and concern may have been directed more prominently to 'insiders' than to 'outsiders', the basic negative prohibition of 'thou shalt not kill' was upheld by prominent halakhic authors in Spinoza's cultural context, in relation to both insiders and outsiders, tracing back to the rabbinic notion of all humanity as constituting the 'image of God'.[29] Thus, while Jewish texts may have displayed

---

[29] Cf. Mekhilta de-Rabbi Ishmael, Mishpatim 4, to Ex. 21:14, on the prohibition of murdering non-Jews as well as Jews, and the ways in which this prohibition was understood by major commentators (including Rashi, Maimonides, and Joseph Karo) in the centuries prior to Spinoza. See (Bleich 1989, pp. 15–17). On elements of classical Jewish sources in Spinoza's educational context, see (Nadler 1999, pp. 63–65).

various particularistic formulations, those same texts, when examined more closely, can be understood as enjoining a practical orientation marked by a fundamentally universalistic ethic with regard to physical harm and oppression. Thus, in addition to the Jewish social circumstances in which Spinoza was acculturated, Spinoza's engagement with the Jewish textual tradition may also have contributed to his development of a universal ethical orientation, regardless of whether Deutscher—or Spinoza himself, for that matter—consciously recognized these dynamics of universalism within Jewish culture, texts, and praxis.

In a similar manner, we can consider the ways in which the Marrano dynamics that Yovel sees as contributing to Spinoza's attitude towards tolerance and against religious persecution may also have correlates in broader Jewish tradition and cultural situatedness. Yovel presents Marranos as living according to laws of the dominant society that are at odds with the Marrano's own inner convictions. Yet, this notion of a gap perceived truth and outward circumstances also corresponds to the rabbinic notion of *dina de-malkhuta dina*, 'the law of the (gentile) kingdom is the law'.[30] In rabbinic conceptuality, the 'true law' is found in the commandments of the Torah—but, the theological and practical conditions of Israel's exile means that Israel is not in a position to enact all the laws of the Torah as the fully determining factor of their outward practical life, and must instead submit to the laws of the gentile kingdoms in which they live. While Israel may continue to study all the laws of the Torah and thus to identify itself with those laws in terms of inner identification, the rabbinic stance holds that Israel's outward life is to be shaped to a significant degree by the legal regimes that presently hold sway, despite the false or idolatrous basis of such political-power structures. While God will one day overturn these 'false' structures, God's current will for Israel is to 'tolerate' and adapt important aspects of its practical life (although not all aspects) to these erroneous regimes in this pre-messianic and pre-redemption era.

In this framework, Israel does not impose the 'true law' on others, and indeed even submits to the 'false laws' of others in Israel's own daily life. This stance of 'tolerance' thus corresponds both to the material circumstances of Jews in Europe as well as to an inner rabbinic theological attitude.[31] We can accordingly discern a close parallel to Spinoza's attitude in which the wise person may be in possession of the unique truth, but does not inherently seek to impose it on all others, and will instead live with a tolerant stance towards the errors of those who lack the truth.

By contrast, the dominant practical and theological stance in Christendom was that 'religious truth' is something to be imposed by force on society as a whole. To take one prominent example, Thomas Aquinas, in relation to the question, "Should heretics be tolerated?," held that heretics who do not repent should not only be excommunicated, but should also be put to death.[32] Such attitudes not only played a role in giving rise to the Inquisition's use of physical force against recalcitrant theological deviants, but also contributed to a more general sense that it is normal and proper to combat 'departure from the truth' by means of coercion.

Thus, when Spinoza opposes the tendency of the Inquisition and of Christendom more broadly to impose 'religious truth' by force, he can be viewed as enacting a stance derived not only from a Marrano orientation but also from core Jewish-rabbinic theological and practical sensibilities. Even if Spinoza was himself excommunicated from the Jewish community (thus pointing to certain dynamics of internal intolerance within early modern Judaism), the basic ideological and material stance of that community was nevertheless one that held that truth is to be affirmed by the minority community

---

[30] See (Schwarzschild 1970; Shilo 1974; Graff 1985).

[31] Moreover, while there may have been elements of imposed coercion *within* Jewish communities in the Middle Ages, previous classical rabbinic texts themselves were likely written in a context in which rabbinic authority was enacted primarily in a context of 'voluntary adjudication.' See, e.g., (Lapin 2012, p. 113ff). This earlier historical context may also have contributed materially to the shaping of the theological trends that I describe.

[32] Thomas Aquinas, *Summa Theologiae* II-II, q. 11, a.3.

that acknowledges it, but is not to be imposed on broader society as a whole.[33] Just as Israel, in this unredeemed world, is to live alongside the dominant Christians whom it views as holding false or heretical views, so too Spinoza can be understood as rendering this stance into a philosophical principle wherein the wise person is to live alongside those who hold false views concerning the truth. Thus, while Spinoza may oppose the Jewish community's practices of excommunication vis-à-vis 'heretics' within its own minority community, his stance can simultaneously be seen as recapitulating the Jewish community's stance of 'toleration of error' in relation to the dominant Christian culture.

Likewise, the basic Marrano sense of the 'hiddenness of the truth' can also be understood as having already been conceptualized within previous Jewish tradition. Commenting on Gen. 1:16, Genesis Rabbah links the moon with Jacob (and thus with the community of Israel), and the sun with Esau (and thus with the dominant Roman Empire, including its transformation into Christendom), stating, "Rabbi Nahman said: as long as the light of the bigger one [i.e., the sun] is present [*qayyam*], the light of the smaller one [i.e., the moon] is not publicly visible [*mitparsem*], but when the light of the bigger one sets, the light of the smaller one is publicly visible. Likewise, as long as the light of Esau is present, the light of Jacob is not publicly visible, but when the light of Esau sets, the light of Jacob will be publicly visible, as it is said, 'Arise, shine, for thy light is come, [and the glory of the Lord is risen upon thee]. For behold, darkness shall cover the earth [and gross darkness the peoples; but upon thee the Lord will arise, and his glory shall be seen upon thee]' (Is. 60:1–2)."[34] Here, while the 'light' of Jacob/Israel is expected to shine forth in the messianic future, the operating assumption is that it is expected *not* to be shining forth in the pre-messianic era. Rather, in the unredeemed present, it is the light of Esau/Rome/Christendom/'the nations' that is expected to be prominent and visible. Thus, from an uninformed outsider perspective, it could easily appear that Israel has been cut off from truth and divine glory. The midrash seems to be associating public visibility with the current 'victorious' imperial stance of Rome/Esau, in contrast to the defeated and oppressed stance of Israel. However, the midrash asserts that in reality Israel retains its 'light', but that this light is not able to be *perceived publicly* at present. In this portrayal, Israel as a community should persist in its inner, non-public knowledge of its light, even though it must do so in a context in which public appearances seem to indicate that it is Esau that possesses the light. Thus, even beyond the question of imposing truth on others or tolerating error, this orientation points to a Jewish self-understanding that sees its own 'truth' not only as lacking coercive power, but as functionally 'invisible' and hidden, with no expectation that it would be able to be perceived by others.

In this sense, when the Marranos were compelled to preserve their sense of Jewishness 'in secret,' and so developed a hidden or esoteric conception of truth, they can be understood as adapting an already-prevalent Jewish stance. It may that scholars like Yovel fail to highlight this continuity due to the fact that 'regular' Jewish communities were allowed to practice their religion more openly, whereas Marranos, due to persecution, were compelled to hide their rituals and beliefs more actively. However, this difference, while important, should not distract from the fact that Jews in Europe, while permitted to carry out the outward forms of their religion, were nevertheless theologically and materially cast by dominant society in a position of subordinated untruth. While Jewish practices were not forced into an 'invisible' position, Jewish truth, ideologically speaking, most certainly was. Jewish communities thus had to operate in a material context in which, however much they might affirm their 'truth' within their communities, that truth was officially invisible and hidden in relation to the broader cultural context. Jewish communities accordingly had to develop a self-perception that took into account the fact that the truth that they affirmed had no visible public status, and indeed would have been treated publicly as having a status of non-truth and falsehood. Thus, while Yovel may be

---

[33] Michael Broyde notes that, apart from Maimonides, most of the rishonim held that Noahide law is not to be imposed by force on non-Jews even in the theoretical circumstance of Jews being in a position of power. See (Broyde 1997, pp. 124–29). For an early rabbinic theological formulation of non-imposition of religious truth by force, see Mishnah Avodah Zarah 4:7.

[34] Genesis Rabbah 6:3.

correct in drawing a connection between Marrano 'esotericism of truth' and Spinoza's 'esotericism of truth', one can also draw a connection between Marrano 'esotericism of truth' and a more basic Jewish-rabbinic 'esotericism of truth.' As such, while Spinoza's orientation to the public hiddenness of truth may stem in part from his Marrano familial-cultural connections, it may also have an important material and theological basis in the Jewish-rabbinic context in which he was raised.

4. Spinoza and Jewish Universalism

Let us now reconsider Spinoza's thought in light of these Jewish religious and cultural dynamics. We have seen that previous Jewish tradition can be understood as affirming and enacting a practical 'universal ethic,' which refrained from engaging in forms of ethically-particularistic killing and warfare across geographic-national boundaries and which thus functionally enacted an ethical 'unity of humanity'. This stood in contrast to the dominant material-cultural structures of European Christian countries and kingdoms, in which each country considered it to be ethically normal and proper to carry out forms of killing and warfare against human beings in other countries, even when that same country would view the other countries as ethically unjust and unwarranted in waging war against *it*. Likewise, in terms of truth and tolerance, the Jewish cultural orientation related to truth, in both practical and theological terms, as something to be affirmed by oneself (as a minority community) but not as something to be imposed on society as a whole. By contrast, the theological and political structures of Christendom tended to view it as a matter of importance that theological truth be imposed on society more broadly, and through the use of physical force and coercion if necessary.

To be sure, the Jewish tradition also contains various aspects that stand out as 'particular', and these may be the elements that could strike some observers as more prominent, particularly if one thinks of Judaism in relation to the Hebrew Bible alone, considered apart from the way this text was understood and interpreted in rabbinic literature. Thus, a reader of the Hebrew Bible could remark upon the ways in which the text could seem to encourage the violent destruction those who engage in idolatry and 'false worship' within Israelite society, or upon the ways in which the Israelites are encouraged to wage violent warfare against other nations. When these are combined with the biblical range of distinctive 'ritual' practices (such as circumcision and dietary restrictions), a reader could (and readers have) come away with a sense of 'Judaism' as quite distanced from the type of 'universalism' that one associates with Spinoza.

Yet, when we consider the theological and material aspects of rabbinic-Jewish tradition considered above, a different picture may emerge, which may contain elements of ritual particularity and cultural separation, but which simultaneously operates on a fundamental basis that rejects particularistic inter-group oppression and warfare and which also shuns coercive imposition of 'religious truth' on society as a whole. To the extent that these latter dynamics *are* preserved in the tradition, the dominant rabbinic tendency either restricts them to the biblical past or suspends them until the future messianic redemption, instead affirming a norm for the present according to which these elements are specifically removed from Israel's ethical-practical activities and interactions with other groups.[35] Thus, the rabbinic tradition can already be seen as actively recasting the tradition in a manner that removes these elements and leaves in place a functionally universalistic existential ethos in these regards.

Thus, Spinoza can be viewed as having been acculturated into this existential ethos, and as reformulating its practical-theological universalism in the language of a philosophical-theoretical universalism. Instead of a norm in which *Israel's special calling from God for the present* entails enacting a stance that rejects imposition of truth and geographically-particular ethics, Spinoza presents a norm in which it is *atemporal reason* that entails enacting a stance that rejects imposition of truth and geographically-particular ethics. Spinoza's immersion in the Jewish material and theological context can be understood as having made it more existentially 'intuitive' for him to imagine a society without

---

[35] See (Berger 2007; Neusner 1987; Weiss 2015).

the enactment of ethically particularistic violence and without forced imposition of religious truth. While the form in which he presents this ethos is new and different in various regards, the basic substance of his stance can be seen as standing in practical continuity with the Jewish tradition out of which he emerged. He can therefore be understood as taking the Jewish existential stance and philosophically extending it to society as a whole in the name of reason.

At the same time, when Spinoza himself puts forth his universalism in the name of 'reason,' he asserts the latter to be specifically separated from all historical-particular elements. Such a notion may appear to differ from the Jewish universalism put forth in the name of an historical-particular-revealed 'Torah.' And indeed, Spinoza's own presentation of Jews and Judaism presents a sharp contrast between his reason-based universalism and the historically-bound (and thus historically-outmoded, after the destruction of the ancient Israelite state) status of "the Law of Moses."[36] Similarly, he sees the election of "the Hebrew nation" as presently having lapsed.[37] To be sure, in rejecting the continuing validity of the historically-particular dimensions of the Hebrew Bible, Spinoza simultaneously sees the same Hebrew Bible itself as proclaiming a "divine universal law," which still remains valid even after the destruction of the ancient Hebrew commonwealth.[38] In this sense, Spinoza can be seen as indicating an awareness of a potential relation between universalism and Jewish tradition. Yet, by portraying the Bible's universal elements as fully separable from the historical-particular aspects of Judaism, he presents a picture in which there is no apparent positive role to be played by Jewish particularity in relation to the task of promoting or upholding the divine universal law. Indeed, he criticizes "the Jews" as failing to recognize the properly universal dimensions of their own scriptural tradition.[39] In this presentation, it would seem that any universal dimensions might that still be found among 'the Jews' would be present in spite of, and not in substantive relation to, the specifics of Jewish tradition.

As such, it could appear that whatever the functional universalism of the Jewish ethos, in connection with its material circumstances, it cannot properly be described as a 'rational' universalism, to the extent that Jewish tradition still upholds the divine normativity of historically-particular practice and identity. However, such an assertion may overlook the crucial distinction between a form of reason that strives to separate itself from all historical-temporal traditions, and a form of reason that can be understood as operating within a historical-temporal tradition. If Jewish tradition operates with concepts of a 'God of all the world' in a manner that enacts an ethical oneness of humanity, cutting across geographic borders and boundaries, and which, while holding to historical-particular norms, theologically rejects the imposition of these on society as a whole, then one can posit—in order to account for the possibility of the phenomena observed—a dynamic of reason at play as that which gives rise to these universal orientations. By contrast, to the degree that the culture of Christendom enacted ethically-particular forms of violence or coercion, we can posit a dynamic of parochial unreason as that which gives rise to these non-universal orientations. Indeed, the Jewish tradition may point to a specific conception of reason, understood not in terms of *imposing upon all people* that which is claimed to be rationally true (an imperialistic notion of reason), but rather in terms of *rejecting the imposition on others* of that which is historical-particular and thus not rationally-universally true. Far from existing in spite of cleaving to historical-particular practices, this alternative mode of reason may in fact be closely bound up with the double dynamic of strongly asserting of the value of historical-particular elements for one's own community while simultaneously

---

[36] For Spinoza's assertion of the outmodedness of the 'Law of Moses,' see (Spinoza 2007, p. 71 [5:5]).
[37] (Spinoza 2007, p. 54 [3:11]).
[38] (Spinoza 2007, pp. 70–71 [5:5]).
[39] See (Spinoza 2007, p. 79 [5:19]), where Spinoza asserts that 'the Jews' (and particularly Maimonides) view salvation as achievable (even in connection to the Noahide laws) only through the divinely revealed Torah and specifically not through universal natural reason. Again, particularly in relation to the latter accusation, even if there do exist certain particularist streams or dynamics within certain Jewish texts or figures, this does not in itself rule out the possibility of universalist streams or dynamics alongside them, and so Spinoza's picture is misleadingly one-sided.

rejecting the imposition of those particularities on others. We can thus view not only the universalism but also the rationalism that Spinoza champions as present in important ways in previous Jewish tradition and practical ethos. While Spinoza himself may not necessarily have fully recognized these dynamics, and while his account of rational universalism may enact certain changes to the previous Jewish dynamics of rational universalism, it is highly misleading to say that his construction of a universal and rational philosophy is accomplished by moving beyond the supposedly non-universal and non-rational structures of traditional Judaism. Again, as stated in the introduction to the present essay, this latter assumption may be more characteristic of recent scholarship on Spinoza than of portrayals of Spinoza in eighteenth-, nineteenth-, and early twentieth-century Jewish thought, but it remains an assumption that stands in need of being challenged today.

5. Jewish Conceptuality as Marrano Conceptuality, Marrano Conceptuality as Jewish Conceptuality

In light of the above analysis, we can reconsider Yovel's construal of Spinoza as "a Marrano of *reason*, rather than of some revealed religion."[40] By this, Yovel intends to distinguish Spinoza from the historical Marranos, who kept their Jewish belief and identity secret while outwardly living within a Christian societal context in which such views were disallowed. By contrast, Yovel holds that while Spinoza likewise holds a 'Marrano-shaped' inner commitment at odds with the dominant view of the society in which he lived and wrote, it is an inner commitment to universal reason, and not to a historical-particular 'revealed religion' such as Judaism. While this description may indeed illuminate Spinoza in important ways, both components of the phrase 'Marrano of reason' can lead to a problematic understanding Spinoza's relation to Jewish tradition. First of all, we have seen that Jewish tradition itself shares key elements with a Marrano orientation, including attitudes towards imposition of truth by force and towards expectations of truth's hiddenness. Thus, when Yovel says that Spinoza enacts 'Marrano' dynamics, but in the name of reason, one could, in many regards, likewise view those same Spinozan data points as enacting 'Jewish' dynamics in the name of reason. Similarly, we have seen that many aspects of Spinoza's rational-universal approach have important resonances with previous Jewish tradition and ethos. Thus, just as Jewish tradition may be 'Marrano' *avant la lettre*, it may also 'rational-universal' *avant la lettre*. At a minimum, treating 'Marrano' versus 'Jewish' or 'universal-rational' versus 'Jewish' as contrast-pairs rather than as overlapping family-resemblance-pairs may obscure more than it clarifies. As such, while Spinoza may indeed be a 'Marrano of reason,' he may also be a 'Marrano of Judaism', as well as a 'Judaizer of reason'—or even a 'Judaizer of Judaism'.

In this sense, while Yovel, as well as Deutscher, may be correct in asserting that Spinoza engages in a rational-universal critique of particularity, they may fail to recognize the extent to which Jewish conceptuality and social-cultural context had already been functionally enacting a universal-rational critique of particularity, and that this may have played a material role in giving rise to Spinoza's ideas. It may be that they, as well as other scholars, take their cue about the relation between Judaism and universalism from some of Spinoza's own explicit (but misleading) statements, and consequently turn instead to 'Marranism' (or other forms of 'marginal Judaism', such as Sabbateanism) as constituting potential sources for or parallels to Spinoza's critique. Instead, it may be that many of Spinoza's universalist dynamics may already have been present, quite close to the surface (even if not fully *on* the surface), in 'mainstream' rabbinic culture and material circumstances, and may not have required all that much of a push for them to be activated in the way that Spinoza does.

A key difference between Spinoza and previous Judaism may be found not in the ethos of his writing but in its implied audience. If universalist dynamics were already enacted in a Jewish context, they were primarily aimed only at the Jewish community itself, whereas Spinoza's reformulation in terms of philosophical reason now enjoins that ethos 'for all,' or at least all students or lovers of reason.

---

[40] (Yovel 1992, p. 37, italics in the original; see also pp. 31, 215).

In this sense, rather than viewing him as going 'beyond both Judaism and Christianity,' he can be seen as transferring the universalist ethos of rabbinic Judaism into a context of Christendom that had been marked, at least since the merging of Christianity with the Roman Empire, by a more particularist and parochialist ethos, linked to ethical differentiation dependent on geographic borders and to imposition of religious truth on general society.[41]

Finally, if Spinoza's approach can be understood as coming not only from his Marrano cultural background, but also, or even more so, from his Jewish background in a more basic sense, this can afford us a similarly broadened perspective on the history of Jewish thought and philosophy after Spinoza as well. It may well be the case that dynamics of universalism akin to those found in Spinoza can also be found in thinkers who engaged in philosophical discourse from out of a Jewish cultural background, even when those thinkers did *not* reject affiliation with Judaism—as in the case of Moses Mendelssohn and Hermann Cohen, to take two especially notable examples.[42] If the wider history of Jewish philosophy in modernity can be interpreted in terms of 'Marranism', as Agata Bielik-Robson has fruitfully done,[43] then it may also be possible to narrate a history of universalism and rationalism in modern Jewish thought in terms of a related dynamic of 'rabbinism,' as the present article attempts to gesture towards. If Deutscher cast Spinoza within a modern intellectual chain of tradition of the 'non-Jewish Jew', then recasting Spinoza more specifically as a 'Jewishly non-Jewish Jew' can in turn give rise to richer understandings of Spinoza, of Judaism, and of modernity, in which dynamics of universalism and rationalism, in a non-imperialist mode, can be understood as arising precisely from out of, rather than in spite of, the historical-particular dynamics of previous Jewish thought and material culture.

Funding: This research received no external funding.

Acknowledgments: I thank the anonymous reviewer for helpful feedback on an earlier version of this article.

Conflicts of Interest: The author declares no conflict of interest.

References

Berger, Michael S. 2007. Taming the Beast: Rabbinic Pacification of Second-Century Jewish Nationalism. In *Belief and Bloodshed: Religion and Violence across Time and Tradition*. Edited by James K. Wellman Jr. Lanham: Rowman and Littlefield, pp. 47–61.

Berkovits, Eliezer. 2002. *Essential Essays on Judaism*. Edited by David Hazony. Jerusalem: Shalem.

Bielik-Robson, Agata. 2014. *Jewish Cryptotheologies of Late Modernity: Philosophical Marranos*. London: Routledge.

Bleich, David. 1989. Jewish Terrorists. In *Contemporary Halakhic Problems*. New York: KTAV, vol. 3, pp. 12–18.

Broyde, Rabbi Michael J. 1997. The Obligation of Jews to Seek Observance of Noahide Laws by Gentiles: A Theoretical Review. In *Tikkun Olam: Social Responsibility in Jewish Thought and Law*. Edited by David Shatz, Chaim I. Waxman and Nathan J. Diament. Northvale: Jason Aaronson, pp. 103–43.

Deutscher, Isaac. 1968. The non-Jewish Jew. In *The Non-Jewish Jew and Other Essays*. Edited by Tamara Deutscher. London: Oxford University Press, pp. 25–41.

Erlewine, Robert. 2010. *Monotheism and Tolerance: Recovering a Religion of Reason*. Bloomington: Indiana University Press.

Farber, Samuel. 2017. Deutscher and the Jews: On the Non-Jewish Jew—An Analysis and Personal Reflection. In *Jews and Leftist Politics: Judaism, Israel, Antisemitism, and Gender*. Edited by Jack Jacobs. Cambridge: Cambridge University Press, pp. 331–49.

---

[41] On rabbinic views of the 'parochialization' entailed by the Christianization of the Roman Empire, see (Weiss 2018). By contrast, the pre-Constantinian Christian ethic (and thus the ethic displayed in the New Testament) may have had more in common with the rabbinic ethic described in the present essay.

[42] See footnote 23 above.

[43] (Bielik-Robson 2014).

Fogel, Jeremy. 2019. Universalism and the Highest Good in Moses Mendelssohn and Hermann Cohen: A Study of Values and Revaluations. Ph.D. dissertation, Tel Aviv University, Tel Aviv, Israel.

Goetschel, Willi. 2004. *Spinoza's Modernity: Mendelssohn, Lessing, and Heine*. Madison: University of Wisconsin Press.

Goetschel, Willi. 2013. *The Discipline of Philosophy and the Invention of Modern Jewish Thought*. New York: Fordham University Press.

Graff, Gil. 1985. *Separation of Church and State: Dina De-Malkhuta Dina in Jewish Law, 1750–1848*. Tuscaloosa: University of Alabama Press.

Hess, Jonathan M. 2002. *Germans, Jews and the Claims of Modernity*. New Haven: Yale University Press.

Lapin, Hayim. 2012. *Rabbis as Romans: The Rabbinic Movement in Palestine, 100–400 CE*. Oxford: Oxford University Press.

Levenson, Jon D. 1996. The Universal Horizon of Biblical Particularism. In *Ethnicity and the Bible*. Edited by Mark G. Brett. Leiden: Brill, pp. 143–69.

Nadler, Steven M. 1999. *Spinoza: A Life*. Cambridge: Cambridge University Press.

Nadler, Steven M. 2009. The Jewish Spinoza. *Journal of the History of Ideas* 70: 491–510. [CrossRef]

Neusner, Jacob. 1987. *Vanquished Nation, Broken Spirit: The Virtues of the Heart in Formative Judaism*. Cambridge: Cambridge University Press.

Ravven, Heidi M., and Lenn E. Goodman, eds. 2002. *Jewish Themes in Spinoza's Philosophy*. Albany: SUNY Press.

Reisen, Abraham. 1917. Dem bruder's koylen [Yiddish]. In *Ale verk fun Avraham Reyzen*. New York: Yiddish, vol. 10, pp. 67–73.

Runesson, Anders. 2000. Particularistic Judaism and Universalistic Christianity?: Some Critical Remarks on Terminology and Theology. *Studia Theologica: Nordic Journal of Theology* 54: 55–75. [CrossRef]

Schwarzschild, Steven. 1970. The Imperative of Religious Law. *Washington University Law Quarterly* Winter no. 1: 103–9.

Schwarzschild, Steven. 1990. The Question of Jewish Ethics Today. In *The Pursuit of the Ideal: The Jewish Writings of Steven Schwarzschild*. Edited by Menachem Kellner. Albany: SUNY Press, pp. 117–35.

Shilo, Shmuel. 1974. *Dina de-Malkhuta Dina*. Jerusalem: Jerusalem Academic Press.

Spinoza, Baruch. 2007. *Theological-Political Treatise*. Edited by Jonathan Israel. Cambridge: Cambridge University Press.

Weiss, Daniel H. 2015. Walter Benjamin and the Antinomianism of Classical Rabbinic Law. *Bamidbar: Journal for Jewish Thought and Philosophy* 4: 56–78.

Weiss, Daniel H. 2016. A Nation without Borders?: Modern European Emancipation as Negation of Galut. *Shofar: An Interdisciplinary Journal of Jewish Studies* 34: 71–97. [CrossRef]

Weiss, Daniel H. 2018. The Christianization of Rome and the Edomization of Christianity: *Avodah Zarah* and Political Power. *Jewish Studies Quarterly* 25: 394–422. [CrossRef]

Yerushalmi, Yosef Hayim. 1997. Exile and Expulsion in Jewish History. In *Crisis and Creativity in the Sephardic World: 1391–1648*. Edited by Benjamin R. Gampel. New York: Columbia University Press, pp. 3–22.

Yovel, Yirmiyahu. 1992. *Spinoza and Other Heretics: The Marrano of Reason*. Princeton: Princeton University Press.

religions

MDPI

Article

Atheism of the Word: Narrated Speech and the Origin of Language in Cohen, Rosenzweig and Levinas

William Large

Department of Liberal and Performing Arts, University of Gloucestershire, Cheltenham GL50 4AZ, UK;
wlarge@glos.ac.uk

Received: 13 November 2018; Accepted: 4 December 2018; Published: 7 December 2018

check for
updates

Abstract: Kant marks a fundamental break in the history of philosophy of religion and the concept of God. God is no longer interpreted as a being necessary to understand the existence of a rational universe, but as an idea that makes sense of our morality. Cohen supplements this idea with the concept of personality, which he argues is the unique contribution of Judaism. For Rosenzweig and Levinas, the monotheistic God is neither a being nor an idea, but the living reality of speech. What would the atheism be that responds to this theism? Linguistics makes a distinction between direct, indirect, and free indirect speech. In the latter form, the origin of speech is not a subject, but narrated language. It is this difference between direct and indirect speech that is missing in Rosenzweig and Levinas's description of God. It would mean that God is produced by language rather than the subject of language. What menaces the reality of God is not whether God exists, or is intelligible, but the externality of language without a subject.

Keywords: Cohen; Rosenzweig; Levinas; God; atheism; language

1. Introduction

Is there a Jewish philosophy that would be "other" than philosophy? But how can that be the case, because if it were truly other then it would not be philosophy at all, but something else? It must be both philosophical and non-philosophical. It would speak the language of philosophy, but at the same time, smuggle Jewish content into the heart of philosophy and thereby transform it from within into something other than itself. An example of such a trafficking would be Hermann Cohen's *Religion of Reason out of the Sources of Judaism*, whose title explicitly announces such an operation. In the introduction to his book, Cohen argues that a religion of reason is separate from the history of religion. History does not determine the concept of reason, rather reason determines the concept of history. If we are to understand the concept of a religion, like Judaism for example, then we cannot just rely on literary sources, because to interpret them the religion we are investigating must already have a meaning for us. We must already have a concept of Judaism even before we approach the religious texts of Judaism. This other source is reason. *"The concept of religion,"* Cohen writes, *"should be discovered through the religion of reason"* (Cohen 1995, p. 5) [Emphasis in the original]. Only then does religion become a properly philosophical problem. Yet what does any religion contribute to the universality of reason except its own particularity? The answer to this question is each particularity expresses its own universality. In form at least, Cohen's strategy is the same as Kant's in *Religion within the Boundaries of Mere Reason* for Christianity, where Kant claims that Judaism, like Islam, is a mere statutory faith, and thus a particularity that only expresses the particularity of its literary sources,

Cohen will claim that Judaism has a universal significance different from Christianity. The universal, paradoxically speaking, is not a unity, but a plurality.[1]

There must be a way in which a religion can state a universal truth, but, at the same time, not lose its specificity. Each religion speaks a universal truth to humanity as its own truth. What, then, is the truth of Judaism? It is, Cohen answers, its ethics, but an ethics of a specific kind. For Kant, religion is subordinated to the universality of the moral law, which has its concrete form in the state and eventually a cosmopolitan order. Yet this sacrifices the particularity of the individual for the sake of a totality, however just that totality might be. Kant's morality only recognizes the 'I' as a member of humanity, but not as an individual. The objective form of the universal ideal of humanity is the state. What is lost in this objectification is the 'you' of the individual who stands before me. In the totality of the state, every person becomes a 'he', which is almost indistinguishable from an 'it'. What Judaism recognizes beyond Kant's morality and politics, is the individuality of an 'I' beyond abstraction. "Is it not precisely through the observation of the other man's suffering," Cohen asks, 'that the other is *changed from the He to the You*" (Cohen 1995, p. 17) [Emphasis in the original. Translation modified]. To preserve the specificity of Judaism is, then, to save the plurality of the other from the universality of the moral law and the state. The universal particularism of Judaism is the reclaiming of particularity of the individual. This is the specific contribution of the religion of Judaism to the universality of reason. It is the paradoxical expression of particularity as universal, as opposed to the universalism of the universal of Christianity, where each of us belongs to the same idea of humanity. In Judaism, each of us are singular, but universally so. The universalism of the universal is the politics of the state, whereas the universalism of the particularity of the ethics of religion.[2] Judaism is the universalism of the particular, whereas Christianity is the universalism of the universal. The universality of reason, which is now plural, requires both.

The difference between Rosenzweig and Cohen is not so much the idea of the universalism of particularity as a resistance to totality as the truth of Judaism, but the form of its presentation, and this changes the relation between religion and reason. If Cohen rejects the literary sources of Judaism for the sake of reason, then Rosenzweig does precisely the opposite. He discards reason for the sake of literary sources. The only meaning of Judaism, in its particularity, is its literary sources. Cohen can translate the particularity of Judaism into the universality of reason because he has already sacrificed the particularity of Judaism by turning it into a philosophy that can be added onto the history of philosophy. If Cohen is still writing a philosophy of religion and preserving Judaism much in the way that Kant saves Christianity, though as the universalism of particularity that preserves the individual within the universal, then Rosenzweig's *Star of Redemption* is a "cryptotheology" against philosophy, and like every "cryptotheology" what it appeals to against philosophy is a particularity that cannot be taken up by a universal that claims to be the origin of every particularity.[3] Both Cohen and Rosenzweig

---

[1] For Kant, the superiority of Christianity over Judaism is that it is a moral and not learned religion based on books. He will go as far as to say that Judaism is not a real religion at all, but merely a political constitution that expresses the will of a people (see Kant 1998, pp. 130–33). It is for this reason that Cohen, who argues that Judaism does have a universal significance, like Christianity, claims there must be a universal concept of Judaism separate from its literature. The source of Kant's anti-Semitism is the universalism of reason. If reason is defined, in advance, as the universality of the moral law, which conceals the particularity of Western philosophy, then any other culture must be found wanting.

[2] There is another politics in *Religion of Reason*, which is messianic. There is a tension in this book between the politics of the state and the politics of religion. Socialism is both the politics of the state and religion. It is a politics of the state because it is part of contemporary politics, but it is also a politics of religion because it works toward a future of justice for all, and the latter requires more than the action of a state. Messianism is an "ethical socialism" (Cohen 1995, p. 311).

[3] It is a "cryptotheology" and not a theology because it shatters the universality of philosophy from within. If Cohen attempts to universalize the particularity of Judaism, then Rosenzweig 'particularizes' the universal. Every universal is a hidden particularity, even the apparent universality of philosophy. It has no more claim to universality than any other particularity. The universal is then transformed into a patchwork of particularities in relation with one another. Cohen sees the particularity of Judaism taken up into the unity of reason, Judaism adds what philosophy lacks through its Greek heritage, whereas Rosenzweig understands the plurality of the universal as heterogenous. The universal is universal as the plurality of particularities and there is no vestige of a universality that communicates between them. There is no "meta-universality". There is no universalism of the universal. This mirrors the difference of their presentation of particularity. For Cohen,

are appealing to a particularity of Judaism, but one from the viewpoint of the universality of reason so the particularity of concept can be subsumed into a universal, whereas the other appeals to a particularity against every concept, even the idea of the unity of reason. If a religion is to claim its own particularity against the universality of reason, then it does so by appealing to the distinctiveness of its own experience. As soon as it enters the field of the universal, then it has already lost. But it also must show that that the universal of philosophy too hides its own particularity. There is no universality of reason that is not the triumph of a particularity over all other particularities. The history of reason is always the history of a tradition that conceals its own particularity by claiming its universality as its origin rather than the result of its history.

For Cohen, Judaism is a concept, however paradoxical that concept might be, but for Rosenzweig, it is an experience of a revelation, and a literary tradition that preserves the particularity of this experience. The difference between the "I" and the "you", this "relation without relation", which is the particularity of Judaism, is not conceived by reason, but is produced through the concrete living reality of speech.[4] Cohen still thinks of the other as another "I" through the concept of individuality, which would be the same for both me and the other, whereas for Rosenzweig, the other is different from me because they speak to me before I have any thought of them, which would make us equivalent. In this address, I am transformed from the indifference of the third person, where everyone is interchangeable, into a singular "you". "The I discovers itself," Rosenzweig writes, "at the moment where it affirms the existence of the you, through the question of the 'where' of the you" (Rosenzweig 2005, p. 189) [Translation modified].

There is a difference between speaking and what is spoken about. In speaking, the individuality of the speaker is revealed, as opposed to the universality of the concept. The living reality of speech is the existence of the "you" who speaks to an "I". Living speech, as opposed to the dead speech of concepts, is a dialogue. Someone is speaking to someone else. Thinking thinks thinking. It imagines itself as a monologue, but there can be no speaking without someone being spoken to. It is not that I relate to you and recognize your particularity, rather a "you" addresses me first and through that address the "I" is produced. The "I" is second, not first. This asymmetry of ethical relation in living speech is repeated in Levinas's description of the ethical relation. The other speaks. The other is present in the words they speak. Only in this way can we distinguish between ethics and ontology. Ontology belongs to the visible; ethics to speech. The difference between Levinas and Rosenzweig is that Rosenzweig begins with God and ends with the other, whereas Levinas starts with the other and ends with God. The first relation of speech for Levinas is not between God and me, but the other who addresses me, and only subsequently do I arrive at an ethical meaning of God.[5]

In Kant, God is an idea as part of the universal value of humanity. The universal value of humanity is expressed concretely in the real possibility of a just world whose existence is only possible through God's providence. In Judaism, God is not an idea, but a proper name. God is a relation to an individual

---

the particular is still a concept, for Rosenzweig it is an experience. There are vestiges of Cohen's approach in Rosenzweig, however, where some particularities are not particular enough to participate in this plural universality, which explains the belittling of Islam throughout the *Star of Redemption*. The universalism of the particular significance of both Judaism and Christianity is explained against the "false" particularism of Islam, which echoes Kant's own criticism of Judaism as merely a religion of books. "Islam," Rosenzweig writes, "is a religion of the book from the first moment" (Rosenzweig 2005, p. 180). For the significance and meaning of "cryptotheology" for Jewish philosophy (see Bielik-Robson 2014). Our aim in this essay is to show that no religion can escape a religion of books. Rosenzweig's heterogeneity is a bounded one, which only allows Judaism and Christianity, and does so by defining Judaism specifically as living speech opposed to the unitary rational universality of Christianity.

4   This does not mean that Cohen never refers to speech in the *Religion of Reason*, but it is a speech as a "rational speech" and not concrete living speech (see Cohen 1995, p. 81).

5   As Shmuel Trigano argues, Levinas is unique in Jewish philosophy in that God is revealed in the other person and not the other person in God. In Rosenzweig, God reveals Himself to me, but in Levinas, revelation occurs in the one who receives, and not the one who gives. The other is not revealed in God, but God in the other. "What, earlier, in classical Jewish-philosophy, was attributed to God or dissociated from this infinity—insofar as it is turned toward the human being—seems, in Levinas' thought, to have to do as much with man in his moral life as with God" (Trigano 2001, p. 296).

and not the manifestation of being. This relation to God as an individual is the universal meaning of Judaism. The uniqueness of God is not that of an idea, but of an individual. Since God is an individual, the relation to God is one of love rather than thought. In thought, I compare one individual to another, whereas I love a singular individual. The universality of Judaism is the universality of the particular, which is both the particularity of the individual other, and the individuality of God. In Kant, the individual is subsumed into the particular, since everyone only has a meaning as part of a totality, but for Judaism, the particular has a universal meaning as a particular. Every individual is unique, as God is. The universal is a plurality rather than a unity. The universality of Western philosophy is as much a particularity, as the particularity of Judaism. If philosophy has a universal meaning to everyone, then so too does Judaism.[6] The universal is not made of one voice, but many voices. When Western philosophy claims to be the only voice, it is because it conceals its own particularity in the universal, and at the same time represses the plurality of its own tradition. Each philosopher, when they create their own concept, retrospectively creates the unity of the history of philosophy in the image of their thought, but the history of philosophy, too, is a plurality of voices. There is no "metaphilosophy" of philosophy.

If the relation to God is love in Judaism, then the expression of that love is speech. God speaks to me as a unique individual and I respond. The universal particularity of Judaism is not the concept of the individual, as it sometime seems to be in Cohen, but the experience of the living speech. It is a "cryptotheology" of the word, but not the word as logos, but as speech. The relation to the "you" and the "I" is asymmetrical. The "I", then, is not an individual as an act of self-positing, but is produced through its relation to another who orders them. The archetypal form of this relation is the relation to the unique God who commands me in speech through His love for me. In thought, every "I" is identical to every other "I", but only in this relation of God to me is the "I" a real existing singular individual. It is not consciousness that is the origin of the singularity of the individual, but speech, and the first speech is the words of God to me.

If living speech is the Judaic "cryptotheology" at the heart of philosophy, since it reveals philosophy as a particularity rather than the universalism it claims to be, then what is the atheism that would respond to this theism? Atheism is not something that assails this "cryptotheology" from the outside, for it is not the atheism of an idea. Kant's moral theism is a reaction to the threat of nihilism occasioned by the success of the materialism of science. In an indifferent material universe, what value could humanity have? It could only be moral one, and religion expresses this moral significance through Christianity stripped of any supernatural and institutional excess. Yet this is the religion of an idea, and not the religion of Judaism. If Judaism is the correlation between the individual and God in speech, then both terms of the relation must be separate from one another if they are not to form a totality. The first word of the individual in response to God's demand is not "yes", but "no". The separation of the individual is atheism. As Levinas writes in *Totality and Infinity*, a "faith purged of myths, the monotheistic faith, itself assumes metaphysical atheism" (Levinas 1969, p. 77) [Translation modified]. Yet is metaphysical atheism the only atheism? Is there not another atheism, an atheism of the word, which neither Rosenzweig or Levinas are aware, or if so, only fleetingly, which threatens only when it is immediately warded off?

For both Rosenzweig and Levinas, the origin of language is the speaking subject, but there are two problems with this. First, this places the origin of language outside of language. The subject speaks, but the speaking subject is not an element of language. Secondly, there is a self of language

---

6   In his preface to the French translation of Mendelssohn's *Jerusalem*, Levinas stresses that the universalism of the Jewish people is its singularity. "In his universalism," Levinas writes, "he [Mendelssohn] does not forget the singularity of the Jewish people and its universal significance, which stems from that very singularity: Israel is still necessary to humanity's monotheism" (Levinas 1994b, p. 144). There is a difference between this universalism of the particularity of Judaism, and the universalism of the universal of Kant's description of Christianity. In the former, the universal is heterogenous, whereas in the latter it is homogenous.

that is not a speaking subject and that is the narrated self. If God is a proper name, rather than an idea, then God can only be a narrated self and not a speaking subject. Yet the origin of the narrated self is not a speaker exterior to language, but words, whose origin can only be other words. Both Rosenzweig and Levinas displace the priority of the "I" of representation and thought for the sake of other who addresses me in speech, but the other who speaks, speaks in the first person. The other or God addresses me as another "I", even though this "I" is not the "I" as an idea. Someone is speaking to me, but this someone is not anonymous. It is this person here speaking to me now in the present, or it is God speaking to me. Levinas describes the Other in *Totality and Infinity*, as being present in the word they speak. "Speech," Levinas writes, "consists in the Other coming to the assistance of the sign issued, attending his own manifestation in signs, remedying the equivocal by this attendance" (Levinas 1969, p. 91) [Translation modified]. What is this "attendance", but the origin of language in the speaking subject? Yet this would be to define the origin of language by that which is outside of language, for the presence of the other in speech is not the words spoken, but a revelation. Even though he defines ethics as language, Levinas will still speak of it as an "optics".[7] It is as though, at this point, with the origin of language itself, the difference between speaking and seeing no longer holds. Although speaking is not the visibility of being, the origin of language is still the visible presence of the speaker in speech, whether as the other or God, outside of the words spoken.

What matters in living speech is the presence of the speaker in their speech. Both Levinas and Rosenzweig decry the written word, for in writing, the speaking self is not present.[8] Yet there can be no God as a speaker, for all God's speech is reported speech. If God speaks to me, then God does so only through the literature of Judaism. There is no direct address of God to me in the way that the other addresses me in conversation. God speaks through the literature of Judaism, through the Talmud, or the Hebrew bible, or the liturgy of the synagogue. Nowhere, in either Rosenzweig's or Levinas's writing, does God address them directly. Indeed, you could claim that such a direct address by God would be prohibited by Judaism. Though Rosenzweig presents God's as speaking in the second part of *The Star of Redemption*, and revelation is explained as living speech, it is in fact by analogy with human speech, for God never speaks as a speaking subject, but always speaks as a narrated self. Linguistics makes a distinction between direct discourse, indirect discourse, and free indirect discourse.[9] In direct discourse, the speech of the other is directly represented from the point of view of the speaker: "He said, 'I was tired.'" In indirect discourse, the speaker is represented from the position of the narrator: "He felt tired". In free indirect discourse, however, there is no point of view, neither of the speaker nor the narrator: "He thought/said he was tired". The narrated self is the narration of speech and thought, but without a speaker. The origin of such a narrated self is not the presence of speaking subject in the words spoken, but the written words themselves. Is there not an atheism of the word, which would not be the same as the metaphysical atheism of a separated subject? For God as a proper name, the narrated God of Jewish "cryptotheology", would find its origin in these words, and not in a

---

[7] "Ethics", Levinas writes, "is spiritual optics" (Levinas 1969, p. 78) [Translation modified].

[8] "The unique actuality of speech," Levinas writes, "tears it from the situation in which it appears and which it seems to prolong. It brings what the written word is already deprived of: mastery. Speech, better than a simple sign, is essentially magisterial" (Levinas 1969, p. 69). As we have already noted, Judaism is differentiated from false monotheism of Islam by Rosenzweig because it belongs to writing. See footnote 3.

[9] For an analysis of these linguistic distinctions and their relation to Biblical Hebrew, see (Van Wolde 1995). As Van Wolde reminds us, free indirect discourse is not possible in Biblical Hebrew, and God generally speaks in direct discourse, which is marked by the Hebrew phrase, וַיֹּאמֶר, 'and He said'. It is for this reason that Rosenzweig always represents God as speaking directly, though of course this is always reported speech through the written word. What if we were to think of language through a free indirect discourse only made possible through writing, rather than the direct speech, where free indirect discourse would merely be an anomaly? Language would then no longer be tied to the speaking subject, but to the exteriority of words. As Foucault writes of the poetry of Roussel, "Language has become circular and all-encompassing; it hastily crosses distant perimeters, but is always drawn by a dark center, never given, always elusive—a perspective extended to infinity in the hollow of words, just as the perspective of the whole poem opens both to the horizon and the very middle of the text" (Foucault 2004, p. 137) [Translation modified].

speaker, divine or otherwise, a language Blanchot describes as, "the murmur of the incessant and the interminable" (Blanchot 1982, p. 48).

2. Living Speech

It is not ideas that explain the origin of speech, but speech the origin of ideas. Speech is the creative origin of meaning, which is always in movement and never fixed once and for all. The reality of meaning is determined by speech, and without speech, meaning would not exist. Speech is the coming into existence of meaning through words. Words are always someone speaking to someone. Speech is always a dialogue within a given concrete social situation. Speech is always about something, and that "something" can be an idea, but speech is never just about something. It is spoken to someone. Speaking speaks to speaking. This is the genesis of every idea. Words must be captured by ideas to have a stable meaning, but stable meanings have their source in speech, which is always changing. It is because meaning has its source in speech, that the belief in fixed essences of words is a philosophical illusion.

The "I" responds to the other who speaks to them. It is the "speaking to" that is the ethical moment, and not "what is spoken about". It is I who responds to the other and not the other who responds to me. The other commands or orders me to respond. It is not I who command or order them. Such an asymmetry, where both the "I" and the other are in a relation, but not unified in a totality mediated by a third term, is only possible within of speech. In vision, individuals are reduced to attributes, which are defined in common. What is visible is not the same as speaking, even though the visible can be a theme of speaking. Echoing Rosenzweig, Levinas emphatically writes that "*the absolute experience is not disclosure but revelation*" (Levinas 1969, pp. 65–66). Revelation only occurs in speaking and not in seeing. It is first an orientation of the "I" and the other before anything is spoken about. The other addresses me and I respond. If it is a conversation, then it is not a conversation of equals. I do not address them first. The reason for this is that the "I" of speech is produced through the relation to the other. There is no "I" first in speech. This would be to confuse the "I" of speaking with the "I" of thought, as though, as Levinas puts it, in one of his Talmudic readings, there was "an inversion of the normal order" and "acting" preceded "understanding" (Levinas 1990, p. 42).

There is a truth of speech, which is not the same as the truth speech speaks about. If Levinas describes the relation of speaking first as the relation between the "I" and the other, then Rosenzweig does so through the "I" and God. Rosenzweig starts with the relation to God, and then proceeds to the social, whereas Levinas starts with the social, and then goes onto God. The form of revelation for Rosenzweig is love, but love is expressed only through speech. If creation is the visible world in which God is hidden, then in revelation, God is present as someone who speaks to me, but He speaks to me out of love for me. This does not mean that love is an attribute of God, as we speak of other attributes of God, like "All-Knowing" or "All-Powerful". To speak of God in terms of attributes is to speak of him as an object of knowledge, and not as a relation between a lover and a beloved. I do not love someone because of their attributes, rather they become beloved through this relation. "Love," Rosenzweig writes, "is not an attribute but an event", and as an event it is speaking (Rosenzweig 2005, p. 177). I know God loves me, because God speaks to me as an individual. I am addressed by God, or not at all. I hear God, or I do not. God speaks to me, or God does not. This speaking has nothing to do with whether I affirm God's existence from His essence. God is not an idea of consciousness, which I then go out looking for and find no confirmation. God first speaks, and then he exists for me, but only in that moment. It is perfectly possible that in the next moment, God will not exist, if I do not hear God's word. God "is" for me only to the extent I respond to God's word. The lover exists in the faithfulness of the beloved. As Rosenzweig cites from a passage from the Midrash, "If you testify to me, then I shall be God, otherwise not" (Rosenzweig 2005, p. 185).[10] There is only God because we believe; we do not believe because there is a God.

If God only exists because I respond to God's love for me, then this "I" only truly exists in this response. Revelation is a dialogue and not a monologue. God speaks first, but I reply to God. God calls to me in His love for me, but I only come into existence by responding to this call. There is only an "I" because of a "you". The origin of the "I" who hears God's word is not the self-reflexivity of the "I think", but the "I" who responds to an address of God by answering the question, "where are you?" Only this "I" is really personal, because it is the individual who is addressed and not an abstraction. I love this person not all persons. To love all persons is meaningless, unless you love this one person before you individually. The "I" as the object of thought is only a label common to every "I" that thinks. The "I" of the "I think" is everyone and no-one. It has no name. Only in being addressed is the "I" authentically personal and individual. It is the "I" of my proper name, and not an abstract concept.

Just as I am addressed as a proper name in the question, 'who are you?', then so too does God speaks to me in his proper name. In his essay, "'The Eternal': Mendelssohn and the Name of God", which concerns the translation of the word, "God", in the Hebrew bible, Rosenzweig tells us that when God spoke to Moses, God did not speak to him as a necessary being, in the way philosophy talks about God, but through the three dimensions of direct speech: Addressing, being addressed, and as a theme (what is spoken about in speaking to someone) (Rosenzweig 1993). God's direct speech, however, is reported through writing. Reported speech can only report the shock of the revelation of direct speech by distorting and doing its own violence to it. Mendelssohn's translation of God's name as "the eternal" is still too determined by his rationalism. For this reason, Rosenzweig explains it is better to translate the word "God" as 'Lord', rather than "Eternal", because "Lord" still contains the notion of an address. In Biblical Hebrew, אֲדֹנָי means 'my Lord', where the first person singular pronoun, enclitic has a sense of a vocative "offering". The revealed God of biblical monotheism is not the manifestation of a being, nor the intelligibility of an idea, but the proper name of a God who addresses me and to whom I respond.

By referring to the Hebrew expression, אֲדֹנָי, Rosenzweig is alluding to the prohibition of pronouncing God's name in Judaism, where rather than uttering the name of God as it is written in the Tetragrammaton, you say, "my Lord".[11] Levinas too explains that the meaning of this ritual is to remind Jews that the name of God is a proper and not a common name (Levinas 1994a, pp. 116–28). A proper name, as Kripke argues, is different from a common one, because it is not a definition of someone, but names an individual (Kripke 1980). If we think of Aristotle as the man who taught Alexander, then he would still be Aristotle, even if we subsequently found out that he had not. The name sticks to an individual in an original act of baptism by a community that bestows it on them, and then it is passed down from one generation to the next, who remembers them. Proper names, precisely because they are passed down in this way, can too be forgotten and misplaced. The question for Levinas is not "does God exist?", but "why should we remember God's name?". Levinas refers to the answer given in verse Genesis 18:3, and its Talmudic reading in *Shevu'oth* 35b. אֲדֹנָי does not invoke the name of God as a being or an idea, but as the ethical obligation to the strangers who Abraham welcomes into his tent, and offers shelter and food, because his hospitality is a response both to God's word and theirs. Through the demand they make upon him, the trace of an absent God is present.[12] "The transcendence of God," Levinas writes, "is his actual effacement but this obligates us to men" (Levinas 1994a, p. 125).

---

[10] "And if you are not witnesses, it will be as if I am not your Lord" *Pesikta de Rav-Kahana*, 12.

[11] The Masoretic text of the Hebrew bible places the diacritics (*nikkud*) of אֲדֹנָי under the Tetragrammaton to remind the reader of this proscription. What is written is not what is read out aloud. This was then mistakenly transliterated as Yahweh or Jehovah, as though the Tetragrammaton were pronounced as it was written.

[12] I have examined Levinas's description of the proper name of God, and its relation to Kripke's explanation of proper names as 'rigid designators', in (Large 2013).

In both Levinas and Rosenzweig, narrated speech is subordinated to direct speech, yet God's word is only accessible to us through narrated speech. We do not hear God speak, but we read about those, like Moses or Abraham, who have. All testimony is through the written word. We bear witness to the proper name of God through writing (the difference between how Tetragrammaton is written and how it is pronounced can only be produced through an effect of writing). What is the relation between narrated and direct speech, and is direct speech always the origin of narrated speech, or can it be the other way around, where direct speech can only be narrated, because when we pass down the word of God, we can only do so through writing? Would such a necessity change the way we think about language, and its relation to a community? A community of speakers only survives because of the narrative of God's word. It is the written word that makes this possible and not direct speech. Does this priority of writing over speech change the way we think about language, community, and the tradition it passes down?

3. Narrated Speech

The proper name of God is fixed by a community of speakers who remember the original baptism of the name. If this ritual is not passed from each generation to the next through the rituals of the prohibition of pronouncing the name and its effacement, then it will be forgotten. The memory of the direct speech of God is only possible through the written word. Even when Rosenzweig describes the dialogical relation between God and humanity, as the revelation of direct speech, then God always speaks through the written word of the Hebrew Bible and the Talmud. God speaks to Moses and Moses speaks to the Israelites, but this is the reported speech of the biblical verse. God never speaks to us directly. As Stéphane Moses, reminds us, the direct speech of God in *The Star of Redemption*, is always the reported speech of the written word. God does not speak to us, except through reported speech, which is witnessed and written down.[13]

The origin of language in direct speech is the speaking subject. It is only because I speak to you that that there is speech at all, and even the other addresses me from their own subject position. Is this the case with indirect speech? In indirect speech, there are two lines of communication. There is my speech and the speech of another. I am speaking to you of what someone else has said. I say or write, "He said". Yet, in narrated speech, there is a further distinction to be made. Not only can I report what another says, but I can write in the voice of another. Linguists make a distinction between direct, indirect (or reported speech), and narrated or free indirect speech. In reported speech, I repeat what has been said by another. All direct speech has this element of reported speech, because all direct speech has a theme, which is the reported speech of another even if they are not named. Narrated speech, however, is a unique case of reported speech, whose effect can only be indicated in writing. In narrated speech, the syntactical and semantic signs of reported speech are omitted, but, more importantly, so too is the focal point of speech in a speaking subject. What is important in narrated speech is not just that I am speaking or representing the voice of another, but this voice does not have its origin in a speaking subject. The self is narrated, but there is no speaker. The narrative voice is anonymous.

It is in literature, and especially the development of the novel, that we see the most extensive use of narrated speech, and where the line between who is narrating and what is being narrated becomes increasingly blurred. In the earliest forms of the novel, the narrator speaks in the voice of the characters, and usually we jump from both voices in the same passage without any sign we are doing so. In the development of the modern novel and narrative not only is the focus on the character or narrator indistinct, but the narrator too becomes lost in the narration. Take, for example, the famous opening of Kafka's *The Trial:*

---

[13] 'Entre l'expérience personnelle de la Révélation et l'impossible saisie de *ce* qui se révèle, le texte biblique interpose son discours métaphorique comme une instance médiatrice' [Between the personal experience of Revelation and the impossible grasp of *that* which it reveals, the biblical text interposes its metaphorical discourse as a mediating instance] (Mosès 1977, p. 517) [Emphasis in the original].

Jemand mußte Josef K. verleumdet haben, denn ohne daß er etwas Böses getan hätte, wurde er eines Morgens verhaftet [Someone must have been telling lies about Josef K., for without having done anything wrong, he found himself arrested one morning]. (Kafka 1989, p. 7)

Who does this 'someone' refer to? You might think it refers to Josef K., or to an absent narrator who is telling the story and perhaps is a 'stand-in' for the real Kafka. Because we tend to think of literature as though it were like a kind of telling similar to speaking, we jump over the detail that this 'someone' has no source in a speaking subject. There is a narrated self, but these is no speaker. The shift from the first to the third person is not just a change in a point of view of a speaking subject, but the effacement of the subject as the origin of language. No one is speaking, though speaking is represented. If we think of narration as a kind of telling, then we think of language as primarily spoken, and literature as merely one possible form of spoken language, but this is to deny any difference between narrated and spoken language. In narration, language can contain sentences without a speaker, so that the question "who is speaking" becomes impossible to determine.[14]

The origin of subjectivity in narrated language is not a speaker, but the narration of a self, which cannot be traced back to any point of view. In spoken language, we can distinguish between speaking and subjectivity. If I define language as essentially speaking, then this subjectivity determines language externally since speech is an expression of subjectivity and not speech subjectivity. Subjectivity defines what it is to speak. This is the meaning of living speech. If language is essentially speaking, then speaking must be spoken by someone to someone. The expressivity of language is paramount in defining language as speech. Narrated speech demonstrates that language does not require a speaking subject. In narration, language is neither primarily spoken nor subjective because the narration of speech and thought does not require a self to embody it. It is a narrated self, made up of words, rather than a speaking subject, as the origin of the words it speaks.

To determine language by the speaking subject is to make the origin of language external to language. For the speaking subject is a point of view before it speaks. What is important is not the words spoken, but the relation of the subject to those words. I am addressed by another. It is the difference between the addresser and addressee, which expresses the essence of living speech, and not any of the words said. Moreover, this living speech is defined by the specific relation the addresser has to the words only they speak, and which the addressee lacks, which is a command or injunction. Authentic speech, as we have already seen in Levinas description of the ethical relation, and Rosenzweig's explanation of revelation, is defined by the presence of the speaker, even if that speaker is God, attending or attesting to the words they speak, rather than the words themselves. Even if a verbal expression is referred to, then it is not the words that are significant, but only the demand invoked by the presence of the speaker coming to their aid. The difference between Rosenzweig and Levinas, is that for Rosenzweig, God is a speaking subject present in his command to me. God is "I" and I am "you". God's response to Moses from the burning bush is "I will be that I will be" (Exodus 3:14). For Levinas, on the contrary, it is the other who is the speaking subject, and the proper name of God only has a meaning after this ethical relation.

Do we think language must have its origin in the speaker or words? If literature gives us an example of narrated speech, then we can generalize it to think about language as a whole. Deleuze explains that language for Foucault does not have its origin in a speaking subject, as a specific case of narrated language, but in every instance of subjectivity (Deleuze 1988, pp. 55–57). As I write this sentence to you now, I am a narrated self. The grammatical form of the speaking subject would not be the essence of language, but what language, without a speaking subject, generally makes possible.

---

14 It is important not to confuse the narrator's voice with the author's. The narration of speech and thought is not the direct address of the writer. To identify the one with the other would be to deny the difference between direct and narrated speech. What distinguishes narration is that language can contain sentences without a speaker. The "he" of narrated speech does not refer to an effaced narrator (See Banfield 1982). For the philosophical implication of this, (see Blanchot 1993, pp. 379–87). What I am here calling the "atheism of the word", Blanchot would name the "neuter".

It is not the subject of enunciation that that is the condition of the statement, but it is a variable of the statement or a given arrangement of statements. Rather than the subject being the origin of the statement, it is anonymous and impersonal *on parle* (one speaks) that speaks through the subject. The essence of language is language, and not a subject that exists outside of language and anchors it in an "I speak". It is not "I speak", which is the condition of "one speaks", but "one speaks" is the condition of the any self speaking as a self. The being of language is historically determined. There is not a universal "one speaks" that speaks through every subject, like there is one transcendental self that determines every empirical self. Rather, there is an assemblage of texts, phrases, and statements that belong to a given epoch, but this historical formation can never be traced back to a single statement by a speaking subject. The regularities of an epoch have their source in language that make possible the position of a speaking subject, but these regularities themselves emerge out of a background of an indeterminate "one speaks" or "it speaks", which in turn is historically dated. It is this impersonal or anonymous speaking that speaks through literature. Literature would not just be a special case of language, but is the being of language.

The other and God speak, but it is not what they say that is important. What is important is the presence or the revelation of the other, or God, in speech, and not the words spoken. The other or God does not babble. Narrated language reverses the relation between language and the speaker. For the narrated self has its origin in words and not a speaker, and these words have their source in a social milieu (the "there is speaking", rather than "I speak"). It is not the narrated self that is a limited case of language, and which is defined in opposition to living speech, but living speech that is the rare instance of language. For the origin of the subject that speaks is not consciousness, but inner speech, and inner speech always emerges from a social milieu. Words speak to words in a ceaseless flow of becoming, and only subsequently can language become the expression of a speaker in relation to a "you". Books, other people's words, thoughts in my head, all have the same reality. The opposition between the individual and the social is a false one, because the individual is social through and through. Speaking then speaks out of the background of an anonymity of language, where there is no conjunction of a speaker and a self, and out of which narrated selves are constructed. If Levinas and Rosenzweig say that the presence of the speaker must attend the words they speak, then we can turn this around, and reply that without the accompanying words there would be no expression. It is not the speaking subject that is first, but the narrated self. It is the social milieu, whose origin is narrated language, that makes self-expression possible, and not expression the social milieu. I speak to you, because there is speaking, words speaking to words, and not because there is an original subjective point of view who speaks, whether this point of view is the "I", the other, or God.[15]

God is not a speaking subject, but a narrated self, and if God is a proper name, then He is only so as narrated speech and thought, and not as a speaker. If God is a narrated self, then God exists only in the words others speak of him in writing. If God is no longer narrated, then he ceases to exist. God is not external to language speaking the words to another, but internal to a narrated language. In the former, God is transcendent in relation to language, whereas in the latter, God is immanent. He either speaks the words to me, as any speaking subject would, or He is spoken about. Rosenzweig writes about God as though he were an "I" speaking to a "you", but in the actual writing of *Star of Redemption* God is a "he", which is just the same as any "he" of narration.

---

[15] Heidegger was right to insist in *Being and Time* that authentic speech is a modification of "idle chatter", which is the anonymity of language that no one speaks, but he is wrong to valorize the one above the other as the being of language, for this would be to make the essence of language what lies outside of language, which would be the subject of enunciation. Heidegger ends up in the same impasse as Rosenzweig and Levinas, where language is defined by what is not language, which is the presence of a speaker in language. The essence of language then becomes silence. The authentic speaker who silently converses with themselves. It is no surprise that "idle chatter" is too associated by Heidegger with writing. "This idle talk is not confined to vocal gossip, but even spreads to what we write, where it takes the form of 'scribbling' [das 'Geschreibe']" (Heidegger 1962, p. 212).

Religions **2018**, *9*, 404

Everything depends on whether the other or God is a speaking subject. If the speaking subject is not the origin of language, then all language is exposed to drift and decline, because there is neither a subject nor visible world to fix the meaning of words outside of language. If direct speech comes second rather than first (the "I" speaks because of inner speech, and inner speech has its origin in the narrated self of the social milieu), then what is fixed by a community of speakers, which is how Rosenzweig defines eternity as the continuity of generations, is always open to the ceaseless becoming of words.[16] There is a subtle difference between the Levinas of *Totality and Infinity*, who is largely inspired by Rosenzweig, and the later Levinas. Rosenzweig's God speaks in the first person, but the same cannot be said of Levinas after *Totality and Infinity*, where dialogue and living speech are no longer the exemplary form of alterity.[17] Levinas writes, in his essay "God and Philosophy", that the transcendence of God is a "he", rather than a "I" or a "you", since God commands me to be good through narrated language, and "is neither object nor interlocuter" (Levinas 1998, p. 69). He describes this transcendence through the neologism "illeity", which he adds is "transcendent to the point of absence, to the point of possible confusion with the agitation of the 'there is' (il y a)" (Levinas 1998, p. 69) [Emphasis in the original]. From Levinas's earliest work, the "there is" is the anonymity of being that is broken by the speech of the other who commands me. Being is neutral. Being does not speak, and rather than expressing my singularity, it overwhelms and submerges me. Why then would God be closer to the "there is" rather than the living speech? Because the proper name of God only exists in words, and the first word is spoken by no-one. We are all surrounded by words, swirling around us, and speaking through us, words endlessly responding to words, which is the "there is" of language. We are all babblers and stutterers when it comes to God. God never addresses me directly. God only has a meaning indirectly through narration, a self without subjectivity, and is always exposed to the immanent atheism of the word out of which any meaning emerges, always changing and never permanent, and forever running the risk of oblivion. Judaism lives on because of writing, but what written marks have not been forgotten? Is not this forgetting the real meaning of atheism, and not whether God exists or not, or whether we have an adequate idea of God?

Funding: This research received no external funding.

Conflicts of Interest: The author declares no conflict of interest.

References

Banfield, Ann. 1982. *Unspeakable Sentences: Narration and Representation in the Language of Fiction*. London: Routledge.

Bielik-Robson, Agata. 2014. *Jewish Cryptotheologies of Late Modernity: Philosophical Marranos*. London: Routledge.

Blanchot, Maurice. 1982. *The Space of Literature*. Translated by Ann Smock. Lincoln: University of Nebraska Press.

Blanchot, Maurice. 1993. *The Infinite Conversation*. Translated by Susan Hanson. Minneapolis: University of Minnesota Press.

Cohen, Hermann. 1995. *Religion of Reason out of the Sources of Judaism*. Translated by Simon Kaplan. Atlanta: Scholars Press.

Deleuze, Gilles. 1988. *Foucault*. Translated by Seán Hand. Minneapolis and London: University of Minnesota Press.

Foucault, Michel. 2004. *Death and the Labyrinth: The World of Raymond Roussel*. Translated by Charles Ruas. London: Continuum.

Heidegger, Martin. 1962. *Being and Time*. Translated by John Macquarrie, and Edward Robinson. Oxford: Wiley-Blackwell.

Kafka, Franz. 1989. *Der Prozeß*. Frankfurt am Main: Fischer Taschenbuch.

---

[16] "He who is begotten as a Jew bears witness to his faith by continuing to beget the eternal people" (Rosenzweig 2005, p. 363). Rosenzweig writes that the Jew does not require words, but only existence, but how can there be existence without words?

[17] The difference between the "saying" and the "said" is not between living and narrated speech since the "saying" is "anterior to verbal signs" and is the disruption of the speaking subject from within (Levinas 1991, p. 5) [Translation modified].

Kant, Immanuel. 1998. *Religion within the Boundaries of Mere Reason and Other Writings*. Translated by Allen Wood, and George Di Giovanni. Cambridge: Cambridge University Press.

Kripke, Saul A. 1980. *Naming and Necessity*. Oxford: Blackwell.

Large, William. 2013. The Name of God: Kripke, Lévinas and Rosenzweig on Proper Names. *Journal of the British Society for Phenomenology* 44: 321–34. [CrossRef]

Levinas, Emmanuel. 1969. *Totality and Infinity: An Essay on Exteriority*. Translated by Alphonso Lingis. Pittsburgh: Duquesne University Press.

Levinas, Emmanuel. 1990. *Nine Talmudic Readings by Emmanuel Levinas*. Translated by Annette Aronowicz. Bloomington: Indiana University Press.

Levinas, Emmanuel. 1991. *Otherwise than Being or Beyond Essence*. Translated by Alphonso Lingis. Dordrecht: Kluwer Academic Publishers.

Levinas, Emmanuel. 1994a. *Beyond the Verse: Talmudic Readings and Lectures*. Translated by Gary D. Mole. London: Athlone Press.

Levinas, Emmanuel. 1994b. *In the Time of the Nations*. Translated by Michael B. Smith. London: The Athlone Press.

Levinas, Emmanuel. 1998. *Of God Who Comes to Mind*. Translated by Bettina Bergo. Stanford: Stanford University Press.

Mosès, Stéphane. 1977. Révélation et dialogue chez Franz Rosenzweig. *Revue des Sciences philosophiques et théologiques* 61: 513–31.

Rosenzweig, Franz. 1993. "The Eternal": Mendelssohn and the Name of God. In *Scripture and Translation*. Translated by Lawrence Rosenwald, and Everett Fox. Bloomington: Indiana University Press, pp. 99–113.

Rosenzweig, Franz. 2005. *The Star of Redemption*. Translated by Barbara E Galli. Madison: University of Wisconsin Press.

Trigano, Shmuel. 2001. Levinas and the Project of Jewish Philosophy. *Jewish Studies Quarterly* 8: 279–307.

Van Wolde, Ellen. 1995. Who Guides Whom? Embeddedness and Perspective in Biblical Hebrew and in 1 Kings 3:16–28. *Journal of Biblical Literature* 114: 623–42. [CrossRef]

religions

MDPI

Article

The Seduction of the Name: Universal Marranism and the Secret of Being-in-Language

Adam Lipszyc

Institute of Philosophy and Sociology, Polish Academy of Sciences, 00-330 Warsaw, Poland;
adamlipszyc@gmail.com

Received: 27 September 2018; Accepted: 12 November 2018; Published: 14 November 2018

check for
updates

Abstract: The author combines Walter Benjamin's speculations on language, naming, and horror with Jean Laplanche's general theory of seduction and his notion of the enigmatic signifier in order to reconstruct what he identifies as the primal scene of initiation into language. Further, the author develops this construction by linking it to a similar structure which he extracts by means of interpretation from Jacques Derrida's commentaries to the Biblical stories of the Tower of Babel and of the Binding of Isaac. Finally, the author shows how the primal scene thus reconstructed should be seen as the transcendental condition of being in language as described by Derrida in his seminal essay on *Monolingualism of the Other* and how this very condition should be understood as a universalized form of the Marrano condition. The most far-reaching conclusion of the argument is, then, that at least for Jacques Derrida, every subject of language is a Marrano.

Keywords: Marranism; language; deconstruction; psychoanalysis; Walter Benjamin

Some time between 1920 and 1922 Walter Benjamin wrote down two brief notes titled *Über das Grauen I* and *Über das Grauen II* (Benjamin 1991, pp. 75–77). Short and sketchy as both pieces are, together they record a splendid speculation concerning the interrelations between affect, body, and language. As such terms as 'eidetic' suggest, in these two pieces Benjamin is playing with phenomenological categories and strategies. However, he uses them in his own, highly idiosyncratic manner, and intertwines them with a number of rather startling notions of his own making.

What Benjamin presents is a quasi-phenomenological analysis of the state of 'horror' (*das Grauen*). Rather surprisingly, according to him, the very essence of the phenomenon comes to the fore in a very peculiar situation: namely, when somebody is woken up by his/her mother from the state of deep meditation or sleep. Strictly speaking, it is the mother's face that, on such an occasion, produces the eidetically pure effect of horror. Even more surprisingly, according to Benjamin, at the moment of such an awakening the mother's face turns into a mirror. In other words, in the state of horror the subject does not really perceive his/her mother, but—due to a curious hallucination—a doppelgänger, a copy of his/her own face that suddenly wakes him up.

The effects of this extreme experience are twofold. First, the horror of awakening affects our body and leads to its 'depotentialization' or even 'disembodiment'. Obviously, it does not mean that our body gets dematerialized. Rather, when we are struck by horror, what crumbles is what Benjamin calls our *Leib*, leaving only the so-called *Körper* as the result of the collapse. These are, again, phenomenological categories, roughly mapping the distinction between the living body and the material flesh, but Benjamin uses them at least partly in his own way. The most elaborate discussion of this distinction in his writings can be found in a slightly later piece titled *Outline of the Psychophysical Problem* (Benjamin 1991, pp. 78–87; 1996, pp. 393–401). What emerges from the latter, dense note is the following conceptual structure.

The notion of *Leib* refers, indeed, to the living body which is identical with the embodied spirit. Such a body is endowed with a general form and clear delineation. It is with and through this body that we participate in society and in the immanence of the historical process. In other words, *Leib* is our body as entangled in the symbolic order. *Körper*, on the other hand, is a paradoxical entity. It is the aspect of our being through which we are riveted to materiality, but it is also through *Körper* that we are subject to God—and only this type of body can be expected to resurrect, whereas our *Leib*, enmeshed in the network of signs as it is, will surely disintegrate. *Körper* is the stamp of our aloneness and singularity, and yet it lacks clear form or delimitations. Moreover, it is not to be perceived as a primitive entity which then gets tattooed with symbols. *Körper* does not precede *Leib*; rather, indeed, it is the residual product of its decomposition. We experience it in pain or pleasure, and as the receiver of perceptions. Also in this text Benjamin claims that we are most powerfully communicated with our *Körper* when we perceive someone else's face. The note on horror teaches us that this very experience is at its most acute when we are confronted with our mother's face at the moment of awakening.

Thus, we can appreciate the full meaning of the first effect of horror. In horror, our structured body (*Leib*) trembles and gets depotentialized, momentarily turning into a shapeless, residual flesh (*Körper*), the material, borderless singularity which is subject to God. Secondly, the experience affects our linguistic capabilities. In horror, we are temporarily devoid of speech. Benjamin discusses this crucial effect in the final paragraph of the first note on horror and devotes to it the whole, shorter note no. 2. Both passages are sufficiently lucid and inspiring to be quoted in full. Here is the ending of *Über das Grauen I*: 'Very important: together with the depotentialization of the body in the state of horror, the other pole, that of language, is dropped, too. What is meant is not only the acoustic speech, but language as such in the broadest sense of expression. From that moment on the very possibility of language seems an incomprehensible act of grace and the feeling that it is something natural seems like a sleepwalker's stroll over a tightrope' (Benjamin 1991, p. 77). This striking idea is further developed in the second note. For here is the full text of *Über das Grauen II*: 'The muteness in the state of horror is a primitive experience. Suddenly, with other capabilities intact, amidst other people, in broad daylight, you are devoid of language, of any capability of expression. And that consciousness: that this muteness, this incapability of expression is rooted in man as deeply as—on the other hand—the capability of speaking which permeates him; that this impotence was bequeathed to him as an atavism by his ancestors' (ibid.).

It would be tempting to compare (and possibly contrast) this eccentric and rich speculation with a number of theories that relate language to affect and the maternal. Julia Kristeva's understanding of the semiotic as well as her vision of the abject comes to mind as a natural candidate for such a promising exercise (Kristeva 1982, pp. 1–32; 1986, pp. 89–136). Here, however, I would like to link Benjamin's speculation to another scene taken from a quite different author. The thinker I have in mind is the great psychoanalyst Jean Laplanche who has developed an original vision of the birth of human sexuality known as the general theory of seduction, elegantly summarized in his *New Foundations for Psychoanalysis* (Laplanche 1989, pp. 89–151). Famously, at the beginning of his career, Sigmund Freud tended to believe in the factuality of the 'seductions' (i.e., rapes and/or intrusive sexual encounters) that his patients told him about, and naturally saw them as traumatic and pathogenic. Later, Freud rejected this stance to a large extent and claimed that his patients' stories about seduction reflect their own unconscious fantasies, rather than actual events. Laplanche laments this change, while pointing out that until the very end of his career Freud did insist on the reality of certain primal, traumatic and seductive scenes in his patients' stories. Following this streak in Freud's thinking Laplanche claims that the category of seduction should be kept. However, it should not be applied to the more or less common pathological situations, but to the inevitably premature and traumatic birth of human sexuality as such. It is the adults that initiate us into the world of sexuality when we are not yet ready for this. When it comes to sexuality, it is always to early for us, while—on the other hand—we are always too late: this social-sexual play had started always already before we appeared on stage and thus, before we can become mature players, our first loves must end in misunderstanding, pain and catastrophe.

More precisely, according to Laplanche's general theory of seduction, our sexuality is born due to the always premature encounters with the so-called enigmatic signifiers, the sexually charged messages or interpellations sent to us (usually unconsciously) by the adults. These messages are both traumatic and seductive. Internalized and repressed, they form the very sources of the sexual drive understood as a distortion of, and a deviation from, our simple biological instincts. Thus, our unconscious is not 'ours', as it is formed by the contingent, enigmatic, traumatic encounter with others, the first of them being usually our own mother or, rather, the mother's breast. Moreover, the enigmatic message may be recognized as the transcendental origin of our linguistic capabilities. According to a number of (otherwise very different) psychoanalytic thinkers we actually acquire spoken language as a never-satisfactory substitute for the loss of the primal object, i.e., the maternal breast itself (e.g., Abraham and Török 1994, pp. 127–28). However, the act of seduction as described by Laplanche marks the more originary origin, both transcendental and contingent at the same time, which can be recognized as such only belatedly and after the event. The enigmatic message has seduced us both into the world of sexuality and signs in the first place. The symbolic system thanks to which we map the world, others and ourselves, can be seen as stable and consistent only thanks to the partial assimilation (or, as Laplanche says, translation) and a partial necessary repression of the originary enigma. The enigmatic signifier reappears as such an origin only when the surface of the signifying speech gets radically broken by the return of our unconscious sexual desire.

If we permit ourselves to combine Benjamin and Laplanche, we can see their speculations as curiously complementary. In particular, the scene of horror as described by Benjamin can be seen as a belated reactivation of our catastrophic encounter with the full power of the seductive, traumatic enigma as described by Laplanche. Ironically but adequately, the Benjaminian scene appears as a dialectical reversal of, and a complement to, the Lacanian mirror stage. According to Lacan's classical speculation, in the early mirror experience we narcissitically identify ourselves with our own image; this experience integrates our body and enables us to form relatively stable I, even if at the price self-alienation (Lacan 2006, pp. 75–81). Instead, Benjamin's mirror stage disintegrates our body. It leads us back to the more originary origin than the primary narcissism—the one described by Laplanche—when we were struck with otherness and seduced both into the world of sexuality and into the world of signs.

More importantly for our purposes, one is tempted to link this primal scene of seduction to Benjamin's own theological speculations. As we have seen, Benjamin's meditations on horror themselves are not free from a theological element: *Körper* which comes to the fore in this experience is what can be called the theological body of man, a body that marks his/her absolute singularity and his relation to God. For his part, Laplanche himself points out that the asymmetrical relation between the adult and the child in the scene of seduction may be seen as analogous to the equally asymmetrical relation between the eminent reality of God and the being of the created world, as described by the Cartesian tradition (Laplanche 1989, pp. 123–24). And, in a different context, Eric Santner has already suggested a fruitful isomorphism between Laplanche's vision of the enigmatic signifier and Gershom Scholem's famous idea of the 'nothingness of revelation' as developed in Scholem's letters to Benjamin himself (Santner 2001, pp. 33–40).

In his seminal essay *On Language as Such and on the Language of Man*, Benjamin claims that at the moment of his creation man was given that very same language which God used when creating the world (Benjamin 1996, pp. 62–74). According to the second version of the creation story, alone among the created beings, man is created out of a material. This seeming inferiority is, in fact, a mark of his superiority, for it means that man was not created through word and was not subjected to the creative language by naming. Rather, an originarily and essentially nameless being, he now completes the work of creation by naming other entities himself with the very same language they were created through. The purity of this language and man's linguistic bliss get lost only at the moment of the Fall which for Benjamin finds its logical completion in the destruction of the Tower of Babel. In fact, the two events, unrelated in the Bible, can be seen as two aspects of the same catastrophe.

However, combining Laplanche's vision of the enigmatic signifier with Benjamin's phenomenology of horror opens a path toward a most natural revision of this theological pattern. It enables us to see man as receiving language in an act of original revelation at the same moment he is subdued to it. This revelation/subjection can be perceived as the very act of naming man by God that Benjamin so forcefully denied to have taken place. Moreover, the now-triple act of revelation, subjection and naming is to be seen as the traumatic interpellation, the seduction by the enigma of the name, which throws us into language, orders us to speak, while making it impossible for us to control the origin. If so, then there is no need for the hypothesis of the Fall which subverts man's almost divine sovereignty—almost divine and not divine proper only because it manifests itself only in naming and not in creation itself—for the very act of receiving language questions human sovereignty and thus it is indistinguishable from the Fall. And if the scene of horror and trembling as described by Benjamin is the originary repetition of such a primal scene of seduction understood as the psychotheological description of the origin of our being-in-language, then we have to revise the point that Benjamin makes in his second note on horror. It is not only that 'this muteness, this incapability of expression is rooted in man as deeply as—on the other hand—the capability of speaking which permeates him'. Rather, now we can see that these two qualities that ultimately define our humanity spring from one and the same though divided origin: it is the enigma which introduces us to language, but which—when confronted in repetition or belated reactivation—robs us of any capability of speaking and leaves our bodies in horror and trembling.

Now, I believe that this primal scene of language which emerges if we combine Benjamin on horror with Laplanche on seduction, should be further combined with a parallel scene which emerges from the work of Jacques Derrida. This scene can be reconstructed from a number of his writings, in particular from the essay *Des Tours de Babel* and from his book on *The Gift of Death*. Briefly speaking, Derrida can be read as linking three Biblical locations: Sinai as the site of revelation, Babel as the site of destruction and Mount Moriah as the site of secret and trembling.

The link or, simply, identification of Sinai and Babel rather obviously emerges from the opening pages of Derrida's essay on the Towers (Derrida 2002, pp. 104–11). In this essay, taking Voltaire's commentary on Babel as his point of departure, Derrida argues that God destroyed the Tower by naming it with his own revealed name which thus can be identified as 'Confusion': 'Babel means not only confusion [. . .] but also the name of the father, more precisely and more commonly, the name of God as name of father. The city would bear the name of God the father and of the father of the city that is called confusion. God, the God, would have marked with his patronym a communal space, that city where understanding is no longer possible' (ibid., p. 105). Thus revealed, the divine Name ruins the Tower of the homogeneous, potentially universal empire and breaks the equally homogeneous language which from now on will be always infected with the virus of *differance*. Thus, whereas actually and factually language does exist earlier, the moment of destruction of the Tower can be seen as the return of the more originary origin of speech, the one which establishes it and disestablishes it at the same time, an act which is to be identified with the revelation on the uncontrollable Name, the only Sinai you can count on Derrida's world.

However, this scene at Babel-as-Sinai is to be further linked to the moment of Akedah as read by Derrida in *The Gift of Death* (Derrida 1996, pp. 53–81). Famously, in his *Fear and Trembling* Kierkegaard argued that Abraham's decision to obey God and sacrifice his son marks the leap that the knight of faith makes when transcending the talkative logos of the ethical stage of existence and entering the utter secrecy and silence of the religious stage. In his deconstructive reading of Kierkegaard's reading of Abraham's story, Derrida argues that, paradoxically, in order for the argument to hold the ethical stage must be transcended and kept at the same time: 'Abraham must assume absolute responsibility for sacrificing his son by sacrificing ethics, but in order for there to be a sacrifice, the ethical must retain all its value, the love for his son must remain intact, and the order of human duty must continue to insist on its rights' (ibid., p. 66). Thus, the so-called religious stage cannot be seen as a separate domain over and above the ethical. Rather, we should see Abraham's decision as a disruptive inscription in the very field of the ethical, with the silence of Abraham as the deconstructive moment of secrecy which troubles the domain of language and the ethical law, permanently reopening them to the moment of alterity and justice. What injects this moment of silence and secrecy into human language and into the field of ethical law is the call of God or, again, his Name: 'One must behave not only in an ethical or responsible manner, but in a nonethical, nonresponsible manner, and one must do that *in the name of* duty, of infinite duty, *in the name of* absolute duty. And this name which must always be singular is here none other than the name of God as completely other, the nameless name of God, the unpronounceable name of God as other to which I am bound by an absolute unconditional obligation, by an incomparable, nonnegotiable duty' (ibid., p. 67).

We can conclude, then, that the Name of God, which as the virus of deconstruction and confusion inserted itself into human language with the destruction of the Tower of Babel, reappears and receives its true ethical significance in God's address to Abraham. Moreover, it is received and responded to in the very silence and secrecy to which Abraham was forced when travelling to the Mount Moriah. And it is this very secrecy that causes literal trembling which marks the permanent return of the disruptive Name: 'A secret always makes you tremble. [...] It suggests that violence is going to break out again, that some traumatism will insist on being repeated. [...] We tremble in that strange repetition that ties an irrefutable past (a shock has been felt, a traumatism has already affected us) to a future that cannot be anticipated' (ibid., pp. 53–54).

So here is the sequence of equations that I insist on. On my reading, the Benjaminian scene of horror is to be seen as the repetition of Laplanche's scene of original seduction. This scene, in turn, is to be equated with the revelation of God's Name in Babel and on Mount Moriah as understood by Derrida. What emerges from this complex sequence is the psychotheological primal scene of the original introduction to language, a scene which precedes the time when we actually start speaking. The scene marks the moment of seduction by the Name—which, combining revised Benjamin on language with unrevised Derrida on Babel, we can now recognize as being *both* God's name *and* the true name of the first man. It is also the moment of making and breaking the language as such, of inscribing the aspect of secrecy and muteness into its very texture, and act of infection which only establishes language properly as the element potentially subject to the permanent deconstructive opening. Only naturally, then, the trembling collapse of our structured bodies and the mute oppression that Benjamin describes in his notes on horror can be perceived as our belated confrontation with the divided origin of our being-in-language, which is responsible both for our linguistic capabilities and for our muteness.

One can note that coherent as the above argument may be, it involves a curious gender mess. Both Benjamin (when discussing horror) and Laplanche (when discussing seduction) focus on the relation between the subject and the maternal. The cluster of arguments that I point to in Derrida at least seem to be focused more on the paternal regime, with God as the terrible father who seems to appear also in Benjamin's own theological speculations on the origin of language. However, if we follow Derrida more closely, the centrality of the paternal figure in his argument may appear as much less certain. For both revelatory scenes we have pointed to in Derrida—while linking them to each other—that is, the Babelic and the Akedic moment, concern the ultimate subversion of phallocentric paternality rather than the establishment of the absolute phallus called God. His or her name is confusion: s/he seduces us into language by naming us and disestablishes every phallic sovereignty without establishing his/her own. Moreover, it is to be noted that at least in one important text Derrida explicitly focuses on the link between language and the maternal, clearly understood along the lines of the above argument. Namely, in an infinitely long footnote to the book on *Monolingualism of the Other*, he discusses Hannah Arendt's attitude to her German *Muttersprache* during the Nazi times and her defensive dictum that it was not the language that has gone mad. Derrida remarks that what Arendt does not take into account is that language as such can be mad after all in a different sense and that, moreover, as he says alluding to his own *Circumfessions*, 'the mother of the language called "maternal"' may 'be able to become, to have been, mad (amnesiac, aphasic, delirious)' (Derrida 1998, p. 87). Thus, the relation to the maternal is not that of the original coziness and of a natural bond which makes us feel at home in our mother tongue. Even though unique and constitutive for the subject, the relation as Derrida describes it is marked by originary otherness and contingency, we might say: by the originary colonization.

Now, I believe that it is precisely *Monolingualism of the Other* that in a particularly lucid way shows the very dynamics of the linguistic existence inaugurated by the primal psychotheological scene I have been reconstructing so far. In other words, my claim is that the linguistic predicament that Derrida analyzes in this text implicitly assumes the traumatic and destructive seduction by the divine Name as the transcendental condition of its possibility and as its (belatedly recognized) origin. Moreover, my ultimate claim is that even though in *Monolingualism of the Other* Derrida does not explicitly refer to the Marrano phenomenon that he discusses in other texts so sympathetically (e.g., Derrida 2007, p. 13), in this very book Derrida can be seen as presenting the very being-in-language of any human subject as a universalized Marrano predicament marked by inherent secrecy which is initiated by the primal scene of naming. *For Derrida, every subject of language is a Marrano.*

Daringly, Derrida takes his private biographical trajectory as the blueprint for his general vision of the constitution of the linguistic subject as such. The trajectory is that of a Franco-Maghrebian Jew and a patriot—or a 'matriot'—of the French culture in general and of the French language in particular. As far as the status of culture is concerned, Derrida universalizes his predicament into the radical statement concerning its inevitable colonialism. He writes: '"Colonialism" and "colonization" are only high points, one traumatism over another, an increasing buildup of violence, the jealous rage of an essential *coloniality* and *culture*, as shown by the two names. A coloniality of culture [...]' (Derrida 1998, p. 24). And further: 'All culture is originarily colonial. In order to recall that, let us not simply rely on etymology. Every culture institutes itself through the unilateral imposition of some "politics" of language. Mastery begins, as we know, through the power of naming, of imposing and legitimating appellations' (ibid., p. 39). And finally, in a most lucid way: 'The question here is not to efface the arrogant specificity or traumatizing brutality of what is called modern colonial war in the "strictest definition" of the expression ... On the contrary. Certain people, myself included, have experienced colonial cruelty from two sides, so to speak. But once again, it reveals the colonial structure of any culture in an exemplary way' (ibid., p. 39). Thus, every being in culture, even in the 'maternal culture', which is constitutive for the very emergence of the subject, is marked by originary contingency and violence. In Derrida's words, it has the structure of 'alienation without alienation' (ibid., p. 25), for there is no subject prior to it to be considered alienated by the originary colonialism.

This originarily colonial nature of any culture finds its most vivid expression in the relation between subject and language. Derrida suggests that his position within French language can be defined by the paradoxical formula which gets repeated throughout the text like a magic incantation: 'I only have one language; it is not mine' (ibid., p. 1). Again, ostensibly, this formula refers to a most peculiar Franco-Maghrebian-Jewish predicament which marks Derrida's own biography. It is the predicament of a radically decentered minority which—having no specific language of its own—breathes the linguistic element of an empire which it does not 'own'. Derrida says: 'As for language in the strict sense, we could not even resort to some familiar substitute, to some idiom internal to the Jewish community, to any sort of language of refuge that, like Yiddish, would have ensured an element of intimacy, the protection of "home-of-one's own" against the language of official culture, a second auxiliary in different socio-semiotic situations' (ibid., p. 54). However, Derrida does not hesitate to universalize the formula which defines his personal position. For if any culture is colonial, then whatever my geo-ethnic position, even my mother tongue, the language that, deep down there, I can call my only language, is not my own. Thus, Derrida may say quite explicitly: 'Consequently, anyone should be able to declare under oath: I have only one language and it is not mine; my "own" language is, for me, a language that cannot be assimilated. My language, the only one I hear myself speak and agree to speak, is the language of the other' (ibid., p. 25).

The biographical, historical and political coloring of Derrida's argument notwithstanding, this is precisely the condition of the subject introduced to language on the primal scene described above: the scene which seduces us into the world of signs, but at the same time disinherits us, makes it impossible for us to feel at home in our only language and to control the origin. If we 'owned' our language, if we controlled its origin, we would have been gods and the catastrophe of the Tower would have been undone. But the origin, the moment of naming, is also the moment of absolute alienation and subversion of any subjective sovereignty that we might ever aspire to. A vivid sign of this initial catastrophe of naming which turns us into speaking subjects is the speechless horror we feel when confronted with the origin once again.

And it is this very linguistic predicament that, I believe, should be identified as universal Marranism. Of course, it is a peculiar, deconstructed and deconstructive form of Marranism, freed from the limitations of its original, historical form. If Marranism means keeping your secret Judaism within the official element of Christianity that one officially professes, then—obviously—neither Derrida is a Marrano, nor—even more obviously—is he treating this condition as universal. Moreover, this is not the case even if being a Marrano means (slightly more metaphorically) that you are keeping a secret yet well defined identity within the element of Christianity, Islam, Judaism or any other religious or atheist/republican discourse, an identity which connects you to a community you have been cut off from or at least defines you as a stable, consistent individual. However, in his book on Marranism considered as the model of modern identity, Yirmiyahu Yovel suggests that even the historical Marranos should be studied as forming a peculiar group of individuals with distorted identities rather than simply as people who were 'in fact' Jews. Yovel stresses the extent to which the Marranos were dramatically estranged from Judaism itself which at least some of them desperately tried to keep on practicing. Thus, without finding their home in the religion they have converted to, at least some of the Marranos were losing a stable identity that could be really cherished in secret and so they were becoming 'heretics to all religions' (Yovel 2009, p. 164).

If we think about Marrano condition along these lines, but move even further away from well-defined subjective identities, we can ultimately arrive at the proper understanding of what I perceive as Derrida's universal Marranism. What is crucial for the deconstructive Marranism is precisely the condition of the subject who, though submerged in the element s/he finds himself/herself alienated in, nevertheless is constituted by this very element and has no private, secret language of his/her own. The secret that the deconstructive Marrano keeps is not a set of propositions or ritual gestures, it is the very condition of alienation without alienation, of that infinitely small, secret fold of subjectivity within the language that constitutes it, a fold that, in turn, is constitutive for language as such as infected by the virus of *differance*. This very subjectivity comes into being (into being-in-language) by the primal scene of scene of seduction and naming described above, which is both the act of initiation and estrangement. And if Derrida is right in *Monoligualism of the Other* and, indeed, if he is right in everything he tried to say about language from the very outset of his project, then the Marrano condition thus defined is, indeed, the condition of every subject of language.

How does this non-propositional, non-essentialist, universal, deconstructive Marranism manifest itself? In the last section of *Monolingualism of the Other* Derrida answers this question in a particularly vivid way. It does not come as a surprise (and agrees fully with what Walter Benjamin told us) that if every subject has one language which, however, is not his/her own, then—paradoxically, but logically—Derrida can identify every subject of language as, in a sense, marked by secret aphasia. He takes this keen observation as the starting point for a striking idea. Namely, that when the linguistic/aphasic subject, rather than pretending that s/he fits nicely into his/her mother tongue like a glove, is true to the secret fold that s/he is, then s/he acts as if s/he were trying to do something impossible: to translate from a language to come into the language s/he speaks. Thus, Derrida can offer one of the most powerful definitions of deconstruction as such: 'That too is a peculiar phenomenon of translation. The translation of a language that does not as yet exist, and that will never have existed, in any given target language. This translation translates itself in an internal (Franco-French) translation by playing with the non-identity with itself of all language. By playing and taking pleasure' (Derrida 1998, p. 65). Incidentally, I would not hesitate to identify the pleasure Derrida is talking about with sexual enjoyment that, according to Jean Laplanche, returns within the breaks of discourse. However this may be, though, it is only by means of that internal, deconstructive translation that each time reopens our present language, our law, our home to what is to come—a translation which is both an act of playful pleasure and an ethical act of justice—that we remain true to our secret Marrano condition and to that primal scene that introduced as to being-in-language: to that horrifying seduction of the Name.

Funding: This research was funded by the Polish National Science Centre, grant number UMO-2017/25/B/HS2/02901.

Conflicts of Interest: The author declares no conflicts of interest.

References

Abraham, Nicolas, and Mária Török. 1994. *The Shell and the Kernel*. Translated by Nicholas T. Rand. Chicago: The University of Chicago Press.

Benjamin, Walter. 1991. *Gesammelte Schriften*. Frankfurt am Main: Suhrkamp Verlag, vol. 1.

Benjamin, Walter. 1996. *Selected Writings*. Edited by Marcus Bullock and Michael W. Jennings. Cambridge: The Belknap Press of Harvard University Press, vol. 1.

Derrida, Jacques. 1996. *The Gift of Death*. Translated by David Willis. Chicago: The University of Chicago Press.

Derrida, Jacques. 1998. *Monoligualism of the Other; or, the Prosthesis of the Origin*. Translated by Patrick Mensah. Stanford: Stanford University Press.

Derrida, Jacques. 2002. *Acts of Religion*. Edited by Gil Anidjar. London: Routledge.

Derrida, Jacques. 2007. Abraham, the other. In *Judeities*. Edited by Bettina Bergo, Joseph Cohen and Raphael Zagury-Orly. New York: Fordham University Press.

Kristeva, Julia. 1982. *Powers of Horror. An Essay on Abjection*. Translated by Leon S. Roudiez. New York: Columbia University Press.

Kristeva, Julia. 1986. *The Kristeva Reader*. Edited by Toril Moi. New York: Columbia University Press.

Lacan, Jacques. 2006. *Écrits*. Translated by Bruce Fink. New York: W.W. Norton & Co.

Laplanche, Jean. 1989. *New Foundations for Psychoanalysis*. Translated by David Macey. Oxford: Basil Blackwell.

Santner, Eric L. 2001. *On the Psychotheology of Everyday Life*. Chicago: The University of Chicago Press.

Yovel, Yirmiyahu. 2009. *The Other Within. The Marranos: Split Identity and Emerging Modernity*. Princeton: Princeton University Press.

MDPI

Article
Benjamin's Profane Uses of Theology: The Invisible Organon

Francisco Naishtat [1,2]

1   Instituto de Investigaciones Gino Germani, Facultad de Ciencias Sociales, Universidad de Buenos Aires, Uriburu 950, 6° Piso, Ciudad de Buenos Aires C1114AAD, Argentina; fnaishtat@gmail.com;
    Tel.: +5411-4508-3815 or +5411-4899-5400
2   Member of the Carrera del Investigador Científico (CIC), Consejo Nacional de Investigaciones Científicas y Tecnológicas (CONICET), Godoy Cruz 2290, Ciudad de Buenos Aires C1425FQB, Argentina

check for updates

Received: 24 October 2018; Accepted: 27 January 2019; Published: 2 February 2019

Abstract: Invisible, but suggestive and fruitful; deprived of any reference to doctrine or ultimate assertive foundations, but nevertheless used in Benjamin like written images, crystallized as "images of thought"; as doctrinally mute as it is heuristically audible, Benjamin's use of theology reminds us of the ironical use that Jorge Luis Borges himself made of theology and metaphysics as part of his own poetic forms. As such, these images of thought are located both in the place of philosophical use and in the one of methodological cunning or *Metis*, across the various levels of the corpus: a metaphysics of experience, literary criticism, philosophy of language, theory of history and Marxism. Therefore, accepting that *criticism* (*Kritik*) is the visible *organon* and the *object* of Benjaminian philosophy, is not theology, then, its *invisible organon*? What seems to be particular to Benjamin, however, is the agonistic but nevertheless heuristic way in which he intends to use theology in order to upset, disarray, and deconstruct the established philosophy, and specially its dominant trends in the field of the theory of history: historicism, positivism, and the evolutionary Hegelian–Marxist philosophy of history. In this article we try to demonstrate how this theological perspective is applied to a Benjaminian grammar of time. We conclude agonistically, confronting the resulting Benjaminian notion of historical past against Heiddeger's own vision of historical time.

Keywords: invisibility; heresy; disguise; disruptive; Marxism; messianism; historical time; past; redemptiveness; language

1. Introduction

Hannah Arendt wrote that Benjamin felt more attracted to theology than to religion, even though he "was no theologian" (Arendt 1969, p. 4). There is in Benjamin, in fact, a productive use of theological images which deviates from the conventional context of the history of religion, but which injects theology into his thinking as an antidote to the conformist and "bourgeois"[1] worldview of his time and to their respective academic ideologemes. The figures of hell, paradise, fall, guilt, eschatology,

---

1   Benjamin early on contrasted "the mystical" with "the bourgeois" (*bürgerlichen Ansicht*): in his 1916 essay on the philosophy of language, he opposed in fact the "mystical theory of language" (*mystische Sprachstheorie*) to the "bourgeois theory" of language (GS-II.1, p. 150). Shortly afterwards, in the *Theological-Political Fragment* (1921–1922), he states that the relationship between the Messianic (*das Messianische*) and the profane (*das Profane*) "is one of the essential teachings of the philosophy of history. It is the precondition of a mystical conception of history" (*mystische Geschichtsauffassung*) (GS-II.1, pp. 203–4 and SW-3, p. 305). Both his reflections on language and those on history already reveal the sharp edge noted by Benjamin in theology as an intensity factor agonistically inscribed against conformism (we will hereafter call GS the *Gesammelte Schriften*, the title of Walter Benjamin's complete works (7 volumes, 14 books), edited by Rolf Tiedemann and Hermann Schweppenhäuser in Suhrkamp, Frankfurt am Main, (Benjamin 1972–1991). Volumes are referred to in Roman numerals; books, when more than one, after a full stop in Arabic numerals; and we will indicate the page(s), after a comma, in Arabic

---

creation, redemption, last judgment, Adam, Messiah—to cite but the most important ones in the Berlin-born philosopher's oeuvre—are recurrent in his work. While theology does not appear in the Benjaminian corpus as a thematic section, it nevertheless permeates the whole of Benjamin's oeuvre, spreading throughout regardless of themes or explicit references.

Thematically or from a doctrinal point of view, however, his theology is invisible. This 'invisibility' of theology in Benjamin does not mean the invisibility of the theological marks, which are on the contrary disseminated throughout the entire corpus. Therefore the expression 'theological invisibility' must be taken here with some caution; it paradigmatically refers to different figures:

(a) The well-known conclusive formula of the first thesis from *On the Concept of History*, where Benjamin prescribes that historical materialism "enlists the services of theology, which today, as we know, is small and ugly and has to keep out of sight" (*nicht darf blicken lassen*) (GS-I.2, p. 693; SW-4, p. 389). Adorno, commenting on this fragment soon after Benjamin's death, wrote in a letter to Horkheimer that "theology cannot enter as such in the written text because its 'invisibility' has become the hallmark of its truth" (*die Theologie nicht in den geschrieben Text einzugehen, da ihr 'Unsichtbarwerden' heute zum Kennzeichen ihrer Wahrheit geworden ist*) (Letter from Adorno to Horkheimer of September 4th 1941, quoted in (Pangritz 2000, p. 819)).

(b) This sort of cryptical invisibility is well depicted in Benjamin's famous declaration on his relation to theology (PW N7a7; Benjamin 1999, p. 471). By way of comparing theology with ink, and his own thinking with the blotting pad, Benjamin emphasizes that the latter is saturated with the former, but he observes, nevertheless, that "were one go by the blotter, however, nothing of what is written would remain" (*nichts, was geschrieben ist, übrig bleiben*). Therefore his standpoint is that whereas the traces of theology indeed fully impregnate his thinking, theology survives in the latter only at the prize of being completely reshaped, reminding us the beautiful title by Irving Wohlfahrt in a paper on Benjamin: "Re-Fusing Theology", not of course as a *refusal* of theology but as *re-fusing*, namely *fusing* it again and on a different basis with his thinking itself (Wohlfarth 1986, pp. 3–24).

(c) This figure leads us to a third plane of invisibility which is the one of the Kabbalah: in his *Erinnerungen* (Memories), Max Rychner pointed out that Benjamin told him that "only someone familiar with the Kabbalah—the sacred texts of the Jewish mystical tradition—could understand the notoriously difficult of the "*Erkenntniskritische Vorrede*" or "Epistemo-Critical Prologue" to his *Origin of the German Trauerspiel*" (Wolin 1994, n. 7, p. 286). Furthermore, in his dedication to Gershom Scholem's personal copy of the *Trauerspiel*, Benjamin wrote "Donated to Gerhard Scholem for the ultima Thule of his Kabbalah library" (Scholem 1975, p. 158). Indeed, as early as in 1918, in *On the Program of the Coming Philosophy* (SW-1, pp. 100–10; GS-II.1, pp. 157–71), Benjamin promoted the abandonment of the enlightened mathematical–mechanical conception of knowledge in favor of a linguistic–critical method based on the philosophy of language. But precisely his philosophy of language, developed since 1916 in his essay "On Language as Such and on the Language of Man" (SW-1, pp. 62–74; GS-II.1, pp. 140–57), so important for Benjamin's thought, is rooted both in the scriptural Jewish tradition and in the tradition of the Kabbalah. A technique of allegory and paradoxical sense, which will later shine in the *Trauerspiel* book, already finds all its space in the previous decade, in terms of a linguistic articulation between the sacred and the profane that can be neither self-evident nor transparent, but esoteric and fragmentary.

Therefore, it makes no sense to seek to reconstruct, against the background of Benjamin's fragmentary thinking, a visible and explicit theological core that may provide an ultimate interpretation or foundation that are lacking in philosophy. Theology in Benjamin is neither an all-encompassing key of unity, or a concealed integration of meaning, nor a content of hope capable of offsetting, like a religious counterbalance, his intellectual pessimism. However, on the other hand, there are

---

numerals. For the English edition of the work, we will, unless otherwise specified, refer to the one edited by Michael Jennings, in four volumes, in the Belknap Press of Harvard University Press, Cambridge, Massachusetts, 1999–2003, named *Selected Writings*, and we will abbreviate SW, indicating the volume with Arabic numbers, followed by the pages' numbers.

theological motifs and references scattered throughout his oeuvre. How then should we read this relationship between the corpus and theology? How is the "task of the critic" [2] articulated with this disguised theology once we have dismissed the view of a theological basis of the work? The answer, if any, is not simple or paradox free, as shown in the already-mentioned passage of the *Passagen-Werk* (*Konvolute* N7a, 7):

> My thinking is related to theology as blotting pad is related to ink. It is saturated with it. Were one to go by the blotter, however, nothing of what is written would remain (*nichts, was geschrieben ist, übrig bleiben*). (PW N7a7; Benjamin 1999, p. 471).

Invisible, but at the same time impregnating and fruitful; deprived of any reference to doctrine or ultimate truth, theology seems to be in Benjamin an implicit *organon*—namely, an implicit heuristics of thought—simultaneously located in the place of philosophical use and of methodological cunning or *Metis* across the various levels of the corpus: a metaphysics of experience, literary criticism, philosophy of language, theory of history and Marxism. If theology does not belong to a religious interpretation, as it would happen with a theological hermeneutics of the corpus—which seems, in our opinion, inappropriate here[3]—, it is however seen in Benjamin's uses of language and frameworks of thought. As stated by Günter Hartung (Hartung 2001, p. 424)[4], Benjamin's Messianism and theology do not define contents of faith or of religious doctrine, but *contents of thought*. The latter should be captured in the modes, allegorizations (*Sinnbilder*) and images (*Denkbilder*) that constellate the Benjaminian fragments.

In his above-mentioned first thesis of *On the Concept of History* (1940), Benjamin, inspired by Poe's short story about the chess-playing automaton, suggests placing theology "at the service" (*Dienst*) of the "puppet called 'historical materialism'":

> One can imagine a philosophic counterpart to this apparatus. The puppet called "historical materialism" is to win all time. It can easily be a match for anyone if it enlists the services of theology, which today, as we know, is small and ugly and has to keep out of sight. (GS-I.2, p. 693; SW-4, p. 389)

Benjamin, like Kant in his 1793 text on religion (Kant 2008), inverts here the *ancilla* formula that defined the relationship of theology with philosophy in medieval tradition (*philosophia ancilla theologiae*—"philosophy the servant of theology"). However, while in Kant the practical use of religion visibly and expressly provides a dimension of intentional hope that opens a horizon of intentional meaning to moral duty, offering a supplement of world to the emaciated transcendental rigorism, in Benjamin, far from that, the theological use is neither explicit nor does it aim at operating as a promise in the way of future expectation. Paradoxically, instead, this use of theology in no way dilutes Benjamin's visceral pessimism or faithlessness, but rather reinforces them, as shown early on by his radical rejection of any *finalistic* or *teleological* perspective in any form: theodicy, theocracy, historicism

---

[2] Benjamin's fragment entitled "The Task of the Critic" (1931) was only posthumously published. Let us point out that Benjamin was fond of using the term "task" (*Aufgabe*) for characterising a series of actions considered necessary with relation to both theoretical and political activity: we can see it in the name he gives to his famous 1923 essay on translation (*Die Aufgabe des Übersetzers*) (GS-IV.1, pp. 9–21), as well as in his eighth thesis of *On the Concept of History* (GS-I.2, p. 697), where he refers to "our task" in a clearly political sense. As for "The Task of the Critic" see (*Aufgabe des Kritikers*, GS-VI.1, pp. 171–72; SW-2, pp. 548–49).

[3] In his letter to Gershom Scholem dated 11th August 1934, Benjamin writes: "I consider Kafka's constant insistence on the Law to be the point where his work comes to a standstill (*den toten Punkt*), which only means to say that it seems to me that the work cannot be moved in any interpretative direction whatsoever from there" (Benjamin 1978, Band IV, p. 479). I think that this hermeneutic self constraint concerning the theological interpretation of Kafka, may also be valid for Benjamin's oeuvre: there is no theological interpretation, which however does not at all reduce the impact of theology on the method and the development of the contents of thought. From this last point of view, theology does not only operate as a "revelation" of writing but also as the negative of revelation or, to use a suggestive term by Danielle Cohen-Levinas, inspired by the Scholem's notion of the "nothingness of revelation", as an "irrevelation" (Cohen-Levinas 2013, p. 315).

[4] Cited by Erdmut Wizisla (Wizisla 2013, p. 308).

or the philosophy of progress, as illustrated by the *Theological-Political Fragment* (1920–1921) and his other youth writings up to his 1940 theses *On the Concept of History*. We should therefore take care not to associate the concealment of theology in Benjamin with the teleological tradition of the "invisible hand" (i.e., God's or Providence's) which characterized modern philosophy from Leibniz' theodicy to Hegel's "cunning of reason" (*List der Vernunft*), not to mention the immanent teleology of the market in the liberal school or the philosophy of progress in "vulgar Marxism" (*vulgärmarxistische Begriff*) (GS-I.2, p. 699).

Accepting, then, with Adorno that in Benjamin "the invisibility of theology has become the distinctive feature of its truth" ("*da ihr Unsichtbarwerden heute zum Kennzeichen ihrer Wahrheit geworden ist*") (Pangritz 2000, p. 819), what is this truth and how does it move with relation to Marxism and to philosophy in order to play the double role of "being at its service" (*in ihren Dienst nimmt*) and, paradoxically, of being like its living, thinking organ, that is, the one that "pulls the strings" (*und die Hand der Puppe an Schnüren lenkte*)? To which truth, in short, does this overshadowed inscription, proper to cabalistic graphology, correspond, "counter-writing" its marks on blotting paper, turned into a dissimulator of writing not to be shown? Accepting with Uwe Steiner, on the other hand, that *criticism* (*die Kritik*) is at the same time the *organon* and the *object* of Benjaminian philosophy,[5] isn't theology, then, its *invisible organon*[6]? Or, if one prefers, *its heretic, disguised organon*, a *photographic negative* of philosophy, or the *counterfugue* to its materialistic discourse? Then, instead of clinging to a binary logic, which in the name of the "excluded third" would suppress theology for Marxism or, inversely, Marxism for theology, Benjamin would be operating with a baroque counteroffensive, consisting in simultaneously combining the two opposing fronts.[7] This heretic, disguised, and invisible organon is negatively characterized:

(1) It is not metatheoretically separable, like the Aristotelian "Organon" or Descartes' "rules of method";

(2) It is not "*inner life*", like "thought" as an intellectual basis (*Nous*, *Esprit*, *Cogito*, *Geist*, *Mind*) that has distinguished dualistic gnoseology;

(3) It is not an *interiority of religious faith*, like a Pascalian or Kierkegaardian interiority[8];

(4) It is not "*Leitfaden*",[9] a Kantian guiding thread or a Hegelian–Marxist theodicy, in a teleologically providential sense of nature or history.

---

5   "Kritik ist aber nicht nur Organon theoretischer Reflexion, sondern zugleich auch ihr Gegenstand" (Steiner 2000, p. 479).
6   The idea of theology in Benjamin as an *organon* (i.e., an "instrument" in Ancient Greek) is suggested by Wolfgang Ullmann (Ullmann 1992, p. 99), who highlights the heuristic and methodological side of theology in Benjamin, possibly inspired by Franz Rosenzweig, who saw theology as a method far more than as an object of philosophy. We could, in turn, rely on the notion of "philosophical Marranism", recently introduced by Agata Bielik-Robson (2014), to account for the type of invisibility we deem it appropriate to associate with what we intend here to call "*invisible organon*". It seems equally suggestive to resort to the second Wittgenstein and to his notion of grammar: in fact, theological invisibility does not work in Benjamin as a phantasmal subject or inner "interiority" as "spirit", "Geist", "Intention", "daemon", or "Intellect", but rather as a *deep grammar* of language and writing, under the form of a palimpsest or of a scriptural watermark, but always *in use*. That is why the chess-playing automaton that pulls the machine strings should not be thought of in a dualistic, substantial way as "the ghost in the machine", as Gilbert Ryle (2000) caricatures Cartesian *res cogitans*, but rather in the manner of the second Wittgenstein, as *philosophical grammar* (Wittgenstein 1958). But just like Orpheus' Eurydice, this invisible *organon* will be veiled and even, in order to keep the Orphic parallelism, monstrously deformed, if we try to make it visible directly as doctrine or as independent methodology, as opposed to what happens with the Stagirite's logical and methodological treatises, which commentators Alexander of Aphrodisias and John Philoponus had early grouped under the name of "organon" ("instrument").
7   Ecuadorian philosopher Bolívar Echeverría, a translator and author of several studies of Walter Benjamin, who has also developed his major research on the topic of the Baroque and the Counter-Reformation in Spanish America, makes clear precisely, within what he calls *baroque ethos*, a logical structure consisting in the rejection of the principle of the "excluded third" and of Aristotelian logic (Echeverría 1998, pp. 199–221). Echeverría does not, but we might well state beyond him that the simultaneous use of theology and Marxism in Benjamin would thus enter the matrix of a *baroque ethos*.
8   In his well-known "Epistemo-Critical Preface" to the *Origin of the German Trauerspiel* (1925–1928), Benjamin claims: "*Die Wahrheit ist der Tod der Intention*" GS-I.1, p. 216 ("Truth is the death of Intention"), deviating from the model of the reflectivity of consciousness and of interiority for the benefit of an idea of truth that can be at the same time articulated with the reality of language and with the Platonic metaphysics of ideas, as if transcending any subjective and individualising interiority.
9   "*Leitfaden*" (guiding thread) is the expression used by Kant when introducing his propositions aimed at making universal history intelligible, through a teleological regulating idea (Kant 1922, p. 152).

But to these features that negatively define the use of theology we could add a clear positive attribute: theology is crucial in the creation of a *grammar of time*, under which, throughout the *corpus*, the figure of "Messianic cessation" (*messianischen Stillstellung*) (GS-I.2, p. 703) will be articulated; a form discovered early on by Benjamin in his youth writings, especially in *Trauerspiel und Tragödie* (1916; GS-II.1, pp. 133–37; SW-1, pp. 55–58), which germinates in his works as if in a spiral, crystallizing in the last five theses from *On the Concept of History* (GS-I.2, pp. 701–4).

2. Results

2.1. Early Benjaminian Theologumena—A Technique of Crisis

Jacob Taubes once argued that, for Benjamin and his generation, the reference of a Messianic event is no longer found at the virtual level of the regulative ideal but in the exceptional present time of the historical events they witnessed: the First World War, the October Revolution, the catastrophe of fascism (Taubes 1993). From this point of view, according to Taubes, what has been decisive in the framework of Benjaminian Messianism is the historical experience that affected his generation. Hence the arc drawn by Taubes between Benjamin's Messianism and Pauline *Kairos*, lies in the idea of the "(exceptional) present time", to which Taubes associates the Benjaminian notion of "now-time" (*Jetztzeit*) that refers to suspended or stopped time, "a present that is not transition" (*einer Gegenwart, die nicht Übergang ist*) (theses XIV, XVI, and XVIII, *On the Concept of History*, GS-I.2, pp. 701–3).[10]

In his early 1915 text titled "The Life of Students" (*Das Leben der Studenten*), Benjamin surprises us by placing the Messianic and the historical side by side, when he literally writes "Messianic kingdom or the idea of French revolution" (*messianische Reich oder die französische Revolutionsidee*), clarifying that it is not a "formless tendency of progress" (*gestaltlose Fortschrittstendenz*), but that which is "deeply rooted in every present in the form of the most endangered, excoriated and ridiculed ideas and products of the creative mind" (SW-1, p. 37). Benjamin then explains that "the historical task" (*geschichtliche Aufgabe*) "is to disclose this immanent state of perfection and make it absolute" (*Den immanenten Zustand der Vollkommenheit rein zum absoluten zu gestalten*), "to make it visible and dominant in the present" (*ihn sichtbar und herrschend in der Gegenwart zu machen*) (SW-1, p. 37; GS. II-1, p. 75). This passage anticipates Benjaminian inflection and reconfiguration of the Kantian figure of the endless task, which had been reappropriated by Hermann Cohen in the context of his peculiar synthesis between Kant's philosophy and Jewish Messianism, laying emphasis on the notion of hope (Cohen 1924; Abadi 2014, pp. 69–99). Benjamin will not stop settling accounts with Neo-Kantianism throughout his work. In his last thesis «On the Concept of History», Benjamin will in fact clear up the prejudices underlying the conception of time in Neo-Kantianism and in German social democracy around the notions of "ideal", "progress" (*Fortschritt*) and "endless task" (*unendliche Aufgabe*), whereby he reveals the structure of an eternal postponement.

> The ideal was defined in the Neo-Kantian doctrine as an "infinite [*unendlich*] task" (*unendliche Aufgabe*). And this doctrine was the school philosophy of the Social Democratic Party—from Schmidt and Stadler to Natorp and Vorländer. Once the classless society had been defined as an infinite task, the empty and homogeneous time (*die leere und homogene Zeit*) was transformed into an anteroom (*Vorzimmer*), so to speak, in which one could wait for the emergence of the revolutionary situation (*revolutionäre Situation*) with more or less equanimity. In reality, there is not a moment that would not carry with it *its* revolutionary chance

---

10　At the time of the war, a certain Messianic juvenilism crossed the Atlantic without its bearers on both sides having always kept direct relationships, as if generational constellations transcended individuals: The then young Argentine philosopher, contemporary of Benjamin, Deodoro Roca, a mentor of the University Reform of Córdoba in 1918, advocated ideas that were very close to the young Benjamin's reflections in texts such as "The Life of Students" ("*Das Leben der Studenten*", GS-II.1, pp. 75–87) and "The Metaphysics of Youth" ("*Metaphysik der Jugend*", GS-II.1, pp. 91–104). Roca talks in his writings of the "bankruptcy of civilization", drawing from the world crisis and catastrophe between 1914–1918 the political energies of a Liminal Manifesto with Messianic and at the same time revolutionary hints (Roca 1999, pp. 77–82; Roca 1999, p. 102).

(*revolutionäre Chance*)—provided only that it is defined in a specific way, namely as the chance for a completely new problem [*Aufgabe*]. (SW-4, pp. 401–2; GS-I.3, p. 1231)[11]

But, more than two decades before that, in the fragment titled "*Trauerspiel* and Tragedy" (*Trauerspiel und Tragödie*, 1916, GS-II.1, pp. 133–37, SW-1, pp. 55–58), not published during the author's life, Benjamin had already pointed out, like in his youth writings above mentioned, the need for another grammar of time. On this occasion, the Berlin-born philosopher placed his problem on the demarcation of history, namely the singularity of historical experience and time in the semantic network of the notions of "Messianic time" (*messianische Zeit*) and of "Baroque drama" (*Trauerspiel*), thereby deviating from the paradigm of mechanical time already disqualified with the same epithets of "homogeneous", "continuous" and "empty" that he would use two decades later in his theses of *On the Concept of History* to refute the model of historicist time and of vulgar Marxism.

> For we should not think of time as merely the measure (*Maß*) that records the duration of a mechanical change (*mechanischen Veranderung*). Although such time is indeed a relatively empty form (*relativ leere Form*), to think of its being filled makes no sense (*keinen Sinn bietet*). Historical time, however, differs from this mechanical time. It determines much more than the possibility of spatial changes (*Raumveränderungen*) of a specific magnitude and regularity—that is to say like the hands of a clock—simultaneously with spatial changes of a complex nature. And without specifying what goes beyond this, what else determines historical time—in short, without defining how it differs from mechanical time—we may assert that the determining force (*bestimmende Kraft*) of historical time (*historischen Zeitform*) cannot be fully grasped by, or wholly concentrated in, any empirical process (*von keinem empirischen Geschehen völlig erfaßt*). Rather, a process that is perfect in historical terms is quite indeterminate empirically; it is in fact an idea. This idea of fulfilled time (*erfüllten Zeit*) is the dominant historical idea of the Bible: it is the idea of messianic time. (SW-1, pp. 55–56; GS-II.1, p. 134)

This passage by the young Benjamin focuses on the understanding of historical time, and on the very characterization of history: what is it that makes an event or an experience be considered historical? This refers to the contrast with time in natural science. However, for Benjamin's demarcation of the historical, the idea of the Messianic, as noted in the conclusion of this passage, plays a key role. In fact, the historical does not lie for Benjamin in the raw empirical datum, but in the "idea", which, as Benjamin states here, is what fulfills (*vollendet*) the "perfect happening" (*vollkommen Geschehen*), saving it from the flow of "empirical events" (*empirischen Geschehen*). Only what the idea gathers, so to speak, makes sense from the point of view of history (*im sinne der Geschichte*). Later, in his famous "Epistemo-Critical Preface" (1928) to the book on the German Trauerspiel ("*Erkenntniskritische Vorrede*", GS-I.1, pp. 207–37), this "idea" will be understood as what "saves" (*retten*) the unique phenomenon and, let's say, inscribes the event in the constellation of a historical truth (GS-I.1, pp. 214–15). Therefore, we should take care not to confound this 'idea' with what the southwest *Baden School* of Neo-Kantian philosophy understood as "value relation" (*Wertbeziehung*), a subjective axiological charge that creates historicity and its meaning. Indeed, for the southwest German school of Neo-Kantianism, values are immanent to intentionality and as such belong to the historian's subjective burden, ultimately resulting in a relativistic perspectivism that will end up crystallizing with Max Weber on a Nietzschean plane of immanence, abandoning the remains of a Kantian transcendentalism that were still to be found in Rickert. For Benjamin, on the other hand, the "idea", as a Messianic figure, draws its absolute and infinite redemptive strength from a transcendent Neo-Platonic realm, radically reformulated

---

[11] This fragment belongs to the preparatory notes for the theses *On the Concept of History*, the so-called "Paralipomena", and it is noted *XVIII'*; in fact it was discovered by Giorgio Agamben in 1975 within a typewritten version of Benjamin's theses—*Handexemplär*—that the Italian philosopher found among George Bataille's papers in the latter's office at the National Library in Paris (Raulet 2010, p. 172).

through the Benjaminian notion of Constellation (*Konstellation*), which is one of the keystones for his "redemptive criticism" (Wolin 1994, pp. 29–77). Therefore the Messianic is already understood in the path of the historical happening (Friedlander 2012, pp. 200–1), i.e., as profane theology, creating paradoxical inversions and polarizing political and religious extremes into one another, a divide but also an allegorical articulation (Wolin 1994, pp. 29–77) between history and theology as it is indicated by Benjamin in 1921 through his *Theological-Political Fragment*:

> The secular order (*Ordnung des Profanen*) should be erected on the idea of happiness. The relation of this order to the messianic (*das Messianische*) is one of the essential teachings of the philosophy of history. It is the precondition of a mystical conception of history (*mystische Geschichtsauffassung*), encompassing a problem that can be represented figuratively. If one arrow points to the goal toward which the secular dynamic acts, and another marks the direction of messianic intensity (*messianischen Intinsität*), then certainly the quest of a free humanity for happiness runs counter to the messianic direction. But just as a force (*Kraft*), by virtue of the path it is moving along, can augment another force on the opposite path, so the secular order (*die profanen Ordnung des Profanen*)—because of its nature as secular—promotes the coming of the Messianic Kingdom (*das Kommen des messianischen Reiches*). The secular (*Das Profane*), therefore, though not itself a category of this kingdom, is a decisive category of its most unobtrusive approach. (SW-3, p. 305; GS-II.1, pp. 203–4)

Benjamin's understanding of Messianic time, initially with an altered Platonic bias, draws therefore the line of an integral historical experience dissolving the conventional understanding of secularized history as being void of theology, and opposing to it an invisible theology of history (Bolz and Reijen 1996, p. 16), not to be confounded with theocracy. If the theocratic view of history is purposively or teleologically understood in terms of a historical realization of the Messianic kingdom, either asymptotically or effectively, Messianism is experienced by Benjamin not as a goal or future-oriented state of facts, but as an interruption of time, in terms of remembrance and translation of the past, anchored in a polarity of justice that obstructs the profane, opening a "mise en abîme" or *Aktualisierung*, by way of trace, ruin and spectrality (Derrida 1994, p. 165; Derrida 2002), favoring interruption (*Unterbrechung*), and suspension (*Stillstand*) of our present as well as profane illumination (*profanen Erleuchtung*).

2.2. Hope in the Past[12]—Towards the Notion of Messianic Time

In order to capture the entire peculiarity of Benjamin's early understanding of messianic time, it is important to briefly address the German debate from the end of the nineteenth century and the beginnings of the 20th around the status of historiography and the *Geisteswissenschaften*. In fact, the problem of the uniqueness of historiography and its regional ontology had already shaken German social sciences reaching the center of the controversy known as *Methodenstreit* ("method dispute") which marked the epistemology of social sciences and hermeneutics, questioning thinkers of the stature of Dilthey, Windelband, Rickert, Lask, Simmel, and Weber (Oakes 1986). If for the Neo-Kantian school of southwestern Germany (Windelband, Rickert, Lask), and for Dilthey's Hermeneutics, the demarcation of history with respect to natural sciences lies at the bottom of their epistemological understanding, the criterion underlying this demarcation remains within the frame of the intentionality of consciousness. In particular, the young Heidegger, whose Habilitation dissertation was supervised by Heinrich Rickert, focused his lecture precisely on the issue of time in historiography. His lecture was titled "The Concept of Time in the Science of History" (Heidegger 2011) and was given at the University of Freiburg on 15 July 1915, that is, some months before Benjamin wrote his fragment on *Trauerspiel and Tragedy* (1916). At first sight, upon comparing both texts, we can see a striking

---

[12] *"Hoffnung im Vergangenen"*, Peter Szondi's eloquent formula to characterize Benjamin's notion of time (Szondi 1961).

affinity between the two thinkers: namely, the express opposition of historiographical time against the "homogeneous", "mechanical", and "continuous" time of natural sciences rendered in quite analogous terms (Heidegger 1978, pp. 415–25). A more cautious look, however, reveals great discontinuities between both perspectives, and that clarifies the Messianic understanding of Benjaminian historical time. In fact, the paths of both thinkers radically fork upon confronting the ontology and knowledge of the past. To Heidegger, the "historical object" "no longer exists":

> The historical object, as historical, is always past: in the strict sense it no longer exists. A temporal divide [*Zeitferne*] separates the historian from the past. The past has its meaning always and only when seen from the present. When viewed from our standpoint, the past not only no longer is; it also was something other than we and our present-day context of life are. This much has already become clear: time has a completely original meaning in history. Only when this qualitative otherness between past times and the present moment breaks into consciousness does the historical sense awaken (...).

> We may say, then, that the starting point of time-reckoning manifests the principle that controls all concept formation in history (*das Prinzip der historischen Begriffsbildung*): relatedness to a value (*die Wertbeziehung*) [emphasis in the original]. (Heidegger 2011, pp. 68–72; Heidegger 1978, pp. 427–33)

Heidegger extracts from this premise two fundamental conclusions: (i) the past has meaning only in the present; (ii) this past is not for us what it was for itself (Heidegger 1978, p. 427). He thus asserts that: (iii) therefore, there is a temporal distance (*Zeitferne*)—even an abyss (*Kluft*)—between the historian and the past, which can only be covered by means of the values (*Werte*) of the present, namely a resolution by the historian mediated by *relatedness to a value* (*Wertbeziehung*), in a similar way to Heinrich Rickert, who had considered since 1902 the selection and knowledge of the historiographical object; (Heidegger 1978, p. 433; Rickert 1913). Thus, Heidegger's position in 1915, already moving towards the idea of temporalization in *Sein und Zeit* (1927), is that it is through the future—namely by means of our present value-orientation allowing historiographical selection—that it is possible to cover the historical gap between present and past. Walter Benjamin, in his letter to Gershom Scholem of November 11, 1916, commenting on Heidegger's text, points out that the Conference "documents precisely how this subject should *not* be treated" (Adorno and Scholem 1994, p. 82 [emphasis in original]). This brings us back again to Benjamin's *Trauerspiel und Tragödie* (1916), not published, as we observed above, during Benjamin's lifetime. Although setting the issue of historical time as his focal point, Benjamin nevertheless refers in this crucial early text to the consideration of death in Tragedy and death in *Trauerspiel* (mourning play). These forms therefore lead to two dramatic figures where the notions of *erfüllt* (fulfilled) and *unerfüllt* (unfulfilled) play a central function: while recognizing that the trajectories of tragedy and of historical time overlap—something that is grounded in the actions of heroes (SW-I, p. 55), Benjamin makes indeed a consideration that will completely take another turn: he observes that "Historical time is infinite (*unendlich*) in every direction (*in jeder Richtung*) and unfulfilled (*unerfüllt*) at every moment (*in jedem Augenblick*)" (SW-1, p. 55; GS–II.1, p. 134), and then he radically distinguishes two sorts of time-fulfillment—namely *individual tragic time*, and *messianic historical fulfillment*. Only the latter could properly lead to messianic or fulfilled historical time. Therefore, despite the above affirmation concerning the overlapping between the tragic genre and historical time, no individual or tragic fulfillment of time could by itself determine historical meaning, which instead could only be constituted through messianic fulfillment:

> Moreover, the idea of a fulfilled historical time is never identical with the idea of an individual time. This feature naturally changes the meaning of fulfillment completely, and it is this that distinguishes tragic time from messianic time. Tragic time is related to the latter in the same way that an individually fulfilled time relates to a divinely fulfilled one. (SW-1, pp. 55–56).

So, we have here two forms of time—the tragic and the messianic—that for Benjamin fit with two forms of fulfillment: the individual and the divine respectively. It seems as if the tragic, restricted to the individual plan of the hero, could neither achieve nor fulfill the historic, whose fulfillment relates to the messianic. In the second part of his text, Benjamin complicates this first sketch with the introduction of a third form, the mourning play, or *Trauerspiel*, as a transitional device: "the mourning play is in every respect a hybrid form" (SW-I, p. 57). The specification of this form is obtained through the contrast between two figures of death, the 'tragic' and the *Trauerspiel's* 'figure of death'. While the former is governed by the law of fate and corresponds to the individual fulfillment of time by the hero's death (SW-I, p. 56), the latter is governed by the law of repetition, where death is only the spectral transition to a form of continuity mediated by a mirror image, defined by Benjamin with Aristotle's 'metabasis of life' (*eis allo genos*)—transformation into another type or sort (SW-I, pp. 56–57). This defines *Trauerspiel's* 'death' as a non-conclusive death. It means that *Trauerspiel* corresponds to a form of expansion and dissemination (SW-I, p. 57) that is typical not only of baroque time, but of modern time, as one which lacks meaning and conclusiveness, and as a time of desolation and dissolution (Caygill 1994; Sagnol 2003). In front of that it is not the tragic fulfillment of the individual heroic death that will carry out the restoration of historical meaning, but the messianic fulfillment belonging to the historical rescue itself. This messianic time however is not literally visible in the *Trauerspiel* but only allegorically indicated by way of the allegorist's work of art. Ultimately, the messianic is not visible at first sight but only through redemptive criticism. As such, it belongs to the *Afterlife* (*Nachleben*) of the play (Sagnol 2003, p. 53; Wolin 1994, pp. 29–77). It is as if the messianic, from then on, remained for Benjamin a keystone, at the top of his earliest phases but not least of the latest context of his thesis *On the Concept of History* (1940), moving on to counterbalance, through a theological plane of *redemptive criticism* (*rettende kritik*) (Habermas 1972; Wolin 1994, pp. 29–77), the hermeneutics of meaningful individual heroes and future-oriented subjectivity.

Heidegger for his part did not publish anything between 1916 and 1927, year of the edition of his magnum opus, *Time and Being* (*Sein und Zeit*—SuZ, Heidegger 2006) whose second section is dedicated to the temporalization of *Dasein* and where he reformulates his approach to historical time further distancing himself from the epistemological context of his work of 1915. In *Sein und Zeit*, Heidegger distinguishes the past as 'ontic', meaning a time that would simply be a 'succession of nows' (*Jetzfolge*), from a past that Heidegger calls 'ontological', as being reflexively maintained in the present of oneself through its own moving towards the future, for a self that temporalizes itself into the projection that Heidegger calls *Ekstasis*—being at the same time its own past and anticipating its future, but in a way that being projected (*Entwurf*) is the possibility of gathering its own time. Here, Heidegger takes from Wilhelm Dilthey the expression "connection of life", (*Zusammenhang des Leben*) for this maintenance of the past in the present under the possibility opened through projection. Like Giorgio Agamben said (Agamben 1978), Heidegger's originality is to propose historical time from the assumption of the temporalization of *Dasein*, and the latter through the figures of resoluteness (*Entschlossenheit*) and instant (*Ekstasis*), as attached to the same being of *Dasein*. Then, the figures of *Zeitigung* and *Entschlossenheit* are linked to the care (*Sorge*) and authenticity (*Eigentlichkeit*) of the figure of being-towards-death (*Sein zum Tode*), which is the keystone to the projectivity of *Dasein*. We exist towards death, and that allows us to live our past as being from birth to death within the structure of finitude. For Heidegger death is not an event: it is a phenomenon that must be understood existentially (SuZ, p. 251). The issue of death lies at the core of temporalization, and therefore, of Heideggerian historicality—something that Adorno criticized in his famous *The Jargon of Authenticity* (Adorno 1973). Being-towards-death is for Heidegger inherent to the *Geworfenheit*, of our being thrown and our finitude as facticity. The authentic choices of *Dasein* projected in a singular destiny (*Schicksal*) are interwoven in order to form the fate (*Geschick*) of a people (*Volk*). The coincident interweaving of fates finds its locus in the figure of generation (*Generation*). Some scholars agree nevertheless that there is a vagueness and incompleteness in the term *Generation* used by Heidegger (Barash 2003, pp. 170–73). Indeed, we wonder here about the gap that Heidegger crosses in the second Section of

Sein und Zeit, by moving without a sentence from the level of individual existence to the plane of historical collective sociality, namely the *Volk*, or the *Generation*, precisely in relation to matters such as past, future, and the pole of death. Actually, the collective level does generate a structural asymmetry in relation to an anthropological reality such as death. There is a tale by Kafka named "An Imperial Message" (Kafka 2009) that Benjamin selected during his radio shows on the Czech writer (GS-II.2, pp. 676–83), in which a messenger is summoned to the Chinese emperor's deathbed. The prominent court men around the emperor open his way and the emperor whispers a secret in his ear—words that no one else hears—and asks him to transmit those very same words to someone who awaits the message on the other side of the empire. After saying these words, the emperor dies. The Chinese messenger's dread is proportional to the immensity of his urgent task due to the fact that just to leave the capital of the empire he must go through countless human barriers composed of the subjects of the crown that are there to be with the emperor during his last breath. The difficulties multiply as the messenger tries to open his way and he soon realizes that he will never be able to personally deliver the message to its receiver. Concerning this story, we could think about the problem that has often been ignored by hermeneutic tradition: the problem of the danger surrounding transmission, and therefore the main task of rescuing the message inherent to its transmission, transmissibility, and linguistic revelation. After all, the god Hermes, out of whom Hermeneutics takes its name, was a messenger. Transmission, transmissibility, and linguistic revelation are always for Benjamin threatened and in danger, and the task of interpretation belongs to the dimension of survival and *Afterlife* (*Nachleben*) of rescuing and saving (*Rettung*) an oppressed tradition whose transmissibility and revelation demands to "brush history against the grain" (*die Geschichte gegen den Strich zu bürsten*) as it is concluded in the Thesis VII in *On the Concept of History* (GS-I.2, p. 696; SW-4, p. 392). Therefore, while in Heidegger, under a tragic perspective, the main issue of the finite historicality is destiny, marked through the death pre-orientation of *Dasein*, in Benjamin it is not destiny but danger that is the main condition surrounding transmission and interpretation which are always under the threat of disappearance or mythical disfiguration; and the answer to danger is not the epic authenticity of the hero who resigns in silence to destiny, but the interruption of destiny in terms of a messianic break through our experience with past and remembrance. The threat against transmission may be each time dismantled in Benjamin through the figures of rescue (*Rettung*) and *Afterlife* (*Nachleben*), as the creatural and profane plane of experience and language, therefore not as *Erlebnisse* or inner states of consciousness, but as *Erfahrung* or transindividual experience, like constelled instances and monades that are heterogeneous, yet at the same time articulated and scattered in a mesh of experiences in time that relate to the translation of different languages, the rescue of different strata of time, and the different disposals and ruins from the past that claim to be rescued through language by commentary, criticism, translation, remembrance, and revelation at the core of Benjaminian profane figures of theology and interpretation.

This is the way in which Benjamin pursued his research beyond his early production of the years 1913–1916: trying to think of a decentralized notion of experience based on transmission rather than on inner-consciousness; on languages and translation rather than on authenticity and selfhood; and on materials and ruins in danger, rather than on heroes and destiny. In this sense, it is with the notion of "remembrance" (*Eingedenken*, according to the neologism introduced by Benjamin himself) that there emerges at last a Messianic grammar of the time of history and a relational conception of the past opposed to the axiological *presentism* of intentionality. Remembrance is not simply a layer of the intentional consciousness, but it is made up of the involuntary memory, dream contents and the *moment of its recognizability* (*Augenblick seiner Erkennbarkeit*, GS-I.2, p. 695; SW-4, p. 390) that combine with the reflective work inherent in *Eingedenken*. Hence, remembrance is telescoping of the past through the present, so that it is more a "translation" of the past into the present (Friedlander 2012, p. 198) than a mere repetition based on the identity of memory contents susceptible of empathic experience, like the one we can see in the *Einfühlung* tradition, proper to Dilthyian *Geisteswissenschaften*. But to speak here of *translation* is consistent with the fact that Benjamin, like early romantics, views the epoch as a text (Bolz and Reijen 1996, p. 5), and its interpretation as the experience of being able to *read what has never been written*, as Benjamin wrote after Hofmannsthal in his fragment *On the Mimetic Faculty* (SW-2, p. 722). Needless to say, we can bridge this textual and reading paradigm to the Kabbalistic tradition of commentary and *Haggadah*, more made up of anecdotes and stories of the rabbinic literature than of the direct teaching of the Mosaic Law (*Halakhah*)—difference that was crucial for Benjaminian's interpretation of Kafka's literature (SW-II.2, p. 679; SW-2, p. 496; Br VI-1938–1940, p. 113). Therefore, through this figure of *Eingedenken*, Benjamin introduces an entirely original idea of the past, as something persistent in the present and, contrary to Heidegger, totally irreducible to intentionality, as follows from the early Benjaminian assertion that "Truth is the death of intention" (*Die Wahrheit ist der Tod der Intention*) (GS-I.1, p. 216). However, along the path of the assertion of this unfinished past, Benjamin not only confronts Heidegger, but also Horkheimer, whose letter dated 16 March 1937 Benjamin recalls in the following fragment of *The Arcades Project* (*Das Passagen-Werk*):

> On the question of the incompleteness [*Unabgeschlossenheit*] of history, Horkheimer's letter of 16 March 1937: "The determination of incompleteness [*Unabgeschlossenheit*] is idealistic if completeness [*Abgeschlossenheit*] is not comprised within it. Past injustice has occurred and is completed [*abgeschlossen*]. The slain are really slain ... If one takes the lack of closure [*Unabgeschlossenheit*] entirely seriously, one must believe in the Last Judgement ... Perhaps, with regard to incompleteness [*Unabgeschlossenheit*], there is a difference between the positive and the negative, so that only the injustice, the horror, the sufferings of the past are irreparable [*irreparabel sind*]. The justice practiced, the joys, the works, have a different relation to time, for their positive character is largely negated by the transience of things [*wird durch die Vergänglichkeit weitgehend negiert*]. This holds first and foremost for individual existence [*im individuellen Dasein*], in which it is not the happiness but the unhappiness that is sealed by death".

(*Das Passagen-Werk, Erkenntnistheoretisches, Theorie des Fortscritts*, [N 8, I]); (Benjamin 1999, p. 471).

Benjamin's answer to Horkheimer follows immediately in the same fragment, but here theology jumps to the forefront through the very movement of remembrance:

> The corrective to this line of thinking may be found in the consideration that history is not simply a science but also and not least a form of remembrance [*eine Form des Eingedenkens*]. What science has "determined" ["*festgestellt*"], remembrance can modify [*kann das Eingedenken modifizieren*]. Such mindfulness [*Eingedenken*] can make the incomplete [*das Unabgeschlossene*] (happiness) into something complete [*Abgeschlossenen*], and the complete [*Abgeschlossene*] (suffering) into something incomplete [*Unabgeschlossenen*]. That is theology [*Das ist Theologie*]; but in remembrance [*im Eingedenken*] we have an experience [*Erfahrung*] that forbids us to conceive of history as fundamentally atheological [*atheologisch zu begreifen*], little as it may be granted us to try to write it with immediately theological concepts [*so wenig wir sie in unmittelbar theologischen Begriffen zu schreiben versuchen dürfen*].

(*The Arcades Project*, N, On the theory of Knowledge, Theory of Progress, [N 8, I]; *Das Passagen-Werk, Erkenntnistheoretisches, Theorie des Fortscritts*, [N 8, I]); (Benjamin 1999, p. 471).

In this exchange, whose importance we cannot overestimate, not only does Benjamin cast a line separating history and science through the function of remembrance (*Eingedenken*), as the corner stone of history, but he advocates for the understanding of remembrance in terms of theology, and nevertheless the use of theology in history, not through "immediately theological concepts" (*unmittelbar theologischen Begriffen*). What is then this use of theology forbidding the "immediately theological concepts"? This is what Theodor Adorno, in a letter to Benjamin of 17 December 1934, commenting on Benjamin's essay on Kafka of that year, has named "the coded character of our theology" (*Chiffernwesen unserer Theologie*), recognizing that "the image of theology in which I see with pleasure that our concepts are hidden is none other than the one that spice up your thoughts", and declaring that "it can be called Inverse Theology" (*es mag wohl "inverse Theologie" heißen*) (Adorno and Benjamin 1994); it is also worth on this topic of the Adornian *inversed theology* to see (Bolz and Reijen 1996, pp. 13–20) and (Pangritz 2000, pp. 788–89). Somehow we anticipated above this figure of inversed theology both with the device of theology's invisibility, through the figure of the "hunch backed dwarf" (*buckliger Zwerg*), concealed master of chess on the first thesis of *On the Concept of History* (GS-I.2, p. 693; SW-4, p. 389), and the function of *Haggadah*, opposed by Benjamin to *Halakhah* in the Benjaminian interpretation of Kafka (SW-II.2, p. 679; SW-2, p. 496; Br VI-1938–1940, p. 113), namely through the total Benjaminian transposition and reshaping of the theological motives into the profane realm. Moreover, the movement of remembrance (*Eingedenken*), as theologically articulated, is condensed both as what makes history irreducible to science, and as what opens the "chamber of the past" (GS-I.3, p. 1231; SW-4, pp. 401–2). The past bears in itself a demand (*Anspruch*) which we can take up from the present inasmuch as we have been endowed with a "weak Messianic power" (*schwache messianische Kraft*) (GS-I.2, pp. 693–94; SW-4, p. 389).

2.3. Theology of History and Theology of Language: Rescuing in Translation

There is an "experience with the past", that should not be understood as a direct or immediate theological writing of history but as an indirect theological method, inasmuch as "method is detour" (*Methode ist Umweg*), as affirmed by Benjamin in his *Erkenntniskristische Vorrede* to the *Ursprung des deutschen Trauerspiels* (GS-I.1, p. 208). Then the paradigm of translation, drawn from Benjamin's philosophy of language, can help us understand this relationship between present and past: it is not about repeating or reviving an identical past through empathetic identification with it but about "translating" past into the present, so that, in being reconfigured in translation it breaks in the present offering us a disruptive experience through revelation in language. But, unlike the unilateralism of the intentional relationship established by the value paradigm (*Wertbeziehung*), the translation paradigm must rely on otherness and maintain with it a relationship that is not egocentric, seeking to save in one's own language the foreign ground where it encounters and receives otherness. But such disposition, in Benjamin, is theological since it stems from the common loss in one's own language and in the foreign language of the original pure language. It is therefore through shared absence and loss and not through community sameness and community identity that the translatability of secular languages (*Übersetzbarkeit*) appears in Benjamin as the primordial linguistic fact through the possibility of a rescue and redemption of otherness (GS-IV.1, pp. 9–21). Analogously, it is the Benjaminian inachievement (*Unvollendung*), incompleteness (*Unerfüllen*) and inconclusiveness (*Unabgeschlossenheit*) of the historical past (GS-II.1, pp. 133–37; PW N8,1), actualized in the spectral and *undeconstructible* idea of "past claim" (*Anspruch*) (GS-I.2, p. 694) (Derrida 1994, pp. 35–40) that the community of experience between past and present is possible. This spectrality, always exceeding law and history, is neither a regulative *telos* nor a "reified" realization of justice, but always an opening and an excess of now-time (*Jetztzeit*) itself (SW-4, pp. 401–2). Toward the end of his *On the Program of the Coming Philosophy* (1918), Benjamin places religious experience and the philosophy of language next to each other, at the same time positioning both of them in the trail of Johann Georg Hamann (1730–1788), Kant's contemporary and rival, precursor of the *Sturm und Drang*. However, in a text written just before the "Program", namely, *On Language as Such and on the Language of Man* (1916) (GS-II-1, pp. 140–57) Benjamin had already drawn from Hamann and Genesis a *naming* theory of the origin of languages and a concept of man's exit from paradise as the loss of the original language and the decline of languages (based on the biblical legend of Babel), which then give up their rescuing role of Adamic naming to adopt a merely communicational, instrumental role. Here Benjamin opposes communication "*through* a language", giving rise to what he calls "the bourgeois theory of language", to communication "*in* a language", leading to what he calls "the mystical theory of language", raising the latter, non-instrumental figure, to the rank of "the linguistic being of things", and of the "spiritual essence of man". The biblical event of the *fall* and the expulsion from paradise hence appear in the treatise on philosophy of language as the key step since it is connected not only with the proliferation of languages based on communicating "something", and the concomitant notion of "chatter" (*Geschwätz*) (GS-II.1, p. 153) taken here from Kierkegaard, as language degraded by guilt, good and evil, or losing oneself in the frenzied world of the reification of language, but also, on the flipside, with the idea of translation—*Übersetzung*—and "translatability" (*Übersetzbarkeit*), as the (possibility of) restoration of the original language trace: "translation attains its full meaning in the realization that every evolved language (with the exception of the word of God) can be considered a translation of all the others (GS-II.1, p. 151 et seq.). Also, through this relationship of languages as a center of varied thickness: Benjamin says, "the reciprocal translatability between languages takes place." Subsequently, this reappears through a philosophy of translation in his famous text *The Task of the Translator* (1923) (GS-IV.1, pp. 9–21). Here the Jewish theological image of the *Tikkun* is key: this element, which in Lurianic Kabbalah refers to a shattered vessel that claims restoration, is the figure of the restitution of harmony to the world. In Benjamin's view, the task of the translator is not to conquer the foreign language by assuming that there is a common sense beyond linguistic difference, but to penetrate one's own language to the bottom to find the traces of the foreign language in order to propose in the end a new form just like the claim for piecing together the broken vessel. Translating does not mean making what is strange in the foreign language sound familiar, but rather making one's own language strange until one finds in it, by penetrating its foundations, the forgotten traces of the foreign language. In his well-known "Epistemo-Critical Preface" to the *Origin of the German Trauerspiel*, Benjamin acknowledges again his naming theory of language, making a statement that has not gone unnoticed, namely, that Adam is not only the father of all men but also the "father of philosophy" (GS-I.1, p. 217) since through the imposition of names, the restoration of the linguistic essence of the idea and the fight against the instrumental value of words lies with him. What should maybe be read here as a watermark is the figure of Adam as the first expression of the ontological difference in language between what is merely ontic, such as losing oneself and sinking into "chatter" (*Geschwätz*) or into "communicating something", and what is ontological, where naming is understood as communication *in* the language of each creature and hence, as the very ontological expression of spiritual revelation through language among creatures. As Bolz and van Reijen affirm "language should not–or should not principally be understood as the reporting of thoughts or experiences, but as the form—and this is not meant metaphorically—of all that exists" (Bolz and Reijen 1996, p. 21). The productivity of Benjamin's reading concerning this articulation can also be seen with respect to other problems when, in *Goethe's Elective Affinities* (1922–1925) the distinction between fallen language and true language returns to literary criticism in order to distinguish between the conditions of an "apparent" and a "true" reconciliation between lovers. Examining the behavior of the characters in Goethe's short story *The Wayward Young Neighbours*, Benjamin describes the impossibility of reaching true reconciliation between lovers who all the time seem to want to avoid true fight—like the calm before the storm (Pangritz 2000, pp. 778–81). A safe, bourgeois love bond such as the one Goethe seems to offer, in Benjamin's point of view, is a bond that has produced " … the complete silence of all emotions" (GS-I.1, p. 184) and therefore can only seek apparent reconciliation. True reconciliation, on the contrary, should be able to deal with a mystery: that of love and beauty, divine grounds for "the hope of redemption we still cherish for all the dead" (GS-I.1, p. 200). Later on, in his *Erkentnniskritische Vorrede* introducing his *Ursprung des deutschen Trauerspiels* (GS-I.1, pp. 207–37) these initial intuitions are revealed as the scholastic term "treatise" is used to refer "albeit implicitly, to those objects of theology without which truth is inconceivable". Indeed, we are confronted here with a notion that stems directly from his first philosophy of language and nevertheless becomes a theological key with relation to his later philosophy—the Babelic notion of the fall. In the same way that for Benjamin Babelic languages of the Fall, namely the profane languages, admit something as a *character of translatability* (*Übersetzbarkeit*) which is constitutive of their linguistic character and prior to their actual translation and revelation through translation, our secular and profane past belonging to historic time admits something of a *moment of its recognizability* (*Augenblick seiner Erkenntnisbarkeit*) which is constitutive of their historic character. If in both cases existence comes to revelation through language, specially through the *Tikkum* rescue inherent to the Fall, then the *Irrevelation's* side of revelation (Cohen-Levinas 2013) as a ruin or as the fogged negative of revelation is the failed side of history that cries out for its redemptive rescue through an inversed theology involved in the profane realm. This is *spectrality*. At some point we could say here that theology in Benjamin is heretically interwoven with a sort of spectrology, and their common medium is language together as a theological, magic, and cognitive device.

3. Conclusions

As we said above, the "invisibility" of theology in Benjamin does not mean the invisibility of its theological marks. On the contrary, the latter are disseminated throughout the entire corpus. Nevertheless, we have proposed here the figure of theology as an "invisible organon", intending to productively decline this device through Benjamin's redemptive criticism.

This was clear through the first thesis of *On the Concept of History*, where Benjamin prescribes that historical materialism "enlists the services of theology, which today, as we know, is small and ugly and has to keep out of sight" (*nicht darf blicken lassen*) (GS-I.2, p. 693; SW-4, p. 389). We attached to this plane the Adornian formula of an "inversed theology" (Adorno and Benjamin 1994), which means the reshaping of theology through the profane, like in Kafka's own Haggadah, being an indirect way to imply the theological language in the reading of the historical material content, however in the frame of a rescuing and redemptive horizon. This sort of cryptical and encoded invisibility is well depicted in Benjamin's famous declaration on his relation to theology (PW N7a7; Benjamin 1999, p. 471). By way of comparing theology with ink, and his own thinking with the blotting pad, Benjamin emphasizes that the latter is saturated with the former, but he observes, nevertheless, that "were one go by the blotter, however, nothing of what is written would remain" (*nichts, was geschrieben ist, übrig bleiben*). Therefore, his standpoint is that whereas the traces of theology indeed fully impregnate his thinking, theology survives in the latter only at the prize of being completely reshaped, like Irving Wohlfahrt's own expression of "Re-Fusing Theology" (Wohlfarth 1986, pp. 3–24). This figure led us to another plane of invisibility which is the one of the Kabbalah. As early as in 1918, in *On the Program of the Coming Philosophy* (SW-1, pp. 100–10; GS-II.1, pp. 157–71), Benjamin promoted the abandonment of the enlightened mathematical-mechanical conception of knowledge in favor of a linguistic-critical method based on the philosophy of language. But precisely his philosophy of language, developed since 1916 in his essay "On Language as Such and on the Language of Man" (SW-1, pp. 62–74; GS-II.1, pp. 140–57), so important for Benjamin's thought, is rooted both in the scriptural Jewish tradition and in the tradition of the Kabbalah. In the last part of our paper, we then used Benjaminian philosophy of language and Benjaminian idea of translation to complete our sketch on a Benjaminian theological grammar of historical past that we had previously opposed to the Heideggerian idea of historical time as something being extracted out of *Dasein's* intentionality. It is worth here—in order to conclude—to quote Benjamin himself, coming back in his last period to confront Heidegger precisely on historical time, through a well-known fragment of *Das Passagen-Werk*:

> (Heidegger seeks in vain to rescue history for phenomenology abstractly through "historicity".) [...]. Every present day is determined by the images that are synchronic with it: each "now" is the now of a particular recognizability. In it, truth is charged to the bursting point with time. (This point of explosion, and nothing else, is the death of the *intentio*, which thus coincides with the birth of authentic historical time, the time of truth.). It is not that what is past casts its light on what is present, or what is present its light on what is past; rather, image is that wherein what has been comes together in a flash with the now to form a constellation. In other words: image is dialectic at standstill. For while the relation of the present to the past is purely temporal, the relation of what has been to the now is dialectical: not temporal in nature but figural <bildlich>. Only dialectical images are genuinely historical—that is, not archaic—images. The image that is read–which is to

say, the image in the now of its recognizability—bears to the highest degree the imprint of the perilous critical moment on which all reading is founded. [PW, N3,1] (Benjamin 1999, pp. 462–63)

Funding: This research was funded partially by CONICT and Project PICT 2014-02968.

Conflicts of Interest: The author declares no conflict of interest.

References

Abadi, Florencia. 2014. *Walter Benjamin: Conocimiento y redención. De Kant al surrealism.* Buenos Aires: Miño y Dávila.

Adorno, Theodor. 1973. *The Jargon of Authenticity.* London: Routledge & Kegan Paul.

Adorno, Theodor, and Walter Benjamin. 1994. *Briefwechsel 1928–1940.* Frankfurt am Main: Surkamp Verlag.

Adorno, Theodor, and Gershom Scholem. 1994. *The Correspondence of Walter Benjamin 1910–1940.* Edited and Annotated by Gershom Scholem and Theodor Adorno. Translated by Manfred R. Jacobson, and Evelyn M. Jacobson. Chicago: The University of Chicago Press.

Agamben, Giorgio. 1978. *Infanzia e storia.* Bologna: Einaudi.

Arendt, Hannah. 1969. Walter Benjamin: 1892–1940. In *Walter Benjamin, Illuminations.* New York: Schocken Books, pp. 1–55.

Barash, Jeffrey Andrew. 2003. *Martin Heidegger and the Problem of Historical Meaning.* New York: Fordham University Press.

Benjamin, Walter. 1972–1991. *Gesammelte Schriften.* Bände I–VII. Frankfurt am Main: Suhrkamp.

Benjamin, Walter. 1978. *Gesammelte Briefe.* Herausgeber Gershon Scholem und Theodor Adorno. Frankfurt am Main: Suhrkamp Verlag.

Benjamin, Walter. 1999. *The Arcades Project.* Translated by Howard Eiland, and Kevin McLaughlin. Cambridge: Belknap Press of Harvard University.

Bielik-Robson, Agata. 2014. *Jewish Cryptotheologies of Late Modernity: Philosophical Marranos.* New York: Routledge.

Bolz, Norbert, and Willem Van Reijen. 1996. *Walter Benjamin.* Atlantic Highlands: Humanities Press.

Caygill, Howard. 1994. Benjamin, Heidegger and the Destruction of Tradition. In *Walter Benjamin's Philosophy. Destruction and Experience.* Edited by Benjamin Andrew and Osborne Peter. London: Routledge, pp. 1–31.

Cohen, Hermann. 1924. *Jüdische Schriften.* Berlin: Schwetschkke & Sohn.

Cohen-Levinas, Danielle. 2013. Révélation et Irrévélation. Walter Benjamin et Gershom Scholem devant Kafka. In *Walter Benjamin.* Edited by Patricia Lavelle. Paris: Éditions de L'Herne, pp. 314–25.

Derrida, Jacques. 1994. *Force de loi.* Paris: Galilée.

Derrida, Jacques. 2002. *Fichus.* Paris: Galilée.

Echeverría, Bolívar. 1998. *La modernidad de lo barroco.* Mexico: D.F., Era.

Friedlander, Eli. 2012. *Walter Benjamin. A Philosophical Portrait.* Cambridge: Harvard University Press.

Habermas, Jünger. 1972. Bewußtmachende oder rettende Kritik. In *Zur Aktualität Walter Benjamins.* Edited by von Siegried Unseld. Frankfurt am Main: Surhrkamp.

Hartung, Günter. 2001. Jacob Taubes und Walter Benjamin. In *Abendländische Eschatologie. Ad Jacob Taubes.* Under the Direction of Richard Faber, Evelyne Goodman-Thau and Thomas Macho. Würzburg: Verlag Königshausen & Neumann.

Heidegger, Martin. 1978. Der Zeitbegriff in der Geschichtswissenschaft. In *Martin Heidegger, Gesamtausgabe, Band 1, Frühe Schriften.* Frankfurt am Main: Vittorio Klostermann, pp. 357–433, Original published as 1916. *Zeitschrift für Philosophie Kritik (Formerly Fichte-Ulricische Zeitschrift).* Leipzig: Verlag von C. E. M. Pfeffer, vol. 161, pp. 173–88.

Heidegger, Martin. 2006. *Sein und Zeit.* Tübingen: Max Niemeyer Verlag.

Heidegger, Martin. 2011. The Concept of Time in the Science of History. In *Becoming Heidegger: On the Trail of His Early Occasional Writings, 1910–1927.* Edited by Kisiel Theodore and Sheehan Thomas. Seattle: Noesis Press, pp. 60–72.

Kafka, Franz. 2009. *Selected Shorter Writings.* Translated by Ion Johnston. Nanaimo: Vancouver Island University, Available online: http://johnstoniatexts.x10host.com/kafka/kafkatofc.html (accessed on 8 November 2018).

Kant, Immanuel. 1922. *Idee zu einer allgemeinen Geschichte in weltbürgerlicher Absicht*. Edited by Schriften. Berlin: Cassirer. First published 1784.

Kant, Immanuel. 2008. *Religion Within the Limits of Reason Alone*. New York: Harper One, First published 1793.

Oakes, Guy. 1986. Rickerts's Theory of Historical Knowledge. In *The Limits of Concept Formation in Natural Science. A Logical Introduction to the Historical Sciences*. Edited by Heinrich Rickert. Cambridge: Cambridge University Press, vols. vii–xxxi.

Pangritz, Andreas. 2000. Theologie. In *Benjamins Begriffe*. Edited by Erdmut Wizisla and Michael Opitz Herausgegeben. Frankfurt am Main: Suhrkamp, pp. 774–825.

Raulet, Gérard. 2010. Kommentar. In *Werke und Nachlaß. Kritische Gesamtausgabe, Über den Begriff der Geschichte*. Edited by Gérard Raulet. Berlin: Suhrkamp Verlag, pp. 159–379.

Rickert, Heinrich. 1913. *Die Grenzen der naturwissenschaftlichen Begriffsbildung*. Tübingen: Mohr, Translated by Guy Oakes. As 1986. *The Limits of Concept Formation in Natural Science*. Cambridge: Cambridge University Press.

Roca, Deodoro. 1999. Ciencias, maestros y universidades. In *Deodoro Roca, el hereje*. Edited by N. Kohan. Buenos Aires: Biblos, pp. 99–108. First published 1915.

Roca, Deodoro. 1999. "La juventud argentina de Córdoba a los hombres libres de Sudamérica" ("Manifiesto Liminar de la Reforma Universitaria", June 21 1918). In *Deodoro Roca, el hereje*. Edited by N. Kohan. Buenos Aires: Biblos, pp. 77–82.

Ryle, Gilbert. 2000. *The Concept of Mind*. London: Penguin Books.

Sagnol, Marc. 2003. Temps mécanique et temps historique. In *Tragique et Tristesse. Walter Benjamin, archéologue de la modernité*. Edited by Sagnol Marc. Paris: Les Éditions du Cerf, pp. 35–54.

Scholem, Gershom. 1975. *Walter Benjamin: Die Geschichte einer Freundschaft*. Frankfurt am Main: Suhrkamp Verlag.

Steiner, Uwe. 2000. Kritik. In *Benjamins Begriffe*. Edited by Erdmut Wizisla and Michael Opitz Herausgegeben. Frankfurt am Main: Suhrkamp, pp. 479–523.

Szondi, Peter. 1961. *Hoffnung im Vergangenen. Über Walter Benjamin*. Zürich: Neue Zürcher Zeitung, October 8.

Taubes, Jacob. 1993. *Die Politische Theologie des Paulus*. Munich: Wilhelm Fink Verlag.

Ullmann, Wolfgang. 1992. Walter Benjamin und die jüdische Theologie. In *Aber ein Sturm weht vom Paradiese her. Texte zu Walter Benjamin*. Edited by Michael Opitz and Erdmut Wizisla. Leipzig: Reclam, pp. 99–101.

Wittgenstein, Ludwig. 1958. *Philosophical Investigations*. Translated by Gertrude Elizabeth Margaret Anscombe. New York: Basil Blackwell.

Wizisla, Erdmut. 2013. Renoncer à produire du rêve? Le messianisme politique chez Benjamin et Brecht. In *Walter Benjamin*. Edited by Patricia Lavelle. Paris: Éditions de L'Herne, pp. 303–8.

Wohlfarth, Irving. 1986. Re-Fusing Theology. Some First Responses to Walter Benjamin's Arcades Project. No 39. Second Special Issue on Walter Benjamin. *New German Critique*, 3–24. [CrossRef]

Wolin, Richard. 1994. *Walter Benjamin. An Aesthetic of Redemption*. Berkeley: University of California Press.

religions MDPI

Article

Ernst Bloch as a Non-Simultaneous Jewish Marxist

Przemyslaw Tacik

Institute of European Studies, Jagiellonian University, Gołębia 24, 31-007 Kraków, Poland;
przemyslaw.tacik@uj.edu.com

Received: 30 September 2018; Accepted: 3 November 2018; Published: 6 November 2018

check for
updates

Abstract: The paper attempts to reassess the fundamentally paradoxical position of Ernst Bloch in 20th century philosophy in the light of the Marranic condition. Indebted, among others, to Jewish heritage and Christian tradition, Bloch considered himself primarily a Marxist. Bloch's uniqueness consists in the stunning equiponderance of the currents he drew from. Contrary to a classic model of modern Jewish philosophy, inaugurated by Hermann Cohen, Bloch's thinking does not allow of easy juxtaposition of "sources" with languages into which they were translated. In this sense, Bloch cannot be easily compared to Franz Rosenzweig, Emmanuel Levinas or even Walter Benjamin (although he bore some striking similarities with the latter). His position at least partly stems from a specific form of directness with which he often used these languages, composing his philosophy in quite an anachronist manner. For this reason his thinking—in itself *"die Gleichzeitigkeit des Ungleichzeitigen"*, as one of his key concepts theorises—is a very modern, internally incoherent space of cross-fertilising inspirations. The paper demonstrates two levels on which Bloch's indebtedness to Judaism might be analysed and then re-assesses his Marxist affiliations as a kind of modern faith which, in a specifically Marranic manner, seals the simultaneity of the non-simultaneous.

Keywords: Ernst Bloch; Jewish philosophy; Marranism; Messianism; Marxism; utopia; Lurianic Kabbalah

1. Introduction

Among other modern philosophical Marranos Ernst Bloch occupies an uneasy and paradoxical position. At least at first sight little digging is required to find traces of Jewish inspirations in his writings; quite often they are either openly admitted by the author or simply self-evident. For this reason it might seem that Bloch performs too little hiding to be taken for a Marrano, especially in comparison with such masters of concealment and play as Jacques Derrida (Derrida 1993, p. 170). To make the situation more complicated, Jewish inspirations not only do not seem to be predominant in Bloch's work, but occasionally are overtly downgraded. They are intermingled with innumerable sources of multifarious origin: Marxism, German Idealism, utopianism, political journalism, philosophy of music, expressionism, etc. which are juxtaposed with little, if any, ambitions of attaining coherence. Consequently, the disclosed but clear structure of translation[1] (or encryption) that we might expect from the Marrano phenomenon—which might be viewed as negotiating one's own idiom on the basis of Jewish inspirations and the language of Western philosophy—is here at

---

[1] As Agata Bielik-Robson puts it, "We can thus see 'Jewish philosophy' as a primarily linguistic problem: speaking one language with the help of another, a case of an instantaneous bilingualism. This brings us immediately to yet another metaphor coming from the Jewish tradition, namely that of Marranos, the Spanish Jews forced to convert to Christianity, who nonetheless preserved their secret Jewish faith: the Marranic 'Judaism undercover', where the unspoken Hebrew shines through but also subverts the overtly spoken dialect of the imposed 'speech of strangers', in this case the Christian religion. It is not an accident that the first Jewish thinkers who entered the world of modern Western thought were mostly of Marrano origin … " Bielik-Robson declares that the goal of philosophical Marranos is "to marry the speech of strangers and let the Hebrew talk through it: to do counter-philosophy with the help of philosophy." (Bielik-Robson 2014, p. 4).

least distorted, if not inexistent. In the incessant stream of Bloch's writing, not rarely bordering on logorrhoea, all the sources mix in unexpected proportions and combinations. Jewish inspirations appear out of nowhere and, at least at first reading, do not seem to provide a broader pattern that could solidly inform interpretation of Bloch's thinking.

Moreover, even if we stick to religious sources which are present in his writing, Judaism is merely one tradition among others. It has been often suggested that Bloch was at his heart a modern Gnostic greatly indebted to Basilides and Marcion, particularly in his vision of vengeful God, the role of cognition in bringing about redemption (Christen 1979, p. 61) and apocalyptic demand for destruction of this world in the name of justice (Boldyrev 2014, pp. 92–95). Nevertheless, much as Bloch overtly confesses his interest in Gnosticism, the exact influence of this current—complex in itself—on the totality of Blochian thinking is difficult to pinpoint. Apart from Gnosticism Bloch delighted in combining other religious traditions: the impact of Christianity on his work is overwhelming to such an extent that sometimes Judaism seems to pale in comparison with it. It needs to be admitted that this Christianity is interpreted in a very specific way—namely as a tradition which accomplishes the whole potential of rebellion present in Judaism and declares human independence from the dead God (Bloch 2009, pp. 122–23)—but even this Hegelian-Nietzschean twist in the perception of Christ cannot diminish the overall domination of Christianity in Bloch's thinking. Even if we take into account how meaningless deathbed confessions sometimes might be, the declaration of deep indebtedness to Christianity that he made shortly before his death (Boldyrev 2014, p. 106) must make his Marrano status somewhat unsure.

To sum up, the unprecedented variegation of the used sources makes Bloch's work profoundly paradoxical. On the one hand, all the ingredients are still recognisable in the incoherent and sometimes shapeless stream of Blochian writing, which makes discovering Jewish inspirations an easy, perhaps all-too-easy task. On the other hand, this patchwork conceals a few major philosophical complexes of ideas whose roots are more unclear. Therefore, I suggest, re-reading Bloch in the light of the Marrano phenomenon must consist of two layers: the epithelial and the deep. The first offers the reader philosophical miracles, but made of tombac; the second is more promising, but requires more risky interpretation. The (post-)deconstructionist self-awareness cannot make any of them prevail only by virtue of their own respective positions. Contrariwise, it is their mutual entanglement that makes Bloch a special Marrano who cannot be saved from the conundrum of Jewish inspirations and Western philosophy by any kind of translation.

These observations determine the research programme for confronting Bloch's thinking with the Marrano metaphor. Firstly, the epithelial level—Jewish traces in his life and writings—will be examined. Secondly, I will attempt to undertake a more perilous path of interpretation in order to re-construct the very core of Bloch's thinking as a form of Lurianism. Finally, I will explore relations and tensions between the two in order to find the appropriate form of Marranism which would be pertinent to Bloch. The overarching framework of this exploration will be provided by one of his best known concepts: *die Gleichzeitigkeit des Ungleichzeitigen*, the simultaneity of the non-simultaneous.

2. The Epithelial

The epithelial level of Bloch's specific Marrano position is determined by a few grounding characteristics of his life and thinking. It is in this perspective that Jewish sources and inspirations stand out as clear references in Bloch's work. All that is necessary at this level is a comprehensive reading: shards of Judaism are easily identifiable.

2.1. An Overtly Marranic Life

To begin at the very obvious level, Ernst Bloch received a Jewish religious upbringing, but to little avail. Just after his bar-mitzvah, he stated publicly in the synagogue three times that he was an atheist (Münster 2001, p. 34). Often repeated as an anecdote, this story conveys much more than a simple tale of a rebellious teenager. Declaring one's atheism after (not during) the bar-mitzvah is a fundamental inconsequence: why should he take part in the religious ceremony of attaining adulthood and assuming responsibility for his life before God, if he did not believe in God? His behaviour might be obviously interpreted as paying lip service to the community only to break out and rebel afterwards, but the stunning temerity of combining bar-mitzvah with a confession of atheism makes it more fascinating. Perhaps this paradox augurs incoherences in Bloch's future thinking: he both confesses and denies, uses a source to twist its meaning, declares his loyalty to a given idea only to juxtapose it with something most foreign to it. At this level, there is hardly any reconciliation between contradictory ideas. They appear one after another. In Bloch's texts they are joined by the common thread of writing, just like the author joined his bar-mitzvah with a declaration of atheism.

This anecdote bears an intriguing affinity to another quality of Blochian thinking. He was very eager to pour new wine into old casks, turning trite concepts into their opposites. Perhaps the best example is the central concept of Bloch's reflection: utopia. Inherited from authors largely fallen into oblivion apart from their role of dummies in handbooks of political philosophy, and at best treated with suspicion and mockery (Sorel 1999, p. 28), utopia was in Bloch's re-reading eviscerated of the legacy of exemplary naiveté. The new approach to utopia strips it of unpractical details full of daydreaming in order to turn it towards the future. From that moment utopia is transformed from a static vision of what should be attained to a dynamic power which is always future-oriented and whose particular manifestations—from Campanella and More to Owen and Fourier (Bloch 1995, pp. 479–589)—are just temporary moments which express the general struggle in particular circumstances. This reinterpretation of utopia demonstrates that Bloch was willing to appropriate numerous concepts just in order to use them for his own purposes. Some of these concepts might be unexpected in a Jewish Marxist, for example the idea of *Heimat* (Bloch 1995, pp. 711–45; Miller Jones 1995, pp. 39–54; Jay 1984, pp. 188–89), a term notoriously appropriated by volkists. Nevertheless, Bloch combines in a unique way his conceptual omnivorousness with the skill to reinterpret categories to his own taste and finally juxtapose them in the incessant tapestry of his verbose writing.

Bloch's life displays analogical tendencies. He was considered an instinctive heretic by most people who had a longer contact with him; many commentators return to this observation in order to find for him a fitting category (Hudson 1982, pp. 49, 210; Münster 2001, p. 16; Walser 1968, p. 14). He never found an intellectual milieu in which he felt fully at ease. He missed both of the two best chances he had: among Jewish intellectuals in the interwar period (Georg Lukács, Martin Buber, Walter Benjamin, Gershom Scholem, Franz Rosenzweig, Siegfried Kracauer, Theodor W. Adorno and Max Horkheimer) he was received with suspicion and distrust, whereas the official Marxism to which he attempted to pledge allegiance obviously could not accommodate his excursions into the realm of philosophical daydreaming. Benjamin seemed for a certain time his best kin (Miller Jones 1995, p. 25; Hudson 1982, p. 8; Thompson 2013b, pp. 84, 98; Münster 2001, pp. 128, 135; Münster 1985, pp. 111–24; Boldyrev 2014, pp. 114–58), but the Christian flavour of some of Bloch's writings (especially of *The Spirit of Utopia*) made him ultimately keep his distance (Münster 1985, p. 113). Close contact with Lukács, who in a certain epoch considered Bloch his greatest influence, ended up with feuds over interpretations of Marxism. Lukács accused his friend of pre-Marxist and pre-materialist positions, mysticism and mythology (Hudson 1982, pp. 34–40; Münster 2001, p. 179). Bloch's relationship to the Frankfurt School was very strained (Münster 2001, pp. 210–14), not only because of his unorthodox and non-academic (to put it mildly) writing, but also due to his staunch support of communists and the Soviet Union (to the point of notorious endorsement of the Moscow trials (Miller Jones 1995, p. 19)) which Adorno and Horkheimer deemed unacceptable.

Consistent loyalty to communist parties and state socialism was also warped by Bloch's gut heterodoxy. His consecration as the leading official philosopher of the GDR in 1947—parenthetically, his nomination for Leipzig University was the first academic position he ever obtained, at the age of 62—soon turned sour and Bloch left the GDR in 1961 after spending a few years in the limbo of dissidence, persecution and smear campaign (Münster 2001, pp. 250–74). Yet even when he defected to the West and took a position at the University of Tübingen, he went against the grain and taught staunch Marxism (Münster 2001, p. 313), becoming for students rebelling in 1968 the only credible member of the academic staff. Upon his death in 1977, he might have said after Septimius Severus: *omnia fui*, although contrary to the Roman emperor's disenchanted conclusion ("*nihil expedit*"), Bloch seemed to have preserved the very same level of satisfaction with his work that he displayed consistently throughout his life. The position of an irredeemable heretic was something he made peace with, remarking in the preface to the German edition of *Atheism in Christianity* that "The best thing about religions is that they produce heretics."[2] (Bloch 1968, p. 15).

His life was similar to his writings: long, inconsistent, full of sudden twists, rejected by priests of all orthodoxies, but unified by the same persistent struggle for his cause and unabating hope. All his formal allegiances to intellectual currents failed in the eyes of his collaborators and friends, because Bloch was apparently unable not to (mis)understand each tradition in his own way. Nonetheless, just as the anecdote about his bar-mitzvah suggests, all the time he needed to feel part of some spiritual community, as if the inevitable rift with it was something that kept happening to him most inadvertently and unintentionally. In this stream Judaism—or, more broadly, Jewish inspirations—were a recurring theme, but never a unique or dominant source of thinking. Moreover, Bloch explicitly disavowed his indebtedness to Judaism, claiming that he was no Buber (Münster 2001, p. 373). He was concerned not to be perceived as determined by one tradition, especially Judaism. For this reason all references to the Kabbalah or, broadly speaking, Jewish spirituality are given equal rights in his works as, say, mentions of Thomas Müntzer, Jakob Böhme, Kant, Schelling, Hegel, Gottfried Keller or even Karl May. In this sense, his intellectual tastes were immune to hierarchies and decorum: everything could be mixed with everything, just as in his life he might have been a professor of philosophy at the Marxist university in the GDR and teach more about Hegel and Böhme than about the official Marx.

In a sense, but perhaps within a superficial perspective, Bloch's life epitomises the exile of Jewish intellectuals in the desert of modernity. The world seemed to him a hostile place, the past sources of spirituality ran dry a long time ago. But with the benefit of materialist hindsight, everything that preserved traces of vitality and hope might have been recovered. With this insight, Bloch lived his life—full of adversities, failures and injustices—with amazing belief in a better future. There was hardly any Marranic tension in it, but perhaps unconquerable hope, Bloch's emblem, could be seen as an utterly secularised Jewish faith, which does not need to hide behind the official dogma that rules the world, because they both overlapped to the point of their indifferentiation.

At the beginning of his philosophical path Bloch wrote a famous letter to his friend Lukács, in which he attempted to define his role and position:

> Ich bin der Paraklet, und die Menschen, denen ich gesandt bin, werden in sich den heimkehrenden Gott erleben und verstehen. (Bloch 1985a, vol. II, p. 66)

> [I am the Paraclete and the people to whom I was sent will experience and understand in themselves God returning to his homeland.]

"Paraclete", in koine Greek "a helper", "a comforter" or "an advocate" (in this sense contemporary Hebrew still uses a descendant of this word for some legal professions), is nowadays a term of distinctively Christian flavour, referring usually to the Holy Spirit. Bloch could hardly have been more explicit in the choice of his affiliation. But once again he borrows an established term for his own goals, this time arrogating the position of the Paraclete. In this strange mixture of German Idealism, Christianity and Gnosticism one thing is certain: Bloch's unshakeable faith in the future and his own mission. Perhaps then the worldly masks that he puts on are of lesser importance; what counts is the faith that the point in which return and ultimate novelty coincide is always before us. If one wants to

---

[2] "Es ist das beste an der Religion, daß sie Ketzer hervorruft."NOTE: all Bloch's texts whose translations to English have not yet been published are quoted from original German versions and followed by the author's own translations in brackets. If official translations exist, they are quoted without citing original texts.

apply the category of Marranism, Bloch would be in this regard a Marrano exiled into the conundrum of capitalist modernity,[3] in which all the sources and currents have been confused. The underlying substrate to which he pledges his ultimate loyalty is the future, which is the true meaning of God, as evidenced by his own self-definition in the formula of אהיה אשר אהיה from Shemot 3.14 (Bloch 2009, p. 79).

2.2. Judaism in Bloch's Writings

References to Jewish thinking and spirituality are interspersed throughout all Bloch's writings from the *Werkausgabe* from the very beginning (*The Spirit of Utopia*) up until the end (*Experimentum Mundi*). Apart from *Atheism in Christianity*, in which ancient Judaism and the milieu of budding Christianity is analysed with greater detail (Bloch 2009, pp. 17–179), these references do not form a solid block of comprehensive reflection. They crop up and vanish without much cohesion, as if Bloch deliberately wanted to attract attention to a theme which might be taken, against his intentions, for a central motive of his thinking.

Even if Bloch's interest in a broadly understood Jewish tradition is rather selective, it began early in his intellectual career. It seems that apart from his patchy religious upbringing he returned to Judaism in 1910–1911, while studying in Berlin, Munich and Würzburg (Münster 2001, p. 44; Münster 1985, p. 108). He was interested not only in the Kabbalah, but many other currents of Jewish spirituality, including Zionism, already in full swing at that time among German Jews. Nevertheless, it is difficult to determine which sources he had firsthand experience with and which ones were filtered through syntheses and interpretations, especially German ones—by Jakob Böhme, Georg von Welling, Franz Hartmann, Franz Joseph Molitor and Franz von Baader (Boldyrev 2014, p. 92). It is worth noticing that he had begun his studies before Gershom Scholem's revival of Kabbalah studies, which naturally meant that any non-professional interest in this area must have been more sketchy and selective. As confirmed by references in his later writings, he probably read Zohar (Bloch 2009, p. 139; Münster 1985, p. 108). It seems nonetheless certain that Bloch's interest in the Kabbalah was devoted not solely to this tradition, but was part of his broader studies in theosophy, mysticism and heterodoxy—including such diverse authors as Meister Eckhart (for Bloch a long-lasting inspiration for conceiving relations between deity and human soul), Schelling and Rudolf Steiner. Apart from the Kabbalah, in the 20s Bloch drew heavily from Chassidism (appropriated via Buber), which particularly marked his *Spuren* (Münster 2001, p. 141; Moltmann 1976, p. 16).

In the 60s Bloch famously told the Israeli ambassador to Germany that he was not an assimilated Jew, but rather that he was assimilating into Judaism (Boldyrev 2014, p. 100). Enigmatic as this formula might sound, it seems that Bloch perceived Judaism not as a tradition that he was brought up in, but rather one of the currents that he selectively appropriated. The same applies to particular currents of Jewish spirituality and thinking. The influence of the Kabbalah on his writings seems rather limited (Münster 1982, pp. 134–37): at least in a literal reading, it seems that Bloch borrowed some particular concepts from this tradition rather than being more comprehensively shaped by it. Key moments in which the Kabbalah explicitly returns in his writings concern the origins of matter in the fall (in *Materialismusproblem*), *unio mystica* of the soul and God's presence modelled after the Shekhinah (even if Boehmian influence is here clearly detectable) and the idea of self-encounter (*Selbstbegegnung*), probably borrowed from Abraham Abulafia via Moses ben Jacob of Kiev (Münster 1982, p. 137; Münster 2001, p. 71; Münster 1985, pp. 42, 106–7; Boldyrev 2014, p. 105).

Apart from these rather patchy references, Bloch's long-lasting interest in Lurianic Kabbalah is noticeable. He explicitly considered Luria one of the greatest Kabbalists (Boldyrev 2014, p. 131), but judging by the sheer number of references in Bloch's work, the master from Safed was clearly

---

[3] As Wayne Hudson put it, "His aim was to develop a philosophical modernism with a theurgic effect: a modernism directed against the "occlusion of the subject" under capitalism." (Hudson 1982, p. 28).

the most important Kabbalist for him. Yet even Bloch's eulogy of Lurianism in *The Principle of Hope* sounds ambiguous:

> One of the greatest Cabbalists, Isaac Luria (1534–1572), introduced the idea of exile even into the teaching of the creation itself and thereby changes it completely; bereshith, the beginning, the word with which the Bible opens, thus became the beginning not of a creation but an imprisonment. The world came into being as a contraction (tsimtsum) of God, is therefore a prison from its origin, is the captivity of Israel as of the spiritual sparks of all men and finally of Yahweh. Instead of the glory of the alpha or morning of creation, the wishful space of the end or day of deliverance presses forward; it allied itself to the beginning only as to a primal Egypt which must be set aside. Little though such ramifications of Mosaism accord with the solemn hymn of Genesis, they correspond precisely to the original God of exodus and the Eh'je asher eh'je, the God of the goal. So Deus Spes is already laid out in Moses, although the image of a last leader out of Egypt, i.e., of the Messiah, does not appear until a thousand years later; messianism is older than this religion of the Messiah. (Bloch 1995, vol. III, p. 1237)

Taking Luria's concept of *tsimtsum* for a clear-cut theory of exile and imprisonment is a very strong Gnosticism-flavoured interpretation, stronger even than Scholem's rendition of the original *tsimtsum* as God's withdrawal (Schulte 2014, p. 385). What follows is a series of equivocations which blur the interpretative richness and vagueness of the original *tsimtsum*: Bloch sees in it "the captivity of Israel as of the spiritual sparks of all men and finally of Yahweh." For unknown reasons, God comes last (referred to with an interpretation of Tetragrammaton, a gesture uncommon even for non-religious thinkers indebted to Judaism). Then Bloch immediately twists *tsimtsum* to his own purposes, trying to show that it expresses nothing more than a primordial push forwards from the origins which are tantamount to imprisonment. Finally, Lurianism is blended without any explanation into the classic doctrine from the Torah. It is therefore difficult to take this reference to Luria as a well-informed inspiration: it is rather playing on a motive that Bloch did not know thoroughly and was not willing to study with due diligence.

Bloch quite often returns to Lurianic motives. Nevertheless, they always have some admixtures of other content which makes the final effect ambiguous and open for interpretative twists. It seems therefore right to point to various elements of Blochian imagery as having Lurianic connotations—for example his use of the concept of sparks dispersed in the vile and negativity-based world which retain the paradoxical memory of redemption that is to come, as well as the vision of human duty consisting in amassing shards of light, *reshimu*, in preparation of the Messianic moment (Boldyrev 2014, p. 104; Thompson 2013b, pp. 84–85). The image of sparks disseminated in the adverse world may, however, be indebted not only to Luria (Thompson 2013a, p. 17), but also (or even predominantly) to Gnosticism, of which Bloch was notoriously fond. Therefore, the position of the Kabbalah among Bloch's inspirations depends heavily on the interpreter's choice and it might be equally substantiated to view him, as Jürgen Habermas and Peter Sloterdijk did, as a "Marxist Schelling" (Habermas 1968, pp. 69–80; Sloterdijk 2016, p. 157). At the level of explicit references, the usage of Kabbalah is rather scarce and, as demonstrated earlier, fairly superficial. Bloch's voice is persistently polyphonic, which is why the Marranic tension does not appear in his direct Kabbalistic inspirations.

Consequently, if we take into account the epithelial layer of influences, it is hardly justified to view Bloch as a modern Marxist Kabbalist, although such claims were occasionally propounded (Münster 1985, p. 108). Naturally, it might be said that it is a matter of personal interpretation how much weight one attributes to a given current of inspirations in Bloch's thinking, but precisely the gesture of taking the Kabbalah for the central inspiration goes against the author's explicit statements and dissimulates the paradoxical inconsistency of his work. The same applies to loose associations between Bloch's style of writing and Kabbalistic inspirations made by Wayne Hudson:

Bloch uses cabbalistical and non-discursive techniques to refer indirectly (*Umweg*) to levels of experience under-represented or repressed by positivist epistemology. (Hudson 1982, p. 2)

The persistence of Bloch's style—almost always (with the notable exception of his Leipzig lectures on the history of philosophy) ravaged with notorious flaws, such as overcomplication, poetical ellipsis bordering on kitsch and amateurish inconsistency—is hardly an intentional application of Kabbalistic techniques. It rather seems that his innate convolutedness of expression produces a mysticising effect which might be taken for a Kabbalistic inspiration. In this sense, it might be argued that Bloch would be to 20th century philosophy what Kabbalists were to Rabbinic Judaism, but this analogy obviously does not make him a Kabbalist in himself.

3. Into the Deep: Bloch's Key Concepts in the Dispersed Light of Lurianism

If the epithelial level of Bloch's writings contains rather superficial references to Jewish spirituality and, more specifically, the Kabbalah, then tracing influences and borrowings yields somewhat unsatisfactory results. We can establish that Bloch mentioned Luria, referred to the Zohar and Jewish apocalyptic visions, but pinpointing the exact stream of influence seems a rather hopeless task. It is in this regard that Bloch's self-proclaimed "assimilation into Judaism"—absorbing its philosophical and spiritual heritage via other sources—bars the way to detecting (or rather re-constructing) the Marranic phenomenon. There can be no translation where the supposedly "original" language is appropriated lately and through multifarious mediations. The patchy tapestry of Judaism-related citations in Bloch's work hardly proves anything truly interesting, especially philosophically. It is certainly evidence of Bloch's acquaintance with some currents of Jewish spirituality, but deducing from it his essentially Kabbalist position would be a gross overstatement.

Are we then lost in the inconclusive tracing of references? Not necessarily, if only we modify the method and attempt to analyse some of Bloch's key concepts as sovereign formations which might be nonetheless interpreted as resounding with Lurianism. In this chapter I will propose their re-reading. It seems that by doing so we are going into the deep: yet in this depth—contrary to the epithelial level—all clearly traceable references are cut. As it will turn out, what we are left with is an undecidable possibility of Lurianic interpretation.

3.1. The Darkness of the Lived Moment as the Perpetual Tsimtsum

The darkness of the lived moment is a concept which stands at the beginning of the schematic exposition of Bloch's thought. Indebted in this to Schelling and Böhme (Bloch 2009, p. 206; Hudson 1982, pp. 26, 73) and possibly to Kierkegaard (Münster 2001, p. 42), Bloch theorised the present as an occluded, permanently shifting moment which conceals impenetrable darkness. The concept itself recurs throughout Bloch's whole work. Let us begin with a fragment from *Atheism in Christianity*:

> There is much that contrasts with a mere Beginning, a simple Has-been. First of all there is the darkness of the present Moment, always impinging but never grasped, never in possession of itself. The darkness which means that every real beginning is a future thing, alive in the past as a fore-shadowing of the future. Or, to put it in other words, the veiled presence of the future here-and-now *is* the open-ended darkness of each present Moment, *is* the pregnant state of all that it contains. (Bloch 2009, p. 206)

With imagery modelled after German Idealism,[4] Bloch points to the radical ungraspability of the present moment which never squares with itself (Bloch 1975a, pp. 14–15). It comes as a surplus to the

---

[4] In *The Phenomenology of Mind* Hegel describes the insufficiency of language (or, to put it more broadly, the symbolic) in exhausting the qualities of a given particularity: "If nothing is said of a thing except that it is an actual thing, an external object, this only makes it the most universal of all possible things, and thereby we express its likeness, its identity, with everything, rather than its difference from everything else. When I say "an individual thing", I at once state it to be really quite a universal, for everything is an individual thing: and in the same way "this thing" is everything and anything we like.

already-happened, which is why past categories cannot describe it adequately. Bloch assumes that happening is a permanent rupture that at each given moment offers radical novelty which cannot be satisfyingly subsumed under any category which is already in use. Therefore each moment contains an element of radical future, which begins now, in the cut that keeps happening. This observation has a significant subjective dimension, because in the present moment we are estranged from ourselves:

> Ich bin. Aber ich habe mich nicht. Darum werden wir erst.
>
> Das Bin ist innen. Alles Innen ist an sich dunkel. Um sich zu sehen und gar was um es ist, muß es aus sich heraus. (Bloch 1985h, p. 13)
>
> [I am. But I do not have myself. This is why we first become.
>
> The "am" is inside. Everything inside is dark in itself. In order to see oneself and what is around, it must get out of itself.]

Existing in a given moment is nothing but persisting in the total darkness, in which we are an undifferentiated mass of innerness without possession of itself. Having oneself can take place only through becoming: in this regard we are not different from anything that exists through the openness to becoming. It is worth noticing that the darkness of the moment defies continuity of history and of the self: it opens everything towards the future and makes each being discordant with itself at the deepest level. One can exist only through becoming, just as if time were a powerful thrust that opens a hole in all beings (including us) and drags their existence into the future (Bloch 1985i, pp. 218–20).

Contrary to the well-known Hegelian theme (Miller Jones 1995, p. xiv), there is no final reconciliation, at least not before the messianic era. Each being can find itself only in its being-towards-the-future, which is why in every given moment it is a mutilated, incomprehensible darkness. Understanding arises in history; whenever a being is wrenched out of it, it means nothing. In order to describe the subjective effect of this vision, Bloch distinguishes two German words deriving from the same stem: *leben* (to live) and *erleben* (to experience, "to live-through") (Bloch 1975a, p. 50). The first one pertains to mere existence, the second—to comprehension of it:

> Was lebt, erlebt sich noch nicht. Am wenigsten in dem, daß es treibt. Wodurch, worin es also beginnt, noch ganz unten und doch in jedem Jetzt pulsend. Genau dieses anstoßende Jetzt ist dunkel, unser unmittelbares Bin und das Ist von allem. Was daran innen ist, wühlt als dunkel und leer.
>
> ... Alles was lebt, muß auf etwas aus sein oder muß sich bewegen und zu etwas unterwegs sein, die unruhige Leere sättigt draußen ihr Bedürfnis, das von ihr kommt. (Bloch 1985h, pp. 14–15)
>
> [What lives is not yet experienced. Least of all in that it pushes on. Through which, in which it thus begins, still underneath, yet pulsating in every now. It is precisely this pushing now

---

More precisely, as this bit of paper, each and every paper is a "this bit of paper", and I have thus said all the while what is universal. If I want, however, to help out speech—which has the divine nature of directly turning the mere "meaning" right round about, making it into something else, and so not letting it ever come the length of words at all—by pointing out this bit of paper, then I get the experience of what is, in point of fact, the real [*in der Tat*] truth of sense-certainty. I point it out as a Here, which is a Here of other Heres, or is in itself simply many Heres together, i.e., is a universal. I take it up then, as in truth it is; and instead of knowing something immediate, I "take" something "truly", I per-ceive (*wahrnehme, per-cipio*)." (Hegel 1977, p. 160). In Hegel's view individuality is a trap: either we accept its description in the universal language, which is always general, or, if we want to seek "true particularity", we are doomed to endless search, because individuality defies universal language. Bloch's vision might be interpreted similarly: the present is ungraspable and inenarrable; it gains sense only when juxtaposed with other moments as one among many. Nevertheless, what makes Bloch different from Hegel in this regard is his stress on the radical novelty of each present moment: at any given point, something new appears which might totally transform the meaningful continuity of history. In this sense, the darkness dissipates into the light of its future explanation.

that is dark, our immediate "am" and the "is" above all. What is inside, rummages as dark and empty.

... Everything that lives must be on the lookout for something or must move and be on the way towards something, the restless emptiness outside satisfies its need that comes from it.]

Living is pushing on in its obfuscated happening; experience of what happened comes later. For this reason the present is a beating moment that keeps thrusting forward in a permanent insatiable need. But even if the moment gets somehow meaningfully melted into later history, it is always in a sense inexhaustible. In his Tübingen lectures Bloch speaks about "primordial darkness of the already lived moment" [*Das Urdunkel des gerade gelebten Augenblicks*] (Bloch 1985h, p. 273), which suggests that the present moment is shrouded by irremovable darkness. As Anton F. Christen pointed out, each interpretation of it is somehow false (Christen 1979, p. 167), as if the ontological rift between the present moment and its experience could never be adequately fulfilled.

With this twist, the darkness of the lived moment is elevated to the rank of pulsating and indefatigable source of the world at the crossings of the object and the subject. "*Urdunkel*" is something more than elusiveness of the present: it is a form of how the origin of the world appears to us, in its obfuscated form. The true origins in Bloch's vision—just as in Benjamin's *Agesilaus Santander* (Benjamin 1999, pp. 712–16)—are before us: only after history comes to its end will we know them, at the very moment when we reach them again and for the first time. But until history ends, we know the origins only under the guise that they take within it: and this guise is precisely the darkness of the lived moment. Consequently, the present, always shrouded in darkness, begins to resemble Cartesian *creatio continua*, albeit this time not begetting (and thus conserving) a perfect world, but being in itself a process of disintegration that expels towards the future the shards of its own restoration. In *The Principle of Hope* Bloch formulates a similar suggestion:

> The start of the beginning and the starting-point called origin and world-ground is to be found in precisely that Now and Here which has not yet emerged from itself, i.e., which has not yet moved from its place at all. This origin in the strict sense has itself not yet arisen, arisen out of itself; its Not is therefore in fact precisely the one which is ultimately driving history and tailoring historical processes to its requirements, but which has itself not yet become historical. The origin remains the incognito of the core which moves throughout all times, but which has not yet moved out of itself. Every lived moment would therefore, if it had eyes, be a witness of the beginning of the world which begins in it time and time again; *every moment, when it has not emerged, is in the year zero of the beginning of the world*. The beginning occurs in it time and time again for as long as it takes until the undefined Not of the That-ground is decided, through the experimental definitions of the world-process and its forms, either as definite Nothing or definite All, according to its content; *every moment therefore likewise potentially contains the date of the completion of the world and the data of its content.* (Bloch 1995, pp. 307–8)

The lived moment is therefore not only the obfuscated origin of the world, "a witness of the beginning of the world" that keeps happening over and over again, but also the concealed potentiality of the world's end. In a sense, in each moment everything is ready for the completion of the world: it does not happen due to a primordial deferral that wrenches the content of the moment from it and scatters it over the future. Nonetheless, it is only by this deferral that we might understand it; distance is necessary for knowledge, whereas nearness—although it contains the solution of the riddle—appears only as darkness:

> the darkness of the lived moment is depictive for the darkness of the objective moment. That is, for the Not-Having-Itself of that intensive time-element which has itself not yet unfolded in time and process as manifested in terms of content. Not the most distant therefore, but *the nearest is still completely dark*, and precisely because it is the nearest and most immanent; *the knot of the riddle of existence is to be found in this nearest*. (Bloch 1995, p. 292)

Habermas interpreted this concept as indebted to Schelling (Habermas 1968, p. 71), but above the level of direct inspirations the (pra-)darkness of the lived moment can be read with a Lurianic spin. In Chaim Vidal's portrayal of the *tsimtsum*, God's initial contraction has two concurrent consequences: first, it empties the space for the creation of the world and second, it expulses the powers of דין, the judgment, out of God (Fine 2003, p. 130; Schulte 2014, pp. 67–68). The powers of the judgment in most versions of the *tsimtsum* give rise to matter, from which the created world is formed (Fine 2003, pp. 131–34).

Naturally, in Bloch there is no *Ein-Sof* per se, but the darkness of the lived moment conceals pleromic nearness which cannot support its own weight:

> [D]as Jetzt ist die letzte Tiefe, ist der nicht nur alles bewegende, sondern auch alles enthaltende Augenblick, das noch verhüllte omnia ubique jedes Objekts. (Bloch 1985i, p. 114)

> [The Now is the ultimate depth, is not only all moving, but also all-containing moment, the still veiled omnia ubique of every object]

The explosion which takes place in each given moment is thus equivalent to the *tsimtsum*, but in a reversed way, adequate to Bloch's reversal of the role of the past and the future. Whereas the Lurianic *tsimtsum* contracts the fullness of the *Ein-Sof* in order to open the space for creation, the Blochian lived moment crushes and contracts the stiff amassment of the past in order to pave the way for the radically new. The past is contracted and thrust open, with its content forcefully pushed into the future. It is in this sense that everything that exists finds its meaning only through what it will become, as if ultimately the origin of the world was not at the beginning, but at the end of the world. If so, then each moment of the present would be a contraction of the past, a kind of incessant *tsimtsum* which creates empty space for the radical novelty of the future. Simultaneously, it contains all potentialities of what a given thing might and will be: in this sense, it is equivalent to *Ein-Sof* which contracts itself in order to release the potential of beings. In this process matter plays a special role, to which I will return promptly.

Bloch is a consistent atheist; his God is nothing but a human creation, even if effectively an immensely powerful one. But if there is no God and no primordial act of creation, the *tsimtsum* cannot be a one-off prelude to it. Nonetheless, nothing better than this concept depicts the cut between fullness and openness that arises out of contraction. It seems therefore that Blochian ontology can be described as based on the ongoing rather than a one-off *tsimtsum*. Coming strikingly close to Benjamin, Bloch rejects the idea that the past is a closed totality, let alone one that burdens the present. On the contrary, the past never squares with itself, is never full or accomplished, because the Blochian *tsimtsum* pushes its content into the future. We are thus never indebted to the past in the sense of a Nietzschean burden of history: rather the past is indebted to us. The present in its darkness tears apart all cohesion of the past and makes it dependent on the future in which its guts are scattered.

3.2. Cracked Ontology and the Need of Tikkun

If we accept this vision of Blochian *tsimtsum*, it transpires that it is the fundamental condition of freedom, hope and utopia are born of the contraction of the stifling past. In *The Principle of Hope* Bloch remarks:

> Only with the farewell to the closed, static concept of being does the real dimension of hope open. Instead, the world is full of propensity towards something, tendency towards something, latency of something, and this intended something means fulfilment of the intending. It means a world which is more adequate for us, without degrading suffering, anxiety, self-alienation, nothingness. However, this tendency is in flux, as one that has precisely the Novum in front of it. The Where To of the real only shows in the Novum its most basic Objective determinateness, and it appeals to man who is the arms of the Novum. (Bloch 1995, vol. I, p. 18)

The darkness of the living moment is thus double-faced: on the one hand, it has dramatically destructive potential, being a sombre spectacle of annihilating the past by an ungraspable power that eludes our understanding due to being in the greatest proximity to ourselves; on the other hand, it opens the new, bringing about the best of what was trapped in the past. To borrow one more term from the Lurianic repertoire, the contraction of the present produces sparks of light—of hope and utopia—dispersed in the emptiness that it opens up. Without this gaping openness of the future, being is almost nothing. In a brief fragment "An Sich", reprinted in his *Literarische Aufsätze*, Bloch remarks:

Man ist. Das ist zu wenig, ja das wenigste. (Bloch 1985d, p. 11)

[One is. That is too little, indeed, the least.]

Existence in itself is the poorest ontological level. It might gain in meaning only when it is future-oriented, pregnant with its own tendency. Consequently, to grasp a being it is necessary to perceive it within the time dimension: at a given moment it is nothing. No being squares with itself, no being has its essence here and now or has a positive ground (Hudson 1982, pp. 51, 121). In a conceptual short-circuit of his philosophy (a kind of Hillel's one-leg-jumping summary) Bloch summarises this vision with a formula playing on one of the classic sentences of the predicate logic: "S is not yet P" (Bloch 1985h, pp. 246, 274; Miller Jones 1995, p. xiii; Münster 1985, p. 74; Münster 2001, p. 89). A being never overlaps with its characteristics, because it is internally delayed due to the *tsimtsum* which delaminates it into elements trapped in various moments of time.

"*Noch nicht*", one of the central Blochian concepts (Siebers 2012, p. 403; Bloch 1975a, p. 28), is an ambiguous term which might simultaneously mean "not so far", "not yet", "still not" (Hudson 1982, p. 20). Even against the background of Heidegger's radical historicity, "*noch nicht*" is a far-fetched attempt to introduce the dimension of temporality into the heart of being. It inaugurates a future-oriented ontology, which does not begin with solid beings that change or move in time, but with beings whose very essence stretches over time. At any given moment beings are "not yet", awaiting the moment of their completion, split by what Johan Siebers calls "ontological interspace" [*ontologischer Zwischenraum*] (Siebers 2012, p. 403). Their identity, instead of being given at the very beginning, is the highest and most ungraspable moment of utopia (Hudson 1982, pp. 126–27; Siebers 2012, p. 406) which will come only in the final messianic times, after the inner rift in beings is redeemed. Each moment of what has happened, once produced by the shifting of the dark present, falls into the mass of the past with its unrealised Messianic spark: it is the task of the future to return to it, bringing redemption (Bloch 1985h, p. 366). We, as human beings, are equally internally dispersed and hidden from ourselves; Bloch uses the term *homo absconditus* to describe this trait of human condition (Bloch 2009, p. 246; Daly 2013, p. 117). "*Dies septimus nos ipsi erimus*", says Bloch after Augustine (Bloch 1968, p. 25), pointing to the fact that our identity will appear only at the final messianic day. Till then, as he claims in *Geist der Utopie*, "we carry sparks of the end on our way" (Bloch 1971, p. 383).

Therefore Bloch's philosophy is always future-oriented. The past can never be understood in itself; its legacy is crucial not even for the present, which contracts it, but for the future, in which it will be accomplished (Raulet 1982, p. 43). As it will be argued later, Bloch perceives Marxism as a tradition which is epistemologically privileged to decode the past and the present with the perspective of the future ("*Only the horizon of the future, which Marxism occupies, with that of the past as the ante-room, gives reality its real dimension*" (Bloch 1995, vol. I, p. 285)), but concentration on the future might be viewed as a generalised form of Messianism (or "messianicity" in the generalised Derridean sense). Bloch openly embraces this idea:

Everywhere one looks, the Messianic is the last handhold of life and the ultimate resultant of the light of Utopian truth. To the clever that is folly, to the pious it is a pre-fabricated house, but to the wise the sense of Utopia is the most real and pressing problem of an unsolved world. It follows that life itself has sense inasmuch—precisely inasmuch—as it forms itself in dissatisfaction, in work, in rejection of the inadequate and in prophetic premonition of the adequate. Man does not lose himself in these heights; he surpasses himself. (Bloch 2009, p. 239)

This sursum corda applies all the more when heaven is certainly not an existing Utterly Different but, as new heaven, new earth, is set as a utopian task; the sursum corda thus bears precisely the religious, i.e., messianic inherited—substratum. Founders of religion had behaved messianically long before the Jews took the messianic at its word, made it into the fundamental reduction of the religious, into the creation of kingdom per se. *Messianism is the salt of the earth—and of heaven, too; so that not only the earth but also the intended heaven should not become stupid.* The promise the numinous made, the messianic aims to keep: its Humanum and the world adequate to it are not only the thoroughly unfamiliar, the thoroughly unbanal, but the distant coast in early morning light. (Bloch 1995, vol. III, p. 1201)

Utopia is therefore not a property of any religion or spiritual tradition; it is part and parcel of generalised Messianism, which stems from the displacement of the past and the present in relation to the future. The past is being permanently constricted and thrust into the future, but the latter is not be feared. Bloch's *tsimtsum* is a thoroughly positive process, by virtue of which the past finds its accomplishment in the future thanks to the utopian drive. In this manner the cracked ontology, itself result of the *tsimtsum*, is structurally linked to the necessity of utopia:

Utopia presses forward, in the will of the subject and in the tendency-latency of the process-world; behind the cracked ontology of a supposedly attained, even finished There. Thus the path of conscious reality-process is in fact increasingly one of the loss of fixed, even hypostatized static being, a path *of increasingly perceived Nothing, though consequently also of utopia.* The latter now completely encompasses the Not-Yet and the dialecticization of the Nothing in the world; but it just as little suppresses in the Real-Possible *the open alternative between absolute Nothing and absolute All.* Utopia, in its concrete form, is the tested will towards the Being of the All; the pathos of Being is therefore now at work in it which was previously devoted to a supposedly already completely founded, successfully existing world order, even supernatural world order. (Bloch 1995, vol. II, p. 312)

The cracked ontology in Bloch's thought means that no being can be adequately grasped as such. In order to see it in its proper dimensions, it is necessary to take into account the wake it leaves in the future—but not when it is evidently discernible, that is after a certain period of time, but already at its beginnings. Bloch is far from the banal argument that the essence of a process can be understood only after it takes place. Neither does he mimic Hegel in claiming that everything is a process and reveals its essence in time. For Bloch the future is what the past is to ordinary intuitions: an already readable dimension, in which everything that exists has its roots. It is for this reason that the future needs to be fundamentally trusted: it is not a terrifying dimension into which we are thrust from our cosy home, but our real homeland to which we travel from the unhospitable world of the past. It is only with reference to the future that we can be ourselves; it is only at the very end of it that we will gain our identity. Bloch's ontology introduces a crack into beings that Aristotle imagined as substances surrounded by a solid wall: from this crack it is dragged into the future. Within a given moment, the future inhabits beings under the guise of possibility (Bloch 1971, p. 335). Things might change, taking different paths of their possibilities. In this sense, the world is an ongoing experiment (Bloch 1985f, p. 413) that the future performs on the present. The ontology of "not yet" is always at the front of the coming novelty:

Utopische Ontologie hat als solche der Front und des Novum Unentschiedenheit, also Kampf vor sich, das durchaus noch ungelungene Reale des "ontos on", des wahren, wirklichen Seins steht in ihr offen.

... Ontologie des Noch-Nicht-Seins steht auf dem Niveau der alten Metaphysik, mit völlig verändertem Gebäude; neue Metaphysik und konkrete Utopie sind dergestalt Synonyme, geeint in *Transzendieren ohne Transzendenz.*

... Item: jedes Ding kann genauer, kann besser gedacht werden als es schon ist. Werden wäre ein sinnleerer Begriff, wenn das, was herauskommt, schon da wäre. Der Nerv des rechten historischen Begriffs ist das Novum, des rechten philosophischen das bessere Novum. (Bloch 1985h, pp. 355–56)

[Utopian ontology has, as such, undecidedness of the front and of the new, has thus struggle before itself, the still totally unrealised reality of the "ontos on", of the true, real being, is open in it.

... ontology of not-yet-being is at the level of old metaphysics with a completely different building; new metaphysics and concrete utopia are synonyms, united in *transcendence without transcendence.*

... Item: each thing can be more accurate, can be thought better than it already is. Becoming would be a meaningless concept if that what came out was already there. The nerve of the right historical concept is the novelty, the better novelty of the truly philosophical.]

If each being has its roots in the future, it may be understood not through ordinary recollection (which would apply if it was embedded in the past), but in *Eingedenken*, paradoxical remembrance-of-the-future:

Wenn Erinnerung voraussetzt, daß etwas vergessen worden ist, so ist Vergessen insgesamt die Unterlassung, woran und wogegen Erinnern und Hoffen als *Besinnung* sich letzthin begegnen. Vom Ausfall Vergessen her erscheint Erinnerung als *Mahnung*, Hoffnung als *Eingedenken* ...

... Vergessen ist ein Modus der Erinnerung wie des Eingedenkens, ist jenes Defiziens, das im Gedächtnis Verlassen, im Eingedenken Verrat heißt. Vergessen ist so Mangel an Treue und wieder nicht einer Treue gegen Erloschenes, sondern gegen Unabgegoltenes. (Bloch 1985h, p. 282)

[If recollection presupposes that something has been forgotten, forgetting altogether is the omission in which and against which remembering and hoping as reflection will meet in the end. By failure of forgetting recollection appears as admonition, hope as *Eingedenken* ...

... Forgetting is a mode of recollection, just like *Eingedenken*, it is that deficiency which is called abandonment in memory, and treachery in *Eingedenken*. Forgetting is lack of loyalty and again not loyalty to the extinct, but to the unfulfilled.]

The Jewish injunction to remember (Yerushalmi 1982) is thus reversed: it no longer concerns loyalty to those who lived and perished or to what existed and disappeared, but to the future that the past bore in itself. *Eingedenken* is both a form of recollection and cognition of what will happen, but is already inscribed in the utopian tissue of the past. Quite clearly *Eingedenken*—and, through its means, recuperation of what remains omitted in the past (Bloch 1971, p. 335), might be seen as a form of *tikkun* (Thompson 2013b, pp. 84–85). Ultimately it is nothing but bringing things to its origin, which is to be sought not before, but after them.

Blochian ontology might be thus read as combining two central Lurianic ideas—*tsimtsum* and *tikkun*—in one and the same device. *Tikkun* in the Lurianic tradition is an act of repairing the damaged world. Being a duty of all exiled Jews, it is meant to glean God's sparks from *kelippot*, evil forces that arose from the excess of severe judgment (Fine 2003, p. 144). The task of *tikkun* makes human beings join the process of redemption: in Bloch's atheist version, the onus is only on them. Recollecting traces of utopia from the inert and stifling mass of the past is like retrieving sparks from *kelippot*: bringing them together materialises the utopian future. No being can exist without this redemption: otherwise it merely subsists, maimed in the disaster-ridden past.

3.3. Matter as Liberating Openness to the Future

The Lurianic reinterpretation of Bloch's utopia brings us to the last concept which I will attempt to view in the light of Kabbalistic inspirations: matter. Bloch is a staunch materialist, who devoted a whole book to a recital of older currents of materialism as viewed from the perspective of 20th century Marxism (Bloch 1972). Like Engels, he believed in materialism as a method of explaining the world with reference only to the world (*Erklärung der Welt aus sich selbst*—(Bloch 1968, p. 20))). In this sense, materialism is a factor of human liberation:

> It is above all fear that keeps men submissive, but even the thought that wishes can be fulfilled from on high makes man a beggar. So it was not impudence that first turned irreligious (for impudence is proper to beggars), but humanness. And in this way materialism has always been endowed with a liberating role for man: it stood upright against the pressure from above, and set knowledge (the *sapere aude*, dare to use your mind) over against fate which, far from being seen through, was even glorified. And upright bearing, then, and the will to know sets the tenor of every great critique of religion ... (Bloch 2009, p. 49)

Materialism is then a particular method of sober thinking which has a cutting blade of anti-religious critique. But, contrary to the stereotypical portrayal of anti-Idealist and positivist materialism, Bloch's matter is not an utterly passive, malleable and dead block (*Klotz*), but an active factor of change (Bloch 1972, p. 126; 1985h, p. 230; Hudson 1982, p. 114). Wayne Hudson goes as far as to identify Bloch's matter with God (Hudson 1982, p. 157), but that seems to have a repositioning effect for the totality of equidistant elements of Blochian thinking. Bloch himself interprets matter as preserving in its latency the utopian potential of the future:

> Matter is latent in these opennesses according to the direction of their objective-real hope-contents: as the end of self-alienation and objectivity encumbered with alien material, as matter of Things For Us. On the path towards this, the objective surpassing of what currently exists in history and world occurs: this transcending without transcendence, which is called process and is accelerated on earth so forcefully by human work. Forward materialism or the warmth-doctrine of Marxism is thus theory-practice of reaching home or of departure from inappropriate objectification; through it the world is developed towards the No-Longer-Alienation of its subjects-objects, hence towards freedom. (Bloch 1995, vol. II, p. 210)

It is precisely in matter that we need to seek fecundity and novelty (Bloch 1995, vol. II, p. 236). In a radically atheist manner, it is conceived as "transcending without transcendence" (*Transzendieren ohne Transzendenz*), that is, having a natural potency to change and bring about an utopian future without being a transcendence to the world (Bloch 1972, p. 478). It is a crucial bearer of what will happen:

> *Without matter no basis of (real) anticipation, without (real) anticipation no horizon of matter is ascertainable.* Real possibility thus does not reside in any ready-made ontology of the being of That-Which-Is up to now, but in the ontology, which must constantly be grounded anew, of the being of That-Which-Is-Not-Yet, which discovers future even in the past and in the whole of nature. Its new space thus emphasizes itself in the old space in the most momentous manner: real possibility is the categorical In-Front-of-Itself of material movement considered as a *process*; it is the specific regional character *of reality itself, on the Front of its occurrence.* How else could we explain the future-laden properties of matter?—there is no true realism without the true dimension of this openness. (Bloch 1995, vol. I, p. 237)

Matter occupies the front of happening, being an active, protean factor of incessant change. Materialism in Bloch's sense does not presuppose the world full of inert substances that interact, but rather a permanent process which happens not only to things, but in them. Matter is full of latent tendencies (Bloch 1972, p. 469) which await realisation: in a sense, it is richer and more inventive than we can be intentionally.

Bloch's materialism can be read in the light of Lurianic Kabbalah as an interpretation of what role God's sparks play in the world. Lurianism presupposes strong division of matter into evil *kelippot* and the scattered pieces of light that are entrapped in them. Matter has generally negative connotations, being a site of fall and sin (Fine 2003, p. 151) which requires acts of *tikkun*. In Bloch's vision, evil is associated rather with the closeness and blindness of human beings than with matter as such. When viewed in the correct light, it discloses its active and utopian potential, as if it preserved the whole richness of permanently happening *tsimtsum*. Only in this sense does matter have a quasi-divine position: in the radically atheist world of Bloch's thinking which keeps being ripped up by each consequent moment of *tsimtsum*, matter is the front of the coming novelty. Therefore it seems to be a God's spark in itself, which demands time and human effort to be brought to the height of its potential revealed in the utopian traces.

It is worth noticing what the absence of God entails in Bloch's thought: it transforms a one-off *tsimtsum* into a permanently recurring process which opens all beings into the future. In so doing he follows in the footsteps of Chaim Vital's interpretation of the *tsimtsum*, which accentuates that God's contraction is permanently renewed in order to allow the world to exist (Schulte 2014, p. 74). Nonetheless, Bloch's matter in its totality is equivalent to the Lurianic *reshimu*, being a silent companion to *tsimtsum* as the active factor of utopian change. There had been no perfect past before the fall, to which the redemption would constitute a match. On the contrary, the best is always still to come; the past had only the pleromic concentration of premonitions and utopian sparks, which will need to develop.

4. Between the Epithelial and the Deep: The Non-Simultaneous in the Marranic Phenomenon

The two previous sections developed two different methods of reading Bloch in search of Marranic traces: the first consisted in retracing his explicit references to Jewish spirituality and the Kabbalah, whereas the second attempted to read three key concepts of his thinking as a profound atheist re-construction of Lurianism. The crucial question which needs to be answered concerns the relationship between the two methods.

Their point of convergence is limited: the first method allows confirmation that Bloch was familiar with Lurianism (albeit it is not certain to what extent and via which sources, as his account of Luria's Kabbalah is somewhat inaccurate), which makes the second method legitimate insofar as it assumes that Luria's teachings might have informed the engine concepts of Bloch's philosophy. Nonetheless, there is no logical bridge between the two. The epithelial approach yields certain, but quite trivial results. The deep approach is far more interesting, but the three concepts discussed above might be equally read as informed by works of Böhme or Schelling. There is no decisive interpretative clue which would make the Lurianic reading fully legitimate. Faith and orientation to the future, the closest contestants for this position, are in themselves too indeterminate to disclose a possible Marranic encryption.

Moreover, there are some significant discrepancies which make such a reading prone to criticism. To name just a few: is taking the darkness of the lived moment for a particular version of the *tsimtsum* not a too far-fetched metaphor? What is the relation between its immanent fullness and the totality of the past that it is supposed to contract? Is atheism a sufficient explanation of Bloch's positive valorisation of matter, so different in tone from Luria's vision? Can the reversal of the ordinary hierarchisation of the past and the future still be inscribed into the framework of Lurianism, no matter how transformed over the ages of interpretation?

One could obviously take this conundrum for a sign that Bloch's Marranic condition reached its fullness, melting with the languages he adopted to the point of undifferentiability.[5] In so doing, Bloch would invent a perfectly universalist language in which all the traces of Jewishness are so well concealed that they can no longer be recognised other than through their re-invention. Nonetheless, such a conclusion does not do justice to the specificity of Bloch's thinking, which does not advance from Judaism to Western philosophy, but rather blends all these languages in a somewhat chaotic manner. Are we therefore doomed to acknowledge the richness of the tapestry of Bloch's writing and desist from seeking in it an overarching framework?

Fortunately, Bloch himself provides a category which might shed light on the specificity of his unbridled multi-discursivism: *the simultaneity of the non-simultaneous.*[6] The concept stems from the very beginnings of Bloch's thought (Bloch 1971, p. 91; Münster 2001, pp. 40–41, 169; Münster 1985, pp. 41–42; Thompson 2013a, p. 15), but it gained its true importance in the analyses of Nazism developed in the late 20s and the 30s, finally published in the volume *Erbschaft dieser Zeit* (Bloch 1985b). In this usage, it was applied to describe the simultaneous co-existence—within one and the same society—of many elements (social strata, customs, ideologies, beliefs, imagieries, etc.) which had their origins in different moments of history. Extrapolating Marx's suggestions, Bloch believed that progress never eradicates the past once and for ever. On the contrary, obsolete elements, once defeated by the force of progress, are pushed aside and subsist at the margins of society (Bloch 1985h, p. 91). For this reason modern society is never properly modern: it also, to a large extent, harbours pre-modern beliefs or prejudices. Society develops by differentiation in time: there are areas which are most up-to-date and those which lag behind. The success of Fascists and Nazis can be explained by noticing that in their political propaganda they addressed the obsolete strata of population via their latent out-of-date content of dreams and phantasies (Bloch 1985b, pp. 98–116; Hudson 1982, p. 44; Christen 1979, p. 106; Münster 1982, p. 241).

In Bloch's theory, all these non-simultaneous elements co-exist at the same time within one and the same society. Consequently, our meaning of time needs to be more complex than just the ordinary mechanical time of clocks (*Uhrzeit*). This time obviously plays an important role, especially in the modern society (Bloch 1985h, p. 130; 1975a, p. 93), but societies and history are shaped by meaningful times of human existence (Bloch 1985h, p. 136). In a crucial move Bloch assumes that times are multiple: each culture is governed by its own (Bloch 1985h, p. 135). Combined with the category of the simultaneity of the non-simultaneous, such an assumption means that different times co-exist within one societal framework. Some strata of the society live closer to the actual front of the present, whereas others are defined by temporal retardation. Nonetheless, they interact, communicate and in this variegation shape social life, even if upon closer scrutiny they are discordant in their temporal dimension.

Therefore, if philosophy wants to recognise history and society in its true form, it needs to adopt multi-dimensional conception of time which Bloch models after Riemann's space. This conception encompasses "non-rigid, polyrythmical historical times" (Hudson 1982, p. 147) that correspond not only to various cultures, but also to different moments in the history of each society (for example, the Russian 1917 is not as dense as the Russian 1967). Moreover, it is necessary to acknowledge the existence of time which is full of curvatures (*krümmungsreiche Zeit*), which can be miraculously shortened in one messianic leap (Münster 2001, pp. 300–1). Bloch finally develops the concept of non-simultaneity to bring it to a sufficiently general level that it could describe, among others, the

---

[5]   Ultimately, for radical Marranos, such as Sabbatians, total concealment of one faith is the desired goal (Scholem 1995, pp. 109–10).

[6]   Bloch's original term, *die Gleichzeitigkeit der Ungleichzeitigen*, has been variously translated into English: as "contemporaneity of the non-contemporaneous", "synchronicity of the non-synchronous" or "simultaneity of the non-simultaneous" (Miller Jones 1995, p. 51). Much as differences between them seem inconsequential, I prefer the last term, because the German word "*gleichzeitig*" or "*Gleichzeitigkeit*" belong to common rather than elaborate language.

complexity of Böhme's thought—drawing from Gnosis, Manicheism and Böhme's own epoch, the Renaissance (Bloch 1985g, p. 228). Simultaneity of the non-simultaneous is thus transformed into a universal theory of multi-dimensional times which interact within cultures, societies or individual thinkers' works, producing unpredictable clashes and synergies (Bloch 1975b, pp. 197–98).

Simultaneity of the non-simultaneous is a concept which lacks one last step: reflective application to Bloch's work as such. This move is not, perhaps, particularly bold, given that the unabating polyphony of his text makes an impression of giving place to the irreconcilable. Bloch audaciously juxtaposes—without melting—inspirations from multifarious spiritual, religious, philosophical and political movements, preserving the multi-dimensional temporality that he himself recognised in thinkers whom he found significant. But this reflexive application is more revealing if we take into account that simultaneity of the non-simultaneous is nothing but a well-thought consequence of the *tsimtsum*, in which the very tissue of time gets ripped up: time is scattered into multiple times which all occupy the same universe. Some among them are like *kelippot*—obsolete, reactionary times which stifle growth and bring human beings back into the obscurity of the past. Some, however, have the position of *reshimu*, residues of divine light. Combining once more Marxism and mysticism, Bloch claimed that dialectical materialism and social strata which correspond to its message—with the particular role of the proletariat—are at the front of contemporaneity (Bloch 1985b, p. 159; Münster 1985, p. 82). They are simultaneous, living up-to-date and reading the signs that the current times give us.

If so, Bloch's thought, which in itself recognises multi-dimensional temporality and applies it in its development, does not apply or interpret the *tsimtsum*, but mirrors it with its own structure. Simultaneity of the non-simultaneous is a concept which refers to societal, ideological and intellectual structuration of temporality, but, *simultaneously*, it is a concept that reveals the heterogenic character of Bloch's thinking. His writing is not "simply" incoherent or patchy: it moves through narratives of different times, which is why it can provide no overarching framework for them. His text bears affinity to the position of simultaneity: it constitutes an empty contingent container, in which discordant contents co-exist. In this sense, precisely by acknowledging non-simultaneity, Bloch elevates his thought to the only contemporaneity that is possible.

In the realm of the non-simultaneous one current is posited as predominant: Marxism.

> Everything that is non-illusory, real-possible about the hope-images leads to Marx, works—as always, in different ways, rationed according to the situation—as part of socialist changing of the world. The architecture of hope thus really becomes one on to man, who had previously only seen it as dream and as high, all too high preappearance, and one on to the new earth. Becoming happy was always what was sought after in the dreams of a better life, and only Marxism can initiate it. (Bloch 1995, vol. I, p. 17)

At least declaratively, Bloch remained a staunch Marxist throughout his mature life. As mentioned previously, his Marxism was as heterodoxical as all his other re-appropriations of intellectual and religious traditions, which had very down-to-earth consequences, especially in relations with GDR authorities. In Bloch's own description Marxism has two main streams: the cold one, concentrated on economy, social structures and abstract analyses, and the warm one which absorbs all the humanistic and utopian impulses that had existed before Marx (Bloch 1995, vol. I, p. 209). Unsurprisingly, Bloch opts for the latter (Bloch 1985c, p. 219; Moltmann 1968, p. 46), simultaneously confessing his deep belief in the accuracy of Marx's insight:

> *The concepts of practice until Marx are therefore completely different from his theory-practice conception, from the doctrine of unity between theory and practice.* (Bloch 1995, vol. I, p. 271)

> It must therefore be repeatedly emphasized: *in Marx a thought is not true because it is useful, but it is useful because it is true.* (Bloch 1995, vol. I, p. 277)

> *Only the horizon of the future, which Marxism occupies, with that of the past as the ante-room, gives reality its real dimension.* (Bloch 1995, vol. I, p. 285)

This heterodoxical Marxism seems to sum up nearly all of Bloch's interests (Habermas 1968, p. 69): utopia, orientation towards the future, class struggle, progress, redemption and the utopian society. Acknowledging Marxist reductionism of complex phenomena to economic materialism and Marxism's deficiency in anthropology, ethics, aesthetics and religion (Bloch 1985e, pp. 475–81), Bloch attempted to enrich it (Hudson 1982, pp. 40–42). It is in this sense that his ontology was meant to be a new metaphysics adapted to Marxism as the only truly future-oriented current of modern thinking (Hudson 1982, p. 104). In Bloch's view, Marxism should absorb all the progressive heritage of the past even in areas which at first sight may seem manifestly discordant with a scientific, atheist and materialist approach, such as religious movements or natural law (Hudson 1982, pp. 160–68).

Ultimately, Marxism is the only constant anchor in Bloch's thinking. Once again the pledge of loyalty is unconventional (but so typical for Bloch), because adamant support of Marxist hardliners (to the point of endorsing Stalinism) in his writings goes hand in hand with embracing the open, humanistic legacy of progressive humanity. It seems, however, that the unbridled simultaneity of the non-simultaneous in his work required some kind of orientation point, which would offer a solid signifier. It is for this reason that Bloch—at least in his own perception—was one of the key Marxist thinkers of the 20th century, even if mainstream Marxism ignored him almost entirely, especially insofar as it concentrated on economic theories. Yet the very heterodoxy of Blochian Marxism proves that it is rather a *space* than a consistent intellectual current. In this way Bloch forces Marxism open: unexpectedly, it is revealed as a part of broader, non-metaphysical ontology. In this form it turns into a uniquely modern kind of Lurianism, in which capitalism is equivalent to the world after the fall, while forces of utopia and communism shine like hidden sparks of God's light. And, unsurprisingly, faith remains the cornerstone of this new kind of Lurianism.

5. Conclusions

If Bloch can be interpreted as a philosophical Marrano, this can be done only after acknowledging his unique position which, in a sense, turns Marranism upside down. The inveterate incoherence of his thinking rules out any Marranic tension between the source and the translation: there is no source and no translation, because all inspirations are juxtaposed with tranquil disregard to their mutual relations.

At the epithelial level, references to spiritual and intellectual currents of Jewish thinking are numerous, but inconclusive. There is hardly anything that makes them more significant than, say, Renaissance utopianism. It often seems that Christian inspirations are more dominant. To make the situation even worse, references to the Kabbalah are somewhat superficial, not to say incorrect. By contrast, at the heart of Bloch's thinking one can discern a powerful philosophical engine which comes most clearly into view through the lens of Lurianic Kabbalah. Such an interpretation, however, forces its way through the dark: there are no definitive clues that would prove any kind of Kabbalistic influence on Bloch's central concepts. Hegelian, Schellingian and Marxist influences might also be used productively to dismantle them.

Yet in this conundrum Bloch's own concept of simultaneity of the non-simultaneous can bring understanding into the patchiness of his work. Even if its interpretation in the light of Lurianism is uncertain, one thing makes it resemble Luria's version of Kabbalah beyond any doubt: fundamental and irreconcilable shattering of the universe into different worlds, each governed by its own respective time. There is no need to find a common ground for all of them, just as there is no need—and no sense—to seek a key to Bloch's writings which would make them coherent. He openly accepts that the universe—perhaps as a result of a specific modern *tsimtsum*—is broken into irreparable pieces. Consequently, his work resembles the world it attempts to grasp, not by interpreting or drawing from Lurianism, but by repeating it with its very structure.

The only thing which remains constant in Bloch's work is faith: faith in the future, in utopia, in Marxism. With its force Marxism itself turns into a generalised future-oriented ontology of the scattered universe. Bloch's faith is unshakable, just as if it flowed from the certainty that there is a structural point in this collapsed world which will never fail. And indeed, the future can never fail, whereas God has failed miserably. The world is pushing forward: is that not a sufficient proof that faith rightly has its object?

"To be open toward the future would be to be Jewish, and vice versa", claimed Derrida in *Fever Archive* (Derrida 1996, p. 74). This is little, very little, especially if this kind of late Jewishness has been already re-appropriated by Western thinking through thousands of re-readings and transformations. Bloch does not require this kind of "secret faith" behind his work. In the immensely rich universe of his writings, faith in the future might be equally Jewish and philosophical. Perhaps if the *tsimtsum* is fully understood and believed in, no Marranic encryption is needed—the very scattering of languages means that they will co-exist and overlap, expressing the *tsimtsum* with their very existence. Faith has truth for its correlate: if one struggles for what is true, philosophy, Judaism and Marxism might be the one and the same without even touching each other.[7]

Funding: This research received no external funding.

Acknowledgments: I would like to express my gratitude for receiving a scholarship of the French government, which allowed me undisturbed work on many projects, including this article.

Conflicts of Interest: The author declares no conflict of interest.

References

Benjamin, Walter. 1999. Agesilaus Santander (First and Second Version). In *Selected Writings. Vol. II, Part 2. 1931–1934*. Cambridge: The Belknapp Press, pp. 712–16.

Bielik-Robson, Agata. 2014. *Jewish Cryptotheologies of Late Modernity. Philosophical Marranos*. London and New York: Routledge.

Bloch, Ernst. 1968. *Werkausgabe Band 14. Atheismus im Christentum. Zur Religion des Exodus und des Reichs*. Frankfurt am Main: Suhrkamp.

Bloch, Ernst. 1971. *Geist der Utopie*. Frankfurt am Main: Suhrkamp.

Bloch, Ernst. 1972. *Das Materialismusproblem, Seine Geschichte und Substanz*. Frankfurt am Main: Suhrkamp.

Bloch, Ernst. 1975a. *Experimentum Mundi. Frage, Kategorien des Herausbringens, Praxis*. Frankfurt am Main: Suhrkamp.

Bloch, Ernst. 1975b. *Gespräche mit Ernst Bloch*. Edited by Rainer Traub and Harald Wieser. Frankfurt am Main: Suhrkamp.

Bloch, Ernst. 1985a. *Briefe 1903–1975*. 2 vols. Frankfurt am Main: Suhrkamp.

Bloch, Ernst. 1985b. *Werkausgabe, Band 4. Erbschaft dieser Zeit*. Frankfurt am Main: Suhrkamp.

Bloch, Ernst. 1985c. *Werkausgabe, Band 6. Naturrecht und menschliche Würde*. Frankfurt am Main: Suhrkamp.

Bloch, Ernst. 1985d. *Werkausgabe, Band 9. Literarische Aufsätze*. Frankfurt am Main: Suhrkamp.

Bloch, Ernst. 1985e. *Werkausgabe, Band 10. Philosophische Aufsätze zur objektiven Phantasie*. Frankfurt am Main: Suhrkamp.

Bloch, Ernst. 1985f. *Werkausgabe, Band 11. Politische Messungen, Pestzeit, Vormärz*. Frankfurt am Main: Suhrkamp.

Bloch, Ernst. 1985g. *Werkausgabe, Band 12. Zwischenwelten in der Philosophiegeschichte: aus Leipziger Vorlesungen*. Frankfurt am Main: Suhrkamp.

Bloch, Ernst. 1985h. *Werkausgabe, Band 13. Tübinger Einleitung in die Philosophie*. Frankfurt am Main: Suhrkamp.

---

[7] In one of his early texts, entitled *Über motorisch-mystische Intention in der Erkenntnis*, Bloch writes: "Der Philosoph also reist nicht wie Münchhausen, von dessen Anwesenheit keines der beschriebenen Länder etwas verspürte, sondern er ist dazu gehalten, Baaders tiefer Forderung zu genügen: gleich einer Sonne über allen Kreaturen aufzugehen, damit er ihnen zur Manifestation eines Gottgleichen verhelfe. Und die ernennende, aufdeckende, schöpferisch informierende, schließlich identifizierende Kraft der Philosophie ist so groß, daß selbst das völlig enthüllte Jetzt, die vollkommene Vergegenwärtigung unserer gelebten Gegenwart, daß selbst noch dieses ehedem als Werk des Messias und der allverwandelnden Apokalypse Gedachte als Werk der Identifizierung ein philosophisches Werk darstellt." (Bloch 1985i, pp. 116–17). [The philosopher, therefore, does not travel like Munchausen, of whose presence none of the described countries was aware, but he is obliged to fulfill Baader's profound demand: to rise like a sun over all creatures, so that he help them come to manifestation of a godlike. And the calling, revealing, creatively informing, and finally identifying power of philosophy is so great that even the fully revealed Now, the perfect visualization of our lived present, that even this work of identification, formerly thought to be the work of the Messiah and the all-transforming Apocalypse, represents a philosophical work.]

Bloch, Ernst. 1985i. *Werkausgabe Ergänzungsband. Tendenz—Latenz—Utopie*. Frankfurt am Main: Suhrkamp.

Bloch, Ernst. 1995. *The Principle of Hope*. 3 vols. Cambridge: The MIT Press.

Bloch, Ernst. 2009. *Atheism in Christianity. The Religion of the Exodus and the Kingdom*. London and New York: Verso.

Boldyrev, Ivan. 2014. *Ernst Bloch and His Contemporaries. Locating Utopian Messianism*. London and New York: Bloomsbury.

Christen, Anton F. 1979. *Ernst Blochs Metaphysik der Materie*. Bonn: Bouvier.

Daly, Frances. 2013. The Zero-Point: Encountering the Dark Emptiness of Nothingness. In *The Privatization of Hope. Ernst Bloch and the Future of Utopia*. Edited by Peter Thompson and Slavoj Žižek. Durham and London: Duke University Press, pp. 164–201.

Derrida, Jacques. 1993. Circumfession. In *Derrida*. Edited by Geoffrey Bennington and Jacques Derrida. London: University of Chicago Press.

Derrida, Jacques. 1996. *Archive Fever. A Freudian Impression*. Chicago: Chicago University Press.

Fine, Lawrence. 2003. *Physician of the Soul, Dealer of the Cosmos. Isaac Luria and His Kabbalistic Fellowship*. Stanford: Stanford University Press.

Habermas, Jürgen. 1968. Ein Marxistischer Schelling. In *Über Ernst Bloch*. Frankfurt am Main: Suhrkamp.

Hegel, Georg Wilhelm Friedrich. 1977. *The Phenomenology of Mind*. New York: Humanities Press.

Hudson, Wayne. 1982. *The Marxist Philosophy of Ernst Bloch*. London and Basingstoke: The Macmillan Press.

Jay, Martin. 1984. *Marxism and Totality. The Adventures of a Concept from Lukács to Habermas*. Berkeley and Los Angeles: University of California Press.

Miller Jones, John. 1995. *Assembling (Post)modernism. The Utopian Philosophy of Ernst Bloch*. New York: Peter Lang.

Moltmann, Jürgen. 1968. Messianismus und Marxismus. In *Über Ernst Bloch*. Frankfurt am Main: Suhrkamp.

Moltmann, Jürgen. 1976. *Im Gespräch mit Ernst Bloch. Eine theologische Wegbegleitung*. München: Kaiser Verlag.

Münster, Arno. 1982. *Utopie, Messianismus und Apokalypse im Frühwerk von Ernst Bloch*. Frankfurt am Main: Suhrkamp.

Münster, Arno. 1985. *Figures de l'utopie dans la pensée d'Ernst Bloch*. Paris: Aubier.

Münster, Arno. 2001. *L'utopie concrète d'Ernst Bloch. Une biographie*. Paris: Kimé.

Raulet, Gérard. 1982. *Humanisation de la nature. Naturalisation de l'homme. Ernst Bloch ou le projet d'une autre rationalité*. Paris: Klincksieck.

Scholem, Gershom. 1995. *The Messianic Idea in Judaism and Other Essays on Jewish Spirituality*. New York: Schocken Books.

Schulte, Christoph. 2014. *Zimzum. Gott und Weltursprung*. Berlin: Jüdischer Verlag.

Siebers, Johan. 2012. Noch Nicht. In *Bloch-Wörterbuch. Leitbegriffe der Philosophie Ernst Blochs*. Edited by Beat Dietschy, Doris Zeilinger and Rainer E. Zimmermann. Berlin and Boston: De Gruyter, pp. 403–8.

Sloterdijk, Peter. 2016. *Was geschah im 20. Jahrhundert?* Berlin: Suhrkamp.

Sorel, Georges. 1999. *Reflections on Violence*. Cambridge: Cambridge University Press.

Thompson, Peter. 2013a. Introduction. In *The Privatization of Hope. Ernst Bloch and the Future of Utopia*. Edited by Peter Thompson and Slavoj Žižek. Durham and London: Duke University Press, pp. 1–20.

Thompson, Peter. 2013b. Religion, Utopia, and the Metaphysics of Contingency. In *The Privatization of Hope. Ernst Bloch and the Future of Utopia*. Edited by Peter Thompson and Slavoj Žižek. Durham and London: Duke University Press, pp. 82–104.

Walser, Martin. 1968. Prophet mit Marx- und Engelszungen. In *Über Ernst Bloch*. Frankfurt am Main: Suhrkamp.

Yerushalmi, Yosef Haim. 1982. *Zakhor. Jewish History and Jewish Memory*. Seattle and London: University of Washington Press.

religions

MDPI

Article

Concerning Some Marrano Threads in The Aesthetic Theory of Theodor W. Adorno

Jakub Górski

Philosophical Department, Institute of Philosophy, Jagiellonian University, 31-007 Krakow, Poland;
jkbgorski@gmail.com

Received: 11 January 2019; Accepted: 5 March 2019; Published: 9 March 2019

check for
updates

Abstract: This article is an attempt to re-read the magnum opus of Adorno's philosophy, namely _Aesthetic Theory_, using an interpretative key offered by Agata Bielik-Robson's book entitled _Jewish Cryptotheologies of Late Modernity: Philosophical Marranos_. This interpretative key, called by the Author _The Marrano Strategy_ implemented to Adorno's late philosophy allows us to investigate the common points of Adorno's theory of art criticism and modern Jewish thought. Therefore the main question of this text concerns the characteristics of Jewishness and messianicity (Scholem, Derrida) in Adorno's _Aesthetic Theory_. The thesis that I am attempting to justify is as follows: the implementation of _Marrano strategy_ to the modern art criticism redefines and reverses the relationship between the particular element and the universal domain. Consequently, this dialectical 'appreciation' of the particular establishes a common conceptual field for critical thinking and traditional, religious motifs.

Keywords: Adorno; Bielik-Robson; Marranism; modernity; aesthetic theory; negative dialectics

---

"The only philosophy which can be responsibly practiced in the face of despair is the attempt to contemplate all things as they would present themselves from the standpoint of redemption. Knowledge has no light but that shed on the world by redemption: all else is reconstruction, mere technique. Perspectives must be fashioned that displace and estrange the world, reveal it to be, with its rifts and crevices, as indigent and distorted as it will one day appear in the messianic light."

Theodor W. Adorno, "Minima Moralia"[1]

The aim of this paper is to present the implementation of the philosophically most important principles of the so-called _Marrano strategy_ in the aesthetic thought of Theodor W. Adorno. My definition of this strategy, or the interpretive key, allowing a different reading of modernity, is based on Agata Bielik-Robson's definition. I attempt to support the author's general thought presented in her paper with examples of specific methodological solutions from Adorno's last book, in my opinion the most important, namely _Aesthetic Theory_. Thus, I point to the legitimacy of this still unpopular "reading" of modernity—its philosophy and art. The work is divided into two main parts. In the first part, I describe the specificity of Jewish thought, as defined by Bielik-Robson, focusing on the answer to the question of how language, interpretation, and criticism are understood in this thought. Against this background, in the second part, I discuss in detail the threads of Jewish nominalism in the concept of Adorno's art, selected and considered by me to be the most important in this context. The thesis that I am trying to justify is as follows: the value that the Marranic interpretation of late modern thought brings is the redefinition and reversal of the relationship between the individual

---

[1] See: (Adorno 2006, Aphorism no. 153, _Finale_, p. 247).

element, the particular element and the universal, general, conceptual domain. Finally, the valorization of what is individual makes it possible to describe the process of acquiring subjectivity as not based on subordination, hierarchy, or exclusion.

1. "Third Language"—Cryptotheology as Modernity Cipher

In the book *Jewish Cryptotheologies of Late Modernity: Philosophical Marranos*, Agata Bielik-Robson describes Jewish philosophy as a "third language". The simplest way to illustrate the specificity of this thought is as follows: if there is a special Jewish perspective of experiencing the world, it is the "place" that corresponds to the "in between" location. It is a crevice in which the falling light of idealistic and post-idealistic Western thought refracts, creating unique constellations, but it does not disappear. Putting aside the metaphors, the Jewishness of philosophy is described by the author as a connection between anti-philosophy and "counter-philosophy". The author defines the philosophy, of which both tendencies oppose when combined, by describing its Greek genesis and special heritage:

> "The mixture of anti-philosophy, which explicitly declares war against the Greek genre of thinking, and counter-philosophy, which implicitly engages in creating counter-arguments, aimed to oppose the Greek vision of the uncreated cosmos, will become a characteristic feature of this uneasy, deeply troubled thing we call, for the lack of a better name, 'Jewish philosophy', from the Hellenistic times of Philo of Alexandria up to the postmodern, neo-Alexandrian times of Lévinas and Derrida."[2]

The vision of the uncreated cosmos, rejected by Jewish philosophy, is described here as a typically Greek amalgam of beliefs about the cyclicality and natural unity of the cosmos. This rejection is simultaneously the "anti-philosophy" element, proposing a different presentation of the myth of the beginning. Using this simple "pedagogical" distinction, she speaks about heritage in the "counter-philosophy" paradigm. The author questions the possibility and further even undermines the necessity and value of rejecting what she calls "the argumentative form of the 'Greek wisdom'". Therefore, the "counter-philosophy" part in the characteristics of Jewish philosophy means that the format of Jewish philosophy is Greek in nature, takes over the ontological-epistemological issues typical of Western continental philosophy, and hence also the above-mentioned form of argumentation. At the same time, it remains the opposite, a "mirror image" of Western thought, a proposal for a different perspective on classical Greek-Christian metaphysical problems. This otherness—peculiarity, to put it more clearly—gives voice to the Jewish thought. The author is convinced that:

> "The situation of 'Jewish philosophy' is exactly like the one described by Reznikoff: it is the singular predicament of the 'third language' in which Jewish thinkers talk Hebrew in words, concepts and arguments bequeathed to them by Greek philosophers. (...) the fusion is inseparable, as indeed in a true marriage, and that 'talking Hebrew in every language under the sun' does not leave the Jewish component untransformed."[3]

For Bielik-Robson, the position of the third language occupied by Jewish philosophy means this "instantaneous bilingualism", the "in-between", influenced by native tradition and orthodox faith in the revealed truth[4], and the freedom of beloved thinking, a freed metaphysical speculation with Greek roots.

Together with the author, we have reached the first important point of these considerations. Bielik-Robson defines the meaning of Greek-Jewish dilation, the third language, by comparing it to the

---

[2] (Bielik-Robson 2014, p. 2).
[3] (Bielik-Robson 2014, pp. 3–4).
[4] As we will see in the further part of the essay, this relationship will be rich in philosophical consequences. Particularly, when we transcribe Scholem's category of commentary into Adorno's concept of art criticism. See: (Scholem 1976), see also: (Adorno 2002, pp. 22–33, 193–97).

principle of Marranism. Marranos, Spanish Jews who were forced to convert to Christianity, retained their traditional faith, Judaism, under the surface of the official religion—they used a language of ideas that was strange to them but thought in Jewish. So, the subversion was bidirectional. The language that was foreign to them "deformed" their learning, and their specific tradition influenced the way they moved around the territory they had inherited, whether they wanted to or not. The last heir of Marranism understood in this way was Derrida, who somewhat ironically called himself Marrano. After all, Bielik-Robson means to narrow the consideration of Marranism to the field of philosophy. The author characterizes his philosophical Marranism, as well as the philosophical Marranism of his predecessors—Spinoza's, or Horkheimer's and Adorno's—in the spirit of the above considerations:

> "The last one of this great philosophical line, Jacques Derrida, openly claimed to be 'a sort of marrane of French Catholic culture', and this declaration prompted him to articulate this peculiar experience of the 'third language', which we would like to call a 'philosophical Marranism'—to denote a type of thinker, like himself, who will never break through the Joycean 'Jew-Greek, Greek-Jew' confusion, but nonetheless will try to turn it into his advantage. That is, to marry the speech of strangers and let the Hebrew talk through it: to do counter-philosophy with the help of philosophy."[5]

The Marranic metaphor best describes the topos and ethos of Jewish philosophy. As I noted, the author writes that the phenomenon of marriage is reflected in deliberations on language. In other words, what defines the specificity of Jewish philosophizing, is in reflection on forms of thinking. The language will also contain the baggage of ideas of strictly Jewish tradition and the method of secretly maintaining them will ultimately be a way they are pronounced, which, by doubling the official discourse, is not available to everyone. The problem, then, will be assimilation in the language without losing what defines a specific identity—a challenge between what is inherited and what is adopted for various historically relevant reasons and goals. As a first step, the nature of the Marrano strategy's "in-between" (full assimilation and orthodoxy) location should also be specified. This is an important problem posed by the philosophical position of the formula of the assumed universality of philosophical language. Universalization, as understood, for example by Hegel, is to be connected with the process of individualization not only of its own, but also of what is particular, detailed, universalized. However, as we know, for example from the *Dialectics of the Enlightenment*, this process historically ends in total failure. This simply happened because the marriage of the universal and the particular was characterized by symbolic, material, and physical violence towards the one striving to be recognized as a unit, an individual, in the name of the generality, such as the state "organism" or the so-called "nation", or this or other political system claiming the right to the only rightful one. The linguistic Marrano strategy, on the other hand, by questioning individualization in terms of the philosophical discourse itself, undermines its founding a priori general position by not directly expressing the subversive formula of the subjectification process: the particular, i.e., non-conceptual, is now to set the direction and to determine the process of individualization. The question emerges and repeats itself along with the need to establish the "identity" of these "strangers", "others" being the philosophical Marranos in Europe, philosophizing Jews who do not accept the conceptually idealistic scheme of unsuccessful individualization. Following the needs of this philosophical diaspora and responding to its mentioned location ("in-between"), the attempts to combine the universal and the particular are not abandoned. The proposal to give subjectivity to the "strange" of Western continental philosophy is one that derives from its Marranic nature, which it wants to preserve not only for its own benefit but also to save the compromised Western culture.[6] The author characterizes this marriage, again using the arguments of Derrida, the last, in her opinion, who used the Marrano strategy to the fullest extent to combine these two tasks:

---

5   (Bielik-Robson 2014, p. 4).
6   (Bielik-Robson 2014, pp. 18–19).

Derrida is particularly useful here, mostly because of his openly declared linguistic promiscuity. By discarding faithfulness to any monolingual tradition, he stands firmly on the post-Babelian grounds of the dispersion of idioms that can approach universality only horizontally: not by assuming a transcendent and superior meta-position, but by engaging in clashes and stormy 'marriages'. There is no such thing as a homogenous universal language. Yet universality can be approached by 'marrying the speeches of strangers', which completes the broken whole on the horizontal level, without usurping the God-like point of view hovering over the clamour of differences. As Walter Benjamin says in 'The Task of the Translator' (...), the only possible strategy of universalization rests on the awareness of particularity of all languages, which then lend themselves to the practices of translation (*Übersetzung*) and completion (*Ergänzung*). The universal can only be made out of the patchwork of mutually strange idioms that are forced into 'marriage' by the translator.[7]

The above-mentioned marriage is characterized by non-hierarchicality, changeability, and openness. Equally important is the leading element in the process of individualization, the process of which this marriage is a "project". If, in the mainstream of Western continental thought (idealistic or, more specifically—Hegelian) it is a general, supra-unit element, then here, the particular, detailed element gains value:

"To reach universality does not mean to escape the confusion in a vertical manner but to stay at its level and work through the differences it creates. This is precisely the paradox of what we will call here a 'Marrano strategy'. The uneasy and deeply problematic discipline of thought called 'Jewish philosophy' became gradually so unhappy with its own nomenclature that it began to claim universality, a true universality, so far unmatched by any language declaring to be universal: philosophy or Christianity. These 'philosophical Marranos', always accused of soiling the universal form of philosophy and its Christian avatar with parochial Hebrew content, eventually turned this accusation to their own advantage and formulated their standpoint as follows: at least we know we are particular and can start from there, while you, our accusers, remain mistaken as to your own alleged universality and thus can never know or doubt your presuppositions. In fact, the whole evolution of modern Jewish thought can be seen as the shift in regard to the issue of universality."[8]

The universality referred to by the author has nothing to do with the order in which the non-conceptual is subordinated to systemic regulation. If universality is to be looked after, it should be its constellationary, messianic formula.[9] The author characterizes the Marrano strategy in such a convention—as a form of messianism—saving what is strange in the face of the assumed universal order, by emphasizing the value of the particular in the process of the multiplication of discourses, that is, as a post-Babelic turn in the very kernel of universalization—towards the primacy of what is strange, different, and special in this process.[10] A life-giving strategy against the ontological status quo, altered for all cases of uniformity and sameness is to turn towards the non-identical, the "non-finalizable", the open. The possible, and what can never be identified in spite of utopia and closed in a single story of reconciliation, is always to take precedence. In this movement, apart from emphasizing the primacy of non-identity and difference, according to the movement of appreciating the particular

---

[7] (Bielik-Robson 2014, p. 5).
[8] (Bielik-Robson 2014, pp. 6–7).
[9] See: (Adorno 2004, pp. 162–66); Adorno took the idea of constellational language of pure names mostly from W. Benjamin. Far more important is that Benjamin was inspired by the Kabbalistic and mystical concept of language. The first is the mystical conception of language by the Magus of the North, J. G. Hammann, as proposed in his *Biblische Unterschungen*. The second is the idea of language held by the Cabbalist Franz Joseph Molitor, expounded in the seventh chapter of his *History of Philosophy* entitled "Über den Ursprung der Sprache und Schrift bei den Ebraern", See: (Jacobson 2003, pp. 114–15); See also: (Benjamin 2003, pp. 27–56; Benjamin 2002a, pp. 62–74); see also: (Scholem 1990).
[10] See: (Bielik-Robson 2014, p. 8).

idiom and preserving the values of universality in memory, the peculiar antinomic place of Jewish truth is also defined.[11] According to Scholem, the memory of it can only be made present in the proleptic movement, a movement of message which is both a movement of forgetting it and hiding. Therefore, its location within the traditional Western philosophical thought (i.e., post-Kantian, Hegelian) only superficially condemns it to subordination, and in reality gives hope for (constantly and continuously delayed and therefore alive) reconciliation of the particular and the universal. As we will see from the example of Adorno, the strictly secularized discourse is ruled by the hidden-under-the-surface, spectral stream of the Kabbalah.[12] Bielik-Robson refers to Derrida in describing this open Judaism in exile with the following words:

> This is what 'constitutes Jewishness beyond all Judaism': 'To be open toward the future would be to be Jewish, and vice versa [. . .] In the future, remember to remember the future' (ibid., pp. 74, 76). And although Derrida quotes Yerushalmi's definitions of the 'Judaism interminable' not without an irony, he nonetheless confirms that what counts in this whole enormous archive, accumulated obsessively by the Jewish archons of memory, is the unique index of its imperative to remember: it is not past-oriented towards the acts of grounding and legitimating a supposedly distinct 'Jewish identity' (for which he gently reproaches Yerushalmi), but future-oriented, proleptic and unprecedentedly open—a *futurité*.[13]

The paradoxical formula of remembrance about the future adopts another condition for the realization of universalization: one should "save" the past, or rather what has been forgotten, because it is subject to the universal laws of history, which is written by the conquerors or their philosophers. At the same time, memory is not Heidegger's pondering but a socially defined form of *praxis*. Benjamin, Adorno, and later Derrida were proponents of such a formula of Jewish philosophy. Summarizing this introductory part of the discussion, the most important features of Marranism can be listed. This procedure is necessary due to the aim of the essay. I would like to remind you that the subject of the dissertation is to define a specific form of this kind of marriage of tradition and modernity in Adorno's aesthetic theory. So, if we want to consider the details, we need to know the "guidelines", the clues that will lead us to answer the main question in this paper.

The most important feature of the Marrano strategy is its secrecy. Secondly, we will "read" it as a kind of crypto-theology[14], according to the slogan: "the less you show yourself as Jewish, the more and better Jew you will be."[15] Thirdly, we will consider this strategy within the question on the specific form of language that creates and "carries" it, being responsible not only for the form but also for the content of the message. What is equally important, this strategy is the result of the "location" between rejection and acceptance of the existing Greek-Christian metaphysical tradition. Finally, the "third language", due to its status as a specific particularity, is still forced to legitimize its universality—it will be an example of the redefinition of an unsuccessful particular-universal marriage. Only when individualization of what is particular goes hand in hand with universalization, can we talk about striving for (endless) reconciliation of the non-reconcilable. Defining the features of this idiom: it should be non-hierarchical, and not based on any existing or planned hierarchy. It is to

---

11 See: (Bielik-Robson 2014, pp. 17–18).
12 See: (de Vries 2005, pp. 235–99); particularly see: (de Vries 2005, pp. 259–61).
13 (Bielik-Robson 2014, p. 18).
14 I accept the concept of "crypto-theology" as defined by Bielik-Robson. The author writes:"I do not use here the word 'theology' in a sense which figures in Lévinas' 'God and Philosophy', i.e., as a being-biased science of God, whose history is the same as 'the history of the destruction of the transcendence' (GP, p. 56). I use it in a much more neutral way, which can also embrace the special slant of Jewish religious thinking, which I have already named as the swerve from the free-fall of indifference towards concern and anxiety, refashioning the world in dynamic terms of ontological insufficiency and the need for redemption. The prefix 'crypto' reflects here the Marrano stance of our thinkers in question, who rarely disclose fully their Judaic sources of inspiration and if so, then usually for the non-religious purposes aiming at the renewal of Western modes of thinking.", (Bielik-Robson 2014, p. 18).
15 (Bielik-Robson 2014, p. 18);

be open: not to exclude but to include, yet with the observation that what is included will not lose its particular meaning. According to Adorno's definition, it is to be "reconciliation in difference".[16] The above-mentioned features of the Marrano strategy do not exhaust its definition, but I consider them to be the most important in the context of these considerations. They allow me to turn to a specific issue: to question the concept of the language resulting from this strategy. Therefore, following the author's example, I will try to bring closer the characteristics of the particular Jewish nominalism. Then, on this basis, I will define the meaning of Jewish linguisticity in Adorno's aesthetic theory and in his concept of art.

2. Jewish Nominalism

At the beginning of chapter 7, entitled "The promise of the Name", the author introduces a working definition of Jewish nominalism, at least to some extent corresponding to specific philosophical concepts by Rosenzweig, Cohen, Benjamin, Scholem, Adorno, and finally Derrida. Important for this definition is the question of one's (own) name and the act of naming, giving names or restoring names as metaphysically expanded acts of communication. The author writes the following:

> "Jewish thinkers I have mentioned can be called nominalists in the traditional sense of the word, but only to a certain extent and with a decisive *clinamen*. Though they all perceive the world as comprised ultimately of singularities, they do not treat names as mere *flatus voci*, i.e., arbitrary conventions that express our cognitive helplessness in the face of the material chaos of things. Far from fostering any kind of magical realism, which would attribute an ontological power to the act of naming, they nonetheless believe that naming as such opens the gate to a special relationship with reality: a relationship maintained not in the mute operations of Ockhamian-Baconian instrumental reason, but in the dialogical process of linguistic communication, where names and naming constitute, in Benjamin's words, in its very essence and true calling of language."[17]

The adoption of a strictly Marranic perspective of language analysis entails a number of structural solutions. At this point, we can notice the connection between naming and rendering the primacy of the particular, the "not-yet-individual" in the act of the linguistic concretization of universalization. Language universalization is to be at the same time individuation both of itself and of the particular. As Bielik-Robson rightly points out, the concept of the language of names comes mainly from Scholem's interpretation of the Kabbalistic concepts of revelation, message, and salvation[18], within which he calls the revelation of the name or names of God a revelation.[19] The concept of nominalism proposed here is thus rooted in the Jewish tradition, where tradition means the message (of the truth of revelation) and the message means creative interpretation, leading through philosophical and aesthetical criticism (Adorno)[20] towards translation-deconstruction led by the imperative of maintaining the memory of Jewish identity as "Jewishness" (vide: Derrida—*Des Tours de Babel*[21], *Archive Fever: A Freudian*

---

[16] Criticizing the Hegelian version of reconciliation in *Aspects of Hegel Philosophy* Adorno implicitly presents his own idea of *Versöhnung*. He writes (Adorno 1993, p. 27): "(. . .) in its emphatic Hegelian version, the concept of spirit is to be understood organically; the partial moments are to grow into and be interpenetrated by one another by virtue of a whole that is already inherent in every of them. This concept of system implies the identity of subject and object, which has developed into the sole and conclusive absolute, and the truth of the system collapses when that identity collapses. But that identity, full reconciliation through spirit in a world which is in reality antagonistic, is a mere assertion. The philosophical anticipation of reconciliation is a trespass against real reconciliation; it ascribes anything that contradicts it to "foul" existence as unworthy of philosophy. But a seamless system and an achieved reconciliation are not one and the same; rather they are contradictory: the unity of the system derives from unreconcilable violence."

[17] (Bielik-Robson 2014, p. 233).

[18] See: (Scholem 1996).

[19] See: (Bielik-Robson 2014, p. 234).

[20] See: (Wasserstrom 2007, pp. 74–76).

[21] See: (Derrida 1985, pp. 165–67).

Impression[22]—the titles first mentioned by Bielik-Robson). What is equally important, another feature of religious origin is the one that defines the function of "naming" (so far its detailed course is not relevant). Therefore, naming is also a creative act, although it is not divine *ex nihilo*, but is its immanent, earthly, and material analogon:

> "God creates by expressing his absolute name, i.e., by leaving his secret signature in all things and thus bestowing upon them their names; creation is but an articulation, both the expression and fragmentation of the divine name. And if Scholem says 'God's language has no grammar', he means that creation does not need any additional metaphysical structure of mediation between the divine source and the created world, no auxiliary scheme of emanation. The relationship between the one and unique God and his creations, conceived in an equally singular way is direct and strictly nominalist. What unites the creation within itself and with its Creator is not the Neoplatonic structure of participation, where all beings share in various degrees the flow of divine power, but language and linguistic communication, in which all of these ontologically separate elements come into a cosmic dialogue. This emphasis on language as the only metaphysical 'glue' of the otherwise fragmented and horizontally diversified universe, accounts also for the special, elect position of man who is the only being capable of using language, that is, of maintaining a relationship with created reality via giving names."[23]

Another noteworthy feature of this kind of nominalism is its separating effect. Contrasting this concept with the idea of "participatory nominalism", the author pointed to the distinctiveness of its Jewish version and its peculiar "nature", alternative to the Christian one. If one of Christian origins recreates the hierarchical dependence of individual entities on the Creator in a conceptual matrix that gives each of them its own meaning, then the Jewish one corresponds more to the horizontal, i.e., not stratifying, structure of particularities.[24] The primacy of what really exists over the concepts that can be read from here is, again, one of the key features of a Marrano language strategy. The non-participatory form of this nominalism results from the non-participatory and non-emanating model of creation, which is defined as follows:

> "in the non-participatory model of creation based on the notion of strict separation, this metaphysical hierarchy is replaced by an anarchic 'ontological multitude' (as Spinoza could have called it), which cannot be ordered according to the modes and degrees of existence because it exists in exactly the same way and manner as the God who created it. In a way, therefore, this vision contains *avant la lettre* the famous prenominalist argument of Duns Scotus, who, in his thesis on univocity (*univocatio entis*) 'equalized' the notion of being against the Neoplatonic tradition of modes and degrees of eminence, still fiercely defended by Thomas Aquinas. Here, creation means making something other than God himself: something truly distinct that, as Lévinas puts it in *Totality and Infinity*, should be able to exist on its own without being a *causa sui*. Just as God is unique and singular (*echad*), bearing a distinct name, so is his creation: equally separate, singularized and free to express itself in the particularity of the name. For, as Isaiah attests, the singularity of everything created is not at all illusory or secondary; to the contrary, it is the most real, because it was the Creator himself who 'called it by name' (Isaiah 43:1)."[25]

A further consequence of such a model is also the "emancipation" of language from general concepts. In other words, the above model can be treated as a hypothetical structure of equally significant

---

[22] (Derrida 1995, pp. 9–63); concerning the differences between Jewishness and Judaism, messianic and messianism—see: (Derrida 1995, pp. 46–50).
[23] (Bielik-Robson 2014, p. 234).
[24] See: (Bielik-Robson 2014, pp. 235–36).
[25] (Bielik-Robson 2014, p. 239).

"singularities"[26] which, paradoxically, because they are named this way, are universalized and thus also the very proposal of metaphysical experience and specific ethos. It is precisely this ethos, as a "serious" action, in a specific social space and context, that will finally—as we will see—be the basis for the negative imperative of Adorno. This philosopher particularly emphasized that the postulated language of names cannot be treated and realized only as an epistemological proposal, but must—according to its Jewish and Marxist genesis—be put into practice. For Adorno, naming would be a kind of a "metaphor" of social criticism, hidden in philosophy or artwork that is subject to interpretation and criticism.

Another, and the last important, feature of the particular language of names discussed here will be the dialectics of secularization[27] which is established and conducted by it. If we consider dialectics, as Adorno and Horkheimer, to be a model of "disenchantment", then a necessary condition for secularization is simultaneous participation in de-secularization. "Neutralization of nihilistic sting of disenchantment"—from Kant to Nietzsche—is only possible by accepting its dialectical marriage with the "object of disenchantment". Thus, this particular object, as in the redefined "particular-universal" marriage, will disenchant the phenomenon of secularization itself, the secularization that strives for universal application, as total, finite, closed:

> "dialectical use of disenchantment is characteristic of those Jewish thinkers who attempted to translate the traditional Judaic critique of myth and magic into modern conditions of secularizing *Entzauberung*, where the latter would be conceived not as an enemy but as an ambiguous ally of religion. Ambiguous—because everything here depends on how we understand the very concept of *Entzauberung* itself. If it boils down to nothing but a dreary form of a 'Urizenic' rationality, reducing being to a machine-like self-sufficiency that blocks any further speculative attempt to achieve any other form of meaning—the view that would immediately conform to what Adorno calls 'the positivistic myth of what is'—then it is definitely more danger than a help. Yet, if it clears room for a new understanding of God's transcendence, no longer in any way enmeshed in the mechanism of being—then it paves a way to a new form of religious speculation which both Adorno and Scholem would very gladly endorse: a version of religious nihilism that interprets the disenchantment of the modern world in theological terms. As Adorno says in his Epigrams: 'No theological content will last untransformed; every single one will have to face the test and enter the sphere of the profane'."[28]

At the same time, unsurprisingly, dialectics allows the two seemingly separate spheres of human spirituality to be mutually defined, while at the same time ensuring their preservation in overcoming [their] abstract separateness. From our point of view, it is important that in this dialectical weave, the form of the Jewish tradition that is being assumed and looked for at first becomes clear. This means that its preservation is only possible as a continuous, open, unfinished redefinition-deconstruction. The concrete "result" of this dialectics determines the assumed form of meaning, assigned to this tradition. A form of meaning in which the emphasis is placed on expressing tension between two dialectical moments is conveyed not as an ontologically marked and separate existence, but as a semantic, language-derived differentiation mechanism.[29] In other words, the condition for the identification of the philosophical Marrano and the world in the process of disenchantment as a Marrano world, is its de-identification, "separation", the life-giving non-identity founded in Adorno's deadly "deserts of abstraction". Bielik-Robson writes:

---

[26] See: (Bielik-Robson 2014, p. 239).
[27] See: (Adorno 2005, pp. 135–43) where Adorno writes on the uneasy relationship between the religion and secularized rationality.
[28] (Bielik-Robson 2014, p. 260).
[29] See: (Bielik-Robson 2014, p. 260).

"in modern Jewish thought—death is a dialectical point of departure beyond the world
of creation, a beginning of the 'path' driving from absolute 'meaninglessness' to equally
absolute 'meaningfulness'; from the mute 'marble-like' existence of death-destined things to
the condition of a dialogue in which every expression acquires a meaning. It is a point of
recognition and clarity that, once all the beautiful and deceptive appearances are gone, lends
a rock-bottom of semantic orientation."[30]

This process, as one may suppose, is not predestined; it does not have a one-way, future-oriented and
fulfillment-oriented, certain goal. It is rather a decentralized movement (expanding from all sides)
of free autonomous seeking of itself.[31] It is only in this liberation that messianic features can be seen.
According to Bielik-Robson, it is only when a man loses the base of a magical bond with the world that
he/she can realize what is at stake in this kind of messianism: individuation or subjectivization, i.e.,
the earthly salvation of himself/herself and silent matter.[32] The Messiah's salvation in its Marrano
form is thus significant for the process of differentiation and separation outlined above, as long as
there is no Messiah anymore, and the uncertainty, which triggers critical vigilance, governs each
subsequent (straying) step.[33] This is neither an active awaiting nor the practice of restoring a lost bond:
in other words, collapse is a necessary condition for being able to grope in the dark.[34] The absence
of God, which is breaking out of this semantic emptiness, therefore has a meaning. If the emptiness
is equal to him, as the philosophical and artistic Marranos see it, then paradoxically—becoming his
trace, allegory, track—it makes him present in this absence.[35] That is to say, if the presence in the
form of a panoptic system of control and the pursuit of hyper-efficiency in each sphere of human
practice is a false form of the omnipresence of the absolute, its "true" presence must be radically
different from that of the all-encompassing and tracking every step of the spectral total power. In such
a dialectical formula, the Marrano nature of the modern "non-existence" of God and the "non-being"
of a Jew/Other/Stranger is enchanted. Here, like the author, I accept the perspective of Scholem,
which was also accepted by Adorno[36]:

"For Benjamin, God the Legislator withdraws, leaving a complete vacuum of 'mere life'
(*blosses Leben*) with its senseless flow-and-fall, unable to produce 'one grain of meaning'.
For Scholem, however, this withdrawal is dialectical: the more God disappears from the
world, the more the world is in the need of revelation, which, in the end, becomes a new
form of revelation that is characteristic of a 'religious nihilist' or a 'pious atheist'. In the
poem dedicated to his friend, Scholem writes: '*Nur den Nichts is die Erfahrung,/Die sie von
dir haben darf*' ('Only nothingness is the experience we are allowed to have of you'). Thus,
while Scholem concentrates on the nothing itself, expecting from it a renewal of revelation,
or a messianic reversal occurring within the Godhead itself, preparing to leap into a new

---

[30] (Bielik-Robson 2014, p. 262).
[31] See: (Bielik-Robson 2014, p. 270).
[32] See: (Bielik-Robson 2014, p. 271).
[33] See: (Bielik-Robson 2014, pp. 272–73).
[34] For Adorno, Auschwitz is the absolute fall of all meanings, teleology and sense, as well as the sense of human bond with
the "divine" order. As the final self-destruction of meaning, semantic silence, (Scholem's "nothingness of revelation" (See:
Scholem 1969), this event is equal to the collapse of the Western civilization. This earthly catastrophe—the absolutely
negative—is a condition and a guarantee of a messianic hope. What is equally important, for Adorno the specific "code of
Auschwitz" determines all possible interpretations of the genocide. Consequently, the thesis that the philosopher assumes
an interpretive model in which "universalizes" this particular and historical event, is acceptable. In other words, one could
agree that the general concept of Adorno's "subvertion of utopia" is founded on this particular event.
[35] See: (Bielik-Robson 2014, p. 276).
[36] As Habermas wrote: "Adorno and Scholem are interested in the possible truth content that monotheistic traditions can
still unfold under conditions of modernity. They are not looking for mythical or pre-Socratic origins. The myth that the
logos of the great world religions had overcome must not "keep the last word". Nietzsche is absent, and the sulfur smell
of neo-Nietzscheanism even more so. The "Transfiguration of Mysticism in Enlightenment" is the place where Adorno
and Scholem meet. He had studied the continuation of the profound teachings of a Luria of Safed in the frankistic sects of
the 18th century and persecuted until the French Revolution. The two are interested in this revolutionary interference of
heterodox teachings in the secular society for various reasons." (Habermas 2015, p. 3).

manifestation (...)—Benjamin is ready only to rely on the 'weak messianic force of the abandoned creatures who must procure the messianic reversal themselves."[37]

Simply put, Marrano dialectics, according to Scholem, will therefore be "the dialectics of absence-presence": the meaning that appears in the place of H/his absence is the almost elusive, emerging bond between the individual and his (divine) designation, his own name. This characteristic corresponds to Adorno's thought, which is why I devoted more space to its presentation. As it will turn out, this is the shortest way to define the "dialectical negativity" of Adorno's philosophy and to combine it through irrevocable marriage with the modern Jewish tradition in order to use such a perverse term.

3. Adorno's *Aesthetic Theory* as the Philosophical Language of Marrano

Once we have the general characteristics of Marrano nominalism and the understanding of language as such, it is possible to consider the specific issue of the title and attempt to highlight the features of a linguistic martial strategy in Adorno's aesthetic thought. It should be added that the indication of a strong relationship between the quasi-religious Marranic strategy and Adorno's aesthetic theory is a certain novelty among the existing interpretations of Adorno's philosophy. In the group of eminent commentators of Adorno's thought, to which I undoubtedly include Martin Jay[38], Roger Foster[39], Jay M. Bernstein[40], or Robert Hullot-Kentor[41], there is no one who develops and describes the abovementioned relationship. Although Jay, for example, writes about mimesis in the context of Adorno's redefinition of the particular-universal relationship, he ignores the question concerning the possible Jewish roots of this idea. Hullot-Kentor, on the other hand, mentions the Greek-Jewish synthesis carried out by Benjamin in the context of the concept of naming in only one place in his work.[42] Similarly, Foster, although he points to the sources of Benjamin's concept of language in Jewish mysticism, doesn't address the issue of Jewishness in Adorno's thought, despite the fact that Adorno can be considered in this context as a continuator of Benjamin's idea.[43] Generally speaking, none of abovementioned authors emphasize the relevance of the Jewish dimension of Adorno's theory. That's why I think it's worth following Bielik-Robson's and Derrida's intuitions. One thing can certainly be said now: the idea behind it will be, in its general expression, identical with the "imperative" of the subversive redefinition of particular-universal marriage and will be understood by it in the context of fulfilling or non-fulfilling the task of social criticism. The totality of the society cannot be rejected in one political "gesture" (that is: revolutionary); similarly Adorno will approach the issue of the relationship between the universal and the particular. The condition for the deconstruction of their marriage is criticism as a medium. Therefore, in the end, he writes that the non-conceptual must be achieved by means of concepts, so that they too, as the general, are open to their "other". Thus, the non-conceptual is a guarantee of the "non-hierarchical", "constellatory" form of the Absolute's non-presence as a personified totality. What "thought-images"[44] of this non-presence are artworks in Adorno's eyes? How do they correspond to the meaning of the Marrano language strategy and what does it mean for them as carriers of potential social criticism and change? Further on, I would like to focus on the answers to the above questions. I will limit myself to the analysis of Adorno's main aesthetic text, namely the unfinished and, according to the author himself, constellational in form,

---

[37] (Bielik-Robson 2014, p. 278).
[38] See: (Jay 1997).
[39] See: (Foster 2007).
[40] See: (Bernstein 1992).
[41] See: (Hullot-Kentor 2006).
[42] (Hullot-Kentor 2006, p. 127).
[43] See: (Foster 2007, p. 60).
[44] See: (Richter 2009, p. 4).

Aesthetic Theory (1969). I believe that, as his last work, it also plays the role of a specific philosophical *resumé* when it comes to issues concerning the relationship of the work and society.

Let me start with the most general remark. *Aesthetic Theory* defines what the work of art is. But, as unfinished, fragmentary, open, it (*Aesthetic Theory* eo ipso) corresponds—albeit unintentionally—to the idea of redefining the marriage of a particular position (thanks to the original idiom) and the general (universal) language of notions it uses. The publishers, closing the work symbolically, quote Adorno' words: "The fragment is the intrusion of death into the work. While destroying it, it removes the stain of semblance." Then they continue: "The text of *Aesthetic Theory*, as it was in August 1969, which the editors present here as faithfully as possible, is the text of a work in progress;"[45] The unfinished, the open, the incidental with which Adorno wanted to measure "vitality", i.e., in his understanding, the social relevance of artworks, refers reflexively to itself. The paradox is that at the same time Adorno activates the dialectics of "death (as) life". In my opinion, this dependence can be directly related to an equally dialectic understanding of the dependence of tradition and what is new in Scholem's understanding, which Adorno took over and developed in *Aesthetic Theory*.[46] I will risk a statement that the death of the master, the Subject, the Narration and the fragmentariness of the argument, which complement each other and at the same time are a peculiar fullness, a whole, deconstruct the notions themselves. Fullness is fulfillment, and therefore the hope; the entirety is fragmentation, so it is not total; closure is the opening, so it is not final—but also vice versa. This kind of dialectics was launched by Adorno in an attempt to fully express his aesthetic concepts, this kind of dialectics, as we have seen, governs the language of philosophical Marranos when talking about their identity. The publishers, quoting from Adorno's correspondence on the following pages, point to another determinant of its endlessness, openness, and verticality, immanent to the work: "It is simply that from my theorem that there is no philosophical first principle, it now also results that one cannot build an argumentative structure that follows the usual progressive succession of steps, but rather that one must assemble the whole out of a series of partial complexes that are, so to speak, of equal weight and concentrically arranged all on the same level; their constellation, not their succession, must yield the idea."[47]

The above introduction and quote contained in it—apart from the fact that it marks a trail leading to several dimensions of the basic analogy, "philosophical Marranism-theory of artwork by Adorno"—will serve as a matrix for this work. The threads will revolve around the assumed analogy, but I will not give any of them the philosophical name of the first, i.e., the most important one. The first, which Adorno himself writes about, is non-philosophical, as a "material" foundation of social conditions, and their historical determinants, broadly understood as "cultural".

3.1. Artwork as a Third Language

At the beginning, I will not implicate the Reader in reflections on the detailed characteristics of Jewish nominalism which describe, in my opinion, also the specific idiom of the language of art with Adorno. However, here I would like to highlight the deep similarities between the location as a third language of specifically Jewish "understanding", "experiencing", "reading" of reality and artwork also as a special kind of understanding and experiencing it. The third language, characterized at the beginning, is the result of the marriage of the Jewish religious tradition and its ontogenetic and soteriological perspective with the western, Greek-Christian metaphysical heritage. The form of this marriage is not insignificant: what is traditionally Jewish remains hidden under the surface of the official discourse. Thanks to this negation, it is preserved. But what defines the specificity of Jewish philosophy here, as I wrote at the beginning, will focus in the final self-referential reflection on the possibilities, moduses of existence of a negated tradition. Language itself will be considered,

---

[45] See: "Editors Afterword. Gretel Adorno and Rolf Tiedemann" (Adorno 2002, p. 361).
[46] See: (Adorno and Scholem 2015), for example, letter no. 2, from Scholem to Adorno, pp. 15–20; or: (Benjamin et al. 1994).
[47] (Adorno 2002, p. 364).

its potential as a carrier of the Word, and the way to "keep it alive", if one can put it this way. Tradition can be preserved by way of hidden expression, "which, by doubling the official discourse, is not available to everyone"[48]. "Starting the play of the inherited and what is accepted for various historically relevant reasons and purposes"—this is the most abbreviated definition of the "location" of the Marranic third language. What similarities does Adorno's language of artwork have with such a location?

The temporal dimension, persistence, transience, anticipation in a modernist artwork is marked on a basic level by dialectics of "tradition—the new".[49] In other words, a modernist artwork negates what has passed as its own condition of socially significant persistence, transience, and anticipation. Adorno, defining this relationship, writes:

> "[T]radition itself, as a medium of historical movement, depends essentially on economic and social structures and is qualitatively transformed along with them. The attitude of contemporary art toward tradition, usually reviled as a loss of tradition, is predicated on the inner transformation of the category of tradition itself. In an essentially nontraditional society, aesthetic tradition a priori is dubious. The authority of the new is that of the historically inevitable. To this extent it implies objective criticism of the individual, the vehicle of the new: In the new the knot is tied aesthetically between individual and society."[50]

Changes within the category of tradition itself are connected with socio-economic ones. Where experience is (slowly) becoming a commodity, there is a lack of objective ground for categories that have leaned into the past. But the past does not die because of commodification and alienation: "Art is modern art through mimesis of the hardened and alienated; only thereby, and not by the refusal of a mute reality, does art become eloquent; this is why art no longer tolerates the innocuous."[51] It is merely a sample of the dialectics which unambiguously indicates the meaning of the presence of what is past in the artwork of modernity as present. The artwork achieves the meaning of this kind through the thematicization of this dialectics: "consideration" of one's own idiom as incorporation of criticism. This, in turn, defines it as a peculiar "language". The importance of the critical self-reflection achieved by the modern artwork can, therefore, be compared to the importance and validity of the "traditional"[52] moment as a reflection on one's own possibility of permanence. Adorno writes "Aesthetic truth content and history are that deeply meshed. A reconciled reality and the restituted truth of the past could converge. What can still be experienced in the art of the past and is still attainable by interpretation is a directive toward this state."[53] However, as long as reality is ruled by antagonisms, the memory of the past and the anticipation of reconciliation must dialectically negate each other in order to preserve this convergence as an opportunity.

Other dialectical pairs that will allow us to define an artwork as a Marranic idiom will be "heteronomy–autonomy" and "mimesis–ratio". I will not discuss here the meaning of these pairs, I will only mention that the first of them defines an artwork as an "object" governed by specific immanent, particular principles of construction and expression. At the same time, it is somehow "externally" determined as a field of play of a socially defined subject and the vision of objectivity promoted by it, as well as the objective social and economic principles—as it is the "market participant". Its double "third" Marranic nature is realized in this context as a unique solution to the "assimilation–orthodoxy" problem[54]. The second pair can be considered as a special consequence of the first one. As a

---

[48] See: p. 1 of this text.

[49] See: (Adorno 2002, pp. 20–21).

[50] (Adorno 2002, pp. 20–21).

[51] (Adorno 2002, p. 21).

[52] The idea of "tradition" here, is founded on Scholem's understanding of tradition as a commentary, transmission. Therefore the inscription into dynamics of historical (socio-cultural) changes is a condition for keeping the category of truth still alive. See: (Scholem 1969).

[53] (Adorno 2002, p. 41).

[54] To compare, see: page 3 of this essay.

proposal of presenting the cognitive aspect of the artwork, it is a criticism of imitation in the way of presentation and understanding, i.e., treating the material and content of thinking as non-mediated, ontologically stable data, the manipulation of which is arbitrary and irrelevant for it. As a redefinition of "non-mediated–mediated" dependence, he points to a dialectical reading of the relationship between the mimetic aspect of an artwork and its structural expression constructed according to the internal logic, thus promoting a critical and non-affirmative model of contact with reality. Striving for reconciliation of what is mimetic with what is "rational" in the artwork and its criticism is, as a consequence, to be a model for cognition in general, promoting the non-hierarchy principle, and the renunciation of thinking founded on ontological priority.[55] Ultimately, it is to be a suggestion of dynamics of impossible/"negative" reconciliation of the other, the particular (here, mimetic) and the familiar, universal (here, rational), which does not give primacy to any of its moments.[56] And as such, it corresponds to the mode of reconciliation proposed by Bielik-Robson's "philosophical Marranos".

3.2. An Artwork—Inversion of the "Particular-Universal" Marriage

If we refer to Derrida's words from a quote from page 3 of this essay that "there is no such thing as homogenous universal language. Yet universality can be approached by 'marrying the speeches of strangers'", and at the same time, we remember about the reconciliation that an artwork designs, the emerging and necessary redefinition will consist of the inversion[57] of importance in the interpretation of "particular-universal" relationship. The supposed effect of this inversion is quite clearly defined by Adorno: the language of the work is to be still a realistically unfulfilled model of relations between what has hitherto been oppressed by the mythically prevailing "reason", and itself as a legislator. Adorno writes: "For artworks it is incumbent to grasp the universal—which dictates the nexus of the existing and is hidden by the existing—in the particular; it is not for art, through particularization, to disguise the ruling universality of the administered world. Totality is the grotesque heir of mana".[58] The task of the work is unmasking the generality, the alleged universality in the particular. How does he propose to discover this? He talks about it directly in another quote: "the artwork that appears as something universal bears the accidental quality of being an example of its genre: It is spuriously individual. (...) Yet the universal becomes substantial in artworks only by its self-transformation. (...) Not only does the dialectic of the universal and particular descend into the depths of the universal in the midst of the particular. At the same time it destroys the invariance of the universal categories."[59] Dialectics, which does not "reflect" the primacy of generality in the administered world, but is guided by the aspiration to express the particular as a conscious entanglement, that is, via *negativa*, critically anticipates, as a model, the achievement of individualization and concreteness also by objects that are not artworks, and thus also by languages of strangers, others, the marginalized. Artworks, therefore, are supposed to indicate the places of entanglement of particular contents or idioms in the generality, consistently—their self-critical thematicization of this entanglement points to the formula of redefining its relationship with the general order—as negative. Ultimately, therefore, the individualization that they try to achieve can only be an awareness of their own negativity, an unfulfilled utopia, if we can put it this way:

> "But because for art, utopia—the yet-to-exist—is draped in black, it remains in all its mediations recollection; recollection of the possible in opposition to the actual that suppresses it; it is the imaginary reparation of the catastrophe of world history; it is freedom, which

---

[55] See: (Adorno 2002), chapter "Semblance and Expression", pp. 100–18.
[56] See: (Adorno 2002) chapter "Universal and Particular", pp. 199–224; On "negativity" of reconciliation, see: (Adorno 2002, pp. 133–36, 189–90, 197, 199).
[57] In my opinion, the most comprehensive definition of inversion in this context is presented by Elisabeth A. Pritchard in her paper entitled: Bilderverbot *Meets Body in Theodor W. Adorno Inverse Theology* (Pritchard 2002).
[58] (Adorno 2002, p. 84).
[59] (Adorno 2002, p.181).

under the spell of necessity did not—and may not ever—come to pass. Art's methexis in the tenebrous, its negativity, is implicit in its tense relation to permanent catastrophe. No existing, appearing artwork holds any positive control over the nonexisting. This distinguishes artworks from religious symbols, which in their appearance lay claim to the transcendence of the immediately present. The nonexisting in artworks is a constellation of the existing."[60]

The works express the universality and commonness of their individualization in themselves and through themselves, at the same time not having the power to make it real. The only possible movement that condemns them to being manifestations of the non-existent and the desire to preserve such an experience of reality that allows keeping the memory of possible reconciliation, is the preservation of their own validity, relevance. Their strength, certainly today, is showing their own strengthlessness in the face of a disastrous circle of exchange. Thematicization should be repeated again and again in line with changing socioeconomic conditions. These repetitions, as each subsequent work, might be interpreted as multiplication of discourses in reaction to real suffering and marginalization, depriving one or another social group of the voice, its degradation. This links the situation of art with the philosophical strategy of the Marranos, described at the beginning of the article. A critical opening of the future makes it possible to preserve the memory of the claustrophobic and violent past and the present day. This form of remembrance is an opening to the possibility of reconciliation of what was, what is, and what will be. Only this form corresponds to the formula of universal subjectification, concretization of each—already existing or not yet existing particularity. This form of particular-universal endless reconciliation in artwork theory is proposed by Adorno, while other philosophical Marranos propose more general tools—e.g., deconstruction.

3.3. The Language of Artwork as a Constellation

It is now possible to answer the question about the linguistic formula of an artwork. The constellationary structure of the language of an artwork most fully expresses the idea of redefining particular-general marriage, which in the Marrano strategy takes the place of the most important regulatory idea. I will now try to justify this thesis. At the same time, the following question must be answered: what does it means that a specific work should be considered as a constellation of its "moments and elements"? Later, it is necessary to show how works as particular "manifestations" of social relations can influence their formation and reformation if they draw the idea of communication with the "outside" from their own "internal" "form and content" relations[61], the relations that Adorno interprets according to the idea of constellativeness. I will begin with an enigmatic statement by the author of *Aesthetic Theory* about the negativity of truth in art. He writes that there is no other object made by man which expresses its conviction of its own constitutive inability to lie. The next statement, however, is even more interesting. Adorno continues: " . . . Unlike anything human, art lays claim to being unable to lie, and thus it is compelled to lie. Art does not have it in its power to decide over the possibility that everything may indeed not come to anything more than nothing; it has its fictiveness in the assertion implicit in its existence that it has gone beyond the limit."[62] The truth expressed by art is mediated by its "invented nature", but otherwise art could not participate in history. This participation is possible only as a form of its criticism, which the works express "with themselves", unintentionally and the "appearance" in which they are. Criticism in this context is a negative projection of the direction of the movement of transcending the *status quo* towards possible (social) change. Although the constellativeness of works has not been defined, we have learned about its very important features: non-intentionality, and action, which is expressed with it through criticism, i.e., transgression. Adorno continues:

---

[60] (Adorno 2002, p. 135).
[61] See: (Adorno 2002, p. 4).
[62] (Adorno 2002, pp. 132–33).

Artworks say what is more than the existing, and they do this exclusively by making a constellation of how it is, "Comment c'est". The metaphysics of art requires its complete separation from the religion in which art originated. Artworks are not the absolute, nor is the absolute immediately present in them. For their methexis in the absolute they are punished with a blindness that in the same instant obscures their language, which is a language of truth: Artworks have the absolute and they do not have it. (. . .) Artworks are a priori negative by the law of their objectivation: They kill what they objectify by tearing it away from the immediacy of its life. Their own life preys on death.[63]

The constellational structure of the work "reveals", in the manner not fully intended by the creating entity, the dependence between what is, how it is reflected (specific socioeconomic conditions) and the "apparently" possible movement that transcends its heteronomy and any relationship between objects and subjects. This very ambitious plan that Adorno draws for art, at the same time, contains a reference to what art has inherited from religion—the imagination of the absolute. The constellational structure of the works does not allow for its direct, that is to say, its imaginary "presence". Objectivization, i.e., unintentional criticism and interpretation (of history), which, according to Adorno, is art, thus brings it closer to the radical formula of Revelation, which Bielik quotes after Scholem.[64] In the context of Marranic thinking, these considerations can be summarized in the following dependence: only the radically hidden presence of the O/other, its actual "non-presence", enables it to be socio-historically relevant. The model of this "non-presence", which for Adorno are works of (modern) art, can be interpreted as axiom of nonidentity. In other words, nonidentity in this context could be "read" as a condition for the coexistence of "others" with those, whose identity is legitimized by official culture. Furthermore, an inversion of importance within the particular-universal relationship, presented by this model, may initiate a debate on the assumed—and culturally inherited—homogenous identity. But first things first.

Thanks to the metaphor of the constellation, Adorno speaks the truth about the spiritual content of the work—that it is "readable" as a code to configure its moments, showing the work as a meaningful whole. Art must include meaning, sense, even as a social untruth, a negation of sense. Otherwise it is trivial. That is why Adorno so eagerly evokes Beckett's art, using the category of the absurd:

"Beckett' s plays are absurd not because of the absence of any meaning, for then they would be simply irrelevant. but because they put meaning on trial; they unfold its history. His work is ruled as much by an obsession with positive nothingness as by the obsession with a meaninglessness that has developed historically and is thus in a sense merited. though this meritedness in no way allows any positive meaning to be reclaimed. Nevertheless the emancipation of artworks from their meaning becomes aesthetically meaningful once this emancipation is realized in the aesthetic material precisely because the aesthetic meaning is not immediately one with theological meaning. Artworks that divest themselves of any semblance of meaning do not thereby forfeit their similitude to language. They enunciate their meaninglessness with the same determinacy as traditional artworks enunciate their positive meaning".[65]

It can be said that the whole, which is made up of constellations, is according to Adorno, untrue. The untruth of the whole speaks a lot about the totality, which, according to a Frankfurt citizen, is the society. Consistently, the category of meaninglessness says a lot about the meaning of what is strange, hidden and non-identical—meaning the strategy of philosophical Marranos—as present and relevant, as "not-identical". Identification with the minus sign, vividly speaking, will be the

---

[63] (Adorno 2002, p. 133).
[64] See: p. 10 of this essay.
[65] (Adorno 2002, p. 153).

principle of totality inversion, the principle governing the constellation, defining it with the principle of "uniting in differentiation", paraphrasing the words of Adorno. The non-identity which is the principle of identity in general, also in this particular case of a constellation, defines its form: openness, which automatically becomes its condition, however, does not mean "spatial" openness. The work as an object is separate. But this abstract autonomy ends when we recall that, in Adorno's opinion, there is no work without interpretation and criticism, without defining it as a product of social and economic play of forces—in other words—as a field of relations. A field whose persistence—as in the case of the discussed crypto-theological form of tradition—ensures openness to the passing of time, that is, to commentary and critique.[66] But it is only thanks to this that Adorno can state that the truth of an artwork lies in its uttered longing for reconciliation, but expressed in terms of what is now, evoked perversely by means of a certain expression of social hopelessness. Consequently, works as constellations are a sign of the time, which they show in its breakdown. A time of profaned myth and rationalized religion or religion of rationality, which they oppose by expressing a subversive longing for the once expressed reconciliation. Non-identity, which they constitute, significantly "speaks"—as an inversion of utopia. Adorno points out that art poses itself a question about its own utopianism through a particular constellation of its elements[67], and the truth of artworks or objects of artistic production is a configuration in which the different emerges from the identical and the defined.[68] Adorno writes the following about the inversion of utopia as configuration-constellation: "The constellation of the existing and nonexisting is the utopic figure of art. Although it is compelled toward absolute negativity, it is precisely by virtue of this negativity that it is not absolutely negative."[69] He adds that it is precisely the social, "revolutionary" power that works draw from within, from this original method of configuring what is social and intra-artistic:

> Art, even as something tolerated in the administered world, embodies what does not allow itself to be managed and what total management suppresses. Greece's new tyrants knew why they banned Beckett's plays, in which there is not a single political word. Asociality becomes the social legitimation of art. For the sake of reconciliation, authentic works must blot out every trace of reconciliation in memory. All the same, the unity that even dissociative works do not escape is not without a trace of the old reconciliation. Artworks are, a priori, socially culpable, and each one that deserves its name seeks to expiate this guilt.[70]

The work finally speaks, becomes "speech-like"—that is, it is considered by Adorno to be successful—thanks to its own immanent way of construction, all directly social content "dies" in it, so that it can be read from the constellation created by the work as a formal-content, non-identical unity.[71] In order to be a "silent" accusation, a work must be "coherent" in this way, control the contradictions that the antagonized society gives it. Thus, the non-identity is not arbitrary and undefined; on the contrary, one can say about the "openness" it provides, about the possibility of thinking and subversive transfiguration of utopia, which it provokes, only when the identity is realized as unity. Conversely, unity only then turns out not to be a closed whole, but a unity in multiplicity: a constellation that binds non-hierarchically what is special and general, as a social negative of the experienced suffering, marginalization. Art as an expression of suffering is not its uncontrollable expression or pure imitation. On the contrary, in order for suffering, as an element of an inverted utopia, to gain expression, i.e., to meet the condition of universalization, it must be transformed, constructed. Experienced and well-considered, but not figured out, it gains in concreteness. The relationship is

---

[66]   See: (Scholem 1969).
[67]   (Adorno 2002, p. 311).
[68]   (Adorno 2002, p. 311).
[69]   (Adorno 2002, p. 233).
[70]   (Adorno 2002, p. 234).
[71]   See: (Adorno 2002, pp. 291–92).

two-sided: the structure gains expression when elements of experience, social antagonisms and the principles of exclusion and marginalization inscribed in it exist as principles of its form:

> In the case of such exemplary artists of the epoch as Schoenberg, Klee, and Picasso, the expressive mimetic element and the constructive element are of equal intensity, not by seeking a happy mean between them but rather by way of the extremes: Yet each is simultaneously content-laden, expression is the negativity of suffering, and construction is the effort to bear up under the suffering of alienation by exceeding it on the horizon of undiminished and thus no longer violent rationality. Just as in thought, form and content are as distinct as they are mediated in one another, so too in art.[72]

4. Conclusions—Art Nominalism and Jewish Nominalism

The analysis of configuration-constellation leads to reflections on similarities between the language and the structure of the work. The thesis to be verified by this analysis speaks of the structural similarity, or even analogy, between the generally discussed Jewish nominalism and the nominalism of the language of art.

In my opinion, the first analogy exists between the meaning of the quasi-creative act of naming, generally discussed in the first part of the text as redefining the relationship between creation and the absolute, and the principle of nominalist art, the principle of creation and the existence of artworks—monads. The idiom of art, distanced from empiria, proposed by Adorno, will be his original proposal of redefining the binding of what is considered universal, i.e., the conceptual language, and every particular idiom, existence, moment, act, expression present in the work. In other words, the work as a "windowless monad" will establish a model similar to the one proposed by e.g., Scholem or Benjamin, considering the possibility of preserving the link between the universal field of theology and religion, tradition and profaned and fatally secularized cultural reality. Adorno, referring to the Jewish formula of preserving tradition proposed by the two thinkers mentioned above, speaks first of the act of naming.[73] For him, it is a link between creation, interpretation, and criticism, mediating in artistic activities and activities defining the duration of the created objects- artworks. For Adorno, the act of naming is an artistic statement and its socio-cultural imprimatur. This kind of linguisticity will be a model of continuous, non-preferential individualization—analogously to the creative model of Jewish nominalism.[74] If we are talking about non-hierarchical unification with a dialectic structure, we assume that individualization includes both the subject and the object. Consequently, the artwork, its specific idiom, will be a field of play between the subjective moment and the objective moment of the aforementioned relation. In his last work, Adorno therefore proposes—and this is my interpretation of the main goal of the *Aesthetic Theory*—a method for fulfilling and implementing the principles of negative dialectics. It is necessary to take a closer look at how he characterizes the specific object of these activities, i.e., artwork.

As I mentioned earlier, the monadology of the artwork determines its idiom distanced from empiria, which in turn marks how subjective-objective relationships within it are arranged. Adorno defines the manner in which the subjective and the socially-inherited elements of the work speak. He thus characterizes this monadology by writing about the intentionlessness and indirectness of pronunciation in the following words:

> The language of artworks is, like every language, constituted by a collective undercurrent, especially in the case of those works popularly stigmatized as lonely and walled up in the ivory tower; the eloquence of their collective substance originates in their image character

---

[72] (Adorno 2002, p. 257).
[73] See: (Benjamin 2002a, pp. 62–74; Benjamin 2002b; Scholem 1990, pp. 97–99); on function of Scripture in Lurianic Kabbalah, see: (Scholem 1996; Biale 1982, pp. 112–47).
[74] See: p. 8, of this essay.

and not in the "testimony" as the cliché goes-that they supposedly wish to express directly to the collective. The specifically artistic achievement is an overarching binding character to be ensnared not thematically or by the manipulation of effects but rather by presenting what is beyond the monad through immersion in the experiences that are fundamental to this bindingness.[75]

In other words, art does not wish to oppose the general, the social and the cultural, but to oppose the specific. This is why the work adopts a monadic idiom in order to de-hierarchize this marriage and to make the other generalities speak with their own language—as it speaks—as a model of such an experience—the work. For art is an unfulfilled promise of reconciliation, and the idea of reconciliation is individualization not based on subordination. In this way, completely convergent with the proposal of the Jewish Marranos, art secularizes the revelation about which Adorno writes that it is both an ideal and a barrier (impassable for) of every work.[76] Again, the fact that art "speaks" as a monad, brings it closer to the language of the Jewish message, a tradition that draws on the idea of creation proposed by the Kabbalah interpreter, Scholem. The presence of revelation is its non-presence or a barrier to the meaning of the work. Adorno writes:

"The contamination of art with revelation would amount to the unreflective repetition of its fetish character on the level of theory. The eradication of every trace of revelation from art would, however, degrade it to the undifferentiated repetition of the status quo. A coherence of meaning—unity—is contrived by art because it does not exist and because as artificial meaning it negates the being-in-itself for the sake of which the organization of meaning was undertaken, ultimately negating art itself. Every artifact works against itself."[77]

The impossibility of reconciliation, about which Adorno further writes, the negation of the unity that the work is, are supported by the truth of the unfulfilled social conditions of the model postulated by every artifact. The artwork is an expression of a lack of unity and sense—it is a monad communicating its own closure, including a social fiasco of subjectification decreed in the notional definitions. So how to read a model of meaning from the negation of sense? If any particular unity read from a work is denied in this identification, then a possible way of "reading" the work will be to incorporate the lack of unity into the process itself. We end up with nothing, or with the space of experiencing the ontological impossibility of any finite narrative. Or the impossibility to transform it into a classic definition. The mechanism of differentiation, about which I wrote in the context of identifying oneself as a Jewish Marrano in the first part of the work, is a model of subject-object relationship postulated in the language of art.

Adorno, as a philosopher reading from fragments of a messed-up life, links the above de-semantic model of meaning, negation of sense and differentiation (as) of identification with a specific event in the history of the West. Auschwitz is a condition of semantic emptiness and eloquent silence as the "language" of 20th-century art[78]. Adorno would also read the preceding works through the prism of radical erasure of what is different from the western cultural tissue—like signs with their inaccessibility proclaiming the need for shelter from real violence. Auschwitz was also the event that most affected the European Jewish diaspora. At the same time, it was an unprecedented genocide in the Western history of those who, for various reasons, were considered the other. They were stigmatized and excluded: symbolically—attempts were made to erase the memory of them—and really, as they were brutally and mechanically murdered, they were eventually deprived even of death.[79] Adorno, who wrote

---

[75] (Adorno 2002, p. 86).
[76] See: (Adorno 2002, pp. 105–6).
[77] (Adorno 2002, p. 106).
[78] Whereas Lacoue-Labarthe has a completely different opinion. As I wrote (see: Górski 2017, pp. 150–54), he defines Auschwitz as the ultimate caesura of any kind of relationship of the universal and the particular, so also critical and artistic; see also: (Lacoue-Labarthe 1990, pp. 41–52).
[79] See: (Lacoue-Labarthe 1990; Vogt 2016).

Aesthetic Theory many years after the war, reconstructed a particular symbolic, or rather allegorical and real, material, bodily marriage. Art is supposed to be a remembrance of suffering, and as such, to carry this suffering within itself, otherwise, it is no longer defensible: "Even in a legendary better future, art could not disavow remembrance of accumulated horror; otherwise its form would be trivial."[80] This means that the expression of the other as concrete, in the philosophical language of the Marrano, and the expression of suffering that monadic work brings in itself and communicates through dissonances, contradictions, antagonism, can be combined with a strong analogy. Nominalism in art, unequal to the philosophical one, due to its dialectic and at the same time monadic attitude towards universality[81], thanks to its similarity to language, shows how to bring together the particular and accidental in a work with the universal. What is more, this bringing together means the only formula of transcendence recognized by Adorno. Adorno writes:

> "In art, universals are strongest where art most closely approaches language: that is, when something speaks, that, by speaking, goes beyond the here and now. Art succeeds at such transcendence, however, only by virtue of its tendency toward radical particularization; that is, only in that it says nothing but what it says by virtue of its own elaboration, through its immanent process".[82]

The expression of suffering is what connects the immanent formula of the work with its tendency to show the possibility of transgression in its closeness and specificity towards the universal. Thus, the work is a model of individualization, a model which closes in a dialectic square of dependencies, where the direction of movement is determined by the dialectics of the notions of immanence and transcendence and its content is determined by a pair of particular—universal notions. The model, impossible to realize, drives the imperative of remembrance of the accumulated terror, the imperative that gives back the meaning to art and restores the "others" the possibility of identification in the tissue of European society—and thus, its constitutive, creative incoherence. Therefore, the topos of art after Auschwitz is equal to the place "reserved" for the Marranos, about which Bielik-Robson writes. The memory of the Other and its prefigurations—about corporeity (vs. conceptuality), about difference and differentiation (vs. identification), about the individual (vs. total), about the open (vs. closed and systemic), etc., is a condition of messianic hope. There is no better way toward an endless reconciliation than the way of social and cultural criticism as a form of remembrance. And the most mature form of this remembrance (and Jewish nominalism) is, in my opinion, the potential of modern artwork described and defined by Theodor W. Adorno in his *Aesthetic Theory*.

Funding: This research received no external funding.

Conflicts of Interest: The author declares no conflict of interest.

References

Adorno, Theodor W. 1993. Aspects of Hegel's Philosophy. In *Hegel. Three Studies*. Translated by Shierry W. Nicholsen. Cambridge, MA and London: The MIT Press, pp. 1–51.

Adorno, Theodor W. 2002. *Aesthetic Theory*. Edited and Translated by Robert Hullot-Kentor. London and New York: Continuum Books.

Adorno, Theodor W. 2004. *Negative Dialectics*. Translated by Ernst B. Ashton. London and New York: Routledge.

Adorno, Theodor W. 2005. Reason and Revelation. In *Critical Models, Interventions and Catchwords*. Translated and with a Preface by Henry W. Pickford. New York: Columbia University Press, pp. 135–43.

Adorno, Theodor W. 2006. *Minima Moralia, Reflections on a Damaged Life*. Translated by Edmund F. N. Jephcott. New York and London: Verso.

---

[80] (Adorno 2002, p. 324).
[81] (Adorno 2002, pp. 199–208).
[82] (Adorno 2002, p. 205).

Adorno, Theodor W., and Gershom Scholem. 2015. *Der Liebe Gott wohnt im Detail, Briefwechsel 1939–1969*. Berlin: Suhrkamp Verlag.

Benjamin, Walter. 2002a. On Language as such and on the Language of Man. In *Selected Writings, Vol. 1, 1913–1926*. Edited by Marcus Bullock and Marcus W. Jennings. London and Cambridge, MA: The Belknap Press of Harvard University Press, pp. 62–74.

Benjamin, Walter. 2002b. The Task of Translator. In *Selected Writings, Vol. 1, 1913–1926*. Edited by Marcus Bullock and Marcus W. Jennings. Cambridge, MA and London: The Belknap Press of Harvard University Press, pp. 253–63.

Benjamin, Walter. 2003. Epistemo-Critical Prologue. In *The Origin of German Tragic Drama*. Translated by John Osborne. London and New York: Verso Books, pp. 27–56.

Benjamin, Walter, Adorno Theodor W., and Scholem Gershom. 1994. *The Correspondence of Walter Benjamin, 1910–1940*. Translated by Manfred R. Jacobson, and Evelyn M. Jacobson. Chicago: The University of Chicago Press.

Bernstein, Jay M. 1992. *The Fate of Art. Aesthetic Alienation from Kant to Derrida and Adorno*. University Park: The Pennsylvania State University Press.

Biale, David. 1982. *Gershom Scholem: Cabbalah and Counter-History*. Cambridge, MA and London: Harvard University Press, pp. 112–47.

Bielik-Robson, Agata. 2014. *Jewish Cryptotheologies of Late Modernity. Philosophical Marranos*. London and New York: Routledge.

de Vries, Hent. 2005. *Minimal Theologies. Critiques of Secular Reason in Adorno and Levinas*. Translated by Geoffrey Hale. Baltimore and London: The Johns Hopkins University Press.

Derrida, Jacques. 1985. Des Tours de Babel. In *Difference in Translation*. Translated by Joseph F. Graham. Edited with an Introduction by Joseph F. Graham. Ithaca and London: Cornell University Press, pp. 165–207.

Derrida, Jacques. 1995. Archive Fever: A Freudian Impression. In *Diacritics Vol. 25, No. 3 (Summer, 1995)*. Translated by Eric Prenowitz. Baltimore: The Johns Hopkins University Press, Volume 25, pp. 9–63.

Foster, Roger. 2007. *Adorno—The Recovery of Experience*. New York: SUNY Press.

Górski, Jakub. 2017. Mimesis, cezura i spekulacja w filozofii Theodora W. Adorna i Philippe'a Lacoue-Labarthe'a. In *Kwartalnik Filozoficzny*. Kraków: Polska Akademia Umiejętności, Uniwersytet Jagielloński, vol. XLV, pp. 135–69.

Habermas, Jürgen. 2015. Adorno und Scholem, Vom Funken den Wahrheit. Available online: https://www.zeit.de/2015/15/theodor-w-adorno-gershom-scholem-freundschaft-briefwechsel (accessed on 8 March 2019).

Hullot-Kentor, Robert. 2006. *Things Beyond Resemblance. On Theodor W. Adorno*. New York: Columbia University Press.

Jacobson, Eric. 2003. *Metaphysics of the Profane, The Political Theologies of Walter Benjamin and Gershom Scholem*. New York: Columbia University Press.

Jay, Martin. 1997. Mimesis and Mimetology. Adorno and Lacoue-Labarthe. In *The Semblance of Subjectivity. Essays in Adorno Aesthetic Theory*. Edited by Tom Huhn and Lambert Zuidervaart. Cambridge, MA: The MIT Press, pp. 29–53.

Lacoue-Labarthe, Philippe. 1990. The Caesura. In *Philippe Lacoue-Labarthe, Heidegger, Art. and Politics*. Translated by Chris Turner. Oxford and Cambridge, MA: Basil Blackwell, pp. 41–52.

Pritchard, Elisabeth A. 2002. *Bildeverbot* Meets Body in Theodor W. Adorno Inverse Theology. In *The Harvard Theological Review, Vol. 95, No. 3*. New York: Cambridge University Press, pp. 291–318.

Richter, Gerhard. 2009. Introduction. In *Language Without Soil. Adorno and Late Philosophical Modernity*. Edited by Gerhard Richter. New York: Fordham University Press, pp. 1–10.

Scholem, Gershom. 1969. Tradition and Commentary as Religious Categories in Judaism. In *Studies in Comparative Religion, Vol. 3, No. 3 (Summer, 1969)*. Bloomington: World Wisdom, Inc., Available online: www.studiesincomparativereligion.com (accessed on 8 March 2019).

Scholem, Gershom. 1976. Offenbarung und Tradition als religiöse Kategorien im Judentum. In *Über einige Grundbegriffe des Judentums*. Berlin: Suhrkamp Verlag, pp. 90–120.

Scholem, Gershom. 1990. On Our Language: A Confession. Translated by Ora Wiskind. In *History and Memory, Vol. 2, No. (Winter, 1990)*. Bloomington: Indiana University Press, pp. 97–99.

Scholem, Gershom. 1996. *On the Kabbalah and Its Symbolism*. New York: Shocken Books.

Vogt, Erik. 2016. The 'Useless Residue of the Western Idea of Art': Adorno and Lacoue-Labarthe Concerning Art 'After' Auschwitz. In *Adorno and the Concept of Genocide*. Edited by Ryan Crawford and Erik M. Vogt. Lieden and Boston: Brill Online, vol. 291, pp. 29–45.

Wasserstrom, Steven. 2007. Adorno's Kabbalah. In *Polemical Encounters, Esoteric Discourse and Its Others*. Edited by Olav Hammer and Kocku von Stuckrad. Lieden and Boston: Brill, pp. 74–76.

religions

MDPI

Article

The Marrano God: Abstraction, Messianicity, and Retreat in Derrida's "Faith and Knowledge"

Agata Bielik-Robson

Department of Theology and Religious Studies, the University of Nottingham, University Park, Nottingham NG7 2RD, UK; agata.bielik-robson@nottingham.ac.uk

Received: 14 November 2018; Accepted: 17 December 2018; Published: 29 December 2018

check for updates

Abstract: This article conducts a close reading of Derrida's 1994 essay, "Faith and Knowledge", devoted to the analysis of what Hegel called 'the religion of modern times'. The reference to Hegel's "Glauben und Wissen" is crucial here, since my reading is meant to offer a supplement to Michael Naas' commentary on "Faith and Knowledge", *Miracle and Machine*, in which Naas states that he is not going to pursue the connection between Derrida and Hegel. It was, however, Hegel who defined the 'modern religious sentiment' in terms of the 'religion of the death of God', and this definition constitutes Derrida's point of departure. Derrida agrees with Hegel's diagnosis, but is also critical of its Protestant–Lutheran interpretation, which founds modern religiosity on the 'memory of the Passion', and attempts a different reading of the 'death of God' motif as the 'divine retreat', pointing to a non-normative 'Marrano' kind of faith that stakes on the alternative 'memory of the Passover'. The apparent visibility of the 'returning religion' Derrida witnesses at the beginning of the 90s hides for him a new dimension of the 'original faith', which Derrida associates with the universal messianic justice and which he ascribes to the paradoxical position of the Marranos: the secret followers of the God 'in retreat'.

Keywords: Derrida; Hegel; Marranos; Faith and Knowledge; messianism; universalism

---

> The feeling that God himself is dead is the sentiment on which the religion of modern times rests.
>
> > G.W.F. Hegel, "Faith and Knowledge"[1]

> How then to think—within the limits of reason alone—a religion which, without again becoming 'natural religion', would today be effectively universal? And which, for that matter, would no longer be restricted to a paradigm that was Christian or even Abrahamic?
>
> > Jacques Derrida, "Faith and Knowledge"[2]

> Claims have also been advanced to the effect that the question of Marranism was recently closed for good. I don't believe it for a second. There are still sons—and daughters—who, unbeknownst to themselves, incarnate or metempsychosize the ventriloquist specters of their ancestors.
>
> > Jacques Derrida, "Marx & Sons"[3]

---

[1] (Hegel 1977, p. 134).
[2] (Derrida 2002, p. 53). Later on as FK.
[3] (Derrida 1999, p. 262).

My aim is to offer a close reading of Derrida's seminal essay, "Faith and Knowledge", the sole subject of which is the analysis of 'the religion of modern times'. Hegel, who coined this phrase in his version of *Glauben und Wissen*, deeply convinced that modern form of religiosity is a true novelty, was still concerned about maintaining continuity with Christian theology in its reformed, Protestant-Lutheran, denomination. Derrida, no longer sharing this concern, experiments with a new concept of a non-normative Marrano religiosity, to which he himself leans in his autobiographical writings.[4] Yet his goal is the same as Hegel's: it is to define *die Religion der neuen Zeiten* in the new condition of 'globalitinization' [*mondialatinisation*] as an ubiquitous presence which spreads its 'good news' through all the possible channels of tele-phonia and tele-vision, making everybody witness its 'miracles' through the medium of the globally operating 'machine'.

In the symphony of voices, which Derrida orchestrates in his extremely rich essay, there is one on which I want to focus here: Hegel, since it is in the polemic with his concept of 'the death of God' and the mournful 'memory of the Passion' that Derrida develops his alternative Jewish–Marrano idea of the 'memory of Passover'.[5] In the text, also traditionally titled "Faith and Knowledge", Hegel refers to the 'modern religious sentiment' as the 'religion of the death of God', and—unlike Nietzsche, who will use this phrase in his critique of monotheism as an irreligious religion without a sense of the true *sacrum*—he connects it to the Christian motif of *kenosis*. The Hegelian God who dies as the sovereign ruler and creator—eternally safe and sound, the very paradigm of indemnity—in order to become contaminated by the creaturely element and work within this condition of impurity as the Spirit, is the kenotic God at his extreme. One cannot imagine a greater 'self-humbling' than the original death, retreat, self-restraint, self-withdrawal, and radical self-negation in which the Infinite becomes ashamed of its unscathed sovereignty and gives up on its perfect pleroma for the sake of the adventure of becoming. This 'kenosis in creation', which Hegel smuggled surreptitiously under the heading of *Entäusserung*—the word meaning 'exteriorization' in the Hegelian vocabulary, but before that used by Martin Luther in his translation of Paul's term *kenosis*—is the divine self-humbling to the point of self-erasure, from which there begins the 'Golgotha of the Absolute Spirit'. It commences with the self-emptying of the First Idea, which gives itself over to the world, loses itself in the alien being in order to resurrect in the future, outlined by Hegel as the dawn of the Absolute Knowledge. In the meantime, however, the Spirit's sacrifice is remembered in the form of the 'infinite grief': the 'religion of modern times' is the religion of mourning.

Hegel would return to the idea of 'the infinite grief in the finite' many times, always accentuating the tragic clash between infinity and finitude, which inevitably demands the sacrifice of the latter. If, as Kant already argued, Christianity is the only 'moral religion', it is because it focuses solely on the act of ethical compensation, in which the believer, following the law of the talion, pays with his

---

[4] Take, for instance, his famous declaration from *Circonfession* written in 1991, three years before the first draft of "Foi et Savoir": "I am a kind of Marrano of French Catholic Culture, and I also have my Christian body, inherited from St. Augustine . . . I am one of those Marranos who, even in the intimacy of their own hearts, do not admit to being Jewish" (Derrida 1993, p. 160). On the significance of Derrida's Marrano declaration see: Helene Cixous, "The Stranjew Body" (Cixous 2007, p. 55); Yvonne Sherwood, "Specters of Abraham", (Sherwood 2014); my introduction to *Jewish Cryptotheologies of Late Modernity: Philosophical Marranos* (Bielik-Robson 2014) and "*Burn After Reading*: Derrida, the Philosophical Marrano" (Bielik-Robson 2017a).

[5] I will apply a similar rule in regard to the symphony of Derrida's commentators and choose one reader, Michael Naas, who devoted the whole book to Derrida's "Faith and Knowledge": *Miracle and Machine* (Naas 2012), later on as MM. Naas, however, makes little of Hegel's presence in Derrida's essay on religion, despite the borrowing of the title. In his "Observation on Hegel", Naas admits that it is always possible that Derrida is hiding his major influence, but "a lot of interpretative work would need to be done to make this case, and even more would need to be done to show that Derrida was trying, in 'Faith and Knowledge', to intervene in the debate between Kant and Hegel. In his attempt to understand the nature of religion today, Derrida had other things in view. For instead of ending his text with a reference to the speculative Good Friday, he concludes with an equally dramatic reference to violence, to ashes, to the massacre at Chatila, and to 'an open pomegranate, one Passover evening, on a tray'" (MM, p. 310). While not disagreeing with Naas, I would like to challenge his dismissal of Hegel, and demonstrate that Derrida constantly refers to Hegel in order to subvert, but to also supplement his 'memory of the Passion' with a different memory of a different mourning, violence, and ashes: a Marrano testimony of the forced loss of God, which created a different kind of memory and commemoration.

'sensuous life' for the loss of the infinite vitality that God had sustained in the process of incarnation. Unlike the 'pagan' cults, therefore, which praise God's infinite vitality, Christian religion consists of a mournful cultivation of the sense of guilt and debt (*Schuld*), which must be duly repayed. The prospect of reconciliation between man and God becomes possible only if man agrees to die in God's image, i.e., to engage in the *imitatio Christi* as the faithful repetition of the 'tragedy of the cross'. For Hegel, faith is precisely this faithful mimesis that occurs in the inner shrine of the soul:

> For the reconciliation of the individual person with God does not enter as a harmony directly, but as a harmony proceeding only from the infinite grief, from surrender, sacrifice, and the death of what is finite, sensuous, and subjective. Here finite and infinite are bound together into one, and the reconciliation in its true profundity, depth of feeling, and force of mediation is exhibited only through the magnitude of harshness of the opposition which is to be resolved. It follows that even the whole sharpness and dissonance of the suffering, torture, and agony involved in such an opposition, belong to the nature of the spirit itself, whose absolute satisfaction is the subject-matter here.[6]

By referring to Freud's famous 1917 essay on *Mourning and Melancholia*, we can phrase the main question of Hegel's philosophy as: can the 'infinite grief' ever be finished? Can it realise itself in a complete work of mourning, or must it perpetuate into infinity as an unworkable burden of melancholy? Hegel is visibly torn between the idea of the infinite process of mourning, which maintains the sacrificial scheme of the 'death of God religion' for ever, and the prospect of the sublation of religion into philosophical knowledge, which simultaneously ends religion/faith with its call for sacrifice and keeps it going on a higher, abstractly ontotheological form. In his own take on *fides et ratio* theme, Derrida points to this aporetic tension in Hegel's logic, which makes 'grief' infinite (i.e., non-sublatable) and temporal (i.e., sublatable) at the same time:

> Infinite pain is still *only a moment, and the moral sacrifice of empirical existence only* dates the absolute Passion or the speculative Good Friday. Dogmatic philosophies and natural religions should disappear and, out of the greatest 'asperity', *the harshest impiety*, out of kenosis and the void of the most serious privation of God [*Gottlosigkeit*], ought to resuscitate the *most serene liberty* in its highest totality. Distinct from faith, from prayer or from sacrifice, ontotheology destroys religion, but, *yet another paradox*, it is also what perhaps informs, on the contrary, the theological and ecclesiastical, even religious, *development of faith*. (FK, p. 53; my emphasis)

And although Derrida does not identify with Hegel's position, which he understands as the full sublation of religion/faith into philosophical absolute knowledge, he nonetheless is willing to pick up the Hegelian thread of the universalizing ontotheological abstraction—and then to play it out differently. Derrida's high argument consists in the attempt to abstract, that is, to detach 'the most serious privation of God' from the tragic remnants of the sacrificial scheme, which linger in the notion of the 'infinite grief'. By simultaneously continuing and correcting the Hegelian analysis of *die Religion der neuen Zeit*, Derrida will thus claim that the current return of the religious 'proclaimed in every newspaper' (FK, p. 43) or this 'machine-like return of religion' (FK, p. 53), which did not disappear despite all the light-therapy applied by Enlightenment, should be challenged by the Hegelian 'feeling that God himself is dead' resulting in the 'harshest impiety'. Far from dismissing the religious as the bygone element of dark ages, scorched out by the modern 'light of the day' (FK, p. 46), Derrida throws himself straight into the Hölderlinian paradox: the coincidence of the highest danger and the growing possibility of redemption, i.e., the aporetic oscillation between 'the most radical evil' and the 'promise of salvation' (FK, p. 43), which he sees as the defining moment of the returning

---

[6]   (Hegel 1975, p. 537).

religion. If 'radical abstraction', by which religion travels today all over the globe thanks to the machine of telecommunication, spells the evil of "deracination, delocalization, disincarnation, formalization, universalizing schematization, objectification" (FK, p. 43), it is also still a possibility of a 'new reflecting faith' (FK, p. 49), which breaks with the dogmatic cult of any sort and opens itself to a universal moral appeal. And if the 'harshest impiety' brought by the Enlightenment may mean the 'war on religion' waged for the sake of 'killing God', it may also suggest a retreat to 'the void of the most serious privation of God', the very 'desert in the desert' in which there is no telling 'what is yet to come' (FK, p. 47): what God, living or dying, might appear on the radically emptied horizon. The proper abstraction could thus still overcome the false one, while a new form of a reflecting faith could form the ground "in whose name one would protest against" the existing form of religiosity which "only resembles the void". This protest against the distorted forms of the modern faith, therefore, is not ventured on the grounds of knowledge, but rather on the grounds of another—withdrawn, invisible, 'harsher'—*foi originaire* which Derrida wants to reveal (as much as it is possible) and defend:

> The abstraction of the desert can thereby open the way to everything from which it withdraws. Whence the ambiguity or the duplicity of the religious trait or retreat, of its abstraction or of its subtraction. This deserted *re-treat* thus makes way for the repetition of that which will have given way precisely for that in whose name one would protest against it, against that which only resembles the void and the indeterminacy of mere abstraction. (FK, p. 55)

1. The 'Deserted Re-Treat': *Kenosis, Tsimtsum,* and *Khora*

But what would be the real void, the true *kenoma*, and not the one which only pretends to be humble and empty? And what would be the mechanism of such pretence? The discussion on globalitinizing Christianity, in which Derrida engages in "Faith and Knowledge" in the first section, written in the Roman Italic as the privileged font of the Global Christian Latin, is organized around these two questions. Derrida's thesis seems to be the following: the merely apparent desert that only 'resembles the void' (FK, p. 55) derives from the falsity of the Christian *kenosis*, which overtly presents itself as an act of self-humbling—the God plunging into the scathed dimension of the finite life—but secretly harbours the inversion where all the pride of the unscathed—the *perfect* self-sacrifice—is still being preserved. The positive thesis is more implicit, more 'secretive', but nonetheless crucial in Derrida's text: the real void, beyond any pretence—and in that sense truly *kenomatic*—is offered by the act of *tsimtsum*, the non-sacrificial re-treat of God, which does not leave creation in the state of the 'infinite grief', and the necessity to repeat the gesture of self-offering.[7] While Christianity follows to tee the logic of 'religion as the ellipsis of sacrifice' (FK, p. 88), this other possibility—which, as I will try to show, Derrida attaches to the modern Marrano experience—allows an exodus out of the sacrificial paradigm, which constitutes the first source of religion, and open it to the second source: the future-oriented messianicity propelled by a single imperative—no more sacrifices!

I have used the Hebrew word *tsimtsum* for a purpose, not only because Derrida's account of Hegel, especially in *Glas*, is secretly lined with Isaac Luria and his dramatic narrative of God, the primordial *Ein Sof*, undergoing a radical contraction in order to 'give place' to the world as the Other. The very concept of withdrawal/retreat, which plays such a fundamental role in "Faith and Knowledge", derives also from the Lurianic kabbalah, which for the first time puts the talmudic term *tsimtsum* [contraction] to metaphysical use, by turning it into the primary creative act: the Infinite

---

7   Although the very term—*tsimtsum*—by which the 16th century kabbalist, Isaac Luria, denotes the 'contraction of God', does not appear explicitly in Derrida's essay (which can also be seen as a typically Marrano manoeuvre of covering up the traces), there is one early text, testifying to his profound knowledge of the theme: "Dissemination", devoted to Philippe Soller's novel *Nombres*, where Derrida states that the idea of *tsimtsum* is "linked to the mythology of Louria" (as he pronounces his name according to the French usage) (Derrida 1981, p. 344). Derrida was also highly aware of the importance of the divine 'retreat' in the work of Lévinas.

receding—withdrawing, retreating—for the sake of the alterity of the finite being.[8] And although Derrida almost never mentions *tsimtsum* explicitly (at least not in "Faith and Knowledge") and even distances himself from the anthropo-theological appropriations of his 'deserted *re-treat*', which he wants to guard in its cold abstraction, it is nonetheless Luria's intervention that is precursorial to all subsequent notions of the self-negating Absolute: Hegel's '*kenosis* in creation', Heidegger's *Entzug des Seins*, as well as Derrida's self-effacing spatiality of *khora*, which, though Platonic in origin, is not described as 'withdrawing' by Plato.[9] In *Timeus*, Plato talks about *khora* as a passive, indifferent and infinitely susceptible 'receiving vessel' capable of accommodate all forms (*pandechos*), and, by calling her a 'nurse of generation', he denies her/it even the slightest activity that is implied by such Derridean terms as 're-treat', 'withdrawal' or 'making-place'. This residual activity imposed on *khora*, in which *khorein* consists in receding for the sake of all things to appear, seems to derive from a different tradition: the one of *tsimtsum* which, in "Faith and Knowledge", will secretly shimmer under the guise of messianicity.

We could even go further and say that Derrida's peculiar idiom of practicing 'Jewish cryptotheology' in a 'greekjew–jewgreek' style culminates precisely in his treatment of *khora*, which is being 'secretly' reinscribed as *makom*, according to "a deep affinity with a certain nomination of the God of the Jews, [where] He is also The Place".[10] While the talmudic tradition of naming God *makom*/place gave canvass to Luria's metaphysical speculation on *tsimtsum* as precisely the act of place-making, this also becomes the main attribute of *khora*, which patiently gives room to everything emerging as a 'pure singularity', and, as such, provides a 'link to the other in general', or a 'fiduciary link' that "precedes all determinate community, all positive religion, every onto-anthropo-theological horizon" (FK, p. 55). There is a good reason why Derrida should conceal the Lurianic source: it is his reluctance to be associated with any particular messianic traditions, the Jewish–kabbalistic included, which all grow out of the kenomatic abstraction of the 'desert in the desert'. In the light of his 'harshest' abstracted messianicity, which relates to the Lurianic messianism in the same manner as the general structure of revealability (the Heideggerian *Veroffenbarkeit*) relates to the concrete revelation (*Veroffenbarung*), *khora* emerges as a better candidate for the second—truly *kenomatic*—source of religion, because it is free of any secondary anthropotheosophic associations. If it gives room/place/space, it does it abstractedly, indifferently, and mechanically: not out of love, kindness, or generosity, which motivate the Lurianic *Ein Sof* in his miraculous act of self-retreat.

And yet, it gives: the machine of ontogeny, inscribed into *khora*, automatically paves the way to messianicity which focuses on the miracle of *tsimtsum*. Even if *khora* itself just "links pure singularities prior to any social or political determination, prior to all intersubjectivity, prior even to the opposition between the sacred (or the holy) and the profane" (FK, p. 55), the messianic promise, which repeats forward the gesture of self-retreat, cannot arise without an ethical interpretation of this gesture which it interprets precisely as—gesture. The miracle is thus in the very machine: that it makes place. This is

---

8   This version of *tsimtsum*, in which God 'takes in his breath' and restricts his glory for the sake of something else to emerge, derives already from Isaiah, as described by Elliott Wolfson in his interpretation of one of the bahiric texts: "The notion of withdrawal, itself withdrawn and thus not stated overtly, is a secret that is exegetically derived from the verse *lema'an shemi a'arikh appi u-tehillati ehetam lakh le-vilti hakhritekha*, 'For the sake of my name I will postpone my wrath and my glory I will hold in for you so that I will not destroy you' (Isa 48:9). The plain sense of the prophetic dictum relates to divine mercy as expressed as God's long-suffering, the capacity to restrain his rage. The expression *tehillati ehetam*, literally 'my glory I will hold in', is parallel to *a'arikh appi*, 'I will postpone my wrath'. One may surmise that at some point in ancient Israel, the notion of a vengeful god yielded its opposite, the compassionate god who holds in his fury" (Wolfson 2006, pp. 132–33).

9   On the significance of the Lurianic heritage, especially for German Idealism, see my "God of Luria, Hegel, Schelling: The Divine Contraction and the Modern Metaphysics of Finitude" (Bielik-Robson 2017b).

10   Jacques Derrida, "Abraham, The Other" (Derrida 2007, p. 33). Michael Naas also notices Derrida's 'jewgreek–greekjew' tendency to produce a dense interference of the two idioms, for instance, in the description of his tallith in "A Silkworm of One's Own" which brings it close to *khora*: " ... and, finally, the tallith, the white tallith, as what belongs to the 'night, the absolute night' also resembles *khora* as 'the place of absolute exteriority', the 'nocturnal source' of both religion and science. The tallith is thus, in some sense, another name for *khora*, the place that gives place and has no name that is absolutely proper to it" (MM, pp. 231–32).

the gist of the Lurianic version of messianism, where the kenomatic 'God of Void' willingly makes out of himself a room for other beings, and by doing so, sets the ethical example for his creation to follow: to always be in retreat and restraint for the sake of the other. Yet not in the sacrificial manner, in which we would 'mourn' the gesture of God's self-offering. In the *tsimtsum* version of withdrawal, there is nothing to mourn: the emergence of pure singularities related to one another by a 'fiduciary link' (FK, p. 55) in the freely 'available space' is an act of the most emphatic affirmation—a truly 'good news' to be rejoiced and not deplored.[11]

Thus, in his deconstruction of the sovereign paradigm of religion, which starts as early as *Glas*, and then continues through "Faith and Knowledge" up to his last seminars, Derrida follows closely Hegel's definition of the modern religious sentiment as the 'religion of the death of God', but he also modifies its affective register. While in Hegel, this sentiment is 'the infinite grief of the finite', the essentially endless work of mourning in which the finite beings are destined to commemorate the dead God, in Derrida's reading, it emerges as a more joyous and future-oriented attitude in which the theological content is offered possibility of a further, albeit secret, *survie*, 'living-on'.[12] Both Hegel and Derrida agree that in order for the singular beings of the world to come to the fore as the proper object of new metaphysics of finitude, God's previously all-powerful and infinite existence has to diminish: its all-pervasive light of *Lichtwesen* must 'set down', and hide from sight. It must commit itself to the self-offering, the 'holocaust', which, at the same time, coincides with the joyous surprise of the 'irruptive event of the gift'.[13] The modern God, therefore, is the hidden God, *deus absconditus*: sent off down to 'under the table' (Benjamin) or straight to the 'crypt' (Derrida), almost—but never completely—erased or forgotten. The modern 'atheism' is thus never pure and simple; it is rather, as in Gershom Scholem's seemingly oxymoronic expression, a pious atheism.[14] A 'harshest impiety', looking straight into the eye of negativity and 'the most severe privation of God'—yet, paradoxically, not without its own pious sense of complicity with God's self-denying intentions.

I have invoked Scholem's name—not in vain. One of the tenets of this essay is to prove—via Derrida's subtle wrestling with Kant, Hegel, and Heidegger—that the 'death of God religion' is not a Christian monopoly. Almost all thinkers that are associated with the 'death of God theology'—Thomas Altizer, Jean-Luc Nancy, Slavoj Žižek—insist on the absolute uniqueness of Christianity as the only religion which harbours atheism structurally within itself, and as such, paves the way to what we tentatively call the modern process of secularization. Yet a similar—even stronger: precursorial—manoeuvre of 'a/theologization' occurs already in the tradition of Jewish messianism, beginning with the Lurianic kabbalah and ending with Derrida's attempt to pluralize the concept of the 'death(s) of God(s) religion(s)' in "Faith and Knowledge". Having learned from Scholem's studies that there is an elective affinity between Lurianism and Marranism, Derrida—obliquely and allusively—calls this heterodox lineage 'Marrano' after the experience of the Spanish and Portuguese *conversos*, forced to convert to Christianity but keeping their Judaic faith undercover or, in the secret imitation of the Lurianic God, 'in retreat'.[15] It is precisely the Marrano 'secret'—almost forgotten, bordering on a/theology or even atheism, yet at the same time, not without its own irregular form

---

11 In Naas' great comment: "Before any social or political space, it [khora] would join or link singularities by saying simply, in an infinitely low voice, and in the name of another tolerance, *Space Available*" (MM, p. 182). Yet, in fact, in order for it to speak with such a 'low voice' (*bat kol*), or to simply speak at all, it already must be partly 'appropriated' by a certain messianic tradition which decides to interpret its passive 'letting-things-be' as an at least vestigially active 'making-place', i.e., to turn its indifference into generosity. In this domain, therefore, everything is contaminated: there is no pure source of 'revealability', and no pure abstraction of 'messianicity'.

12 (Hegel 1977, p. 190).

13 (Derrida 1986a, p. 241).

14 (Scholem 1976, p. 283).

15 Derrida's take on the Marrano secret as simultaneously attacking the religious sovereignty and realizing that the messianic message goes indeed hand in hand with Gershom Scholem who, in his studies on the Marrano theology, wrote: "The psychology of the 'radical' Sabbatians was utterly paradoxical and 'Marranic'. Essentially its guiding principle was: Whoever is as he appears to be cannot be a true 'believer'. In practice this means the following: The 'true faith' cannot be a faith which men publicly profess. On the contrary, the 'true faith' must always be concealed. In fact, it is one's duty to deny it

of piety and memory—that offers the aptest model for the 'religion of modern times'. Just as the Marrano encrypts the Jewish *deus absconditus* in the inner crypt of his seemingly impious self, so does the modern faith hides behind the façade of knowledge and develops further (FK, p. 53), undercover and in secrecy. Knowledge, therefore, not only represses faith in the (once) Living God, but it also protects faith in the second source of the messianic re-treat. This alternative, *fides abscondita*, is not to be dragged out from the shadow of the crypt into the light of presence: if it develops and becomes a new 'religion of the new times' (*der neuzen Zeiten*), it is only thanks to the darkness of the 'desert in the desert', which is its hiding place. The hiddenness is the necessary condition of its survival.

2. Not Kenosis, But Kenoma

What I, following Derrida's logic, propose to call the Marrano *kenomatic* God is a further radicalization of this already radical image of the divine 'ordeal' (*epreuve*): God who not only humbles himself in the act of *kenosis*, but truly 'empties himself out', *entäussert sich*, by transforming into the 'desert in the desert' which the Jewish–Gnostic tradition calls *kenoma–tehiru*: 'the void of the most serious privation of God (*Gottlosigkeit*)' (FK, p. 53). Thus, if Hegel describes 'modern religious sentiment' in terms of the 'abandonement by God', it also—or rather, most of all—means that God had abandoned himself; that he *verliess*, let go and gave up his sovereign Godhead, or, in Derrida's idiom, that God resigned his unscathed purity for the sake of contamination with the alien element of the world.

The crucial step further, therefore, is to 'abstract' this highly vulnerable, non-immune and self-atheologizing deity from the Christian context of *kenosis* that still keeps Hegel in its thrall, by arresting him in the blind spot of the aporia, which he cannot (or will not) solve dialectically. This aporia is a typical 'double bind': on the one hand, *kenosis* implies the highest possible sacrifice on God's part, ending in the Hegelian 'feeling that God himself is dead'—on the other, however, *kenosis* appears always within the Trinitarian 'machine', in which God can simultaneously plunge into the depths of creation as the incarnated Son, and somehow—miraculously and paradoxically—remain unscathed as the first person of the Trinity, God the Father. This Trinitarian trick of God dying and resurrecting at the same time; this 'play' [*Spiel*] in which the 'harm' [*Verletzung*] can be done and undone simultaneously, maintains the kenotic abandonement of the life unscathed still within the traditional scheme, which demands an instant restoration of this very life.[16] This means, however, that while Christianity, especially in its modern version, makes a move towards the acceptance of finitude—it is immediately counteracted by the traditional structure of the Trinitarian compensation, which brings the 'harmed' God back to his untouchable infinity in—literally—no time.[17]

---

outwardly, for it is like a seed that has been planted in the bed of the soul and it cannot grown unless it is first covered over. *For this reason every Jew is obliged to become a Marrano*" (Scholem 1995, p. 109; my emphasis).

[16] As Hegel himself observed in *Phenomenology of Spirit*, calling the 'facile' Trinitarian synthesis *ein eitles Spiel*: "Thus the life of God and divine cognition may well be spoken of as disporting of Love with itself; but this idea sinks into mere edification, and even insipidity, if it lacks the seriousness, the suffering, the patience, and the labour of the negative. In itself, that life is indeed one untroubled equality and unity with itself, for which otherness and alienation, and the overcoming of alienation, are not serious matters" (Hegel 1976, p. 11). This objection, uttered mostly against Schelling's notion of the self-healing Absolute, marks a significant change in Hegel's theological views. Before, i.e., at the stage of "Christianity and Its Fate", he would still maintain the idea of the holy as *das unverletzte Leben*, 'life unharmed'—the obvious prototype for Derrida's *vie indemne*—which excludes by definition any moment of negativity: lack, suffering, or death. It is only in the mature middle phase, when he composes *Phenomenology*, that he opens himself to another possibility: of fully and seriously admitting 'the terrible thought that God himself is dead' and that negativity is not just an attribute of the profane, but also a most holy affair.

[17] The objection that the 'wound' sustained by the Father is merely a *dokos*, a 'facade', all too easily healed in the Trinitarian play, appears often in Derrida's writings, most of all in *Glas* (where it is leveled against Hegel's romantic conception of the self-healing and scarless wounds of the Spirit), as well as in *Dissemination*, where the Trinitarian play is contrasted with the 'real' crisis in the godhead, resulting in the 'real' dispersion of beings, and calling for the 'real' messianic action. In Trinity, therefore, the 'death of God', in which the Father loses his breath/Spirit/*ruah*, remains merely apparent, because the Father "loses his breath in sustaining, retaining, idealizing, reinternalizing, and mastering his seed". In consequence, the crisis is quickly 'mastered', as it "would be acted out [. . .] between father and son alone: aitoinsemination, homoinsemination, reinsemination" (Derrida 1981, p. 45). Whereas, the eponymous *dissemination* is a 'real' loss of integrity, unity, and safety

Contrary to this, the *kenomatic* God, whom Derrida proposes (though merely implicitly, as if, as Michael Naas would say, 'under his breath'), a God truly emptied and harmed (*verletzt*), is absolutely past and beyond the safe and sound of the Trinitarian medicine of self-healing. As such, he promises to go beyond the mechanical horizon of the medicine of salvation as a direct vitalist manifestation of life. Submerged in the sphere of the Hegelian immediacy, religion, with all its mechanisms of spontaneous healing, precludes 'reflection', and as such, is indeed at—not, as in Kant, within—the limits of reason alone. In order to think about religion, one must abstract it from the realm of immediacy and tear it away from the spontaneous vitalist mechanism of the self-healing life. This, however, can only be achieved with that which does not heal, and is the very opposite of the unscathed: an eternal wound and an irreversible trauma, which does not undo its 'damns' and 'harms' in the circular process of pre-historical life, but ventures beyond the biological cycle into History proper.

Thus, while the first source of religion is the *pleromatic* vision of always 'safe and sound' life, in which there is no room for anything else—the second source is the very opposite: it is the *kenomatic* act of radical withdrawal/retreat that makes room for everything else. It is essential to repeat it again and again that the second source is *kenomatic*, and not just *kenotic*: it constitutes an ultimate openness to the 'wound' which is no longer conceived as a sickness-to-be-healed or a crisis-to-be-overcome. No longer a negative concept, it does not denote a *skandalon* (as Saint Paul named the divine incarnation resulting in God's crucifixion) which calls for a cosmic revenge, that is, for the apocalyptic self-annihilation of the world, thus paying back for the sacrificial gift of being and redeeming itself in the symmetrical sacrificial process: offering for an offering, a pure calculation of the salvatory machine based on the *jus talionis*. While Christian *kenosis* still rings with the overtones of the metaphysical scandal, which demands 'the moral sacrifice of empirical existence'[18] as the precisely calculated repayment of the debt, the *kenoma* which God willingly assumes in order to make a room for the otherness of the other—the surprise of alterity, the 'real' product of dissemination beyond any control and mastery—presents the 'death of God' in far less sacrificial manner, and therefore also no longer mechanically inducing sin, guilt, and debt.

This is probably the most crucial moment of the whole reasoning, first announced in "Faith and Knowledge", and then endlessly elaborated in Derrida's last seminars, all devoted—in the most passionate and religious sense of the word—to life. Yet not Life with the capital L, modelling itself after the Hegelian *unverletztes Leben* of the self-healing Trinity, but life of the singular living: finite, precarious and thus always inescapably 'scathed'. Already here we see the transition which Derrida will then restlessly attack and deconstruct: the tacit link between the Christian obsessive 'memory of the Passion' (Hegel again), which in the name of the highest divine life demands sacrifice of the human finite life—and the Christian sublimation of Thanatos, which, by the chiasmatic logic, turns the kenotic 'death of God' into a new, once again unscathed, 'God of death'. The modern Christian God—the one emerging from the writings of Kant and Hegel and their 'certain Christianity' (FK, p. 50)—is the God who dies, but only in order to 'give death': to force the believer to repeat—inevitably, mechanically—the same sacrifice of life: to make him renounce his 'natural' life as pathological and worth only of being offered for the sake of the *restitutio ad integrum* of the lost divine pleroma. For, as Hegel puts it in *Phenomenology*, the only function of the life of the believer is to 'resurrect God daily'.[19] This mysterious leap from the love of the life immortal and unharmed, in which our finite life wishes to augment itself, into a cult of something 'more than life', which turns against the finite life and demands its sacrifice in order to stay whole and healthy, is, according to Derrida, the most dangerous mechanism of religion, and not just the Christian one. The seemingly spontaneous, purely mechanical logic of

---

of the divine which gives itself over to the risk, empties itself out completely, without a remainder, and opens itself to the irreversible process of alienation.

[18] (Hegel 1975, p. 537).
[19] (Hegel 1976, p. 299).

the first pleromatic source, which feeds on all life in order to keep its living plenitude intact, must, therefore, be arrested, that is, made at least 'reflective':

> This mechanical principle is apparently very simple: life has absolute value only if it is worth *more than* life. And hence only in so far as it mourns, becoming itself in the labour of infinite mourning, in the indemnification of a spectrality without limit. It is sacred, holy, infinitely respectable only in the name of what is worth more than it and what is not restricted to the naturalness of the bio-zoological (sacrificeable)—although true sacrifice ought to sacrifice not only 'natural' life, called 'animal or 'biological', but also that which is worth more than so-called natural life. The price of human life, which is to say, of anthropo-theological life, the price of what to remain safe (*heilig*, sacred, safe and sound, unscathed, immune), as the absolute price, the price of what ought to inspire respect, modesty, reticence, this price is priceless. It corresponds to what Kant calls the dignity [*Würdigkeit*] of the end in itself [...] This dignity of life can only subsist beyond the present living being. Whence, transcendence, fetishism and spectrality; whence, the religiosity of religion. This excess above and beyond the living, whose life only has absolute value by being worth more than life, more than itself—this, in short, is what opens the space of death that is linked to the automaton (exemplarily 'phallic'), to technics, the machine, the prosthesis: in a word, to the dimensions of auto-immune and self-sacrificial supplementarity, to this death-drive that is silently at work in every community, every *auto-co-immunity*, constituting it as such in its iterability, its heritage, its spectral tradition [...] Religion, as a response that is both ambiguous and ambivalent is thus an ellipsis: *the ellipsis of sacrifice*. (FK, pp. 87–88; my emphasis)

Yet, Derrida's aim is not just to 'arrest' the sacrificial logic of the first source, which is the cult of the unscathed pleromatic life. Having in mind the second—kenomatic—source, he also immediately asks the question: "Is a religion imaginable without sacrifice and without prayer?" (FK, p. 88). And then we almost hear, 'under his breath': perhaps, perhaps ... Just few pages before, Derrida told us that it is ontotheology which is 'without sacrifice and without prayer' (FK, p. 53): the new philosophical doctrine which, in a semi-Hegelian fashion, sublates/devours the religious content in order to preserve it in the abstracted form. Another subtle gesturing towards this 'perhaps', seemingly in a completely different direction, lurks in the passage in which Derrida describes the challenge to the Christian 'memory of the Passion' posed by Judaism and Islam, the "two non-pagan monotheisms that do not accept death any more than multiplicity in God [...], alienating themselves from a Europe that signifies the death of God" (FK, p. 51). This alienation, however, should not be conceived as a simple reminder that monotheism signifies a 'faith in the living One' (FK, p. 51), but as a prompt suggesting that the 'death of God' itself is not an exclusively Christian affair of the 'tragedy of the cross', and that it can also be thought in terms of God's most surprising survival—of a God-in-retreat, a *tsimtsem* God, who is not to be mourned, but celebrated in his peculiar mode of living-on: among his followers and in the world.

3. The Self-Deconstructing Religion, or the Scathed Life

It is quite justifiable to read "Faith and Knowledge" as the critique of all religions understood as the cults of the unscathed—and Martin Hägglund's *Radical Atheism* is the best example of such interpretation. According to Hägglund, Derrida, who defends the 'time of life' against any eternalizing hypostasis, is the most radical type of atheist, and fundamentally so in the phenomenological sense of the word. His investment in the ever-disseminating temporality, which can only leave a transient trace of its presence, makes Derrida a staunch enemy of any form of the Absolute conceived as a timeless *nunc stans*. By insisting on the inherent connection between transience and life, Derrida dismisses all religious attempts to think in terms of life infinite and immortal as leading out of the domain of life and into the realm of death: the unchanging and untouchable Absolute can never be alive, it is death pure and simple. For, as long as there is life, there is exposure to time, scathedness and vulnerability:

the idea of an Absolute Life, essential to all religions, is thus a *contradictio in adjecto*. Life can only affirm itself as a constant effort of survival, which, according to Hägglund, is the defining feature of radical atheism. It is merely the desire for survival which dissimulates itself as the desire for immortality. However, while it precedes the latter, it also contradicts it from within: "There is thus an internal contradiction in the so-called desire for immortality. If one were not attached to mortal life, there would be no fear of death and no desire to live on".[20]

Hägglund's interpretation aims at re-reading the whole of Derrida's work, from his earliest deconstruction of Husserl in *Speech and Phenomena* up to his latest seminars on the death penalty and sovereignty, in terms of the determined attempt to reformulate our attitude to survival as ultimately positive: "The radical finitude of survival—he says—is not a lack of being that is desirable to overcome. Rather, the finitude of survival opens the chance for everything that is desired and the threat of everything that is feared".[21] Because of that, the very concept of God who is "beyond everything that can be predicated by a finite being" and who cannot die ("If God were not immortal, he would not be God")—must be abandoned.[22] To say, therefore, that 'God is dead', is not enough. According to Hägglund, Derrida radicalizes the atheist thesis by implying that 'God is death', i.e., that he is the direct opposite, as well as the negation of all things alive and finite:

> If to be alive is to be mortal, it follows that to *not* be mortal—to be immortal—is to be dead. If one cannot die, one is dead. Hence, Derrida does not limit himself to the atheist claim that God is dead; he repeatedly makes the radically atheist claim that *God is death*. That God is death does not mean that we reach God through death or that God rules over death. On the contrary, it means that the idea of immortality—which according to Marion is 'the idea that we cannot not form of God'—is inseparable from the idea of absolute death.[23]

This is all very true: if one treats Jean-Luc Marion as the paradigmatic exponent of the religious belief which, following the long tradition of Anselm's ontological argument, imputes the incapability to sustain any 'wound' to the very essence of the pleromatic godhead—then Derrida, indeed, is the radical denier of such faith. But is this the only way possible to conceive God? What if, apart from the 'God is death' of the absolutist theology embraced by Marion, there is also a 'death of God' theology which moves, according to its own self-atheologizing and self-deconstructive rhythm, away from the image of the unscathed Infinite towards the affirmation of the finite? Derrida's critical treatment of the Hegelian–Kantian model of God's demise complicates the dualistic picture painted by Hägglund, based on the simple opposition of the God who by definition cannot die, on the one hand, and the radical atheism which accepts the premise that whatever is alive must be mortal, on the other.

Despite Hägglund's atheistic interpretation, Derrida does not reject all possible religion. Although historically, almost all actual religions tended to define themselves as cults of the unscathed, understood either in the immanentis terms of the invulnerable life or in the transcendent terms of the otherworldly Infinite, he is nonetheless mostly interested in the self-deconstructive tendency of the 'modern religious sentiment' which attaches itself to the motif of the divine 'scathedness', and which the Hegelian Christianity defined—partly rightly, but also partly confusedly—as the 'religion of the death of God'. The question, therefore, is: can there be a religion of the scathed—the vulnerable, finite,

---

[20] (Hägglund 2008, p. 2).
[21] (Hägglund 2008, p. 2).
[22] (Hägglund 2008, pp. 7–8).
[23] (Hägglund 2008, p. 8). The paradox of the deadening idemnification is a frequent subject of Abraham and Torok's reflections on the en-cryption, cryptonymy, and cryptophoria, also commented on by Derrida in his preface to their *Wolf Man's Magic Word*: "A crypt, people believe, always hides something dead. But to guard it from what? Against what does one keep a corpse intact, safe both from life and from death, which could both come in from the outside to touch it? And to allow death to take no place in life?" (Derrida 1986b, p. xxi). Indeed, "day in day out, *the crypt itself remains unscathed*" (Abraham and Torok 1994, p. 152; my emphasis). The 'shell', therefore, i.e., the wall that creates the crypt, not only deadens/oppresses the 'kernel', which lies there deposited, but also protects it and guards it in its hiddenness—which, for Derrida, is precisely the dialectical model for the relation between Knowledge (shell) and Faith (kernel).

exposed—without any recourse to the Absolute? Again, it is Hegel who delivers main categories: just as his 'death of God religion' cuts into the neat dualism of traditional religiosity, sporting the image of the divine sovereign, on the one hand, and atheism resulting from 'Nietzsche's two words', on the other—so does his early concept of *unverletztes Leben*, 'unscathed life', serves to depict the inner mechanism of religious cults. But what if this very mechanism broke? What if it jammed, became 'reflective', and began to self-deconstruct? What if God himself, so to say, stepped down from the pedestal of undamaged vitality (or dead immortality) and let the second, kenomatic, source come more visibly to the fore?

The change which occurs in Hegel's thought between his early theological writings and the inception of *Phenomenology*—the shift from the traditional Christian image of religious community as mirroring the perfect, unscathed life of the godhead to the heterodox Christian-Gnostic notion of God depleting himself and emptying out into creation—can also be seen as the canvas for Derrida's own deconstructive manoeuvre. Far from refuting all 'religious sentiments' as inevitably gravitating towards the 'safe and sound', he, just like Hegel before, aims to distil—abstract—the streak of the other, self-deconstructive religiosity which affirmatively welcomes the finite and scathed. "Faith and Knowledge", therefore, does not deconstruct religion from the outside—the radical atheist position that Hägglund attributes to Derrida—but from the inside, following and enhancing the internal self-deconstructive moment of religion itself, which he—after Hegel (but also, as I insist here, implicitly, Isaac Luria)—identifies with the 'death of God' as the Lord and Master: a self-willed demise of sovereignty, which does not set an example in death, and does not call for the reciprocal sacrifice of life.

The experiment of "Faith and Knowledge", precursorial to his last seminars, is thus to test out for the first time the possibility of a 'modern religious sentiment' which will ultimately free itself from the infatuation with sovereign power: the 'more than life' image of the unscathed absolute to which no harm can be done. Derrida's double portrayal of the second source—the Abrahamic messianicity on the one hand, and the Platonic *khora* on the other—deliberately emphasizes their weakness and vulnerability, not typical for the foundational *arche*: *khora* is an 'open wound' itself, but also the messianic principle is anarchic, swerving away from the royal image of the *melekh ha-olam*, the King of the World, popular in the orthodox Judaism. This rhetoric of weakening aims at presenting these two visions of the second source as equally *kenomatic*: generously self-emptying, self-humbling, self-offering. Yet, this weakness should not be conflated with a mere negative depletion of power. It comes with a twist: with a decisive reversal, allowing for the escape of the discourse of power, vitality, and unscathedness altogether. What thus may appear as being weak and debilitated from the Nietzschean perspective of the *Wille zur Macht*—the ailing Judeo-Christian God laying himself down in the tomb/crypt—announces a radical change of register, which ultimately invalidates the attribute of omnipotence as the criterion of the creative power. Neither messianicity nor *khora* are powerful and pleromatic principles of foundation. They are the self-withdrawn, *tsimtsem*, anarchic 'sources' of the desert, the element of emptiness, *kenoma*—but precisely because of that creative, place-making, letting-be. *Seinlassen* is not a derivative of the infinite power; on the contrary, it involves an element of *Gelassenheit* that is understood as self-abandonement.[24]

It is thus necessary to remember that this self-deconstructive movement within Graeco-Abrahamic heritage occurs not for the sake of weakness issuing in death, but for the sake of 'powerlessness' which lets live life and thus gives life—finite, scathed, and contingent. Hence, the 'weakness' of the Christian Messiah who lays himself in the 'crypt' is not the final word of the 'deconstruction of Christianity',

---

24 For Derrida, the true *Gelassenheit*, therefore, is the art of "abandoning God who abandons himself": not an attempt to cling to him, not even to grasp him—just "not give anything to God, not even Adieu, not even to his name . . . This is how I sometimes understand the tradition of *Gelazenheit*, the serenity that allows being without indifference, let's go without abandoning, unless it abandons without forgetting or *forgets without forgetting*" (Derrida 1995b, pp. 73, 84; my emphasis). He also calls this position, after Leibniz, an 'almost-atheism' (Derrida 1995b, p. 83). In a moment, we shall see that this paradoxical 'forgetting without forgetting' that leads to the 'almost-atheism' characterizes the Marrano 'memory of the Passover', constituting a Derridean alternative to the Hegelian 'memory of the Passion'.

in the way it is envisaged by Jean-Luc Nancy who in *Corpus*, the book written in 1992, finishes it with the 'death of God' and what remains of it—the dead divine *corpus*.[25] This, for Derrida, is the paradigmatic case of the wrong deconstructive move, which ends with the deification of death, and thus reinstates the sovereign status of 'God as death'. Derrida deliberately does not end his essay with the image of the corpse in the crypt, and adds the second section on ' . . . *pomegranates*': the fruit which, according to the Jewish messianic sources, is still hanging on the branches of the Tree of Life.

This unwelcome inversion within the unscathed—from the sovereignty of the 'most living' into the sovereignty of death—is the reason why, in the later book devoted to Nancy, *On Touching*, Derrida fiercely attacks what he calls the Christian *delectatio morosa*, revelling in the 'tragedy of the cross'. Note that, once again, he refers to 'a certain Christianity', which already in "Faith and Knowledge" is accused of the infatuation with the thanatic power:

> *For a certain Christianity* will always take charge of the most exacting, the most *exact*, and the most eschatological hyperbole of deconstruction, the overbid of 'Hoc est enim corpus meum'. *It will still make sacrifice of its own self-deconstruction*. Hey, Sade—go for it![26]

Alluding to Lacan's "Kant avec Sade", which found a sadistic component of *jouissance* in a seemingly purely formal Kantian ethics, Derrida points to the libidinal surplus of enjoyment in the paradoxical pride taken in the absolute uniqueness of Christianity as the religion of the dead/killed God. The whole of Derrida's argument hinges here (as elsewhere) on the notion of sacrifice: *kenosis*, even the most radical, is still God's self-offering, and because of that, a toxic gift, which does not liberate its recipients but enslaves them by a perverse gesture of sovereignty. This is also the reason why, against Nancy's official thesis, Christianity can never fully deconstruct itself into atheism, because it will always be kept on the leash of indebtedness and obligation; a certain bad conscience which keeps returning, more or less involuntarily, in Nietzsche, Heidegger, and Nancy, despite their explicit allegiance to the 'innocence of becoming'. The Christian dead God can never let his people go: he will forever make them *schuldig*. Hence, as we have already suggested, in thinking about God-becoming-finite, we must pass beyond the traps of *kenosis*, which smuggles under its *skandalon* the idea of a cosmic catastrophe, and thus prevents from imagining God's act of finitization as a truly free opening, beyond the economy of debt and repayment. This is precisely where *tsimtsum*—withdrawal/retreat, or another 'death of God'—enters as the non-sacrificial and non-catastrophic gesture of the divine self-limitation: the gift without sacrifice: the gift of life, which releases the donné from the automatic obligation to return life to the donor.

4. Hail to Impurity: The Marrano God

But how is this reversal within the 'modern religious sentiment' to be achieved? The first necessary step is Derrida's deconstruction of the logic of indemnification inherent in all religions as 'ellipses of sacrifice', i.e., the mechanism of the offering for the sake of something that is always more-than-life—beyond harm, *unverletzt*, *indemne*—and hence, made exempt or abstracted from the ordinary fate of all the living. Indemnification is precisely the 'wrong' kind of abstraction, which produces a sovereign exception.

By making analogy with the mechanism of auto/immunity, Derrida demonstrates the double bind that affects all religions as 'religions of the living', that is, ultimately, as the most original expressions of life itself: the aporia between immunization and autoimmunization. The religious indemnification can be regarded here as the extreme of the immunizing tendency in which the religious systems, which invest too much in the ideal of an indemnified purity, are doomed to self-destruct under the weight of their overstimulated self-protection. Just like an organism, which overdefends against infection and

---

[25] See (Nancy 2008a) as well as (Nancy 2008b).
[26] (Derrida 2005a, p. 60; my emphasis).

produces too many antibodies that eventually turn against this very organism, religions overdefend against contamination with anything alien, and by purging all impure elements, also turn against themselves, and then they either stifle or become completely defenceless, which, in the end, amounts to the same thing: the incapability of a further survival, or living-on. The problem with immunization consists, therefore, in the self-destructive coupling of survival with purity, the mechanism that is so well described by René Girard in his scapegoat theory, but also by Mary Douglas in *Purity and Danger*. As an organism, which wants to protect itself, but in the process of building self-protection, it becomes alien to itself, i.e., it alienates the whole of what it actually is for the sake of an abstract ideal of itself, purely in and for itself—religious traditions engage in the same error, by staking their survival on averting all dangers of impurity and contamination, which eventually takes over the whole of their actual life, for the sake of an idealized, abstracted, more-than-life, hyper-pure essence of their identity that, by definition, cannot be touched by anything alien. This abstraction of a pure and indemnified more-than-life, which alienates the whole of actual life of the tradition, demands, therefore, the destruction–sacrifice of all that is alien, life included (precisely as in Kant's and Hegel's definition of 'moral religion' as the one which calls for the sacrifice of the actual—always pathological—'sensuous life'). Thus, instead of securing infinite survival, traditions, fenced behind the all too protective walls, collapse and die—unleashing violent cleansing upon themselves and others. On the other hand, however, the traditions face symmetrical danger coming from the corner of autoimmunization: while they begin to protect themselves against their own overprotection, it may leave them wholly unprotected, and thus unable to survive in their difference; once an organism loses the last traces of self-preservation, it simply dissolves, as a separate living unit, into its surroundings. This way or another, auto/immunity—death by suffocating purification or death by suicidal dissolution—leads to the paradoxical counter-result: not the infinite living-on, but the very opposite of survival. The medicine of salvation turns out to be a lethal *pharmakon*: a deadly poison when, inevitably, overdosed.[27]

Prima facie, Derrida pretends to be fatalistic about it, almost to the point of sighing–whispering, helplessly, with a tragic undertone, as if citing Shelley's poem, *The Triumph of Life* (on which he had written in *Living-On. Borderlines*) 'under his breath': "ah well, religion—ah well, life . . . What can be done about it?" Apparently, not much. The tragic wisdom of the self-dooming cycle of a living thing, which comes to life on the same grounds that then cause its demise, reverberates through Derrida's musings on the self-destructive nature of all living nature, as well as all phenomena that are fashioned after such naturalistic mode of being and its inherently tragic desire to live-on. But it is so only on the surface. In fact, Derrida has something else in store: hidden, disguised, encrypted. However, although delayed and deferred (as all messianic promises), this novelty eventually arrives to the surface, breaks through the concealment of the crypt—and takes the form of the ' . . . *pomegranates*' (necessarily and emphatically with the ellipsis which announces—without announcing—something surprising, unexpected, a pure new arrival). Thus, suddenly, at the very end of his essay, Derrida comes back to the issue of the modern philosophical ontotheology, which sublated and abstracted the language of old 'living religions', transforming them into 'religions of the death of God', and says that it . . .

> . . . en*crypts* faith and destines it to the condition of a sort of Spanish Marrano who would have lost—in truth, dispersed, multiplied—everything up to and including the memory of his unique secret. Emblem of a still life: an opened pomegranate, one Passover evening, on a tray. (FK, p. 100)

---

[27] Naas comments: "It is precisely those discourses of life that believe they can exclude death, those that believe they can return to a life protected from corruption, that often lead to the worst possible violence, the most nightmarish scenes of death and destruction—all fed by the phantasm of a life greater than life, the dream, in short, of a miracle that can do without the machine" (MM, p. 196).

This passage, talking about encryption, is itself deeply cryptic, but the best way to approach it is not to dismiss it as a negative remark. In fact, it is rather an oblique appreciation of the Marrano *conversos*, who, only on the surface, would have lost the inner truth of their Jewish identity (even, as Derrida says in *Circumfession*, in the intimacy of their hearts) but, in fact, would have dispersed it, yet not in the manner of squandering and loss, but in the manner of multiplication which the Biblical topos affirms as the right thing to do, that is, as a mark of successful survival. The *marrano* (in Spanish, a swine) is a symbol of impurity which lost the memory of his uniqueness and betrayed loyalty to his tradition which is no longer One, but inherently *plus d'Un*, multiplied and dispersed also internally, contaminated to the point where it is no longer possible to tell the ownmost proper from the alien. But Marrano is also an emblem of a still life [*nature morte*], which locates itself in between the premodern cult of the Living God and the modern 'death of God' religion: seemingly dead, but—still—a life; still, quiet, restrained, self-withdrawn, and yet—still—a life. A paradoxical emblem of the 'dead nature': no longer natural, but yet un-dead; not a vitalist pleroma of unbound power, yet—still—some kind of denaturalized life that does not equal death, but stubbornly survives. An emblem of a survival, therefore—yet not by purification and indemnification, but by contamination, which nonetheless retains a trace of its original difference, the dim memory of the Jewish rite of Passover. Here it is, shown to you openly and plainly, on a tray. An opened pomegranate: wounded, cut through, exposing its inner flesh to the alien outside, exposing its scatheedness, wound, *blessure*, circumcision ... [28]

There is nothing on circumcision in "Faith and Knowledge", but we know from other texts, most of all *Circumfession*, how important this symbol of a never-healing wound is for Derrida: a symbol of a wounded, self-restrained and self-circumcised, kenomatic second source of religion, which would be even more *kenotic* than the Christian God, even more deipassionistic than in Hegel's description of the modern 'death of God' religion, and even more universally messianic than all of the most radical Jewish, Muslim and Christian messianisms taken together. The true desert source, followed by his true–untrue mis-believing believers, the Marranos, who stay faithful to their tradition only by betraying it, or, as Derrida puts it somewhere else, by remembering in forgetting, because only in this way, one can keep a vestigial memory of the source that self-retreats: "one can only recall it to oneself in forgetting it (*on ne peut se la rappeler qu'en l'oubliant*)".[29] For, if God abandons himself, the only manner to keep him in mind—or encrypt him—is to 'forget without forgetting'.

On the one hand, the second source of religion called *khora* is a wound itself, *l'epreuve*, an ordeal, constant slipping out of being: the open, still-living flesh of the pomegranate—but, on the other, it is also full of still-growing the seeds of what is yet to come. Just as Marranos exited all forms of institutionalized religions, being now neither Jewish nor Christian, so does *khora* remain outside: "It will never have entered religion and will never permit itself to be sacralized, sanctified, humanized, theologized, cultivated, historicized. Radically heterogenous to the safe and sound, to the holy and the sacred, it never admits of any *indemnification*" (FK, p. 58). And just as Marranos are oblivious and unsure of their past and identity, impure and contaminated, universally despised, yet precisely because of that masters of survival, so is *khora*: treated by Plato as being metaphysically inferior,

---

[28] In French, the title of the section is ' ... *et grenades*': a phrase which involves an ambivalence lost in the English translation, but which was well spotted by Michael Naas, who in *Derrida from Now on* writes: "While the latter context [which I have just analysed—ABR] justifies the translation of grenades by 'pomegranates', its context here, in the midst of a text on religion and science, faith and violence, is not so determined as to exclude the other meaning of grenades in French, namely, 'grenades'. Indeed, Derrida appears to have lobbed this word into the middle of the fifty-two sections of "Faith and Knowledge" in order to gather or, rather, disperse many of the themes of the phantasm that we have been following throughout this essay, in order to evoke all the tensions between, precisely, faith and knowledge, nature and culture, the pomegranate of religion and the grenade of techno-science, a symbol of female fertility, of life-giving seed, on the one hand, and an image of masculine violence, of shrapnel-casting death, on the other, the blood-red pomegranate of Persephone, on the one hand, and the army-green hand-held machine of technoscience, on the other" (Naas 2008, p. 205, later on as DFNO). The intimate link between pomegranates and grenades can thus be deconstructed: but it cannot be fully deactivated: whenever the kenomatic source comes into the presence of a revealed religion and its techniques of maintaining this presence in the media machine, the innocent fruit hardens into a potential weapon.

[29] (Derrida 2005c, p. 49).

rejected by Abrahamic monotheisms, *khora* is, in fact, their secret messianic energy without which they turn stale, dead, cultic, too indemnified. It signifies another desert: not the one of a raging jealousy of the One God who cannot stand any rivalry, but the one of an original contamination, heterogeneity, always already 'more-than-one', subtle and generous potentiality that is not yet formed into rigid identities, of a 'still life', but nonetheless always surviving, living-on, always there, in the dark silent background, hidden and secret. If Judaism follows the 'jealous God' who turns the desert into his kingdom (pure absolute Life), and if Christianity follows the 'dead God', who, in the gesture of inverse sovereignty, indebts his believers with the infinite *Schuld* (pure absolute Death)—Marranism can be seen as penetrating deeper beneath those religious fixed identities into the realm of *khora*, where every singular being tolls with the effort of Survival, yet is free from any form of sovereign power.

What Derrida is thus aiming at is neither dualism nor a synthesis of the two sources, but their constant 'impure' oscillation (FK, p. 59) or *Schweben*—the favourite movement of German Idealism, from Kant to Hegel, which already Luther ascribed to *ruah Elohim*, the Spirit of God hovering over but also reflecting, mirroring and thus absorbing the image of the watery abysses below. This is not a God establishing his invincible identity in the gesture of subduing the darkness of *tohu va-vohu*, but a God who gives up on the triumphant integrity of the unscathed; opens himself, like the pomegranate, and exposes to the outmost vulnerability, accident and chance; affirms the wound of the precarious finite life. This messianic God is thus nothing else but the *khora* that awakens from its indifference to self-awareness, and says Yes to itself and its own ordeal.[30] A Marrano God—unstable and internally dispersed, multiplied—who only pretends to be the highest and most perfect *primum ens* of the globalatinized philosophical ontotheology, firmly squatted in the center of the Kingdom of Being, but, in fact, in its hidden depths—or 'under his breath'—is the very opposite: the wound and lack itself, self-emptied *kenoma*, always in the state of revealing and manifesting itself, which inevitably betrays its dark source.[31]

In Scholem's account, "authentic tradition remains hidden"[32], and Derrida shares this Marrano declaration. The 'reflecting faith' (FK, p. 59), which he has in mind as an alternative to its Kantian/Hegelian version, must thus keep close to the clandestine level of revealability, not contending itself with any determinate form of revelation. For, even the humblest and most loving God, when fully revealed in the articulated set of beliefs, tends to lose the kenomatic aspect of retreat, and assumes the pleromatic aspect of visibility and power. The more he comes into light, the more he gains presence, the more he fleshes himself out—the more he falls under the rules of 'ontologism', in which all phenomena want to steal the show: be the only thing of light, presence, being, and vitality, and then 'jealously' guard it only for itself. Very much in and from this world, the revealed God represses the otherworldly source in retreat. To maintain the abstraction of messianicity means, on the other hand, to be faithful to the 'night events' of the hidden and hiding source—and to avoid full identification with any overt theology, or, more generally, with any 'light': be it of the revelation/illumination or of

---

[30] This awakening is a cryptotheological theme of Derrida's essay on Joyce, *Ulysses Gramophone*, where God, implicitly compared to a writer who relinquishes the right of control over his work, pours himself into the creation and then releases it, by leaving only his consenting signature: *Yes, yes*.

[31] Again, it is Michael Naas who seems particularly attentive to Derrida's gnomic, cryptic, and simultaneously hyper-condensed Marrano imagery, which deliberately avoids full articulation. While commenting on the pomegranate 'still life', he states that "faith would be a Marrano that eludes this putative self-presence (like a crypt within ontotheology) and opens this seemingly indivisible identity (like a cut pomegranate) [...] Faith would thus be encrypted like a Marrano within religion, given a chance to circulate within a religion only on the condition of hiding or being concealed within it [...] Faith would be encrypted in ontotheology in this way, sublimated, one might say, *forced underground, forced to go by other names or go about in other guises*, able to reveal its true identity only to other members of the same secret community [...] But the Marrano Derrida is evoking here would be a Marrano, even to this secret community, a *Marrano of Marranos*, then, a secret even for or to those in on the secret, not unlike the desert within the desert that is *khora*. It is in this sense that we must understand why Derrida refers to himself not only as 'a sort of Marrano of French Catholic culture' but, in an untranslatable French phrase, as *le dernier des juifs*, that is, as the 'last of the Jews', 'the least of the Jews', but also 'the most Jewish of Jews', the most because the least, the least became the most, the first because the last, and so on" (MM, pp. 232–33; my emphasis).

[32] (Scholem 1973, p. 264).

the Enlightenment, either the light of the revealed Faith or the light of the enlightened Knowledge. To be faithful to this original night is, therefore, to be nothing else but a Marrano: a forgetful believer of a self-effacing God in denial. Just as *khora* does not enter any explicit theological discourse, so does Marrano stand apart from any revealed religion. However, it is precisely this separation that brings him closer to the ever-receding realm of revealability.[33]

Closer, but still not fully identified with the second source. The complex dialectic—oscillation, *Schweben*—between the two poles of hidden revealability and open revelation comes to the foremost strikingly in the concluding paragraph of the italic section, which once again refers to *khora* and its indifferent, automatic production of beings—but also, more obliquely, evokes the Lurianic heritage of *tsimtsum* as a withdrawal committed out of generosity, in which God dies in his original form, makes gift out of his 'holocaust' (see again *Glas*) and then disseminates its traces/ashes in the world as the seeds of the messianic promise:

> It makes way, perhaps, but without the slightest generosity, neither human nor divine. The dispersion of ashes is not even promised there, nor death given. (FK, p. 100)

Naas says very rightly that "the [Derridean] testament questions even the testament of ash, as if the promise of ashes already promised too much" (MM, p. 242)—yet without this miracle of the promise, there would be no religion, which must always hover in between the two sources: the kenomatic *khora* which, left on its own slides into 'indifference'—and the pleromatic God the Sovereign, who by his own quickening power, easily turns into a 'monstrosity'. The Marranos occupy precisely this troubled, instable in-between.

5. Still Life, or the Marrano Denaturalization

Could this at-once contaminated and abstract messianicity, which would maintain itself in the Marrano middle between no religion of pure revealability and all religions of particular revelations, be the new 'reflecting faith', the coming of which Derrida announces at the end of the Latin–italics section—as if at the end of the age of ontotheology and at the limits of reason alone?

> Respect for this singular indecision/oscillation or for this hyperbolic outbidding between two originarities, the order of the 'revealed' and the order of the 'revealable', is this not at once the chance of every responsible decision and of *another 'reflecting faith'*, of a new 'tolerance'? (FK, p. 59; my emphasis)

If so, then its most suitable bearer would indeed be the Marrano as the universal figure of dispersion and contamination, the very opposite of the identitarian purity: the master of survival, the *mischling* being at home nowhere and everywhere, and the new citizen of the globalatinized empire, carrying his 'secret' difference within himself.[34]

---

[33] See Naas commenting on this ontologistic rule of presence: "The sacred or the holy is related not just to sovereign power but to an exuberant, fecund force capable of bringing to life in a spontaneous and automatic way. The phallus effect or the fecund belly rises up of its own accord, self-seeding and self-bearing—like an Immaculate Conception" (DFNO, p. 204). This is how every *revealed* religion, precisely because of the moment of coming-into-light, necessarily must result in the repression of the kenomatic source for the sake of the visible and monstrable, which automatically tends to assume aspects of pleromatic vitality.

[34] The Marrano context of the modern 'reflecting faith' as being secretly internalized and suppported only by the 'inner heart', itself also prone to forgetting, was spotted very aptly by Yirmiyahu Yovel: "For them [Marranos] authentic religion had been desinstitutionalized and privatized ... , *depending on the inner heart as its almost sole support.* There were, of course, supporting fragments of memory and custom, and the sense of secret fraternity ... In the end, and all along, the person had to face the most important religious truths—decisions about value, and about personal fate in this and the next world—within a private 'inner forum'". This could indeed be a good portrait of Derrida as the Marrano: grappling with the imperatives of the 'inner heart' (in constant polemical reference to Paul and Augustine); resorting to supporting accessories like tallith (as in "Silkworm"); having a sense of secret fraternity (including even *frere* Heidegger, as in *On Spirit: Heidegger and The Question*); bearing witness to the most singular idiosyncrasy that is a secret, even to itself (as in *Archive Fever*); and the play between the 'inner forum' and the 'fors/fortress' of the crypt, in which the Marrano secret has been deposited (as in

As we have seen, Derrida associates the Marrano mode of *sur-vie* with a 'still life', *nature morte*. Neither simply alive nor simply dead, posed in the strange suspension between natural vitality and 'more-than-life' thanatic sublimation, it is life denaturalized—taken out of nature and its vitalistic sacred, yet, at the same time, arrested in what Lacan calls the 'inversion of the desire': a process in which libido turns away from life and the 'sheeplike conglomerations of the Eros', and aims at an identification with the other powerful unscathed, the death-drive.[35] This suspension blocks the mechanism of religious sublimation, which replaces the one unscathed of the infinite Life with another unscathed of the invulnerable Death, and situates itself in the middle of the finite life, understood as the process of survival. This suspension can also be described by the Hegelian term, *die Zerrisenheit—arrachement*—which Derrida reuses, but with a changed dispositif. While in Hegel, it served as a critique of the Jewish religion, which is allegedly accountable for the violent break with nature, hatred for life, and the sin of deracination, in Derrida it denotes a right move—but only provided that it does not end up in the 'counter-fetishism' of the thanatic machine. 'Violent sundering'—yes, but simultaneously *arrested*, caught in the cadre of 'still life', *nature morte*, content with its aporeticity, not trying to resolve it in the symmetrical 'inverted' sanctification of death. Thus, right after the section devoted to the 'Jewish question' and 'Jewish survival', Derrida introduces the 'two figures', which he sees as responsible for the self-destructive logic of the returning religions:

> 1. Violent sundering, to be sure, from the radicality of roots (*Entwürzelung*, Heidegger would say ...) and from all forms of original *physis*, from all the supposed resources of a force held to be authentically generative, sacred, unscathed, 'safe and sound' (*heilig*): ethnic identity, descent, family, nation, blood and soil, proper name, proer idiom, proper culture, and memory. 2. But also, more than ever, the counter-fetishism of the same *desire inverted*, the animist relation to the tele-technoscientific machine, which then becomes a machine of evil, and of radical evil, but a machine to be manipulated as much as to be exorcised. (FK, p. 91; my emphasis)

The first figure alludes to the caricature version of Judaism that is widely sported by 'a certain Christianity' (including Hegel and Heidegger)—the blind and mechanical antithesis towards all living *physis* as the unscathed source of authentic vitality—which Derrida spitefully endorses and intensifies, to the extent of denying the properly 'separated', even the blood line, proper name, and proper memory. The truly 'sundered' and 'separated' one would thus be the Marrano, ultimately and decisively cut from any form of the unscathed that necessarily populate all revealed religions. But to be truly 'separated' also means to be able to live on in the condition of permanent *Zerrisenheit*, to be for ever indifferent to the temptation of counter-fetishization, i.e., to the last remnants of the animistic magic looking for the substitutes of the lost vital sacred—even if, following the Lacanian 'inverted ladder of desire', this replacement is to be found in the dead machine, the mechanical death-drive that is itself incapable of dying. The Marrano type of survival, stubbornly living on in the contaminated and compromised realm between Life and Death, Eros and Thanatos—these two giant powers of the pure and unscathed, which always threaten our singular finite lives—is offered by Derrida, as if on a tray, as a modest possibility of salvation. For all of us.

"Fors", written as a preface to Abraham and Torok's famous book on cryptophoria); and finally, faithful to the 'encrypted' Jewish God, who comes to haunt the living as a *reverant* or ghost/phantom, and who is not 'resurrected daily', as in Hegel, but merely evoked as a spectre (as in *Specters of Marx*). Yovel himself admits it by calling Derrida's 'non-Jewish Jewishness' the very epitome of the Marrano experience consciously turned into a universal condition, where the split, non-integral and unfinished identity becomes a paradigm of the modern subject which, precisely because of that, can only be described in terms of a meta-identitarian remnant (*le derniere des Juifs*): "Derrida considered himself a non-Jewish Jew and a kind of Marrano. He identified in his Jewishness all the marks of dualities and disintegrated identity that his philosophy ascribed to the human condition in general" (Yovel 2009, pp. 88, 367; my emphasis).

[35] (Lacan 1989, pp. 104–5).

Religions **2019**, *10*, 22

6. A New Alexandria, or the Marrano Universalism

"Faith and Knowledge" is not just a theological treatise, it is also a politico-theological one that should be read as the rejoinder to the conception of the 'global Latin empire' put forward by the most influential Hegelian thinker of the 20th century, the founding father of the French Theory, Alexandre Kojève. Derrida's vision of the globalatinized world draws polemically on the Kojèvian precursorial reflections on the nature of late-modern globalization: instead of the 'universal homogenous state', which according to Kojève, will come at the end of history ultimately won by the Western Christianity, Derrida projects a global empire based on the principle of contamination, which will never erase all the differences and impurities without trace. In the new global era, we will not so much all become Christians as rather Marranos, carrying on in our 'inner hearts' the dirty secret of our non-homogeneity.

According to Kojève, history ends with the universal homogenous state where all differences between races, classes, and individuals become irrelevant, and there is no longer any need for the struggle for recognition, which constituted the only fuel of historical development. When the Christian–Occidental model of globalization becomes hegemonic, all individuals all over the world will be granted the same abstract and inalienable rights for which they will no longer have to fight: this is the law of history, executed with mechanical precision and efficiency, which cannot be counteracted. Derrida partly agrees with this diagnosis—he does not contest the efficiency of the globalatinizing machinery imposing hegemonic homogeneity everywhere—but disagrees with Kojève's proposal, in which he tries to rescue the last 'Greek' remnants of the Master and Slave dialectics and its struggle for recognition.[36] For Derrida, it is rather the desire to live on and survive, the desire not to perish in the global dispersion but, despite the dangerous condition of the universal exile, 'save the name' (one of the possible meanings of Derrida's favourite phrase: *sauf le nom*), which can counteract the machine of the 'wrong' Christian abstraction. He thus envisages the global order as a kind of a *New Alexandria*, an empire which stakes on 'mixtures' and thrives on 'contaminations'. Derrida's question is: can we once again engage in the process of contamination, which would reactivate the differences that have been declared invalid in the 'Christian' abstract model of universalization, yet without the reintroduction of the struggle for recognition, which inevitably ends up in non-democratic forms of social hierarchy? Can we have both: the differences that matter and a purely horizontal plane of their encounters, clashes, interchanges, and intermarriages?

Although critical of the post-Hegelian idiom of universality as 'globalatinization', Derrida is also completely against the isolation of cultures, undertaken in the name of their illusory purity. As we have seen, the true danger to the survival of cultures, traditions, and religions lies not in contamination of the proper with the alien, but in the obsessive warding off the spectre of impurity. The 'radical evil' of the process of 'globalatinization', therefore, consists in the violent clash of the two abstractions: the formal purity of 'a certain Christianity', and its strategy of universalization which confronts the self-defensive 'purity' of indigenous cultures. Yet, Derrida is far from dismissing every universalizing strategy. He openly claims that "we also share [...] an unreserved taste, if not an unconditional preference, for what in politics, is called republican democracy as a universalizable model" (FK, p. 47). Thus, while the critical part of "Faith and Knowledge" consists of the deconstruction of the religious phantasms of purity, present not only in the traditional premodern traditions, but also in the abstract 'certain Christianity' of Kant and Hegel—the constructive part consists of turning our attention to the alternative, Marrano-messianic movement of universalization, which constantly occurs in its modern half-secularized variant.

On Derrida's account, all religions contain in themselves an aporetic tension between particularity and universality. Just like the kabbalistic God of Isaac Luria, they constantly pulsate between contraction, where hey defensively withdraw into their 'most proper' identities, and expansion, where they overreach and messianically appropriate the alien element. In Franz Rosenzweig's *Star*

---

[36]   See most of all (Strauss 2013).

of Redemption, which Derrida knew well and often commented upon, this 'oscillation' takes the form of a division of labour within the Judeo-Christian alliance. While Judaism's role is to contract and keep the message of all Abrahamic religions intact and unscathed in its original purity, the role of Christianity is to expand—proselytize, convert, overreach the pagan world—but then also inevitably risk contamination.[37] According to Rosenzweig, Judaism stays pure, but pays for it with the lack of worldly activity—whereas Christianity is messianically active, but pays for it with the hazard of losing itself in the alien. Derrida also thinks in terms of the Judeo-Christian alliance, though perhaps more tense internally, and assigns the roles differently. Pace Rosenzweig, he perceives Christianity—from Saint Paul through Kant to Hegel—as an abstract internalized faith which, by the very nature of its formal abstractedness, resists any contamination with 'impure' elements. If, therefore, this universalizing variant of Christianity involves the radical internalization of morality, then the Jews are the last stumbling block of resistance to it, strangely though, not from without, but from within the Judeo-Christian 'gathering'. That, Derrida claims, was well spotted by Nietzsche: "The Jews and European Judaism even constituted in his eyes a desperate attempt to resist, in so far as there was any resistance, a last-ditch protest from within, directed against a certain Christianity" (FK, p. 50). Following Nietzsche, Derrida portrays European Judaism in Marrano terms as an internal opposition struggling for a different form of Christianity, irreducible to the abstract internalization advocated by Saint Paul.[38] Jews, always accused of their 'carnal' leanings, which would render them material and not sufficiently spiritual, bear the mark of particularity—yet, in Derrida's reading, it is not a drawback but a chance: a chance to rethink positively the moment of contamination against the phantasm of spiritual purism.[39]

Could it be that, in the end, this seemingly most despised Marrano condition offers the key to a new form of universalization—a kind of Marrano universalism? Perhaps, this is what Derrida has in mind when he poses the question:

> How then to think [...] a religion which, without again becoming 'natural religion', would today be effectively universal? And which, for that matter, would no longer be restricted to a paradigm that was Christian or even Abrahamic? (FK, p. 53)

Neither the 'natural religion' of one universal human nature nor the 'revealed religion' of a particular chosen nation (first Jewish, then European–Christian), this newly thought religion is still 'abstract',

---

[37] See (Rosenzweig 1985), especially Part 3, "Redemption".

[38] Perhaps, it is precisely this 'different Christianity' which has not yet revealed its essence, of which Derrida speaks in the *Gift of Death* about his reflections on Jan Patocka's *Heretical Essays* (Derrida 1995a, pp. 6–7).

[39] There is a myriad of meanings of the Derridean use of the term 'machine', and Michael Naas is very good at listing them, but there is one which he omits, and which seems to play a crucial role in Derrida's essay on religion. For, if miracle is indeed 'breath' (*ruah, souffle*) and life of faith, then machine is law and ritual: the pattern of repetition, in which faith confirms itself in the worldly conditions. However, it is precisely this pattern of repetition which rendered Jewish religion susceptible to the accusation of a 'mechanical obedience', which started with Saint Paul and culminated in Hegel's *Early Theological Writings*: one of the tenets of Derrida's essay is to deconstruct this objection levelled from the angle of the 'genuine faith' or the purely spiritual *Innerlichkeit*. The paradox of this 'authenticity' is that while it derives from the 'religion of the death of God', it nonetheless restores God to pure life in the inner shrine of the soul: as I have shown, the Hegelian 'infinite mourning' (which, being infinite, cannot ever become the complete work of mourning) makes God 'resurrect daily' in the nostalgic effort to compensate for the scandal of his sacrificial death. Whereas Derrida's Marrano argument is that there is nothing to mourn or compensate for: God has died for the world to make it possible—make the 'space available'—and there is no need to repent for it; God has given up on the singular miracle of his life, so that the machine of being could go on; or, in yet other words, God has abandoned his unique idiom for the sake of the strange institution called reality. 'Authenticity', and 'pure faith', therefore, would be the internalized variation on the unscathed *unverletztes Leben*, which, being the force of pure life, is also the force of pure death. And since this equation—pure life is the same as pure death—is also a Hegelian formula, one can also read Derrida's essay as a Hegelian correction of Hegel himself, who, otherwise a dialectical thinker of universal contamination, has to be made free of this one phantasmatic blind spot of 'purity': his theologically driven, Lutheran, investment in *sola fide*, 'pure faith'. As Naas very rightly comments: "Hence faith and knowledge, religion and science, the miracle and the machine, must be thought together as a single possibility, a single possibility that divides or fissures already at the origin. They are not the same thing, but they cannot be thought separately. Both are possible only on the basis of a 'testimonial *deus ex machina*', which always already betrays and displays the duplicity of origins, a *deus* that from the beginning becomes *deux*, at once miracle and machine" (MM, p. 166).

staying close to the source of revealability itself. Yet, its abstraction is to be conceived in a different way than in Kant's formalism or Hegel–Kojève's universal sublation in one global 'religion of the Spirit', in which "the moral law inscribes itself at the bottom of our hearts like a memory of the Passion" (FK, p. 50). Although close to the revealable 'desert in retreat', the new religion is not contentless: it urges its believers to 'wander away from their origins' and to engage in the universalizing process, for, as Derrida says, "in uprooting the tradition that bears it, in atheologizing it, *this* abstraction, without denying faith, *liberates* a universal rationality and political democracy that cannot be dissociated from it" (FK, p. 57; my emphasis). The link between abstraction, in which the content retreats from presence, and liberation is absolutely crucial here: just as the Christian 'memory of the Passion' hinders the abstraction, by indebting the creatures with the moral call to self-sacrifice—the Marrano 'memory of Passover', a dim remembrance of Exodus, liberates creation in a truly emancipatory gesture of *khorein / Seinlassen / tsimtsum*, which then becomes a blue-print for all further liberations: the universal rationality and political democracy to come, which, as Derrida says in *Rogues,* will eventually have been 'like the khora of the political'.[40]

It is, therefore, not abstraction as such that implies the risk of the 'radical evil' (FK, p. 43), but only its wrong form. The danger is twofold: either the abstraction is incomplete, because it is hindered by an 'irrational' cultic moment of the 'memory of the Passion'—or it is too complete in its purely formal aspect of aggressive secularization which literally 'kills God' in the manner of radical Enlightenment, by burning all the mystery with its scorching light: 'denies faith', 'uproots traditions', and 'atheologizes' religions by violently forcing them to comply to 'reason alone'. Another abstraction, on the other hand, allows traditions to wander with it, condensed in a sort of a portable version—as the scroll of Torah that must compensate for the loss of the Temple and the death of the present God; a piece of parchment that can be carried into all places at all time by anyone, once the connection with the sacred space harbouring the divine pleromatic presence had been broken; "an opened pomegranate, one Passover evening, on a tray" (FK, p. 100) or some other 'supporting fragments of memory and custom' (as Yovel calls them), which, like Derrida's tallith, would remind him of the self-absented divine spectre.[41]

7. Conclusions

This type of the Marrano abstraction is not a knowledge that is a priori hostile to faith. To the contrary, when it uproots and atheologizises, it also secures the tradition its true survival. Derrida states this very clearly in the fragment devoted to Yoseph Yerushalmi in *The Archive Fever*: it is only the 'portable' Judaism which is a proper 'Judaism unterminable', i.e., the one that is capable of infinite survival.[42] When it is too rooted in its rituals and too caring about its inner purity; when trying too hard to recreate the lost privileged space and time of the Temple and being too deeply buried in its archives, Judaism (which here is just an example of any tradition concerned about its living-on) ossifies, dies, and lays itself in the 'crypt' as 'Judaism terminable': the one that is destined to perish with its own 'death of God', that is, the demise of the visible cult. Only this Judaism which wanders away from its own origins, boldly jumps the 'fences around the Torah', being raised by the all-too protective rabbis, confronts other traditions, marries all languages under the sun, and lets them speak Hebrew as if from within, as the Marranos did, allowing the tradition to survive. This is because tradition, as the very etymology suggests, thrives only on treasons—and dies from too much awe, faithfulness, and untouchable indemnity. This dialectical movement between particularity and universality is what Walter Benjamin, in full accordance with Scholem, defines as the very essence of *Tradierbarkeit*:

---

[40] (Derrida 2005b, p. 44).

[41] It must, therefore, be emphasized that, for Derrida, the tallith is not a symbolic part of the sacramental whole, where the external elements of liturgy complement the internal element of faith. It is not an external symbol of the internal faith, where the two form an integral cotemporaneous totality. Derrida's tallith is detached and 'abstracted' from its religious context, and functions as a mnemonic device, the role of which is to remind of the almost-forgotten, by-gone, and concealed God. In that sense, it is rather a Benjaminian allegory, taken out of the 'tradition in ruins', than a living sacramental symbol.

[42] (Derrida 1996, pp. 74–100).

passing on the tradition through its inevitable betrayal. By opening the traditional isolated 'gene pool' to 'mixture' and 'contamination', translation simultaneously preserves it and puts at risk—yet, this very risk is nothing but life itself.[43] Thus, when contracted–condensed–abstracted to its most dense 'portable' minimum; when shrunk by this radical *tsimtsum*, which separates the Marrano from every visible/revealed cult, the Marrano tradition turns out to be nothing but the teaching of the universal messianic justice, following the example of the ever-retreating kenomatic source: "this justice, which I distinguish from right, alone allows hope, beyond all 'messianisms', of a universalizable culture of singularities, a culture in which the abstract possibility of the *impossible translation* could nevertheless be announced" (FK, p. 56; my emphasis).

In the New Alexandria, therefore, universality can be reached only from a particular standpoint, even though it is a point of departure that is only to be shaken in the final act of 'burning the archives' and letting them survive solely in the scattered form of cinders, which remembers only in and through forgetting. This is the main theme of *The Archive Fever*, but is also the subject of last paragraph of "Faith and Knowledge" which we have already quoted, and which compares the Marrano survival to the 'dispersion of ashes' (FK, p. 100). Here, however, the nostalgic-mournful perspective must be decisively rejected. The Marranos—uprooted from any overt religious identity, atheologized to the limit of the 'almost-atheism', deprived of any cultic piety, and withdrawn into the secret of their 'inner hearts', always on the brink of self-denial and self-oblivion—are not the victims of global modernization, which indeed may be said to have begun with the 15th century 'Marrano experience'.[44] Derrida's intention is to invert this negative image, and to present the Marranos, the people without de-nomination and hence 'without name', as the harbingers of a possible universal faith that will speak simultaneously all the archival, long-forgotten languages (like Hebrew), and a new idiom of the future yet to come:

> On the bottom without bottom of an always virgin impassibility, *khora* of tomorrow in languages we no longer know or do not yet speak. This place is unique, it is the One without name. (FK, p. 100)

Funding: An essay written thanks to the support of NCN Opus 13 Grant: *The Marrano Phenomenon: The Jewish 'Hidden Tradition' and Modernity*, registered in the OSF system as 2017/25/B/HS2/02901.

Conflicts of Interest: The author declares no conflict of interest.

References

Abraham, Nicolas, and Maria Torok. 1994. *The Shell and the Kernel*. Edited and Translated by Nicholas T. Rand. Chicago: The University of Chicago Press, vol. 1.

Benjamin, Walter. 2003a. The Task of the Translator. In *Selected Writings*. Edited by Howard Eiland and Michael W. Jennings. Cambridge: Harvard University Press, vol. 1.

Benjamin, Walter. 2003b. On Language as Such of Man and the Language of Man. In *Selected Writings*. Edited by Howard Eiland and Michael W. Jennings. Cambridge: Harvard University Press, vol. 1.

Bielik-Robson, Agata. 2014. *Jewish Cryptotheologies of Late Modernity. Philosophical Marranos*. London and New York: Routledge.

Bielik-Robson, Agata. 2017a. Burn After Reading: Derrida, the Philosophical Marrano. In *Divisible Derridas*. Edited by Victor E. Taylor and Stephen Nichols. Colorado: Davies Publication Group (Emergence), pp. 51–70.

---

[43] See (Benjamin 2003a, p. 257). For Benjamin, the translation works as *die Ergänzung*, or the completion, where it is simultaneously a contaminating and completing agent, gesturing towards the elusive totality of the 'pure language'—the living *lingua adamica* that Benjamin talks about in his essay "On Language as Such of Man and the Language of Man"—which can only be partly reflected in the fragmented languages of the 'post-Babelian' condition: "All higher language is a translation of lower ones, until in ultimate clarity the word of God unfolds, which is the unity of this movement made up of language" (Benjamin 2003b, p. 74).

[44] See (Yovel 2009, p. 61), where the Marrano is described as the first modern "type [of man] that lives beyond the spheres of conventional belief and mentality".

Bielik-Robson, Agata. 2017b. God of Luria, Hegel, Schelling: The Divine Contraction and the Modern Metaphysics of Finitude. In *Mystical Theology & Continental Philosophy*. Edited by David Lewin, Simon D. Podmore and Duane Williams. London and New York: Routledge, pp. 32–30.

Cixous, Helene. 2007. The Stranjew Body. In *Judeities. Questions for Jacques Derrida*. Edited by Joseph Cohen and Raphael Zagury-Orly. Translated by Bettina Bergo, and Michael B. Smith. New York: Fordham University Press.

Derrida, Jacques. 1981. *Dissemination*. Translated by Barbara Johnson. Chicago: The University of Chicago Press.

Derrida, Jacques. 1986a. *Glas*. Translated by John P. Leavey, and Richard Rand. Lincoln and London: Nebraska University Press.

Derrida, Jacques. 1986b. Fors. In *Wolf Man's Magic Word: A Cryptonymy*. Translated by Nicholas Rand. Minneapolis: Minnesota University Press.

Derrida, Jacques. 1993. Circumfession. In *Jacques Derrida and Geoffrey Bennington, Jacques Derrida*. Translated by Geoffrey Bennington. Chicago: The University of Chicago Press.

Derrida, Jacques. 1995a. *The Gift of Death*. Translated by David Willis. Chicago: The University of Chicago Press.

Derrida, Jacques. 1995b. *On the Name*. Translated by John P. Leavey. Stanford: Stanford University Press.

Derrida, Jacques. 1996. *Archive Fever. A Freudian Impression*. Translated by Eric Prenowitz. Chicago: The University of Chicago Press.

Derrida, Jacques. 1999. Marx and Sons. In *Ghostly Demarcations. A Symposium on Jacques Derrida's "Specters of Marx"*. Edited by Michael Sprinker. Translated by G. M. Goshgarian. London: Verso.

Derrida, Jacques. 2002. Faith and Knowledge. The Two Sources of 'Religion' at the Limits of Reason Alone. In *Acts of Religion*. Translated by Gil Anidjar. New York and London: Routledge.

Derrida, Jacques. 2005a. *On Touching—Jean-Luc Nancy*. Translated by Christine Irizarry. Stanford: Stanford University Press.

Derrida, Jacques. 2005b. *Rogues. Two Essays on Reason*. Translated by Pascale-Anne Brault. Stanford: Stanford University Press.

Derrida, Jacques. 2005c. *Sovereignties in Question. The Poetics of Paul Celan*. Translated by Thomas Dutoit, and Outi Passanen. New York: Fordham University Press.

Derrida, Jacques. 2007. Abraham, The Other. In *Judeities. Questions for Jacques Derrida*. Edited by Joseph Cohen and Raphael Zagury-Orly. Translated by Bettina Bergo, and Michael B. Smith. New York: Fordham University Press.

Hägglund, Martin. 2008. *Radical Atheism. Derrida and the Time of Life*. Stanford: Stanford University Press.

Hegel, Georg Wilhelm Friedrich. 1975. *Aesthetics. Lectures on Fine Art*. Translated by Thomas Malcolm Knox. Oxford: Oxford University Press.

Hegel, Georg Wilhelm Friedrich. 1976. *Phenomenology of Spirit*. Translated by Arnold Vincent Miller. Oxford: Oxford University Press.

Hegel, Georg Wilhelm Friedrich. 1977. *Faith and Knowledge*. Translated by Walter Cerf, and Henry Silton Harris. Albany: SUNY Press.

Lacan, Jacques. 1989. *Ecrits. A Selection*. Translated by Alan Sheridan. London: Routledge.

Naas, Michael. 2008. *Derrida from Now on*. New York: Fordham University Press.

Naas, Michael. 2012. *Miracle and Machine*. New York: Fordham University Press.

Nancy, Jean-Luc. 2008a. *Corpus*. Translated by Richard Rand. New York: Fordham University Press.

Nancy, Jean-Luc. 2008b. *Dis-Enclosure. The Deconstruction of Christianity*. Translated by Bettina Bergo. New York: Fordham University Press.

Rosenzweig, Franz. 1985. *The Star of Redemption*. Translated by William W. Hallo. Notre Dame and London: University of Notre Dame Press.

Sherwood, Yvonne. 2014. Specters of Abraham. In *Judaism in Contemporary Thought: Traces and Influence*. Edited by Agata Bielik-Robson and Adam Lipszyc. London: Routledge.

Scholem, Gershom. 1973. Zehn Unhistorische Sätze über Kabbala. In *Judaica 3, Studien Zur Jüdischen Mystik*. Frankfurt am Main: Suhrkamp Verlag.

Scholem, Gershom. 1976. *On Jews and Judaism in Crisis. Selected Essays*. Edited by Werner Dannhauser. New York: Schocken Books.

Scholem, Gershom. 1995. *The Messianic Idea in Judaism. And Other Essays on Jewish Spirituality*. New York: Schocken Books.

Strauss, Leo. 2013. *On Tyranny: Corrected and Expanded Edition, Including the Strauss-Kojève Correspondence.* Translated by Victor Gourevitch. Chicago: The University of Chicago Press.

Yovel, Yirmiyahu. 2009. *The Other Within. The Marranos: Split Idenity and Emerging Modernity.* Princeton and Oxford: Princeton University Press.

Wolfson, Elliott. 2006. *Alef, Mem, Tau. Kabbalistic Musings on Time, Truth, and Death.* Berkeley: University of California Press.

religions

MDPI

Article

Thank God We Are Creatures: Hannah Arendt's Cryptotheology

Rafael Zawisza

Faculty of Artes Liberales, University of Warsaw, ul. Nowy Świat 69, 00-046 Warszawa, Poland; rafal.w.zawisza@gmail.com

Received: 1 October 2018; Accepted: 13 November 2018; Published: 19 November 2018

check for
updates

Abstract: Main concern of this article is to grasp the interpretative matrix of Hannah Arendt's doctorate, which, I claim, is the central organising net for her other writings. I call this matrix "cryptotheological defence of the secular world". In order to show its functionality, I have to determine the character of Arendt's discourse in relation to theology and philosophy on the basis of her doctoral thesis from 1929. The main attention will be focused on the figure of the neighbour as a singular and the concept of natality. I will show how the critique of theology, often very ironic, serves Arendt to contest the paradigm of the political theology.

Keywords: Hannah Arendt; Augustine of Hippo; creatureliness; neighbour; post-secularism; cryptotheology; marrano; transcendence; singularity

---

> *Die Welt war schlechthin unabsolut geworden. Nicht bloß der Mensch, nein auch Gott konnte außer ihren Grenzen, wenn anders er wollte, Platz finden. Diese metalogische Welt bot aber, gerade weil sie gottlos war, keinen Schutz gegen Gott.*
>
> Franz Rosenzweig, *Der Stern der Erlösung* (Rosenzweig 1921, p. 23)

After having read numerous texts about Hannah Arendt's doctoral thesis *Der Liebesbegriff bei Augustin*, I came to a conclusion that we need a new interpretation of it. It is a rule that scholars insisting on Arendt's secularism do not have an idea how to integrate the confusing dissertation into her oeuvre. There is a temptation to avoid this inconvenience by stating that between the doctorate and her next major work, *The Origins of Totalitarianism*—which means between 1929 and 1951—there was a decisive break. I am not going to contest the facts and claim that there was no change, that the horrific time of totalitarian rulership, exile, and war did not put an imprint on Hannah Arendt. But to announce the break and neglect her first work would be nothing but an excuse. An excuse that makes her work easier to understand, even to use or widespread, nonetheless it would mean that a galvanised image of Arendt as political theorist will become more and more a cliché and an obstacle to revive her thought for future generations.

There is no historical evidence of what motivated Hannah Arendt to choose the topic of the dissertation. Laure Adler claims that it was meeting Rudolf Bultmann at his seminar on the New Testament, which coloured Arendt decision. It was apparently thanks to him that she discovered Augustine for herself (Adler 2008, p. 62). However, other scholars insist on the primary role of Heidegger. Jacques Taminiaux intended to show that Heidegger's lectures on Aristotle made an impression on the young Arendt (Taminiaux 1997). Luca Savarino attempted to underline an impact of Heidegger's lectures from 1920 to 1921 (introduction to the phenomenology of religion as well as the lecture about Augustine and Neo-Platonism), although Savarino emphasises that there is no certainty whether Arendt was familiar with the content of those lectures, which she did not attend (Savarino 1999, pp. 251–61). Various influences do not exclude each other, which is why one may also mention Hans Jonas, who as a very good friend of Arendt's was elaborating his thesis *Augustin und das paulinische Freiheitsproblem: Ein philosophischer Beitrag zur Genesis der christlich-abendländischen Freiheitsidee*, finished in 1930.

Hannah Arendt's doctoral dissertation was defended in autumn 1928 in Freiburg and published by Julius Springer in Berlin in 1929 under the title *Der Liebesbegriff bei Augustin: Versuch einer philosophischen Interpretation*. It was part of a series which was soon to be closed and where Karl Jaspers helped his students to publish their thesis. Scarcity of time, which Arendt complained to Jaspers about, could explain the dense and inconclusive character of the third part: *Vita socialis*. However, there were graver problems that the young author encountered and somehow left unresolved, while still being able to draw up a map, which would delineate her later concerns.

For hermeneutical reasons, there is one decisive issue I have to explain at the start. Hannah Arendt worked on the translation of her dissertation into English in the late 1950s and early 1960s. It was a translation by Ernst Basch Ashton, which she received to approve and which she corrected a lot, going as far as to amend the whole text, except the last part, *Vita socialis*, which she left unchanged. Again, it is not certain why Arendt gave up at certain point, as a result of which the translation needed to wait for publication until 1996. In a letter from 20 October 1965 to Mary McCarthy, Arendt gave an impression of how she felt about the encounter with her prewar text:

> *I got myself into something absurd—Macmillan had asked me years ago for my dissertation on Augustine. I needed the money (not really, but could use it) and said yes. The translation arrived two years ago and now I ran out of excuses and have to go over it. It is kind of a traumatic experience. I am re-writing the whole darned business, trying not to do anything new, but only to explain in English (and not in Latin) what I thought when I was twenty. It is probably not worth it and I should simply return the money—but by now I am strangely fascinated in this rencontre. I had not read the thing for nearly forty years. (Arendt and McCarthy 1995, p. 190)*

The differences between the German original from 1929 and Arendt's amendments from the 1950s and 1960s to the English translation of her dissertation constitute a topic in itself. Here I analyse the final shape of her doctorate, claiming that its complex development only confirmed that what Arendt had written in the late 1920s then became the cryptotheological matrix, where initial intuition only crystallised and from which it was widespread throughout her various writings. I am persuaded that scrupulous, "Talmudic" work on the comparison of the German and English editions, all existing corrections included, is necessary and that it is a work waiting for its author. Yet, as for the aim and structure of my thesis, this is not of high importance. First of all, the most essential part of Arendt's dissertation, namely the third chapter entitled *Vita socialis*, was published in English edition as a direct translation of the original from 1929, because Arendt did not introduce any changes to this part. As for the two previous chapters, I analyse original as well as added fragments, treating them as one migrating entity. What I mean by that is that the ideas present in the first edition were only developed more fully in the 1950s and 1960s, thus there is no break or shift that could make this historical process of migration of ideas problematic for my reconstruction. What constitutes *the* genuine shift already in the 1920s is *Vita socialis*. To summarize, I was considering dividing the material by commenting on the original and on the amendments separately, but I decided that the advantages of this option are few and the risk of producing chaos—quite predictable (due to necessity of constantly clarifying which version of Arendt's dissertation I refer to—and then to integrate some complex lines of argumentation). In my opinion, natalism is the undercurrent of Arendt's thought, originating in her doctoral thesis, that is why it is not controversial to see this in holistic perspective. What would be of high importance is to grasp the moments in her texts written after publication of *The Origins* (1951), which were influenced by her return to her dissertation since the 1950s. I only mark this fact here in order to demonstrate the processes of translations and transmissions. The specific texts at stake are the last chapter of *The Origins—Ideology and Terror*—added to the second edition (1958) but written in the middle in the 1950s as well as *The Human Condition* (1958). *On Revolution* (1963) in this perspective appears as the elaborate response to the dilemmas and aporias which haunted Arendt when she was preparing *Vita socialis*.

Richard Wolin calls Arendt's dissertation "a strikingly un-Arendtian document (…) [in which—RZ] the inflections of her mature philosophical voice are barely audible. It is a work of a disciple, narrowly textual in orientation and focus, devoid of the originality that would characterize her subsequent work" (Wolin 2001, pp. 42–43). Wolin disregards the fact that the whole Arendtian anthropology was germinating in her first book. He uses schematic explanation, which shows how little he understood from *Der Liebesbegriff*; Wolin thinks that because of Augustine's otherworldliness, young Arendt—as lost in Augustinian worldview—could not be reconciled with her later insistence on worldliness. In sum, he overlooks that it was precisely in Augustine that Arendt intended to find commitment to the world despite having declared rejection of it. His second argument, that transcendence contradicts plurality, also shows rather Wolin's own misconception and in consequence it obnubilates Arendt's dialectic attitude towards theological tradition. Only on the basis of his interpretative failure could Wolin not only separate *Der Liebesbegriff* from her later thought, but he could also claim that in *Rahel Varnhagen* Arendt rejected her first work as concentrated on introspection (Wolin 2001, p. 44). I would rather insist that despite her scepticism about the force of inwardness, she did not dismiss its role altogether.

Kurt Sontheimer found *Der Liebesbegriff* more promising, calling it "the first important, but not particularly original step towards intellectual independence" (Sontheimer 2005, p. 31). It is characteristic that the dissertation is underestimated either by the secular interpreters, or by theological ones, who have a tendency to ascribe everything valuable to Augustine and see Arendt in a minor position of, for example, Heidegger's "child" or Augustine's "daughter". John Kiess, as one of the few commentators representing theology, felt compelled to protest against those attempts at diminishment: "as with Heidegger, Arendt appropriated and criticized elements of Augustine's work with the same spirit of independence that will mark her engagement with many other thinkers" (Kiess 2016, p. 21). It is even more than to say that Arendt was "a qualified Augustinian" (Clarke and Quill 2009, p. 254).

It is not unimportant how we understand Arendt's stance towards the Augustinian legacy, and later, how we estimate what happened after World War II at her first encounter with Augustine's thought. I agree with Joanna Vecchiarelli Scott, who states that Arendt's perseverating references to Augustine "are central to her argument and cannot be easily dismissed as scholastic decoration or the afterglow of an early flirtation with idealism for the most part outgrown" (Vecchiarelli Scott 1988, p. 398). As we will see, Arendt built on a certain logic of thought already inscribed in her doctoral thesis. "This text—Étienne Tassin writes—is seminal: it fecundates [irrigue] all the future works, including capturing the distance which it induces" (Tassin and Albanel 2010, p. 11). It was, however, not only the logic of argumentation, but also the set of problems she found in Augustine which she regarded as pressing on her own contemporaneity. The questions were not so much originally Augustinian, but rather revived in different thematic constellations. That is why I abstain from calling Arendt an Augustinian of any sort. She deeply distorted his reflections and did not read him as a theologian. Those who regard *Der Liebesbegriff* as a work dependent on Augustine and theology are probably confused by its form, un-Arendtian indeed. If one does not follow the lines of argumentation rigorously and does not pay attention to the details, it seems that the author of the dissertation is a commentator of the great thinker of the past. By quoting Augustine extensively, Arendt made the impression that she was totally immersed into the analysed material. But this was precisely her strategy: to show, through close reading, inconsequences and aporias. They would not appear as problematic points without Hannah Arendt's unique position of speaking, which gave her freedom to compose Augustine's thought in the way she did it and not otherwise. Arendt's seemingly "humble" role of commentator submerged her extremely critical voice. Yet, again, this voice is so subtly ironic and her criticism so embedded in the structure of the book, that it is easy to disregard it.

Apart from the problem of inventiveness of early Arendt, there are two other issues: her potentially political stance and her attitude to theology. Ronald Beiner writes: "What the Augustine book may indicate is that Arendt was a political philosopher before she knew that she was one" (Beiner 1997, p. 270). My task is to radicalise this statement by showing how deeply political her earliest concerns about the love of the neighbour and relations of the individual torn between God and world were.[1] I am not going to contest the thesis that Rahel Varnhagen's biography was Arendt's first political book, properly speaking (Armenteros 1999, p. 86), and indicated the period when she became politically conscious and began to deal seriously with history, law, and politics. Yet, I strongly disagree with Carolina Armenteros' unjust qualifications of *Der Liebesbegriff* as a "highly abstract existential exercise" (Armenteros 1999, p. 87).

Arendt's doctoral thesis has much to offer when it comes to an *anthropology of political theory*, i.e., more "pre-political" or "meta-political" reflections; however, this does not mean that it is less relevant in that regard. Conversely, what I call "pre-political" is what was reflected by Arendt herself under the term "pre-theological sphere" (*die vortheologische Sphäre*; Arendt 1929, p. 3). The sphere prior to any religion and its theological self-understanding constitutes a battlefield with the paradigm of political theology, which makes politics dependent on certain theological origin.

It is probably not astonishing that Arendt's dissertation has not found its full recognition. Among both religious and secular commentators there is no agreement whether young Arendt was more theological or philosophical. I found some paradox as indicative, namely that a Jesuit claims that "Hannah Arendt never writes theology" (Boyle 1987, p. 96), while a secular scholar does not hesitate to report about "Arendt's youthful flirtation with theology" (Moyn 2008, p. 71). Some resolution would be to count Arendt among "nontheologians practicing theology" (Biale 2011, p. 9), as David Biale shortened Amos Funkenstein's definition of the "secular theology". However, what interests me the most is "her consequent ability to live with creative confusion" (Neiman 2001, p. 72). That is why I am inclined to think about Hannah Arendt as a representative of the group named by Agata Bielik-Robson "the philosophical Marranos" (Bielik-Robson 2014).

Only by referring to this complex approach it would be possible to reintegrate *Der Liebesbegriff* within the context of politico-theological debates of the Weimar period.[2] In order to do that, however, a move backwards is necessary, which grasps the dissertation in its microcosm. The subtlety necessary to decipher Arendtian cryptotheological secularism usually escapes theological interpretations.[3] Even though secular interpretations are closer to the point, they remain incomplete without acknowledgement that, in defending secularity, Arendt sought help by both secular and theological means. That is why Samuel Moyn in his otherwise excellent article about Arendt and the secular marvels over the fact that she acceded biblical provenance for the model of political promise and calls this idea "rather shocking" (Moyn 2008, p. 86). The concept of natality poses a similar difficulty for Moyn, as he thinks that it is too religiously burdened and because of that it incurs a risk of the Schmittian critique (Moyn 2008, p. 96). I claim exactly the opposite: that Arendt's familiarity with theology and her philosophy of birth makes the attack on the political theology all the more crushing. Political theology is deconstructed by the introduction of the third element, preceding both theology and politics: anthropology. What is more, the appreciation of the human birth in its anti-naturalist specificity serves to contest the political implications of the doctrine of the original sin, on which Christian political theology relied.

---

[1] For the picture of the tensions in Weimar Germany due to religious divisions, see the sociological-historical summary of Todd H. Weir (Weir 2015). He depicted intrareligious battles, but also a campaign against secularism, which helped Hitler come to power. The author also described the Catholic ambivalent reaction to Nazism and vice versa, the reasons why Protestants supported Hitler more than Catholics, or how Catholics mimed communist organisations in order to combat them. What is missing in Weir's article is the role of the Jews.

[2] The first step in this direction was already taken, see (Chacón 2012).

[3] The discussion about Arendt and theology did not reach full-scale until Jesuits from Boston edited the volume *Amor mundi* (Bernauer 1987a). Nevertheless, there was no further resonance, probably because this volume, containing many deep insights notwithstanding, is charged by apologetic intentions.

1. Pretheological Sphere

Arendt's dissertation was "guided by the question of the meaning and importance of neighbourly love in particular" (Arendt 1996, p. 3). Knowing her sense of irony, this could implicitly indicate that despite the fact that this was one of Augustine's central concerns, his theological vision of God and its philosophical antecedents had overridden essentiality of the neighbour. The fact that Arendt's recapitulation of Augustine's views was intended to be an accompanying critique from the very beginning is reinforced by the following statement:

> *Augustine's every perception and every remark about love refer at least in part to this love of neighbor. Thus the question about the neighbor's relevance always turns into a simultaneous critique of the prevailing concept of love and of man's attitude toward himself and toward God. (Arendt 1996, p. 3)*

Taking into account her overall deconstruction of the Augustinian concepts, Arendt could not have been much more overt about her intentions in the introduction. Otherwise, it would have been seen as a gross effrontery—after all, she was just a doctoral student at that time.[4]

Arendt's initial remarks conceal a polemical approach, without the detection of which the whole interpretation of her work would bog down. She very often pretended that she was just summarizing Augustine's ideas, while in fact she adopted his views in order to turn them against themselves. For instance, when she said: "This critique will never be an absolute critique from some fixed philosophical or theological standpoint. It is a critique only because the respective concept of love claims to be a Christian one" (Arendt 1996, p. 3). In other words, Arendt's intention is to check to what extent Augustine's argumentation sticks to the teachings of Christianity.

She estimated that Augustine had been "truly religious rather than determined by Neoplatonic Greek influences" (Arendt 1996, p. 4). By saying that Arendt only payed off a debt to biographical truth, to Augustine's inner intentions,[5] which, however, did not find its road to fulfilment throughout Greek categories.[6] Heterogeneous influences together with "heterogeneous intentions" brought about the effect of "disjointedness", and for that reason Arendt applied her "systematic approach in detail" so that "a substantially common base" (Arendt 1996, p. 4) could be grasped. In no case did she intend to synthetize Augustine's divergent trains of thought—on the contrary, she made crevices on this common surface perfectly visible, without any attempt to reconcile them in antithetical or dialectical form. The ironic impetus of Arendt's analysis employs what we could call "double negative dialectics",[7] which is able to maintain contradictions in motion, following life's own rhythm that defends itself from stopping, ending, and dispersing.

Nonetheless, irony does not exclude seriousness, related to this so far quite mysterious "substantially common base" located within "pretheological sphere". Ironic impulses serve to uncover it, yet not allowing to determine it as the ultimate ground. On the other hand, as we will see later, it is just because of this ultimate, drifting ground that the common base could appear as common. Arendt's interpretative strategy relies on "making explicit what Augustine himself has merely implied", meaning that in order to treat him more seriously, one needs a detachment from "Augustine's dogmatic

---

4   I would not, however, go so far as Richard Wolin did, who says: "In certain respects, the work stand out as an embarrassing testimonial to the delusions of assimilationism. It was written at a point in Arendt's life when she still entertained hopes of a university career amid the woefully conservative milieu of German academic mandarins" (Wolin 2001, p. 43). As reflected in her prewar letters with Jaspers, Arendt was very straightforward and fierce in her critique. She quarrelled with Jaspers about his political stance towards Jews in the 1930s. Moreover, Hans Jonas preserved a memory of her audacious behaviour at the university: before joining Rudolf Bultmann's seminar on the New Testament, she as a Jew wanted to make sure that she would not listen to anti-Semitic remarks. Joanna Vecchiarelli Scott poses a rhetorical question, asking who among the Weimar era students dared behave so boldly towards the mandarins of German academia (Vecchiarelli Scott 2010, p. 16)?

5   "For Augustine this relevance [of the neighbour—RZ] was simply a matter of course" (Arendt 1996, p. 4).

6   Arendt explained one of the aporias found in the analysed texts by saying that "the reason for this incongruity lies in Augustine's terminology, which he took from the tradition of Greek philosophy even when he wished to express experiences that were quite alien to it" (Arendt 1996, p. 12).

7   Derived from simultaneous absorption and negation of life's "not yet" and "no more": "This questioning beyond the world rests on the double negative into which life is placed" (Arendt 1996, p. 70).

subservience to scriptural and ecclesiastical authority" (Arendt 1996, p. 4). The thing which from a dogmatic position seems to be ironic, blasphemous, and heretic, could actually be a polemical struggle for true seriousness (in this case: in treating one's own neighbour). Nevertheless, Arendt did not defend any polemics with orthodoxy as simply justified in itself thanks to be antidogmatic. This is crucial, because it is hard to attack her stance as simple reversal, revaluation of values, etc. Instead, she admitted that "such intentional detachment from all dogmatic elements may doom the interpretation of a religious author, but is relatively easy to justify in Augustine's case" (Arendt 1996, p. 4).

The way that Arendt emphasized autonomy of the secular realm against the divine one is so subversive that one can probably understand the following conclusion only as an excuse that could have left a naïve reader mistaken: "Of course, these presentations will not prove whether, in fact, such a pretheological sphere is to be justified as all, or whether the possible being or not being of human existence is truly settled in God's presence" (Arendt 1996, p. 6). Partially, this statement could signify that Arendt's "attempt at an inquiry of purely philosophical interest" (Arendt 1996, p. 6)—as she called her dissertation—does not encroach upon territory reserved for theology. But it is not clear how Arendt could maintain the purity of this division, since she acknowledged that even in his most religious writings Augustine "never wholly lost the impulse of philosophical questioning" (Arendt 1996, p. 6). Moreover, in *Der Liebesbegriff* the essential theoretical battles were conducted precisely in the midst of theology, using theological reasoning, drawing conclusions from it to the point of absurdity.

That Arendt manoeuvred between secular and religious reading of theological discourse, provoking its destabilisation, becomes visible in her introduction of the term the "pretheological sphere". It is not only that she assumed that theological edifice rests on philosophy, but—more profoundly—that it always rests on a certain anthropology, as it derives from anthropological sources, and finally from the time out of mind. That is why, according to the double negative dialectics, she secularised theology, and granted religion a position higher than earthly authority, at the same time dismantling the theocratic stalemate with this singular move. By this I mean that she extracted the most precious element from theology in order to catapult it into "heavens" of ideals. The religious experience and theological discourse are not excluded, but separated. The former concerns strictly inner reality, the latter would inspire the world if it only could illuminate existence without demanding a certain *credo*. Since the second option is barely possible, Arendt chose a philosophical "contraband" instead of a reversal of theology. Those restrictions explain why Arendt's immediate reaction to any possibility of the absolute to appear consisted of strengthening divisions and buffer zones. Arendt quoted Augustine:

> They have not understood that 'Do not do to another what you do not wish to have done to you', cannot be varied in any way by any national diversity of customs. When this rule is applied to the love of God, all vices die; when it is applied to the love of our neighbor, all crimes vanish. (Arendt 1996, pp. 4–5)

However, Arendt's comment distorted the Augustinian text beyond recognition. She wrote:

> Preceding the express commandment of neighborly love is another that is independent of any such explicit divine revelation that has become real in Christ. This is the 'law written in our hearts.' The Christian commandment sharpens this 'natural' law, and thus enhances the human community to its highest reality in which all crimes are extinguished. Therefore, we shall be able to limit the scope of interpretation in two ways without being dogmatic. First, we shall ask about this pretheological sphere. Second, we shall seek to grasp what Augustine's exegesis would regard as the specific novelty in the Christian elaboration. (Arendt 1996, p. 5)

Here, her reading of Augustine, the anti-Pelagian author, is thoroughly Pelagian. In the first quotation, that from Augustine, divine law implants itself on the common moral basis, free from cultural contexts; it is a narrative conducted by the demands of the economy of salvation, which explains how the

Christian faith only strengthens what was already prepared within pagan ethics, waiting for the divine message. Arendt did not undermine this narrative, she just changed perspective: if a "law written in our hearts" lasted for centuries without Christian revelation, this undoubtedly means that it was independent from any revelation. "Through philosophical work with ideas the author wants to justify her freedom from Christian possibilities, which also attract her" (Arendt and Jaspers 1992, p. 690)—as Karl Jaspers wrote in a review, being the supervisor of Arendt's thesis. That is why she emphasised the element as autonomous from excessively demanding Christian ethics, not calling it "pagan" or "Jewish", but rather—"the pretheological", prior to any institutionalized religion, the "natural, prereligious, and secular law" (Arendt 1996, p. 39). Her reservation regarding Christianity is full of respect and justified only from the point of view of a Marranic cryptotheology that Arendt secretly activated in her dissertation. The Christian message is renounced not because it is false, but because it is all too soon.[8] Double negative dialectics allows to keep divinity at distance[9], which is not necessarily an atheistic gesture, but a more pious one than that which is usually taken as religious. To keep God at distance implies prevention of any divinisation of earthly reality. This is the reason why Arendt took "natural" in quotes, using the term "'natural' law" (Arendt 1996, p. 5)[10] (even though in this particular context this natural law would be in tune with her defence of secularity). However, secularity in this version is devoid of sanctity: consequently, secularisation could not be equalled with a robbery, usurpation, or inheritance of any sacral "property". Thus, a "substitutional dilemma" (Moyn 2008, p. 77) could be avoided and not neglected.

2. Nature

De-divinization of nature by means of the notion of transcendent God governs the thinking of Franz Rosenzweig, who was the greatest unmentioned precursor of Arendt when she was preparing *Der Liebesbegriff*. For Rosenzweig, nonidentity of "world" and "nature"[11] (Rosenzweig 2005, p. 23) protects a human being's freedom, ultimately guaranteed in the analogous, paradigmatic separation of God from the world:

> *The condition of creature, which we have claimed for the world in order to save the selfness of man, therefore let God, too, escape from the world. Metaethical man is the fermentation that breaks down the logical and physical unity of the cosmos into the metalogical world and the metaphysical God.* (Rosenzweig 2005, p. 22)

For man confronted face to face with nature renders to be "not a creature, but a part" (Arendt 1996, p. 69), a part of nature whose totality obtrudes as crushing if there is nothing to counterbalance it. It obtrudes itself upon individuality to the extent that it hollows inwardness out, resulting in the denigration of the subject. On the contrary, Arendt emptied individuality out of natural content, leaving free space for ethical life. "If he [man—RZ] could be said to have an essential nature at all, it would be lack of self-sufficiency" (Arendt 1996, p. 19). It means that the human condition is undetermined,

---

8   I will demonstrate the validity of the terms "Marranic" and "Judeochristian" later. Here I may add a hypothesis, which I am unable to prove within the scope of this text, but which, nonetheless, inspired my interpretation, namely that the model of Arendt's hidden theological imagination could be found in the idea of a withdrawn God (*tzimtzum*) as it is known from the Lurianic Kabbalah. The hypothesis is verifiable textually through Arendt's intellectual exchange with Gershom Scholem, which started in the late 1930s. As for the earlier possible sources of this influence one could indicate Franz Rosenzweig. It is also not excluded that Arendt might have inherited certain heterodox ideas through German idealism, especially via dialectical theology, and if so, the term "Judeochristian" would gain additional legitimisation in interpretation of Arendt's oeuvre. All in all, what is crucial for the current presentation is that according to the 20th century re-appropriations of the Lurianic theological narrative by the German-Jewish thinkers, the secular character of secularity seems to be the only trace of divine chosenness. As for the importance of the Arendt–Scholem correspondence for the Lurianic hypothesis, see a marvellous study of Vivian Liska (Liska 2017).

9   I elaborated this idea for the first time in an article from 2012, see (Zawisza 2012).

10   Catholic scholars lament on Arendt and blame her of being ignorant when it comes to the natural law, just like if they were unable to understand that some intelligent people can reject a hypothesis of natural law, having in mind alternative theories of human self-constitution. (See Winters 1987, pp. 197, 203, 217; Kampowski 2008, p. 265).

11   Just like in *Truth and Politics*, Arendt made a distinction between "politics" and "world", seeing the latter as more voluminous.

unknown, but not in a sense that we need more knowledge to capture it fully one day; it is unknown because it is endlessly, irreversibly deepened and complicated by language and enigmatic inscriptions into inwardness. Human being is born as a stranger into nature, and for that reason she can never return to a fictive natural harmony, neither could she recognise a "natural law" emanating from the cosmos, which lost its sacral status after the Gnostic tendency of the "Jewish-Christian teaching" (Arendt 1996, p. 52) had banished cosmotheism. From then on, any normative proposal based on the Greek notion of "nature" (*physis*) and its "pseudo-Christian" (Arendt 1996, p. 30) adaptation under the name of "order" (*ordo*) as an "everlasting, forever lawful structure" (Arendt 1996, p. 61)—is invalid. Paradise remains forever lost.

This problematic finds its realisation in the section of Arendt's dissertation entitled *Ordinata dilectio*. It is the most unpersuasive part of the whole book—not so much because Arendt had no idea how to play it out, but because she was not convinced at all by Augustine's argumentation, and exposed her deep reservation performatively; she seemingly tried to proceed this argumentation, but the way she did so rendered it thin. It is a parody. At first glance, ordered love seems to be an antidote for previously presented, unpredictable bursts of passion towards the Other which ended with self-destruction. It is a perfect "regulatory point of reference" (Arendt 1996, p. 37) providing tools for regulations, adaptations, and ordering, applied according to the "general order of everything that is" (Arendt 1996, p. 39); in other words, according to the vision of a pagan god understood as immutable wholeness or everlasting nature. Arendt's talent for wrongheaded recapitulations made her description of ordered love turn into adverse publicity, with barely pent-up revulsion, since it is "unconcerned objectivity" that determines:

> *what ought to be loved. Love itself is a consequence of this determination. The same is true for the degree of intensity that love will spend on its object, depending upon the order that assigns each to its proper place. Everyone is loved as much as he ought to be, no more and no less. (Arendt 1996, p. 38)*

Nature puts people in their place. No protest, no complaint, no lament is allowed. One could ask to what end such a love is promoted which treats a human being as "a mere 'thing' to be used for the true life to come" (Arendt 1996, p. 38)? The bitter truth is that there is no other answer than that: "the 'highest good' is drawn into the present and can dominate and regulate life in this world" (Arendt 1996, p. 41). It means that the Christian theological concepts of providence, natural law, and *ordo caritatis* are interrelated, forming a dangerous mixture by help of which some people could gain power over another and repress them, "for the good of somebody". Those who command and order, pretending that they know this "good", do not respect enigma of human singularity, fragility, and inimitableness grounded in groundless abyss of the mystery of creation epitomised by each birth. As Arendt concluded, ordered love stays "in flagrant contradiction to the very essence of love in all its forms" (Arendt 1996, p. 42), because it depersonalises the neighbour who is not recognised in his "concrete uniqueness", but "in sublime indifference regardless of what or who he is" (Arendt 1996, p. 43).[12] Christian passion netted by categories of the Greek philosophy squirms in convulsive motion raging from self-sacrifice to indifference—perversion of suffering at its zenith.

It is obviously not only because of the demands of the Greek philosophy, but first of all because of "life's instability" (Arendt 1996, p. 17) that man could not find its final destination. But what Arendt recommends for human condition's instability by no means resembles traditionalist *ordo*. Since it is a creaturely life, finite and thus far from absolute, it needs a proper perspective, which would respect the "limitations of earthly life" (Arendt 1996, p. 27). Therefore, the sense of measure is crucial—measure not derived from extraterrestrial patterns, by means of which life "is looked upon from the outside (from outside the living person)" (Arendt 1996, p. 16), but elaborated on the basis of life's own limitations, to begin with birth and death. Arendt kept persuading that "meeting life from the outside"

---

[12]   On that basis she criticized evocation of love for humankind as abstract in *On Revolution*.

(Arendt 1996, p. 12) results in blaming human life for its finitude, treating it like a malady or calamity, in the end — as evil. If one compares finite life with durability of things, not to mention prevailing forces of nature, human conditionality must look miserable and incurably tragic.

> (...) *upon all this misery, philosophy smiles its empty smile and, with its outstretched index finger, shows the creature, whose limbs are trembling in fear for its life in this world, a world beyond, of which it wants to know nothing at all. For man does not at all want to escape from some chain; he wants to stay, he wants—to live.* (Rosenzweig 2005, p. 9)

Influenced by Rosenzweig, Arendt continued his *neues Denken*, especially when she rotated the perspectives to favour singularity against Wholeness. To do so, she sometimes took liberties mocking sanctity: "For man, eternity is the future, and this fact, seen from the viewpoint of eternity, is of course a contradiction in terms" (Arendt 1996, p. 16). Absurdity helps to show how absurd is to force human beings to imitate idealised projections of absoluteness. For instance, Arendt criticized pure thinking abstracted from a living subjectivity: "From the viewpoint of life this state in which man's spirit relates to itself is a kind of death. For to the extent that we are alive and active (and desire is a form of action), we necessarily are involved in things outside ourselves and cannot be free" (Arendt 1996, p. 21). Cannot be free in an absolute sense, I should add. Our freedom is possible only in the absence of absolute. If in lieu of celebration of this conditioned freedom, man starts to desire eternity, a kind of time without space, then it poisons finitude with nostalgia for an existence freed from any movement and intermingling with matter. To that Arendt responded with a highly polemical sentence interwoven as a counterpoint between verses, in which she depicted trances of Plotinus and Augustine about eternity: "What prevents man from 'living' in the timeless present is life itself, which never 'stands still'" (Arendt 1996, p. 16).[13]

Arendt protected the exceptionality of human condition so that it would not dissipate into shapeless eddying of cosmic becoming. This does not mean that she avoided transcending life, crossing the boundaries of birth and death into two types of nothingness. However, as we will see, the clinching is where the observation post will be located: whether we look at the cold cosmos, or it looks at us and chills the blood.

3. Damned Creatures

Although the central question of the dissertation is neighbourly love, the first part deals with solipsism of the subject desiring God, while the second part concerns inversion of this longing, namely a path that an individual follows backwards, looking through his origin for the Creator. This composition itself outlines Arendt's critical stance: since only the third part opens the possibility of loving one's neighbours, in the previous ones a reader finds nothing but aporias, obstacles, impasses, and contradictions. Happiness turns out to be unreachable, life is bitter, God's grace fades—alienation in full swing. "Can life be said to exist at all?" (Arendt 1996, p. 14)—asked Arendt, leading Augustine's doubts to completion. In her mouth this "doubt" concerning life turns almost into a kind of Docetic heresy: Augustine is accused of hampering the recognition of the carnal, earthly presence of his neighbours.

The problem resides in the ideal of self-sufficiency, *das Autarkieideal* (Arendt 1929, p. 27).[14] Philosophical vision of the absolute inherited by Augustine—immovable, omnipotent, omniscient—hangs over men as a sign that they are always inferior. Consequently, desire of eternal life, with its aspiration of being in God, with God, like God, brings about that "man's present life is being neglected for the sake of its future, and loses its meaningfulness and weight in comparison with that true life" (Arendt 1996, p. 27). Craving for timeless delight "proceeds to strip the world and all

---

13 That is why Arendt was critical about *nunc stans* also in her last work, *Willing*.
14 In the text I use "autarchic" as derivative from "autarchy", although its meaning as "absolute" produces additional aftersound.

temporal things of their value and to make them relative. (. . .) Since they will not last, they do not really exist" (Arendt 1996, p. 14).

The root of the problem lies deeper. Self-sufficiency meets its limits everywhere. Because of the dialectics of life, which continues its development due to changes, to live means to move, never standing still.[15] This provokes frustration. And since God in Augustine is by definition the highest good, the only object to be blamed is life or human being, or—in a refined version—fallen human nature. Thus, Arendt's intuition leads her to locate the source of the problems articulated by Augustine in his very attitude towards life: "Once we assume the perspective that we no longer view life as 'before death' but as 'after death,' death equalizes by devaluing life as such" (Arendt 1996, p. 76).

Although Arendt discussed many influences which shaped Augustinian thought, she never mentioned Manichaeism, neither Gnosticism in general. But here it would be very much accurate to see not only Stoic and Neoplatonic dimensions in the ideal of autarchy, but also the Manichean background of some motives, like regression and withdrawal from the world no less than the shift from total concentration of inwardness to the sacrifice of the self, which Arendt called "pseudo-Christian" (Arendt 1996, p. 30). Later on, she noted the existence of some Christian type of self-denial, but without detail.[16] Nevertheless, Arendt enumerated essential features of love according to Paul of Tarsus, who, unlike Augustine, had claimed: that perfection is possible already in finite life, not only in heaven; that love won't cease in eternity; that in the afterlife God will be loved by the same love through which s/he is loved (Arendt 1996, pp. 30–32). On the contrary, for Augustine the Manichean, world and creatures remain in such a deep debasement that they do not deserve to be loved. "Man should not love in this life" (Arendt 1996, p. 30), because any possible object of love cannot compare with God. Accordingly, love in any case should not be accompanied by enjoyment (*frui*). The only characteristic of *caritas* that provides people with a foretaste of eternity is fearlessness. But disappearance of the fear of death results in forgetting about mortality (Arendt 1996, p. 29), abandonment of the human condition and achievement of ataraxic indifference.[17] This indifference to one's own death, however, could affect attitude towards others. Fleeing from evil nature and avoiding intense relations with people, solipsist subjectivity seeks its only refuge in God. But this god, whom the isolated individual worships so fervently in a language of philosophy, is the ancient cosmos in disguise.

4. Indifference vs. Singularity

Loath reference to life comes from a certain vision of the cosmos treated as a pattern and a fundament which human finitude should depend on. Worse, if the Hebrew God—philosophically dissected by theologians—adopts the attributes from the cosmic Wholeness, which was the case in the Christian theology. "I think, and hope to show, that it is precisely the notion of God as *summum bonum* that creates the difficulty" (Arendt 1996, p. 44)—with this statement which leaves no doubt about her intentions, Arendt closed the first part of the dissertation. In the second, "natalist" part, the quest for one's origin plays the main role. Despite the obvious fact that its appearance seems to be contradistinctively infinitesimal in comparison to the magnitude of cosmos, birth becomes the Archimedean point for a defence of a fragile process of individuation.

In the world constructed by Augustine, nobody is interested in our happiness, everyone lives alone facing death and meanwhile experiencing disillusionment because of desires. "The Creator remains forever identically the same, independent of his creation and whatever may happen within it"

---

[15] Giorgio Agamben cannot be a legitimate continuator of Arendt's for this reason alone that his deconstruction of Western metaphysics contains aversion towards movement and moving (Agamben 2013, p. 95). For Arendt "calm quietude" (Arendt 1996, p. 19) is as rare as love, not to mention the absolute calmness which simply equals death (Arendt 1996, p. 13).

[16] Arendt's general stance towards Christianity one could explain this way: when she wrote that "contempt for the world and its goods is not Christian in origin" (Arendt 1996, p. 20), she did not claim that neither Christian traditions nor ecclesiastical laws are deprived of this *Grundbefindlichkeit*.

[17] These are cryptotheological motives inherited by Agamben from Martin Heidegger; Agamben's elaboration of limbo contains them in a nutshell.

(Arendt 1996, p. 56). Not only does the Creator keep indifference, "the postulated eternity of Being makes beginning and end interchangeable in terms of the temporal creature's reference to its own existence" (Arendt 1996, p. 56). This was another blasphemy for Arendt, even if she was perfectly conscious about its provenance from a different religious sensibility which makes an idol of something the strongest. Having reversed perspectives, Arendt's tenderness focuses on the most unwanted element in nature, abandoned even by "God"—on a singularity:

> *Self-questioning (se quaerere) can thus be doubly guided: man can ask himself both about the 'whence' and the 'whither' of this existence. Although both questions ask about negations of life, the negations differ in kind. The negation 'not yet' denotes the source of life and the 'no more' denotes death. Despite their seemingly identical negativity, the past and future negations are not the same". (Arendt 1996, p. 70)*

It is worth underlining that although an individual directed at origin is favoured over an individual directed at death, the former is not absolutized by Arendt, since the final vision of mankind's community, a possible modest salvation already on earth, we find in the third part of her doctoral thesis. Yet, in the end, without the loved singularities this community could be a catastrophe. That is why Arendt spoke up for any singularity, buffering "the very tendency to be" (Arendt 1996, p. 71) against laminating by cosmic indifference.

To defend singularity as such is not enough, though. Natality towers pure potentiality of becoming.[18] When due to comparison with the vastness of nature "human life is divested of the uniqueness and irreversibility in which temporal sequences follow each other from birth to death", the individual does not necessarily cease to be a singularity (*singulum*) but loses its "autonomous significance" (Arendt 1996, p. 60). Singularities seen from the viewpoint of nature are unreservedly exchangeable "whatever beings", perfectly replicable.[19] That is why they could not be loved, since love *singularizes* (Bielik-Robson 2015). "If man and his life are parts of some encompassing whole, they cannot be said to have an origin and their mortality has become irrelevant" (Arendt 1996, p. 62). When somebody's death does not bother us, it means that we do not love this person.

To singularize someone is like breaking the eternal cycle for a while, in order to offer him a shelter where he would escape from the double threat of nothingness surrounding finite life. The cycle of generation and perishing must be interrupted, to give a breath for life individualised, augmented, irreducible to any other. Only then the highest possible hope of conducting *inimitable life* would shine upon dark horizon. As was said, Arendtian vitalism does not prohibit transgressions beyond both horizons, but only because it is already well "earthed". Singularity can be self-assured always having someone on her side. Through "transmundane recollection" (Arendt 1996, p. 47), inspired and driven by the love of the world, finite life constitutes itself and consolidates, even though it demands accompanying, so that one does not let it out of sight. Perspective makes a difference. When we are imagining singularity and think about the whole time when she had been nonexistent, up until the moment of coming into the world, our concentration condenses myriad coincidences, entwining them more and more tightly and expecting the looming of a beloved shape. However, this attitude is not the first and the only reaction one can develop towards the naked fact of being—it is unpredictable like every singularity. It is always true that it might had been otherwise.

Thus, "to love the other in his mortality" (Arendt 1996, p. 96) does not mean to love death, but to truly love finite condition of creatureliness, despite death, despite everything. It is not love *of* mortality,

---

[18] "The mere potentiality for something is not yet a being-intended for something in such a way that the process of becoming is guided toward it" (Jonas 1996, p. 172). That is why, on the other side of a spectrum, when Arendt conceptualised specific place of natal capacity to begin, "she did not equate spontaneity with contingency" (Kalyvas 2008, p. 224). She was not an enthusiast of contingency—it was, according to her, the price of freedom.

[19] This point is completely overlooked by Agamben and Esposito, who built their theories on Deleuze's notion of singularity. "Pre-existing creation" (Arendt 1996, p. 66) and "pure createdness" (Arendt 1996, p. 68) is just a germ, the daybreak of the odyssey that subjectivity undertakes, not its last chapter.

but of natal singular *in* his mortality. Love of life, even though provoked by death, exceeds mere acceptance and gets stamina from natality. Stubbornly repeating "not yet", it mobilizes all resources of "whence" against dispersion and brings previous obstacles back to prove its strength and durability. Only then challenging the truth that "human existence as such depends on something outside the human condition" (Arendt 1996, p. 49) comes out as not so terrifying. Natality and remembrance stand guard over another truth: "once called into existence, human life cannot turn into nothingness" (Arendt 1996, p. 53). Because the eternal cycle was broken, something really unpredictable came into being. That is why for the philosophy of immanence that ennobles the "sempiternal Becoming" (Arendt 1996, p. 63), natality equals mortality. It is not surprising that Aristotle's god who "never came into being" and is praised for being immutable, could not mourn. He did not risk anything, so he had nothing to lose.

5. BDSM Theology

Hannah Arendt as the thinker of natality does not overestimate living-towards-origin, contrary to what Agata Bielik-Robson claims (Bielik-Robson 2015). For movement directed at beginning could turn out to be "the self-denial of referring back" (Arendt 1996, p. 98).[20] Even in the fragments which seem to be an apology of the return to one's own origin, she maintained awareness that "this approach depends on God's own inclination to the creature" (Arendt 1996, p. 90). But it is already clear: God (of metaphysics) has no inclinations and knows no exception. Arendt's critique is strong, but subtle. For example, she sounds very affirmatively in the statements like: "*Caritas* fulfils the law, because to *caritas* the law is no longer a command; it is grace itself. (…) This loving acceptance reconciles the creature with its Creator" (Arendt 1996, p. 91). However, this is not such an idyll as it might look like. Arendt immediately adds a sarcastic comment: "This self-denial can only be achieved in *caritas*, because nothing else provides a reason for the sacrifice" (Arendt 1996, p. 91).[21] Indeed, love of God has devastating effects for the subject, who "loves himself as God loves him, hating everything he has made in himself, and loving himself only insofar as he is God's creation" (Arendt 1996, p. 91). The extremism visible here is embedded in the conception of the original sin, which attempts the complete disempowerment of man. Of course, Augustine left some division of labour, so that man was not totally passive: what is evil is inscribed at the human's account, what is good occurs in the form of God's grace.[22] From the anthropological point of view, it was detrimental. When in *Willing* Arendt returned once again to Augustine, she criticised him for incorporating "scandalous" dialectics of grace, which encourages to ignite "willed submissiveness" and a delight in painful experiences in the individual (Arendt 1978, p. 90). This comment inspired the present section, which could be

---

[20] Arendt's critique of solipsist individual turned against the world could have had political resonance already within the Weimar context. Arendt developed secularist use of the "unavailable inwardness" (*unverfügbare Innerlichkeit*), while Weimar religious antimodernists (like contemporary ones do) used it for completely opposite reasons—to destroy the autonomous secular realm of the Republic, treated as an imposition of the "Western values": "Social utopias were centered around two poles; on one side around the idea of a strong state, and on the other side around the conception of an individual who should be enabled to voluntarily fulfil his duties towards the whole, based on a religiously founded morality. All of these alternative concepts had a widely identical structural core and were binding ideologies. There was indeed constant talk of freedom, conscience and personality but only in a certain sense. (…) Freedom was for the most part understood as the ability to bind and sacrifice oneself. In defining these binding ideologies—this pious nationalization of conscience—theological conceptions played a central role (Tanner 2012, p. 13). Karl Löwith put things differently, believing in the automatic political significance of inwardness, but his perspective sheds light on the issue of Arendt's early concerns. Criticizing Nazi-influenced philosophical works of the 1920s and 1930s, he stated that "the main losses were the questions regarding individual existence or—religiously speaking—the interest in spiritual salvation. Augustine's '*quaestio mihi factus sum*' (I have examined myself) was no longer voiced by anyone today, but one indeed raised questions about the natural foundations of *völkisch* life: about soil, race, region and blood" (Löwith 1994, p. 53).

[21] This sarcasm is undetectable for a Catholic reader, for whom "truly Christian *caritas*" occurs when a creature regresses to the Creator, "humbly admitting that he has not made himself … " (Kampowski 2008, p. 227).

[22] "To defeat the Pelagian heresy, however, Augustine abandoned a dialectical view of the relation of law to grace. On this new account, in the dialectic of willing and incapacity the latter had finally triumphed. *Homo sub lege*, or man under law, was divested of all capacity to will or do good. His freedom consisted only in the *delectatio peccati*, the lust for the sinful. No longer did Augustine speak of a serious fight against temptation" (Lazier 2008, p. 39).

regarded as prolegomena to the psychotheological critique of religion and unguarded worship of God, which especially in Christianity is at risk of falling into idolatry of the natural order.

The cosmic indifference, represented philosophically, conceptualised divinity as a perfectly autarchic, self-centred Whole. But interconnected with the wilful Hebrew Yahweh, this god becomes monstrous. The theatre of cruelty demands not only "self-hatred" (Arendt 1996, p. 27), but also resignation from activity, since no one is able to deserve salvation (Arendt 1996, p. 29). The intrusive presence of divine grace keeps life in disgrace. "What becomes sinful here is independence as such, not a revolt of the part against the whole, but as an independent performance of submission" (Arendt 1996, p. 87). It means that even a gesture of submission is castigated as much too subjective, not to mention what unbelievable sin it would be not to adapt to the Whole (Arendt 1996, p. 65). Any perversion on the part of the creature is forbidden, so that the Sovereign develops his phantasies about absolute domination without restraint. "Creature has no power over its own being" (Arendt 1996, p. 87), he lives "keeping with (...) newly felt dependence" (Arendt 1996, p. 88), which means "no longer a simple relation to God, but a direct plea for his help" (Arendt 1996, p. 89). "Contempt for self" (Arendt 1996, p. 102) comes from nothing, but a recognition of "the sinfulness of his own incapacity and inferiority to the command" (Arendt 1996, p. 89). Finally, humiliation transforms into experiencing the divine "grace" (Arendt 1996, p. 88) and "love" (Arendt 1996, p. 89). The secret lies in obeying "the command to return to Being" (Arendt 1996, p. 88), i.e., indifference, ruthlessness, and cruelty.

There are certain methods also for those who do not really enjoy pain and suffering. "Cruel lies [*grausam Lügen*; Rosenzweig 1921, p. 9]"[23] (Rosenzweig 2005, p. 10) of philosophy (and theology altogether) are intended to cover a horrific spectacle. "The tool with which philosophy works the obstinate material until it no longer puts up resistance" (Rosenzweig 2005, p. 10), in this case is the ideal of beauty. Augustine emblazoned how cosmos was perfect and spotless so that burke all possible complaints of the creatures, the very germs of critique. "Imperishable harmonious whole" was in Augustine's eyes vested in the "splendor of eternity" (Arendt 1996, p. 59), gleaming with the "admirable beauty of the universal" (Arendt 1996, p. 60). Going from one extremity to another, Augustine, following the Manicheans on the one hand, rejected earthly reality as inferior, if not disgusting, but following Plato, Stoics, and Plotinus on the other hand, he justified overwhelming beauty of the cosmos,[24] claiming that mortals cannot see this perfect, ideal harmony, just because their perspective is much too narrow. With this argument one could show disrespect to every suffering, pain, malady, illness, to any harm done. For that reason, Arendt was merciless in dragging up such horrible quotations as proof of Augustine's indifference. When he tried to explain why God allowed some people to do evil, he said that because "they might decorate the universe" (Arendt 1996, p. 61).[25] Another example, this time summarized in Arendt's words, elucidates why something other than perfect Wholeness should exist at all. The indirect answer seems to be grotesque, well ... , God needed us to get some exercise: "It is the function of the parts to set and keep in motion (*agere*) the whole" (Arendt 1996, p. 58). This sadomasochistic predilection for the Whole, which contradicts any attention for the oppressed creatures, resonates in Plotinus, "whose thought Augustine frequently render almost verbatim" (Arendt 1996, p. 64):

> If one of these parts moves according to its nature, it makes those suffer to whom this movement is
> against their own nature, whereas the former as parts of the whole are well. Those who cannot bear

---

[23] Translation modified.
[24] In the text *Augustin und der Protestantismus* from 1930 Arendt wrote: "Indeed, he never abandoned his Neo-Platonism, the legacy of Plotinus, the last Greek. He never stopped trying to understand and interpret the world in philosophical-cosmological terms" (Arendt 1994, p. 25). That is why Vecchiarelli Scott is wrong when she thinks that Neo-Platonism was one of the many influences which Augustine could balance and choose between, sometimes belittling their strength (Vecchiarelli Scott 2010, p. 15).
[25] From: *The Free Choice of the Will* III, 11, 32.

> *the order of the whole perish [. . .] since they cannot escape the order [. . .]. If, however, they could*
> *fit themselves into the order of the whole they would suffer nothing from it. (Arendt 1996, pp. 64–65)*

I quote extensively in order to make evident what commentators usually prefer to obliterate, namely unconditioned consent to violence and cruelty.[26] The quotation comes from the famous treaty *Against the Gnostics* contained in the second *Ennead*, where Plotinus made transparent what he regarded as the greatest danger associated with the Gnostic rebel against the cosmic piety: "blaming the whole" (Plotinus 1990, p. 249).

6. Redemption through Sin: Defence of the *Saeculum*

Already at the beginning of the dissertation Arendt lost patience, asking whether life is indeed not worth a damn. Whether *vita mortalis* is indistinguishable from *mors vitalis*, a living death? But what if "there [is—RZ] no consolation in death?" (Arendt 1996, p. 11). Whether life is so bitter that one should love death instead? And later on, with disarming sincerity, she nailed Augustine down:

> *Would it not then be better to love the world in cupiditas and be at home? Why should we make*
> *a desert out of this world? The justification for this extraordinary enterprise can only lie in a deep*
> *dissatisfaction with what the world can give its lovers. (Arendt 1996, p. 19)*

She lamented and reproached him, because for him the human being is always "too much" or "not enough". There is any tiny place for "celebrate yourself". It would be better not to be born. What at least about "transient happiness" (Arendt 1996, p. 11)?

Nonetheless, Augustine claimed that earthly love is impossible to satisfy. Arendt lapped it up: love is indefinite which exposes infinity of desire, just as love for the world marks world's incompleteness and openness. It is nobody's fault, it is our chance and only hope. The word *mundus*,[27] which had fallen off theology,[28] Arendt lifted like a precious jewel. It glimmers with verboten glamour. "The world consists of those who love it" (Arendt 1996, p. 66). A chance of reinvention resides solely in them.

Yet, freedom is Augustine's tormentor. As well as desire. "Augustine calls this right love *caritas*: the 'root of all evils is *cupiditas*, the root of all goods is *caritas*.' However, both right and wrong love (. . .) have this in common—craving desire, that is, *appetitus*" (Arendt 1996, p. 17). Why is this so important? Because it secures anthropology from the Manichean tendency within Augustinian thought, which strives for condemnation of the humankind. Thus, Arendt mobilised counterarguments: firstly, in selfhatred man "denies the present, mortal self that is, after all, God's creation" (Arendt 1996, p. 30); secondly, "he who does not love and desire at all is nobody" (Arendt 1996, p. 18); thirdly, "even *caritas* mediates between man and God in exactly the same way as *cupiditas* mediates between man and the world" (Arendt 1996, p. 30); fourthly, there is something more perturbing than discordant desire, namely: isolation, whom both *caritas* and *cupiditas* break (Arendt 1996, pp. 18–19).

The only interpreter who noticed and appreciated Arendt's defence of *cupiditas* is Lucy Tatman.[29] However, I need to disagree at one point with her otherwise illuminating reading. In my opinion, it is

---

[26] Which is not so much a question of temperament—since both serene Plotinus and impetuous Augustine agreed on legitimate violence of the Whole against its parts—but rather a logic of thought which, once set in motion on the basis of a false premise, rams everything on its way. Would it not be justified to read the case of Eichmann this way?

[27] If one wanted to find biographical references, Arendt's insistence on "being of the world", *de mundo* (Arendt 1996, p. 66), could be matched with her predilection for Berlin as a cosmopolitan city, the first metropolis she lived in, see (Steinberg 2007). A flavour of this spirit was preserved in some languages, for instance in German *weltmännisch*, French *mondain* or Polish *światowy*, mirroring the theological anathema put on worldly man. Arendt's biographer characterised her as follows: "Hannah Arendt was a Weimar Berliner in social mores" (Young-Bruehl 2004, p. 240).

[28] Oliver Marchart characterizes Arendt's later notion of the "Earth" as "non-theological"; however, he claims that the origin of her concept of the "world" was double, being a combination of Augustine's and Heidegger's views (Marchart 2005, pp. 33–34). In this way it comes partially from theological discussions—it was extracted from them; hence I would call it cryptotheological.

[29] See especially (Tatman 2013, p. 629).

not fortunate to call what Arendt did the "transvaluation of Augustinian values" (Tatman 2013, p. 630). If we needed to search for her progenitor, then, knowing what Karl Löwith wrote about Friedrich Nietzsche and Franz Overbeck in the end of *Von Hegel zu Nietzsche* (Löwith 1964), I think it would be more accurate to regard Arendt as an Overbeck's heir. It is a question of style, but also of method. In her dissertation, Arendt wrote *within* theology, trying to elbow through dense material and make a place for anthropological, secular sensitivity. It was necessary, because "Augustine proceeds to strip the world and all temporal things of their value and to make them relative. All worldly goods are changeable (*mutabilia*). Since they will not last, they do not really exist" (Arendt 1996, p. 14).

There is no comparison between Tatman's deep understanding and the mistaken theological critiques, like the one, didactic in tone,[30] which sees in *cupiditas* losing the self, isolation and disorientation, confusion caused by desire (Vecchiarelli Scott 1988, p. 409). No doubt, since for Vecchiarelli Scott "*cupiditas* (. . .) is evil itself" (Vecchiarelli Scott 1988, p. 417). I have just demonstrated that Arendt was not terrified by worldly attachments, and did not follow Augustine's panic. For her, it was more dreadful and pernicious isolation than *cupiditas*, which is rather always an engagement into worldly matters.

Moreover, there is the whole affirmative section in *Der Liebesbegriff* about *dilectores mundi*, whom Augustine in his less philosophical tone had regarded simply as sinners. But Arendt's analysis uncovers a positive mode of being in the world, which not only cannot be theologically smashed, but—conversely—needs to be appreciated from a theological point of view. Avoiding to directly address the human fallenness and its cause, she shifted attention and underlined that whatever the cause might have been, it is a matter of fact that humans build the world, although they did not create it. Oliver Marchart uses the concept of co-creation (*mit-schaffen*) in this context, and depicts human activity with the verb *eingreifen*, which promotes understanding of the act of coming into the world as stepping into it, intervention and interference (Marchart 2005, p. 33).[31]

In other words, the distinction between *principium* as creation of the world by God and *initium* as human potentiality to insert new beginnings was not Arendt's warning of man against trespassing the human condition; rather, it is a conservative predilection of reading the history of creation first as a history of men's fall and condemnation. Arendt understood the difference between God and humans without nostalgia or melancholy. Thank God we are creatures, not God himself. It means that we do not need to drag responsibility for the world as it was created, but we are responsible within the horizon of co-creation. Next to a possibility of destroying the world, there are plenty of peaceful and delightful modes of inhabiting the earth. What I think Arendt wanted to regain was closer to the Jewish attitude towards earthly reality, which is not poisoned by the obsessive concentration on human sinfulness and, consequently, does not need to project a vision of God as *summum bonum*. In Arendt's cryptotheological sensitivity, human beings are not totally opposed to God, as thinkers like Augustine, Karl Barth, or Eric Voegelin might suggest—indeed, Arendt rejected Augustine's blackmail of choosing between "contempt of God" or "contempt for self" (Arendt 1996, p. 102). Hence, men can be co-creators, allowed to intervene in the course of events and take responsibility for action. But the first attachment needs to be to the world, not to God. This does not mean that it should be

---

30 Pedagogical simplification is evident in a moralistic reading of *The Human Condition*, which strives to condemn modernity as an error and link *Der Liebesbegriff* to Arendt's later thought in a function of a theological critique of the modern age. According to David Grumett, modern lifestyle epitomises *cupiditas*, which leads directly to the "inversion of the right order of eternal and temporal goods" (Grumett 2000, p. 161).

31 It is impossible to imagine how this vision could be compatible with Augustine's version of God who "hated us as being such as he had not made us" (Arendt 1996, p. 92; from: Tractates on John's Gospel CX, 6). This God wants to see us in pure creatureliness understood as crude misery, the initial poverty and dependence. She behaves like a parent who can't reconcile with her children's maturity, because she feels unnecessary, thus she makes their separation impossible. In misery humankind would pray to God more willingly. That God hates our technique, medicine, our pills, lipsticks and drags. Incidentally, Arendt had her own opinion about the Vatican biopolitics under the pope Paul VI. In a letter dated 21 December 1968, she wrote to Mary McCarthy: "Poor Paul—who in addition to everything else is a political idiot; he could have left the Pill [sic!] very well alone" (Arendt and McCarthy 1995, p. 232).

directed against God. On the other hand, it ought to be directed against any vision of God which would discourage man from taking his earthly finitude seriously, from leaving "human standard" (Arendt 1996, p. 94). No salvation or apocalypse should unbrace human life's rootedness, anchored to the Earth.

I cannot agree with Beiner when he writes: "What Augustine seeks is for human beings to 'crave' the eternal with the same 'appetite', the same intensity of feeling, with which they have always hitherto carved the things of this world" (Beiner 1997, p. 271). It is not so simple: damned creatureliness nudzhs even in *amor Dei*, since "'when I love *my* God'—says Augustine—I love not 'the beauty of bodies, not the splendour of time, not the brightness of light, (. . .) not the sweet melodies of all kinds of songs,' yet I still 'love some kind of light, and some voice, and some odor'" (Arendt 1996, p. 25). Arendt implicitly showed in such fragments from Augustine that his isolationist ideal prevents him from elementary gratitude. He was more eager to concentrate on "independence" of those imaginations from matter, "forgetting" what he had already said about their likeness to the earthly reality. He also "forgot" about himself as an enlivened matter which carries those images.

Appetite is always disturbing, sensual, it reminds of being *de mundo*, merely a creature. Instead, Augustine's obsession with self-sufficiency and animosity towards matter made him dream about freedom from libido (Arendt 1996, p. 20) and pleasure (*voluptas*) (Arendt 1996, p. 24). Arendt ironized that, saying that whereas he had become a thinker after his friend's death, he had become a Christian because of libido (Arendt 1996, pp. 13–14). In general, in Augustine's aversion for life Arendt detected fear of "multiplicity of the world" (Arendt 1996, p. 24), of "dispersion" (Arendt 1996, p. 23), whereas for her "the field of transcendence" (Celermajer 2011, p. 8) was relocated into human relations, as Celermajer rightly observes.

Arendt's unspoken objection was that Augustine's mode of loving was full immersion, which was performed only before God. However, in the second part she evoked a more affirmative constellation of desires within Augustinian frame, swerved slightly by natalist recollection of the self. For desire is defined as certain ability, which should be awakened and inspired thanks to memory: instead of repressing it by *ordo*, desire should seek for happiness (Arendt 1996, pp. 48, 49, 51). Happiness is "always previously given" (Arendt 1996, p. 9), in a sense it is a gift of fate (Arendt 1996, p. 69), since it depends on others, deep relations with our earthly creators, parents, and caregivers, finally on a clandestine transmission of a sparkle of life and enigmatic word about "more life". In sum, reflection on desire beyond object-related pattern[32] leads to the discovery of a "deeper and more fundamental mode of human dependence" (Arendt 1996, p. 49). And this is what an isolated individual exclusively concerned with his soul dreads the most.

It is noteworthy that for Augustine the original sin was transmitted materially by the father's libido and sperm. Only then Arendtian natalism could be properly understood unto its dark provenance. Natalism is an attempt to overcome gnosis, condensed in the Augustinian contempt for body, procreation, and sexuality. What he had called sinfulness, she called "the most crucial determinant of human existence" (Arendt 1996, p. 100). Arendt's seemingly objective description shifts accents from sin to freedom: "Man's origin is at the same time both the beginning of the man-made world in Adam's original sin and the origin of his separation from God. His descent is defined by generation and not by creation" (Arendt 1996, p. 104). To sum up what we have so far: firstly, God's separation of the creatures from nature, then analysis concentrated more on creation than on Creator[33] so that finally could introduce another cut, distancing "degenerated" men from the order

---

[32] It is only for Augustine that relation of happiness and memory demands the model of anamnesis, which links the shape the desire could take with certain divine instruction. Arendt preserved the connection with the past, but for her the fate of desire, the specific direction it heads, is not determined. She pointed at the more fundamental dependence, which results in the general affirmation of life, something occurring before full individuation.

[33] "(. . .) a religious faith not in God but in creation" (Bernauer 1987b, p. 11). On the contrary, as Benjamin Lazier observes, dialectic theologians saved God, but not creation (Lazier 2008, p. 120).

of creation. In order to say that one has to have a different understanding of what Augustine named as original sin. For Arendt it was less dramatic: "The quest for worldliness changes man's nature" (Arendt 1996, p. 18). It is a matter of fact, the fact that "man is not self-sufficient" (Arendt 1996, p. 18), nothing more and nothing less. In other words, we are not guilty that we were born this way.

One could say that Arendt did not allow this guilt complex to actuate the "inner dialectics of faith", thus she turned direction and asked about "the common ground of experience" (Arendt 1996, p. 99). The dilemmas of inwardness, known already, are dismissed here. While the first part unmasked human futuristic desire as underpinned by something that psychoanalysis could call simply death-drive, the second part ended with a failure of another movement towards God, this time origin-oriented one. But Arendt did not condemn those general orientations of the *homo temporalis*;[34] rather, she clarified that what had caused these pointless attempts had been a mistaken starting point—in an isolated individual. For that reason, the third part deals with *inter-esse*, the space in-between where any kind of human relations takes its origin, "tied to the factuality of history and to the past as such" (Arendt 1996, p. 99). Since Arendt wanted to read theologems in the most secular way possible, she chose to follow Augustine in what he taught about *civitas terrena*, earthly city, a condition of social life with horizontal relations and reciprocal interdependence.[35] Nonetheless, the contemporary reception of Arendt understands the shift from the individual to community in a simplistic way: as abandonment and renouncement. What my interpretation regains is that it was a highly dialectical shift, in which the critique of the absolutisation of the subject goes hand in hand with the defence of the process of individuation.

Arendt's analysis focuses on "the common descend from Adam, the foundation of a definite and obligatory equality among all people" (Arendt 1996, p. 100). Even if it could be called "community-in-sinfulness" (Arendt 1996, p. 102), "this *civitas terrena* is not arbitrarily founded and not arbitrarily dissolved" (Arendt 1996, p. 100). Continuity of generations is hard to be extinguished, because "once called into existence, human life cannot turn into nothingness" (Arendt 1996, p. 53)—this fragment clearly shows how Arendt used theological vision of God's own promises and logic of creation in order to protect humankind from God's potential arbitrariness. She grounded this subversion of perspectives in quotidian experience: even if God created us, the first link in the chain of being are our parents, then previous generations back to Adam and Eve. "The primary experience is not that God is imperishable, but that the world is" (Arendt 1996, p. 69). "God (if indeed it is God)" (Arendt 1996, p. 78) should not feel offended that such is the first panorama of a finite being. Creaturely life is by definition limited, and to live one needs a sense of orientation within possibilities, gained by testing the boundaries of reality. The origins are always modest: "The community of all people among themselves goes back to Adam and constitutes the world; it always precedes any city of God (*civitas Dei*). It is a pre-existing community into which the individual comes by birth" (Arendt 1996, p. 103). It is not necessarily directed with arrogance against God—if only this is the God who draws conclusions from his actions and for that reason respects human freedom.

---

[34] The figure of *homo temporalis* appeared on one of the last pages Arendt ever wrote, and Tatman suggests that in *Judging* the author would have been trying to establish a subjectivity based on a temporality of love (Tatman 2013, p. 633). Thus, it is unthinkable what John Kiess writes, whether one understands it theologically or as intellectualisation: "Arendt ultimately seeks to secure a place outside temporal existence" (Kiess 2016, p. 117). That she wanted to rescue singularity from the flux of events, and spontaneity from the dominant forces of causality does not mean that she sought rescue in some kind of *nunc stans*. She was not a dualist to think in terms of either-or.

[35] But horizontal relations between people derive directly from the failure of solipsist, vertical modes of subjectivisation. That is why Bernauer is completely wrong searching for an analogy that could reconcile everything: "As creatures of the same Creator, each individual is also related to all others in an ontological relationship which is called to concretize itself in mutual commitments" (Bernauer 1987b, p. 19). It is evident here how pious intentions of the theologians result in negligence of Arendt's double negative dialectics without which cryptotheological defence of secularity is unthinkable. In the end, maybe there is nothing esoteric in all of that (Kampowski 2008, p. 23), however ... *der liebe Gott wohnt im Detail*.

7. *Vita socialis* (III Chapter)

Arendt, dissatisfied by the outcomes from the first two chapters, posed a question whether one could find in Augustine "another empirical context, different in origin, that would give the neighbor a specific relevance" (Arendt 1996, p. 98). She immediately looked at "the community of faith", first generations of Christians, bonded not even by common descent, not by any "pre-existing reality in the world", but by "a specific possibility"— "the common faith" (Arendt 1996, p. 98). It would seem that a community gathered around "possibility" is an open community, which is true in a sense that it demands sharing belief, disregarding questions of provenance and gender (or at least, this is a radical realisation of community enabled by early Christianity). But this kind of inclusiveness has its hidden agenda, namely that it "demands a total response from each person"—"the community of faith demands the whole man" (Arendt 1996, p. 99). It is an invitation to live "a last and most radical possibility of being human" (Arendt 1996, p. 99), extremely detached from any worldly context.

Another problem which we can decipher as allusive is that this community, however open to converts it may be, renders every individual to be a potential co-fellow in faith (Arendt 1996, p. 99). If I understand Arendt well, she mentioned here a pressure on conversion, especially disturbing for the Jews who did not follow Jesus of Nazareth and saw neither Messiah nor Christ in him. There is no open question about the Jews, but it is obvious that Arendt asked about them too, universalizing her inquiry to "all people, even unbelievers" (Arendt 1996, p. 99), whom she put as challenge to the vision of the community limited to one faith in one God.

Here starts Arendt's *Judeochristian* intervention. After she questioned the boundaries of the newly formed community, whose universalism limits itself only to those who converted, then she tried a mode of interpretation which I call *Marranic*. Before she confronted the event of Christ's revelation, she made sure that even unbelievers (Jews among others—because from the Christian perspective Jews are also unbelievers, since they do not believe in divinity of Jesus of Nazareth) can be treated as neighbours. As we will see, referring to "a historically pre-existing reality, obliging as such" (Arendt 1996, p. 99), Arendt not only wanted to find more universal conception of the neighbourly love than the Christian one, but she did that specifically by starting to investigate new Christians about their most intimate past, reminding them that their "faith is tied to the factuality of history and to the past as such" (Arendt 1996, p. 99). One may like to read those passages philosophically, which is possible, but the very passages oblige us to read them within the context of earthly reality. This reality was the Jewishness of Jesus and Jewish origins of a part of early followers of Christ. What this strong reminder implies is not only certain solidarity and gratitude, but also it opens the ground for theological and historical discussions about the fate of Judeochristianity, a belief that historically did not become dominant, did not crystallize, yet left traces and remained intellectually provocative for both Jews and Christians, who at a certain point found themselves partings their ways.

By calling Arendt's textual strategy "Marranic" I do not claim that she was a Marrano, neither at the time of writing the dissertation nor after. My interpretation refers to the *positing of the author*. First of all, the name she used for Jesus of Nazareth is "Christ", as if she treated him like a Christian. This "as if" is crucial to understand the strategy. It allows Arendt to work within Christian tradition, at its core and Judaizing it. If she marked her (personal) distance from the Christian faith as a Jew (or as an unbeliever, or both), the textual effect would be less disturbing. But here we see how "the author" invades a seemingly alien territory, leaving actual persona of Hannah Arendt, the real author, aside. I call this reading a Marranic one with reference to the actual person, who wrote her dissertation and spent her student years in the context of an officially secular state and university, but actually in an environment when Christianity was still culturally dominant. But when it comes to the internal intertextual context, her dissertation could be classified as Judeochristian, meaning an attempt to imagine the beginning of the new era differently, to reinvigorate a debate about the boundaries of the new creed, its object and horizon.

Hannah Arendt had many objections to the way historical Christianity evolved from these early experiences. She initiated her discussion with the provocative sentence which orients the rest of her investigations: "The redeeming death of Christ did not redeem an individual but the whole (*mundus*), understood as the man-made world" (Arendt 1996, p. 99). Nothing more blasphemous for Augustine, whom the perspective of salvation instructed that it was only the immortal soul and not the world which deserved to be redeemed. And Augustine functions here as a representant of the official Christian theology, not as an extreme exception, but as the rule.

Be that as it may, the first step—claiming that salvation concerns the existing world, and not even mentioning any future one, but claiming additionally that the soul is definitely not at stake—entails the second step, namely turning the perspective from salvation to creation and from Christ to Adam. The typical Christian dilemmas and convulsions of a soul trembling about its future is replaced by the interest in the germ of a social bond, the basis for the neighbourly love, which here is not even love, but "affection" (Arendt 1996, p. 100).

When in *The Origins* Arendt would distance itself from the naturalised conception of equality of all men, it would seem that she left behind equality guaranteed by nature or God. Nevertheless, what she detected in Augustine as "a definite and obligatory equality among all people" (Arendt 1996, p. 100) is not a fact—it is a wish (one should wish others to be equal with her) and an obligation (one ought to do so). Although God created men from one man to give incontestable proof of the common descent, it is not *from* nature, but *through* nature that equality gains its validity: "This kinship creates an equality neither of traits nor of talents, but of situation" (Arendt 1996, p. 100). This situation is mortality, common "fate" (Arendt 1996, p. 100). But it is not to be treated with resignation and sadness—what in Augustine is called "original sin" for Arendt presents itself as just "the most crucial determinant of human existence" (Arendt 1996, p. 100). What she borrows from Augustine—and it will not change after the war—is that equality is not a natural fact, but a question of recognition. Here it is in front of God because it is still a reconstruction of theological texts, but the crucial thing is that even having God the Creator at the bottom of the narrative equality is not a matter of fact, and it cannot be taken for granted. In other words, even if God sees everybody as equal, people are expected to discover equality of sharing the human condition on their own. They are encouraged or obliged to do so. Obligation, however, is understood as wishing others to be equal to myself, believing in that, and actively changing the situation in this direction: "all people were to be united not only by the likeness of nature, but also by the affection of kinship" (Arendt 1996, p. 100).[36]

It will be characteristic for Arendt's understanding of the human rights that although we know today that the genetical unity of the whole humankind is a fact, it could only inspire us to cherish humanity of the species. But it cannot be the decisive argument.[37] Unlike Hans Jonas, who quarrelled with Arendt about that point and who placed ethical grounding in the biology of organic life, she rather thought that this kind of proof is not only unnecessary, but that it contradicts the way human society is being formed. In reference to "mutual interdependence" and social life based on a belief-trust, she wrote: "The continued existence of humankind does not rest on the proof. Rather, it rests on necessary belief, without which social life would become impossible" (Arendt 1996, p. 101).

The proper, radical, otherworldly grounded, thus non-Judaic notion of neighbourly love comes with the revelation of Christ, which Arendt described with certain reluctance, seeing in it—which was already noticed before—the most extreme way of being, but the one which could fail because of its high hopes. Besides, in this fragment Arendt reconstructed Augustine's path of reasoning. But more importantly, it seems that she did not want to simply replace the Jewish model with a Christian one.

---

[36] From: *The City of God*, XIV: 1.
[37] Shin Chiba makes errors twice by stating: "In later years she even has rejected the Judaeo-Christian belief in the unitary origin of the human race, a position that she obviously endorsed in her earliest work, *Der Liebesbegriff bei Augustin*" (Chiba 1995, p. 515). First of all, Arendt did not directly harbour humanity of humankind in the divine origin, even in her dissertation. Secondly, she never abandoned the idea of the unity of humankind. Without the subtlety of cryptotheological inspiration one cannot understand how it was smuggled into her understanding of the human rights.

After a short passage about the new Christian community based on freely chosen commitments and obligations (Arendt 1996, p. 102), she returned to the *saeculum* and the humanity originating in Adam:

> *In the society founded on Adam man has made himself independent of the Creator. He depends on other persons and not on God. The human race as such originates in Adam and not in the Creator. (. . .) The world's independence from God rests on historicity, that is, on mankind's own origin, which possesses its own legitimacy. The world's sinfullness derives from its origin independent of God. (Arendt 1996, p. 103)*

With this passage Hannah Arendt made a shift which by many will be interpreted in terms of total *secularisation* of her philosophy. For me, however, it is a perfect realisation of her *cryptotheology*. God is not rejected or neglected—it is only from a dogmatic position that it could seem to be like that. Conversely, it is the moment when double negative dialectics works within monotheistic legacy in order to legitimize the plurality of mankind. From "the simple sameness of the God" (Arendt 1996, p. 99) firstly sprang Adam, as an idea of mankind unified, and then the dispersion of Men from Man occurred. It is an alternative narrative about Creation, which one may find in Kabbalah (Scholem 1965). There is no contradiction between this version and the fact that at the beginning of *The Human Condition* Arendt opted for one of the two versions of the creation of man in Genesis, which depicted the creation Adam and Eve at the same time (not Adam first and Eve from his flesh), because Arendt referred in *Der Liebesbegriff* to the non-canonical sources too – characteristically, she did not leave any footnote introducing a quaint figure of Adam before Adam. The Adam whom Arendt could have had in mind while writing *Der Liebesbegriff* was Adam Kadmon from the Kabbalah, not the actual Adam from the first couple. Adam Kadmon was a mediator between God's oneness and human plurality. God created this ideal image in his own likeness and then dispersed it indirectly. Although Arendt did not evoke Kabbalistic sources openly,[38] one can understand her otherwise obscure speculation referring to the Jewish traditions:

> *it is the origin of the whole race transmitted indirectly to the individual by generation. The first man, the source, hands down this indirectness by way of all men through the historically made world. Indirectness alone first establishes the equality of all people. (Arendt 1996, p. 104)*

Adam before Adam helps to resolve the problem haunting Christian metaphysics, namely how to explain that something different from God came into being at all. If God is so perfect in his isolation, why did he create the world? Or, how to affirm human plurality contrasting with his oneness? Christian radicalism personified in Augustine had resolved those dilemmas at the expense of man. But in Judeochristian reading which Arendt offered, there is no necessity to contrast human and God like one contrasts evil and good (not to mention that in the Kabbalah the reflection about God's internal evil, hidden and safely remaining in his essence, was not something unheard of). When we change perspective, however, and start with the perception Arendt proposed, what we have at first is human irreducible plurality; going back through generations we could reach the imagined first couple and then, it seems, monotheistic religious imagination needed an image of one man to build a passage between earthly reality (dyadic structure as the simplest one possible to reproduce) and God's inaccessibility. Adam Kadmon would be then a condensation of human dreams about a universal, diverse unity. At the same time, unique status of God is preserved and—looking chronologically this time, in the way his uniqueness is transmitted to men—mediated. Before differentiation in multitude and dispersion there is the last moment, which will remain embedded *in the memory of humankind*, reminding it of the "distinctive human origin" (Arendt 1996, p. 104), a double genealogy. It implies double negative dialectics, which could distance singularity from God in order to secure her "being

---

38   It would have been quite odd after all, analysing Augustine. However, Arendt in her dissertation sometimes seemed to refer to some esoteric thought.

of man among men" (Arendt 1996, p. 104), but also distance her from a given community thanks to referring back to something that exceeds actuality and immanence. According to Arendt, Christianity accentuated rather the latter—"being of man as a creature" (Arendt 1996, p. 104), standing individually before God in isolation and alienation, believing falsely that humans need to imitate autarkic ideal.

The rest of the third chapter Arendt devoted to discussing the Christian community of faith. It is a complicated part, which could be misunderstood without the Marranic hypothesis. The author rarely trespasses mere reconstruction, but from time to time she commented critically. The rhythm of the presentation consists of longer passages of reconstruction, followed by interventions. They do not add much to the arguments gathered so far. It is evident, however, that Arendt completely disregarded taking salvation into account. In her reading, Christianity already entered into the zone of salvation, the Kingdom had already come, so the only important issue is the neighbour. She emphasized that salvation had not abolished mortality. Although she engaged deeply in the meanders of Christian neighbourly love, what counted for her most is that "the neighbor's relevance is not tied to Christianity. The binding power of the common faith in Christ is secondary. Faith in Christ redeems the past and only the common past can make the faith a common faith. This past alone is common to all" (Arendt 1996, p. 107).

8. Whose Is That God?

In the letter from 14 January 1945 to Gershom Scholem, Hannah Arendt presented herself as follows: "Ich bin (…) ein Epikaeures" (Arendt and Scholem 2010, p. 57). It is an epithet iridescent with various meanings, attributed by the Jewish communities to Hellenised Jews, heretics, epicureans or unbelievers. Relying on this polymorphous self-ascription, one should not expect any "religious correctness"[39] from Arendt. She betrayed both traditions, Jewish and Christian, looking for "the speculative conditions for a philosophy of freedom" (Arendt 1978, pp. 145–46).

When it comes to God, she was very fastidious. Her remarks, like: "God (if indeed it is God)" (Arendt 1996, p. 78)—signify "healthy suspicion of the transcendent" (Neiman 2001, p. 70). Arendt did not accept God, who appears as *deus ex machina*, ready to command (Arendt 1996, p. 39). For some people who regard themselves as "orthodox", it could seem to be hutzpah. But I find in her art of distancing oneself from the absolute a kind of respect for God's enigma and a deep understanding of the symmetrical enigma of men. The figure of chiasmus incarnates the way their interconnectedness functions. God of Arendtian speculation resides on the antipodes of the theological vision of divinity preferred by Augustine:

> as Supreme Being, God is the quintessence of Being, namely self-sufficiency, which needs no help from the outside and actually has nothing outside itself. So strong is Augustine's dependence upon these non-Christian currents of thought that he even uses them occasionally for a description of God: 'God needs no assistance from anything else in the act of creation as though he were one who did not suffice himself.' Undoubtedly, insofar as Augustine defines love as a kind of desire, he hardly speaks as a Christian. (Arendt 1996, pp. 20–21)[40]

For Arendt things present themselves contrarily: "Man was originally created into the world and, in spite of this election, this fact of being in the world separates him from God, that is, from pure being" (Arendt 1996, p. 80). For Augustine, to say that God could be deficient was blasphemous. According to Arendt, deficient God would be the only one who could fit to human deficiency, incompleteness, and openness. Creatureliness is torn between two kinds of nothingness. It is neither being, nor

---

[39] This example seems to be sufficient: "The redeeming death of Christ did not redeem an individual but the whole world (*mundus*), understood as the man-made world" (Arendt 1996, p. 99). So much was her attention for the world, that she not only profaned Christian salvation, but also death, which she saw as "the loss of the world" (Arendt 1996, p. 33).

[40] The error made by Danielle Celermajer is, thus, astonishing: "she assumed that the Neoplatonic characterizations of the God of the Jews accurately represented the ontological structure of the Hebraic universe (and God)" (Celermajer 2011, p. 10). Nothing more contrary to everything Arendt said about Neoplatonism.

nothingness, but living in relations (Arendt 1996, p. 52). Living in-between, but at the edge of nothingness, demands some limits and buffer zones, otherwise "conscious entity" (Arendt 1996, p. 50) could not crystallise. This would not be possible without antinaturalism: distant, almost forgotten transcendence sets immanent reality aside. Nonetheless, a God who offered a space for something other than himself does not expect praise. His discreet leaving was intended, instead, to avert human gaze from absoluteness and to concentrate it on the world, inhabited by our neighbours.

Even joking sarcastically, or maybe especially then, Hannah Arendt treated theology seriously, as the absolute can at any moment invade politics in the only form absoluteness comes: violence. For that reason, I am sceptical about Samuel Moyn's recapitulation of Arendt's aim: "Secularization is precisely the attempt not to escape from the authority and the sanction with which the absolute provides politics but to find nonreligious version of them" (Moyn 2008, p. 75). Even if it were so, then, in order to cope responsibly with monotheistic legacy[41] in politics, we need the cryptotheological defence of the secular world.

Funding: Narodowe Centrum Nauki (National Science Centre, Poland): grant no. 2016/20/T/HS1/00244.

Conflicts of Interest: The author declares no conflict of interest. The founding sponsors had no role in the design of the study; in the collection, analyses, or interpretation of data; in the writing of the manuscript, and in the decision to publish the results.

References

Adler, Laure. 2008. *Śladami Hannah Arendt*. Translated by Janina Aleksandrowicz. Warszawa: Wydawnictwo Książkowe Twój Styl. First published 2005.

Agamben, Giorgio. 2013. *Opus Dei: An Archaeology of Duty*. Translated by Adam Kotsko. Stanford: Stanford University Press.

Arendt, Hannah. 1929. *Der Liebesbegriff bei Augustin: Versuch einer Philosophischen Interpretation*. Berlin: Julius Springer.

Arendt, Hannah. 1978. Willing. In *The Life of the Mind*. New York: Harcourt Brace Jovanovich.

Arendt, Hannah. 1994. *Essays in Understanding, 1930–1954*. Edited by Jerome Kohn. New York: Harcourt, Brace & Co.

Arendt, Hannah. 1996. *Love and Saint Augustine*. Edited and with an Interpretive Essay by Joanna Vecchiarelli Scott and Judith Chelius Stark. Chicago: University of Chicago Press.

Arendt, Hannah, and Karl Jaspers. 1992. *Hannah Arendt/Karl Jaspers Correspondence, 1926–1969*. Edited by Lotte Kohler and Hans Saner. Translated by Robert, and Rita Kimber. New York: Harcourt Brace Jovanovich. First published 1985.

Arendt, Hannah, and Mary McCarthy. 1995. *Between Friends: The Correspondence of Hannah Arendt and Mary McCarthy, 1949–1975*. Edited and with an Introduction by Carol Brightman. New York: Harcourt Brace.

Arendt, Hannah, and Gershom Scholem. 2010. *Der Briefwechsel*. Edited by Marie Luise Knott, with Assistance of David Heredia. Berlin: Jüdischer Verlag.

Armenteros, Carolina. 1999. Hannah Arendt, Rahel Varnhagen and the beginnings of Arendtian political philosophy. *The Journal of Jewish Thought and Philosophy* 8: 81–118. [CrossRef]

Beiner, Ronald. 1997. Love and worldliness: Hannah Arendt's reading of St. Augustine. In *Hannah Arendt: Twenty Years Later*. Edited by Larry May and Jerome Kohn. Cambridge: MIT Press.

---

[41] I find Jane Anna Gordon's emphasis put on "Arendt's anomalously positive appraisal of polytheism" (Gordon 2009, p. 330) overestimated and shallow. A statement that "political theology of democratic life" can be built only on polytheistic premises does not exhaust the complexity and ambiguous character of the remarks made by Arendt about religious traditions. Of course, she admitted that the political model of sovereignty, which she contested, is embedded in a monotheistic image of God, but nevertheless—as my interpretative frame aspires to show—it was not a simple rejection of monotheism, but a heterodox pluralisation of this model. Precisely the same efforts of Jewish thinkers were described by Gershom Scholem in his studies on the Kabbalah: to defend the secular world by means of theology, avoiding an accusation of ideological reductionism by indicating the fact that "the hidden tradition" of Hebraic religion encapsulated the impulse of *amor mundi*.

Bernauer, James W. 1987a. *Amor Mundi: Explorations in the Faith and Thought of Hannah Arendt.* Edited by James W. Bernauer. Boston, Dordrecht and Lancaster: Martinus Nijhoff Publishers.

Bernauer, James W. 1987b. The faith of Hannah Arendt: amor mundi and its critique-assimilation of religious experience. In *Amor Mundi: Explorations in the Faith and Thought of Hannah Arendt.* Edited by James W. Bernauer. Boston, Dordrecht and Lancaster: Martinus Nijhoff Publishers.

Biale, David. 2011. *Not in the Heavens: The Tradition of Jewish Secular Thought.* Princeton: Princeton University Press.

Bielik-Robson, Agata. 2014. *Jewish Cryptotheologies of Late Modernity: Philosophical Marranos.* London and New York: Routledge, Taylor & Francis Group.

Bielik-Robson, Agata. 2015. L'amour fort comme la mort: Les Juifs contre Heidegger (sur la question de la finitude). *La Règle du Jeu* 58/59: 529–60.

Boyle, Patrick. 1987. Elusive neighborliness: Hannah Arendt's interpretation of Saint Augustine. In *Amor Mundi: Explorations in the Faith and Thought of Hannah Arendt.* Edited by James W. Bernauer. Boston, Dordrecht and Lancaster: Martinus Nijhoff Publishers.

Celermajer, Danielle. 2011. Hebraic dimensions of Hannah Arendt's thought. *Journal of Modern Jewish Studies* 10: 3–22. [CrossRef]

Chacón, Rodrigo. 2012. Hannah Arendt in Weimar: beyond the theological-political predicament? In *The Weimar Moment: Liberalism, Political Theology, and Law.* Edited by Leonard V. Kaplan and Rudy Koshar. Lanham: Lexington Books.

Chiba, Shin. 1995. Hannah Arendt on love and the political: Love, friendship and citizenship. *The Review of Politics* 57: 505–35. [CrossRef]

Clarke, Barry, and Lawrence Quill. 2009. Augustine, Arendt, and Anthropy. *Sophia: International Journal for Philosophy of Religion, Metaphysical Theology and Ethics* 48: 253–65. [CrossRef]

Gordon, Jane Anna. 2009. Hannah Arendt's political theology of democratic life. *Political Theology* 10: 325–39. [CrossRef]

Grumett, David. 2000. Arendt, Augustine and Evil. *Heythrop Journal* 41: 154–69. [CrossRef]

Jonas, Hans. 1996. *Mortality and Morality: A Search for the Good after Auschwitz.* Edited and with an Introduction by Lawrence Vogel. Evanston: Northwestern University Press.

Kalyvas, Andreas. 2008. *Democracy and the Politics of the Extraordinary: Max Weber, Carl Schmitt, and Hannah Arendt.* Cambridge and New York: Cambridge University Press.

Kampowski, Stephan. 2008. *Arendt, Augustine, and the New Beginning: The Action Theory and Moral Thought of Hannah Arendt in the Light of Her Dissertation on St. Augustine.* Grand Rapids and Cambridge: William B. Eerdmans Pub. Co.

Kiess, John. 2016. *Hannah Arendt and Theology.* London and New York: Bloomsbury T&T Clark.

Lazier, Benjamin. 2008. *God Interrupted: Heresy and the European Imagination between the World Wars.* Princeton: Princeton University Press.

Liska, Vivian. 2017. *German-Jewish Thought and Its Afterlife: A Tenuous Legacy.* Bloomington: Indiana University Press.

Löwith, Karl. 1964. *From Hegel to Nietzsche: The Revolution in Nineteenth-Century Thought.* Translated by David E. Green. New York: Holt, Rinehart and Winston. First published 1941.

Löwith, Karl. 1994. *My Life in Germany before and after 1933: A Report.* Translated by Elizabeth King. London: Athlone Press. First published 1986.

Marchart, Oliver. 2005. *Neu Beginnen: Hannah Arendt, die Revolution und die Globalisierung.* With a preface by Linda Zerilli. Wien: Turia + Kant.

Moyn, Samuel. 2008. Hannah Arendt on the Secular. *New German Critique* 35: 71–96. [CrossRef]

Neiman, Susan. 2001. Theodicy in Jerusalem. In *Hannah Arendt in Jerusalem.* Edited by Steven E. Aschheim. Berkeley: University of California Press.

Plotinus. 1990. *Ennead II.* Translated by Arthur Hilary Armstrong. Cambridge and London: Harvard University Press.

Rosenzweig, Franz. 2005. *The Star of Redemption.* Translated by Barbara E. Galli. Madison: University of Wisconsin Press. First published 1921.

Rosenzweig, Franz. 1921. *Der Stern der Erlösung.* Frankfurt am Main: J. Kauffmann Verlag.

Savarino, Luca. 1999. Quaestio mihi factus sum: Una lettura heideggeriana di 'Il concetto d'amore in Agostino'. In *Hannah Arendt.* Introduction and Edited by Simona Forti. Milano: Bruno Mondadori.

Scholem, Gershom. 1965. *On the Kabbalah and its Symbolism*. Translated by Ralph Manheim. New York: Schocken Books.

Sontheimer, Kurt. 2005. *Hannah Arendt: Der Weg einer grossen Denkerin*. München: Piper.

Steinberg, Michael P. 2007. Hannah Arendt and the cultural style of the German Jews. *Social Research* 74: 879–902.

Taminiaux, Jacques. 1997. *The Thracian Maid and the Professional Thinker: Arendt and Heidegger*. Translated and Edited by Michael Gendre. Albany: State University of New York Press. First published 1992.

Tanner, Klaus. 2012. Protestant Revolt against Modernity. In *The Weimar Moment: Liberalism, Political Theology, and Law*. Edited by Leonard V. Kaplan and Rudy Koshar. Lanham: Lexington Books.

Tassin, Étienne, and de Véronique Albanel. 2010. Préface. In *Amour du monde: Christianisme et politique chez Hannah Arendt*. Paris: Les Éditions du Cerf.

Tatman, Lucy. 2013. Arendt and Augustine: More than one kind of love. *Sophia* 52: 625–35. [CrossRef]

Vecchiarelli Scott, Joanna. 1988. 'A detour through Pietism:' Hannah Arendt's on St. Augustine's philosophy of freedom. *Polity* 20: 394–425. [CrossRef]

Vecchiarelli Scott, Joanna. 2010. What St. Augustine taught Hannah Arendt about 'how to live in the world:' caritas, natality and the banality of evil. *Collegium: Studies Across Disciplines in the Humanities and Social Sciences* 8: 67–85.

Weir, Todd H. 2015. The Christian front against godlessness: Anti-secularism and the demise of the Weimar Republic, 1928–1933. *Past and Present* 229: 201–38. [CrossRef]

Winters, Francis X. 1987. The Banality of virtue: Reflections on Hannah Arendt's reinterpretation of political ethics. In *Amor Mundi: Explorations in the Faith and Thought of Hannah Arendt*. Edited by James W. Bernauer. Boston, Dordrecht and Lancaster: Martinus Nijhoff Publishers.

Wolin, Richard. 2001. *Heidegger's Children: Hannah Arendt, Karl Löwith, Hans Jonas, and Herbert Marcuse*. Princeton: Princeton University Press.

Young-Bruehl, Elisabeth. 2004. *Hannah Arendt: For Love of the World*, 2nd ed. New Haven and London: Yale University Press. First published 1982.

Zawisza, Rafał. 2012. Ocalić to, co się da: Witalistyczna interpretacja rozprawy doktorskiej Hanny Arendt pt. 'O pojęciu miłości u Augustyna'. *Praktyka Teoretyczna* 6: 327–45. [CrossRef]

![religions logo] *religions*

MDPI

Article

Jacques Derrida: The Double Liminality of a Philosophical Marrano

Emilie Kutash

Philosophy Department, Salem State University, Salem, MA 01970, USA; ekutash@salemstate.edu

Received: 28 December 2018; Accepted: 19 January 2019; Published: 22 January 2019

check for updates

Abstract: There is an analogy between two types of liminality: the geographic or cultural 'outside' space of the Marrano Jew, alienated from his/her original religion and the one he or she has been forced to adopt, and, a philosophical position that is outside of both Athens and Jerusalem. Derrida finds and re-finds 'h'ors- texte', an 'internal desert', a 'secret' outside place: alien to both the western philosophical tradition and the Hebraic archive. In this liminal space he questions the otherness of the French language to which he was acculturated, and, in a turn to a less discursive modality, autobiography, finds, in the words of Helene Cixous, "the Jew-who-doesn't know-that-he-is". Derrida's galut (exile) is neither Hebrew nor Greek. It is a private place outside of all discourse, which he claims, is inevitably ethnocentric. In inhabiting this outside space, he exercises the prerogative of a Marrano, equipped to critique the French language of his acculturation and the western philosophy of the scholars. French and Hebrew are irreconcilable binaries, western philosophy and his Hebrew legacy is as well. These issues will be discussed in this paper with reference to *Monolingualism of the Other* and *Archive Fever* as they augment some of his earlier work, *Writing and Difference* and *Speech and Phenomena*.

Keywords: Derrida; philosophical Marrano; liminal; archive; Hebrew; Greek; Monolingualism

The Marrano Jew has been studied from a sociological, historical and religious perspective. The effect of the Marrano 'position' in the later generations of these original peoples, particularly on the work of Marrano scholars, is of interest as well. The term 'Marrano', narrowly defined, applies to Jewish people who were living in the Iberian peninsula in the Middle Ages and were forced to convert to Christianity. Marranos were expelled from the country in which they were acculturated, or they had to assume a position outside the Jewish religion of their ancestors. In either situation they were forced to exist at the margins of the culture in which they lived. The exteriority that goes along with cultural marginalization has had notable effects in shaping Marrano sensibility. Jacques Derrida, a self-proclaimed 'Marrano', merits a careful examination to his work in this regard. As Agata Bielik-Robson discusses, Derrida like other philosophers who were "philosophical Marranos" turned "the Jew Greek: Greek Jew" binary to his advantage" (Bielik-Robson 2004, p. 4). His work will serve here to illustrate how a Marrano mentality can situate a philosopher such as Derrida in a unique position to criticize and analyze the 'host' culture to which he experienced an uneasy assimilation. The marginal position from which Derrida viewed Western philosophy and its Greek inheritance allowed him to claim himself to be neither 'Greek' or Jew but rather exterior to both traditions.

The term 'liminality' from the Latin word 'limen', meaning 'threshold', has the connotation of disorientation between a previous way of structuring one's reality or identity and assuming a new one. For the postmodern philosopher Jacques Derrida, this term can be applied to an analogy that can be made between two types of liminality: the geographic or cultural exteriority of the Marrano Jew–and a philosophical position that is outside of both Jewish and Greek traditions. In fact, Derrida, who is the arch deconstructor of binary oppositions, is outside or external to almost any binary opposition one cares to name. The Marrano Jew is expelled from her original spiritual domicile and alien to the one she has been forced to adopt. Derrida is alienated both from the place of his birth and acculturation, including his only, but still foreign, native tongue and his Jewish heritage. Doubling this exteriority is his philosophical alienation both from the totalizing western/Greek philosophical tradition of his educational nurture, and the Hebraic traditional archive, which, to him, in Zizek's prescient term, is an 'unknown known' (Zizek 2008). Outside of both Athens and Jerusalem, he proclaims he is situated in neither.

Derrida, famously, is often characterized as claiming there is no" hors- texte", nothing outside the texe (Derrida 1976, p. 158). Outside of all disseminating and totalizing 'White Mythology,'[1] and outside the Hebrew texts that comprise the archive of his ancestors, in fact, it is he himself that is hors-texte. He is sans archive; sans a language of his own and sans a believable textual universe of discourse. This is precisely why his *Circumfession*, an autobiographical memoir written later in his career, is a key document that situates him squarely outside of academic writing except when it can function as a record of memory. To occupy that space he had spent a great deal of his career deconstructing the texts of the alien intellectual world to which he had been acculturated. This he had done masterfully throughout his academic life. He could not, however, as he so eloquently expresses, occupy the 'archive' of his own heritage. When he turned to autobiography to make himself immune to discourse that betrays his secret self, he was able to find, in Helene Cixous's words, "the-Jew-who-doesn't-know-tht-he-is" (Cixous 2004, p. 118). The meaning of liminality for Derrida will be taken up here in three contexts: language, archives and philosophical discourse. Derrida's own 'galut' (exile) is neither Hebrew nor Greek.[2] It is a secret place outside of or at the margins of all discourse which discourse he claims, is inevitably ethnocentric.[3]

1. What Does Liminality Mean in Terms of a Language/Mother Tongue?

In *Monolingualism of the Other*, Derrida describes the community of his childhood and acculturation. First of all, it was cut off from both Arabic or Berber (more properly Maghrebian) language and culture. Second, it was also cut off from French, as a European language and culture, the language of what Derrida calls the 'metropole'. His own Algerian French was equally alien to him. Doubling up on this, he was cut off from Jewish 'cultural memory', from the "[h]istory and language that one must presume to be their own, but which, at a certain point, no longer was; namely Hebrew." Where, he then asks, are we? He cannot take refuge in the language or "[i]diom internal to the Jewish community, to any sort of language of refuge like Yiddish, (which) "would have ensured an element of intimacy, (as he put it), the protection of a "home-of –one's own (chez –soi) against the language of the official culture . . . " (Derrida 1998, p. 54). Ladino, a language spoken primarily by Sephardic Jews throughout the Mediterranean was not spoken in the Algeria he knew, as it was not spoken in the bigger cities, where the Jewish population happened to be concentrated. In fact, he bemoans the fact that the Jews of the Mediterranean coastline would probably be more alien to him than those of Christian France (Derrida 1998, p. 55).[4] As a philosopher, he was doubly troubled by philosophical coinages as well as by his spoken language The substantivized abstractions which he systematically dismantled in "White Mythology" and other texts could never, he claimed, produce their intended meanings.

In a footnote to this discussion of his perceived cultural and linguistic exclusion, Derrida elaborates on the issue of being Jewish and being acculturated in a diaspora culture. He cites Franz Rosenzweig who took up the question of Jews and their foreign language. Rosenzweig claimed that "the eternal people have lost their own language (*seine eigne Sprache verloren hat*): "[t]hey have no language that is

---

[1] His term for the abstract 'philosophemes' that dominate western philosophy.

[2] See Miriam Leonard, "Derrida between Greek and Jew" in (Leonard 2010) for elaboration on this theme.

[3] Erin Graff Zivin's collection of essays in the recent book *The Marrano Specter: Derrida and Hispanism* (Zivin 2017) extensively discusses Derrida's preoccupation with secrecy and its relation to his Marrano identity. See for example Peggy Kanuf's preface.

[4] See also (Derrida 1998, p. 55, n. 9).

exclusively their own, only the language of the host . . . ". Even when they speak the language of the host who is accommodating them", they speak a language that is not theirs (Derrida 1998, p. 79–80).[5] As for Hebrew, according to Rosenzweig, the Jewish people speak it only to the extent that it is employed in prayer. Derrida remarks on his own spoken and written acculturated tongue. "My language," he declares, "the only one I hear myself speak and agree to speak, is the language of the other" (Derrida 1998, p. 25). "Alienation without alienation, this inalienable alienation . . . " seems to be the outcome. He associates murder and trauma and collective assassinations with this unchosen language. Language, then, is another space of potential exclusion as was his own expulsion from non-Jewish schools. He had no choice in either case. The subtext attached to this narrative is the danger that lies within a language not one's own: the assumed language is not free of culture or history. There is no non-ethnocentric panoptic metalanguage that can rescue a speaker who is ambivalent about the culture in which he was brought up. Murder, trauma and collective assassinations, which he pins on to his Algerian French, puts Jacques Derrida in a precarious relationship with his native tongue. The trauma of having been expelled from his school because of antisemitism had raised his consciousness of the dangers of a foreign acculturation. This situation in respect to language was precisely articulated by Franz Kafka. In a letter to Max Brod, concerning German Jewish writers and the German language, Kafka claimed, "They existed "among three impossibilities . . . the impossibility of not writing" (as they could get rid of their inspiration only by writing) the impossibility of writing in German . . . (and) "there is also the impossibility of writing differently since no other language was available . . . " (Kafka 1921).[6] Kafka considered their use of the German language as the "overt or convert, or possibly self-tormenting usurpation of an alien properly which has not been acquired but stolen . . . quickly picked up, and which remains someone else's possession." Cynthia Ozick points out that Kafka had attended a German university, studied German jurisprudence and published in German periodicals. He did not write in Czech. The Jews of Prague at that time were German educated from grade school on and yet in this letter, he is expressing, as did Derrida in *Monolingualism of the Other*, a feeling of estrangement from this "available" language.[7]

Derrida discusses the position of Hannah Arendt when, while living in Paris, she was stripped of her citizenship by the Nazis. She later made the claim that deprivation of citizenship should be classified as a crime against humanity (Arendt and Kohn 2018, p. 99) If, as Derrida has claimed, we make a language, written or spoken, the agent of ethnocentrism, (Derrida 1976, p. 3), then German as the spoken language of Hannah Arendt should be also implicated. If, as happened to Derrida, the figure of the other within colonial Algeria can be stripped of the privileges of citizenship, the language itself can become an evil stepmother. Derrida describes his situation while he lived in Algiers. Derrida called France the metropole. It was a fantasy place: "[t]he Capital-City-Mother-Fatherland, the city of the mother tongue . . . a faraway country, near but far away . . . , strange fantastic and phantom-like . . . it represented the language of the master" (Derrida 1998, p. 42). Hannah Arendt, discussed at length by Derrida in the footnote to *Monolingualism*, when asked about Nazism and her attachment to the German language said, "After all, it is not the German language that has gone mad . . . and in the second place nothing can replace the mother tongue" (Derrida 1998, p. 84). Derrida contends that in these simplistic statements Arendt did not see the abyss opening under them. The implication here is that the French language of Derrida's acculturation, as a Marrano Jew, could easily open up the abyss of anti-Semitism and take the ground out from under these 'ex-otic" citizens, as it did during Derrida's youth. Though making no direct connection with the events of Germany in the years before the Holocaust, the analogy is implicit.

Doubling upon Derrida's irreconcilable liminality, from both the France of Algiers and that of the idealized Metropole ("the Capital-City-Mother-Fatherland") is an analogous alienation from

---

[5]   Derrida cites Rosenzweig (1982, p. 354).
[6]   Franz Kafka, Letter to Max Brod, 1921 quoted in Kafka, *Basic Kafka*, (1984, p. 292).
[7]   Cynthia Ozick, discusses this in "The Impossibility of Translating Franz Kafka", (New Yorker, 11 January 1999).

philosophical language as well as from the ancestral archive of Hebrew texts. Philosophical writing is irredeemably metonymic, with no resting place in false absolutes whose meanings disseminate and can be deconstructed. We recall that in an early work, one definitive for his later positions, Of *Grammatology*, (Derrida 1976, p. 3) in an Exergue, Derrida makes it clear that writing is controlled by ethnocentrism. Logocentrism, he says at another point, is an agent of ethnocentrism. As far as the Hebrew textual universe is concerned, Edmond Jabès called these texts "the fatherland of the Jew"—"the sacred text surrounded by commentary" (Jabès 1963, p. 109). Derrida quotes this in his essay on Jabès' *Les Livre des questions* (Derrida 1978a, p. 67). In the case of the so called "fatherland of the Jews", the Hebrew archive, it consists of the written scripture and the so-called oral tradition consisting of the Mishnah, Talmud and later commentary. In addition to Derrida's general suspicion of all written text, for Derrida, there is the uncomfortable possibility that an allegiance to these and other authoritative Hebrew texts would entail a 'particularism' that is in opposition to a more ethical universalism. European language, however, is also subject to a particularism that poses as universal and this is perhaps even more deceptive.

When the valorization of a given language is associated with nationalism, the situation is compounded. It is interesting in this regard to recall Fichte's address to the German People, (an inspiration for one of Heidegger's most pro-Nazi addresses) in which Fichte extols the German language as an authentic language with spiritual qualities (Fichte 1808).[8] When Derrida invokes the word 'fatherland' it has the uneasy overtones of Fichte Heidegger's speech and the Nazi valorization of fatherland and of native tongue. The implication here is similar to that of "Interpretations at War": Kant, the Jew, the German" (Derrida 1991). In this essay, he calls Philo the 'fuhrer' using the German word in the sense of leader but, again, invoking the dangerous possibilities of a Jewish philosopher 'feigning to speak Greek'. In the 1964 essay on Levinas entitled "Violence and Metaphysics," Derrida asks, "[W]ill a non-Greek ever succeed in doing what a Greek could not do except by . . . feigning to speak Greek in order to get near the king (viz. the parricide of the Greek father)?" (Derrida 1978b, p. 89). Here 'Greek' can be considered a metonym for spoken languages, particularly European ones. If, as Jabès claims, it is the Hebrew texts that are the 'fatherland of the Jews', (Jabès 1963, p. 109) those of the French will always be alien, even dangerous, only to be used in the service of parracidic textual deconstruction. With this said, Derrida himself can be held to the same standard as he holds Levinas. He too may be 'feigning' in the language of the other, also known as Greek (a placeholder for western written texts) and has put his efforts aimed at deconstructing western philosophy in the service of "parricide" as well.

The act of reading Derrida as a system of hyperlinks that circle back from later to earlier writings and then back again to later ones is always crucial to interpreting his work and deriving meaning out of his texts. Derrida's early work centered on the deconstruction of the privileging of speech over writing, what he considered a prevalent but unwarranted binary opposition which devalued writing in favor of speech. In *Speech and Phenomena*, he questioned the presence to self of speech. Speech is as devoid of presence as writing and signification always refers to other signs not itself. Spatial and temporal differing defer meaning in a dissemination that leaves only 'traces' of originating meaning. *Monolingualism of the Other* adds a cultural dimension which spoken languages bring to 'speech'. The early disavowal of 'speech' as a privileged connection to the 'signified' as presence is compounded by the addition of the ethnocentricity of language doubling the problematic of s meaning. In *Des tours de Babel*, (Derrida 2002b), Derrida makes it clear that no human language is exempt from a decentered and regional hermeneutic specificity. The situatedness of the subject as speaker of a specific tongue is victim of a tautegorical set of meanings resistant to translation. Derrida will conclude that the acculturated language is always alien, always originates in the 'other' for a speaker, such as himself, who holds an ambivalent relationship to the place of his childhood community. "We only ever speak

---

8   In the fifth, sixth, and thirteenth address Fichte extolls the German language in this way.

one language-and since it returns to the other, it exists asymmetrically, always for the other, from the other, kept by the other" (Derrida 1998, p. 40).

Reading *Gift of Death* in light of the arguments in *Monolingualism of the Other*, allows a contrast between a public discourse, as are all spoken languages, and a private 'self'. Abraham, when complying with the divine command that he sacrifice his son, the biblical drama that Derrida elaborates at length in *Gift of Death* (Derrida 1995b), embodies the singularity, as opposed to the subject of speech and writing, of a silent but authentic subject Abraham enacts this drama within a liminal situation exterior to public discourse, displaying in his silence an abject faith and avowal to the divine command. *Monolingualism of the Other*, makes it clear that spoken language is always at the service of political, ethnic and social factors and is not an independent signifying apparatus. The silence of Abraham at Mount Moriah represents a moment of avowal, outside all and any sociocultural milieu. The 'I' or self that is the subject to the objectifications posited by language is inauthentic and differs according to the ethnically diverse public domains in which they originate. An original or archaic monolingualism as a universally given structure was lost at Babel. The moment of avowal at Moriah, then, holds significance for Derrida as a template for the possibility of a secret self that is genuinely and truly 'outside'.

2. Archive Fever

As Simon Ctitchley explains, Derrida's deconstruction attempts to locate a non-site from which he can question philosophy. It is a place of exteriority, alterity or marginality (Critchley 2014, pp. 29–32). Derrida is not only entrapped in a mono-linguicism that is not his own, but in a philosophical history/archive that is equally a mono-ontology or philsopheme-ology of the other. Derrida's externality, in fact, is at the margin or outside of two completely disparate archives, both outside of Hebrew and Greek. He has a painful sense that the search for origins might, (and he equivocates on this), be futile and therefore precludes the possibility of authenticating either one. On the one hand, there is the Greco-Latin-German idealist tradition of which Plato, Philo 'the fuhrer', Maimonides all the way to o Kant, Hegel, Husserl and Hermann Cohen and on to Heidegger, are the authorizing patriarchs. On the other hand, there is the Judaic archive, as Urbach (1995) tells us which denotes the written scripture and the Sages of the Oral Law: the Mishna, and Talmud, Tosefta, Midrashim, (and the tradition of responsa which continues into the twentieth century with figures such as Moshe Feinstein). The Torah and the Mishna and the sages of the Talmud provide a core reality that is axiomatic to Jewish thought. The heavenly origin of the Torah, the possibility of a messianic age, elected nationhood and other such principles that ground these works, however, leave them outside modern sensibilities and comprehension. In this sense, Greek/Western philosophy and Judaic thought cannot fully coincide since it would be impossible for the former to meet these primal stipulations. Allegory and symbolic interpretation were long ago recognized as precluded from the Hebrew canon and its idiolectic system. '*Chokhmot chitzoniyot*' (foreign wisdoms) are alien to these texts and their interpretive communities just as they were for Crescas when he viewed Maimonides intellectualism as the direct cause of Iberian Jewry's spiritual breakdown.

Derrida is doubly liminal in relation to the two archival histories. The Marrano Jew, in his or her original situation, was only partially removed from the Judaism h/she secretly practiced, recognizing that the culture to which h/she was assimilated was a false identity. Derrida's 'Converso' position is that of someone who is many generations removed from this original set of circumstances. He has never known or meaningfully practiced his Judaism and is alienated from both his ancestral legacy and his sociocultural assimilated Jewish present. The philosophical archive that Derrida acquired during his university education and from his philosophical community, in addition, is irreconcilable with that of the ancestral heritage of which he only possesses traces. Derrida remains outside the reason/revelation binary that allegedly differentiates the two as well. The God of Moses cannot be translated into the temporalized absolute that appears in western philosophical discussions such as in the texts of German Idealists, (Hammer 2011)[9], but neither does the God of the Jewish people make his presence known to Derrida. Derrida joins an ancient and age-old Judaic opposition to philosophy without being able to do it in the name of the traditional sages and medieval Jewish philosophers who opposed so called 'Greek Wisdom'. Their opposition had the imprimatur of Divine Origin and enfranchised interpretation grounded in proof texts such as the written scripture. His finds no such ground. In fact, he deconstructs the whole idea of a ground.

Derrida is situated outside his own tradition, as well, due to the painful fact that the historicity of the Judaic archive is subject to limitations that any kind of modernist criteria for verification would impose. Cultural memory is not history. For both Edmond Jabès, and Derrida, while an allegorical reading of the Torah, thanks to Philo is unacceptable, the concrete literality of the Judaic archive makes it an idiolect, that is equally suspect. The literal reading that is required for a true faith creates an unnegotiable separation between the 'really real' of historicity and the unverified 'historical' 'Book' that is the proof text of all Jewish learning. On the other hand, as Derrida says in the Jabès essay, describing the Jew as a split self, "He, would have no history at all if he let himself be attenuated within the algebra of an abstract universalism" (Derrida 1978a, p. 75). The modernist alienation from the Jewish archives based on rationalist scientific criteria and a passion for historicity does not allow adherence to the biblical texts but 'abstract universalism' is not an option. In *Archive Fever*, Derrida discusses Freud's book on Moses, not as a history but as a novel. The actual biblical narratives might be equally regarded as fictional by a postmodern reader. Scientific validity and philosophical objectivity, on the other hand, have themselves engendered a troublesome progeny. Once again Derrida is caught between a universality that is permeated by false absolutes and an archive which would make him the patron of concrete literalism and an unacceptable particularism. Citing Jabès, this entails "[t]he incommensurable destiny which grafts the historicity of a '*race born of the book*' (*Livre des questions*, p. 26) onto the radical origin of meaning as literality, that is, onto historicity itself." (Derrida 1978a, p. 64).

In *Monolingualism of the Other*, Derrida describes himself as subject to a "radical lack of culture from which I undoubtedly never completely emerged" (Derrida 1998, p. 53). He defines himself by this lack and thus identifies himself as the occupant of a space empty of cultural preconditions. He is without a lens through which he could acculturate. His use of any number of mouthpieces other than himself reflects the fact of his personal residence within a cultural desert where none of the options available to him bear fruit intellectually or make him speak in his own voice. In the Talmud all the arguments are made in the voice of one or another of the Rabbinic sages, while the narrative voice of the redactor is unknown. Derrida, too, makes a cryptic use of mouthpieces thus yielding up traces of the secrets he has contemplated while in retreat to his own spiritual desert. In *Archive Fever* he takes on the voice of Yerushalmi in his book, *Freud's Moses; Judaism Terminable and Interminable*, where Yerushalmi contends that there is some validity to Freud's own secret, that psychoanalysis is a Jewish science, despite the fact that Freud disavows this in his public discourse (Yerushalmi 1991). When Freud does invoke the Jewish archive, in *Moses and Monotheism*, he gives it a pseudo historicity exiling it from the archival account in the Torah and making it live uncomfortably in neither true history nor biblical narrative. In public Freud was a modern sceptic, in private he held allegiance to his Judaism. *Moses and Monotheism* is the uneasy hybrid. If Yerushalmi's account of this matter, then, reflects a position with which Derrida identifies, it is archetypically in Marrano style, passed through the lens of Yerushalmi's discussion of Freud's secret. Derrida remains hidden concerning his own secrets. Throughout Derrida's career, he was preoccupied with secrecy and many of the voices he deploys in his texts mask his own backstage puppeteering.

Derrida's use of Kierkegaard's discussion of the Akedah to expose the idea of what a secret avowal to the wholly Other, God, would look like –sans text, –sans the Hebrew/Greek binaries, is an example of this practice. Derrida reveals, through a presentation of Kierkegaard's treatment of the Akedah in

---

9   See Espen Hammer, Hegel's Temporalization of the Absolute, pp. 71–96. for this general idea of a temporalize absolute.

Fear and Trembling, a secret place. It is a place where the call of the Other qua Other, the Absolute Other reveals "the still Jewish experience of a secret, hidden, separate, absent or mysterious G-d, the one who decrees without revealing his reason demanding of Abraham his impossible sacrifice. All this goes on in secret." (Derrida 1995a, p. 58) "By keeping the secret, Abraham betrays ethics". This moment is outside Western discourse, outside ethics and paradoxically removed from Jewish moral teaching as well. In a technique that Plato used when deploying Socrates as a mouthpiece, Derrida hides behind Kierkegaard, Kafka, and Abraham in rendering the Akedah narrative. It functions as a placeholder for the possibility of an authentic avowal of faith. This "Here I Am" moment in relation to the *toute autre* (the Divine call) may hold Derrida's own secret hints at the possibility of avowal, one which must remain hidden.

The word 'secret' can be treated as a hyperlink in the Derridean corpus that links to the "[p]aradox of faith, that interiority that remains 'incommensurable with exteriority'." (Derrida 1995b, p. 63) (quoting Kierkegaard 1983). The term 'secret' is found again in *Circumfession* (pp. 36, 74, 85 etc.), and all through his writing. It is the backdrop for his disavowal of all spoken and written language and its public and therefore fake reifications, a philosophical language rooted in the substantiations made possible by ancient Greek grammar. From these Abraham is exempt. Abraham is exempt as well from the ethics of law even in the Hebrew archive viz.' Thou shalt not kill". Abraham, in Derrida's account, embodies the singularity, as opposed to the subject of speech and writing, of a silent but authentic subject who possesses a moral code outside the public discourse, outside of law and illustrates that the true authentic self must be silent. All language, law, and ethical doctrine would position him as the subject/victim of origination in the other.[10]

One other factor that places Derrida outside of all archives is their incommensurability with each other and their co-existence in the matrix of what Derrida characterizes as the "ontotheologico-political tradition that links Greek philosophy to the Abrahamic revelations ... " (Derrida 2002c, p. 58) He describes this situation, as resistant to interrogation: "perhaps we must also submit to the ordeal of that which resists such interrogation, which will have always resisted from within or as though from an exteriority that works and resists inside. Chora, the ordeal of Chora." Derrida invokes the term *'chora'* (a spatial figure that Plato used for as a name for the indeterminate receptacle of form and idea in *Timaeus*). He upgrades its use to be deployed as the site that would be resistant to the 'ontotheologico-politica' matrix. It is "[t]he name for place, a place name, and a rather singular one at that, for that spacing which, not allowing itself to be dominated by any theological, ontological or anthropological instance, without age, without history, and more "ancient" than all oppositions ... " (Derrida 2002c, p. 58). Here he is cryptically but unmistakably assuming a position of exteriority. He goes on to identify the "desert in the desert" as that "which contains" [t]hat which is [n]ot reappropriable, even by our memory, even by our "Greek" memory: it says the immemoriality of a desert in the desert of which it is neither a threshold nor a mourning." It is outside historical religions etc. (Derrida 2002c, p. 59). In later writing Derrida will continually refer to the "secret" when discussing his Judaism (Derrida 2007). When this is augmented with the idea of a desert in the desert, it also links to what Derrida refers to as his 'internal desert' (Bielik-Robson 2017, p. 54).[11] Derrida's reference to *'chora'*, the indeterminate receptacle, the desert etc. identifies through spatial metaphors, an exteriority emptied of conventional meanings and/or sociopolitical or ethnocentric context. Without explicit reference, he invokes the Book of Numbers 'B'midbar' (in the desert), the portion of the Bible which describes the forty years of the Jews wandering in the desert after leaving Egypt. On the basis of this positioning, with only a remote hope of liminal reentry and sans archive, neither Hebrew or Greek, Derrida identifies a space

---

10 In later writing on sovereignty the idea of a sovereign nation and its potential for violence is can be seen as a further development of the general mistrust of ethnocentric cultures and languages that makes his own monolingualism potentially dangerous (Derrida 2011).

11 Agata Bielik-Robson, "Burn After Reading Derrida the Philosophical Marrano", p. 54 quoting Derrida (1989)," How to avoid Speaking", in Howard Coward and Toby Foshay, *Derrida and Negative theology* (SUNY Press), 1992.

outside, once again, all binaries. While some scholars have posited that Derrida's 'silence' and secret internal removal are a kind of apophatic theology, it can also be understood in relation to his Judaism. Derrida's secret, viz Judaism, is secret precisely because revealing it would have to subject it to the public domain and to public discourse. A language that is of necessity ethnocentric and political (there is no metalanguage) would violate the secret silence of the radically singular Judaism of faith and avowal, a commitment which must be protected from violence. Thus the 'outside' space, the 'desert in the desert' protects a self that is not subject to a discourse alien to itself. Jewish philosophers who have made common cause with the Western philosophical tradition, on the other hand, have breached the boundaries of this authentic Jewish space, best held in silence.

Any attempts to integrate Greek philosophy and the Abrahamic tradition would be done within a theological- ontological -political matrix and be suspect. The Jewish philosophers who have made common cause with the western philosophical tradition, beginning with Philo are especially suspect. Hebrew and Greek archives are not intertranslatable. The Hebrew archive, (the so-called fatherland of the Jews), in its idiolectic exclusivity, or as Michael Fishbane describes, is an "ontologically unique literature". Externally it wears one of several garments whose layers conceal deeper aspects of divine truth (Fishbane 1992, p. 35). All of the Holy Scriptures and the Oral tradition (the Mishna and the Talmud, which are written accounts of the spoken debates of the sages of the time) are intrinsically connected or hyperlinked to this scripture as proof text and its canonicity, precluding an outside. The Greek archive consists of the entire philosophic tradition form Ionia to Jena, and beyond. In *Writing and Difference*, for example, Derrida refers to "[t]he two Greeks named Husserl and Heidegger" (Derrida 1978b, p. 83. Derrida houses his entire deconstruction of the metaphysics of presence as a project that cannot be disassociated from an exploration of Greek thought (Derrida 1978b, p. 4). As Miriam Leonard claims; "For Derrida it is the non-Greek, the Barbarian, the Egyptian, the Jew and the Christian who; ultimately come to define the contours of the Hellenic legacy of philosophy." (Leonard 2010, p. 5). Derrida achieves his parricide of the Greek father by reading the Greeks and exposing the hermeneutic instability in the western legacy. Dismantling the metaphysics of presence, he uses to Greeks to deconstruct them. He is not so confident when it comes to assaulting his own ancestral legacy. When it comes to asserting his own Jewish identity, he clearly assumes a Marrano position. In 'Abraham, the Other' he states this as follows. "[t]he law that comes upon me, a law that, appearing antinomian dictated to me the hyper-formalized formula of a destiny devoted to the secret-and that is why I play seriously, more and more, with the figure of the Marrano the less you show yourself as Jewish, the more and better jew you will be." (Derrida 2007, p. 13).

Those Jewish philosophes who would contrive illegitimate confabulations composed of Hebrew and archival texts and 'Greek' ideas are misguided and even dangerous. There are no supervening principles to resolve the differences between the two. In' Interpretations at War' (Derrida 1991) he discusses Hermann Cohen, who influenced and mentored a whole generation of German Jewish scholars in Neo Kantian Idealism. Cohen contended that German Jewry is the legitimate offspring, and exclusively so, of the Hellenist traditions. Derrida points out that though anti-Semitism touched Cohen closely in his own institution and took the form of excluding Jewish students from corporate student associations, Cohen only alludes to that briefly. Cohen argues for Jewish German solidarity and even calls Germany the homeland of the Jews. Derrida takes him to task for this insistence on this unhealthy alliance. The false messiah Immanuel Kant and Cohen's abject admiration for him, seen through the eyes of Derrida who has seen the horrific sequel of the fusion between nationalism and German Idealism situates Cohen along the intellectual trajectory that lent support to Nazi ideology. Derrida actually makes an analogy between the Jewish militants of the Front Populaire who during a demonstration in Nice presented a bouquet to Mr. Le Pen, a trivializer concerning the Holocaust, and Cohen who "[p]resents at each moment a bouquet to all the dormant -or rather ever-wakeful-Le Pens . . . " of this world. (Derrida 2002d, p. 166). Even Derrida's good friend Emmanuel Levinas must be implicated as a purveyor of a false coupling between Hellenism and Judaism. Inhis 1967 essay, 'Violence and Metaphysics', Derrida claims that Levinas sought an exit from the "Greek domination the same and The One" in Hebraic alterity (Derrida 1978b, p. 83). He argues that evinas is trapped inthephilsophical language nd is therefore compelled to speak 'Greek'. (Leonard 2010, p. 137). For Derrida even, the idea of otherness, a mainstay of Levinas' ethical admonitions concerning the 'other' is Greek.

For Derrida, then, "the entirety of philosophy is conceived on the basis of its Greek source ... it would not be possible to philosophize ... outside this medium." (Leonard 2010, p. 137). Derrida has positioned himself outside of this western archive while deconstructing it in its own terms. His position of extreme exteriority is not completely Nietzschean (in the sense of assuming a vantage point that allows a negative assessment of all philosophical shibboleths or so called "dangerous old conceptual fictions" as Nietzsche calls them in *Genealogy of Morals* (Nietzsche 1989, p. 119). On the other hand, it is not held in the name of the Jewish defenders of the Talmud who burnt Maimonides books in the Middle Ages in defiance of Greek wisdom. Derrida shares Nietzsche's cynicism in regard to the false absolutes of Western philosophy but never arrives at either the place of 'hidden miracles' as did Nachmanides a medieval Jewish philosopher who opposed Maimonides rationalism) nor the Holy commands of the rabbis. He did not hold to the full extent of Nietzschean negativity either, rather, he regards and analyzes the Western archive and its terminology in the service of dismantling the so called 'metaphysics of presence'. Derrida is sans archive, neither Hebrew nor Greek.

3. Philosophical Liminality

How and where can we find Jacques Derrida, the holder of an interiority that is outside of all cultural binaries? In a not very well-known interview/essay, 'Eating well', Derrida claims that the whole idea of the Subject as it has been contrived by philosophers as diverse as Descartes, Marx, Freud, Heidegger, Lacan, Foucault and others, is a fictitious and fabulated entity. At one point he states, "I don't see the necessity of keeping the word 'subject' at any "price" (Derrida 1991, p. 99). When it comes to his own person, Derrida is outside the binary that is at the heart of modern philosophy: subject and object. Where can Derrida find himself? It must be an internal site that is not a falsely fabulated Cartesian, Kantian, Hegelian or Husserlian subject. In his earliest work, in his deconstruction of Husserl, he makes it clear that the alleged primal moment that Husserl identifies as the last refuge of the metaphysical entails the "I" that can perform the phenomenological *epoché*. It consists of an allegedly authentic comprehension of reality by a subject as distinct from its 'object'. A true 'self' and true inner life, as opposed to the Husserlian 'subject' must somehow be apart from objectification. Thus, in *Speech and Phenomena*, Derrida makes it clear that the very existence of temporality makes the framing of experience in terms of subject and object under erasure at every turn (Derrida 1973). A true self would have to be one that does not undergo a continuous dissolution under the dominance of moveable temporality. The Cartesian/Husserlian subject is a fabrication born of philosophical abstraction, a chimera, and Derrida situates himself outside of it. Not only is it a metaphysical shibboleth on the mythological structure of the individual but its equivalent in public discourse is fraught with dangerous possibilities.

We can now understand that the secret is equivalent to a position that is outside public discourse and outside of western philosophy in its Greek incarnation. Where is he? Where can Derrida be found? Who is in the desert? Who is it that does not possess his own language? It is the Jacques Derrida as the child who was circumcised and did not have the right of refusal, was not an autonomous subject, and did not give informed consent, as he describes in *Circumfession*. This is the self who acquired his Judaism by being born of a Jewish mother, who was given the name Elie and who can be persecuted by anti-Semitism, whether or not he is a believer. Helen Cixous explains "To think he was a Marrano all along and didn't know it. A true Marrano. Don't tell a soul. It's a secret." (Cixous 2004, p. 86). Now it is possible to understand Derrida's gnomic pronouncement that all he has ever spoken about is circumcision (Derrida 1993, p. 70). Circumcision is the wound which signifies his exteriority and brings his 'self' as a subject into question. Who is it that was circumcised and given a Hebrew name? It was not the 'Ich' of the autonomous ego of Kant, it was not the subjectivity that is the opposing subject of the subject/object dichotomy set up by Descartes and which features in Husserl's texts and carries a long history in western philosophy. It is not the Hegelian subjectivity. Derrida is the son of a long line of wandering Jews who have left Harran (Abraham), left Egypt (Moses), left Algeria and now leaves western philosophy. Jacques Derrida is a marked man. Just as Jean Amery in his book, At *the Mind's Limits*, (Améry 1980, p. 94) realizes that he is a Jew when examining the numbers on his left arm after his concentration camp experience, it is interesting to follow Derrida's use the word '*marque*'. His French Algerian experience has marked his body of language, his Jewish identity imposed from without marked his body with circumcision. Circumcision becomes the placeholder for the whole Judaic archive.

In *Monolingualism of the Other*, Derrida uses the word 'marque' in relation to the body of language. He makes an analogy to the wound of circumcision, –"Terror is practiced at the expense of wounds inscribed on the body" A "Franco-Maghrebian martyr" is assigned a single language but prohibited from appropriating it. and is subject to the terror which marks a martyred existence, (Derrida 1998, p. 27) The other marque he finds on his own body. In the *marque* of circumcision there is the trace of the 'unknown known' of his ancestral archive. Both the nonlinguistic language and the circumcision are violent wounds upon him while he, the subject who is not a subject, was not autonomous in choosing or receiving these inscriptions. Finding himself trapped in a language not his own and a mark on his body that he received from without, he is caught between avowing and disavowing. He disavows his given language but never the less writes in French. Like Kafka's Abraham described in his essay, *Abraham the Other*, he hears the call of the *tout autre* but cannot trust the call that he hears.

In "*Circumfession*" and other later writings, Derrida finds a living, confessing 'self' and takes hold of an authentic and personal inner life. Here he confesses and here he can assume an autobiographical 'I', gestated within an interior space where he can elect to be Jewish, without exemplarity and with only an archive of personal memory. Here he can stay outside the binary universalism/particularity where particularity would endorse an ethnocentric position that would exclude others and be ethically questionable. Here he finds, within "a bottomless alienation for the soul a catastrophe that others will also say is a paradoxical opportunity". This circumstance was the "[t]he radical lack of culture from which I undoubtedly never completely emerged . . . " (Derrida 1998, p. 53). This has allowed him the freedom that a Marrano might possess. As a Marrano he is outside of all the constraints of a language not his own, a culture that is alien and a 'faith' free of a publicly endorsed religion.

4. Conclusions

Although it is a commonplace that language is inextricably wedded to spatial metaphor, Derrida's geographical spatial allusions are telling. In his early essay on Jabès, Derrida, in the voice of a poet, names a "site that is "not necessarily pagan". This "[s]ite, is not a site, an enclosure, a place of exclusion, a province or a ghetto" (Algiers, France Europe?). "When a Jew or a poet proclaims the Site, he is not declaring war. For this site, this land, is from beyond memory is always elsewhere. This site is not the empirical and national" (Derrida 1978a, p. 66). Derrida, it seems, has found such a place. Its indeterminateness becomes an opportunity of non-situatedness allowing an unusual perspective. It is a place that symbolizes his own state of being, '*b'midbar*, in a desert but with a promise. "It is immemorial, and thus also a future . . . Freedom is granted to the nonpagan Land only if it is separated from freedom by the Desert of the Promise. That is by the poem. When it lets itself be articulated by poetic discourse, the Land always keeps itself beyond any proximity" (Derrida 1978a, p. 66). Derrida the ventriloquist makes the poet a voice for a wandering Jew "not born here but elsewhere." Derrida, in the name of Jabès, articulates a non-temporal exteriority outside of a promised land. This "land" is one which his universalist, public and ethical European sensibilities relegates to poetic phantasm. It is something other than a place of exclusion- which place would be uninhabitable. He is outside of both *mythos* and *logos* and only a poet, such as Jabès can supply the words to articulate this situatedness.

We must leave Derrida on route, like his father whom he mentions crossed the sea with his tallit. We leave him caressing it, as he describes his relation to that silken prayer shawl m that he keeps and treasures (Derrida 2002a, p. 327). This transitional space is a perpetual transit between modernity and an archive from which he is exiled. In an autobiographical mode, in *Circumfession*, he was somehow able to take leave of his borrowed language and assume his Hebrew name. Still, he remains, as he puts it, never at rest, interminably, "[s]earching for the archive right where it slips away." (Derrida 1995a, p. 91). The marks on him and the ghosts who haunt him make him believe there is a 'really real', even if he cannot appropriate it. As Freud had his ghosts, Jakub Shelomoh, Moses, he himself claims the ghosts of "[J]akob, Hayim, my grandfather Moses and Abraham and a few others" (Derrida 1995a, p. 78). Circumcision, like marked steles that are inscribed with ancient aretalogies, carries the weight of the whole archive that he cannot own. Thus, the place that is assigned to him from without and which endowed him with a language that is not his own leaves Derrida *B'midbar*. He is an inhabitant of a desert in which he can experiment with his secret, assault the identity imposed on him but never enter the spiritual homeland that he never knew. He destroys every effigy of *Amalek* (the term for the perennial enemy of the Jews) but unlike Abraham smashing the idols of his father and leaving Harran, he can smash idols but cannot arrive. Like Moses who leads his followers out of the land of alienation but is himself flawed in the eyes of G-d, he is unable to enter the Promised Land. Jacques Dermda's liminality leaves him, therefore, as the title of an English translation of Edmond Jabès' poetry suggests, wondering, "If there were anywhere but Desert".

Funding: This research received no external funding.

Conflicts of Interest: The author declares no conflict of interest.

References

Améry, Jean. 1980. *At the Mind's Limits*. Bloomington: Indiana University Press.

Arendt, Hannah, and Jerome Kohn. 2018. *Thinking Without a Banister: Essays in Understanding, 1953–1975*. New York: Schocken Books.

Bielik-Robson, Agata. 2004. *Jewish Cryptotheologies of Late Modernity*. Abingdon: Routledge.

Bielik-Robson, Agata. 2017. Burn After Reading: Derrida, the Philosophical Marrano. In *Divisible Derridas*. Edited by Victor E. Taylor and Stephen G. Nichols. Aurora, CO, USA: Noesis Press.

Cixous, Hélène. 2004. *Portrait of Jacques Derrida as a Young Jewish Saint*. New York: Columbia University Press.

Critchley, Simon. 2014. *The Ethics of Deconstruction*. Edenborough: Edenborough University Press.

Derrida, Jacques. 1973. *Speech and Phenomena*. Translated by David B. Allison. Evanston: Northwestern University Press.

Derrida, Jacques. 1976. *Of Grammatology*. Translated by Gayatri Chakravorty Spivak. Baltimore: Johns Hopkins University Press.

Derrida, Jacques. 1978a. Edmond Jabès and the Question of the Book. In *Writing and Difference*. Translated by Alan Bass. Chicago: University of Chicago Press, pp. 64–78. First published 1966.

Derrida, Jacques. 1978b. Violence and Metaphysics. In *Writing and Difference*. Translated by Alan Bass. Chicago: University of Chicago Press, pp. 79–153. First published this edition is published in 1964.

Derrida, Jacques. 1989. *Of Spirit: Heidegger and the Question*. Translated by Geoffrey Bennington, and Rachel Bowlby. Chicago: The University of Chicago Press.

Derrida, Jacques. 1991. "Eating Well" or the Calculation of the Subject: An Interview with Jacques Derrida. In *Who Comes after the Subject*. Edited by Eduardo Cadava, Peter Cernor and Jean-Luc Nancy. London: Routledge.

Derrida, Jacques. 1993. Circumfession: Fifty-nine Periods and periphrases. In *Geoffrey Bennington Jacques Derrida*. Chicago: Chicago University Press.

Derrida, Jacques. 1995a. *Archive Fever: A Freudian Impression*. Translated by Eric Prenowitz. Chicago: Chicago University Press.

Derrida, Jacques. 1995b. *The Gift of Death*. Translated by David Wills. Chicago: Chicago University Press.

Derrida, Jacques. 1998. *Monolingualism of the Other or the Prosthesis of Origin*. Translated by Patrick Mensiah. Stanford: Stanford University Press.

Derrida, Jacques. 2002a. A Silkworm of one's Own. In *Acts of Religion*. Edited by Gil Anidjar. London: Routledge Press, pp. 309–55.

Derrida, Jacques. 2002b. Des Tours des Babel. In *Acts of Religion*. Edited by Gil Anidjar. London: Routledge Press, pp. 102–34. First published 1980.

Derrida, Jacques. 2002c. Faith and Knowledge. In *Acts of Religion*. Edited by Gil Anidjar. London: Routledge Press, pp. 40–101. First published 1998.

Derrida, Jacques. 2002d. Interpretations at War: Kant, the Jew, the German. In *Acts of Religion*. Edited by Gil Anidjar. London: Routledge Press, pp. 135–88. First published 1991.

Derrida, Jacques. 2007. Abraham, the Other. In *Judeities*. Edited by Bettina Bergo, Joseph Cohen and Raphael Zagry-Orly. New York: Fordham University Press, pp. 1–35.

Derrida, Jacques. 2011. *The Beast and the Sovereign*. Translated by Geoffrey Bennington. Chicago: University of Chicago Press, vol. 1.

Fichte, Johann Gottfried. 1808. *Addresses to the German Nation*. Edited by George Moore. Cambridge: Cambridge University Press.

Fishbane, Michael. 1992. *The Garments of Torah*. Bloomington: Indiana University Press.

Hammer, Espen. 2011. *Philosophy and Temporality from Kant to Critical Theory*. Cambridge: Cambridge University Press.

Jabès, Edmond. 1963. *Les Livres des Questions*. Paris: Galimid.

Kafka, Franz. 1921. Letter to Max Brod. In *Basic Kafka*. New York: Simon and Schuster.

Kierkegaard, Soren. 1983. Fear and Trembling. In *Kierkegaard's Writings*. Edited and Translated by Howard V. Hong, Edna H. Hong. Princeton: Princeton University Press, vol. 6.

Leonard, Miriam. 2010. *Derrida and Antiquity*. Oxford: Oxford University Press.

Nietzsche, Frederich. 1989. *On the Genealogy of Morals and Ecco Homo*. Edited by Walter Kaufman. Translated by Walter Kaufma. New York: Vintage Books.

Rosenzweig, Franz. 1982. *L'étoile de l redemption*. Translated by A. Derczanski, and J. L. Schlegel. Paris: Seuil.

Urbach, Ephraim. 1995. *The Sages*. Translated by Israel Abrahans. Cambrige: Harvard University Press.

Yerushalmi, Yosef Hayim. 1991. *Freud's Moses; Judaism Terminable and Interminable*. New Haven: Yale University Press.

Zivin, Erin Graff, ed. 2017. *The Marrano Specter: Derrida and Hispanism*. Fordham: Fordham University Press.

Zizek, Slavoj. 2008. Rumsfeld and the bees. *The Guardian*, June 27.

religions MDPI

Article

Giorgio Agamben—A Modern Sabbatian? Marranic Messianism and the Problem of Law

Piotr Sawczyński

Department of International and Political Studies, Jagiellonian University, Gołębia 24, 31-007 Kraków, Poland;
piotr.sawczynski@gmail.com

Received: 30 September 2018; Accepted: 27 December 2018; Published: 1 January 2019

check for
updates

Abstract: The article analyzes the influence of the kabbalistic doctrine of Sabbatianism on the messianic philosophy of Giorgio Agamben. I argue against Simon Critchley that Agamben's critique of the sovereign law is not inspired by Marcion's idea of the total annihilation of law but by Sabbatai Zevi's project of deactivating its repressive function. I further argue that Agamben also adopts the Sabbatian idea of Marranic messianism, which makes him repeatedly contaminate the Jewish tradition with foreign influences. Although this strategy is potentially fruitful, it eventually leads Agamben to overemphasize antinomianism and problematically associate all Jewish-based messianism with the radical critique of law. In the article, I demonstrate that things are more complex and even in the openly antinomian works of Walter Benjamin—Agamben's greatest philosophical inspiration—Jewish law is endued with some emancipatory potential.

Keywords: Giorgio Agamben; Judaism; messianism; law; state of exception; Marcionism; Marranism; Sabbatianism

---

1. Introduction

In one of his most important early writings, titled *Theologisch-politisches Fragment* [Theologico-Political Fragment], Walter Benjamin famously confronted the problem of political theology. Against those who speak of the religious sense of human history, Benjamin argues that there is no direct ontological connection between the profane and the holy, and—consequently—"nothing historical can relate itself on its own account to anything Messianic" (Benjamin 1991d, p. 203).[1] Jacob Taubes (Taubes 1986) returned to Benjamin's powerful thesis in his polemic essay *Walter Benjamin—ein moderner Marcionit* [Walter Benjamin—A Modern Marcionite?],[2] where he argues that the idea of the ontological separation of creation and redemption bears a strong resemblance to the Gnostic doctrine of Marcionism. Although Marcion (c. 85–160) was "the most resolutely and undilutedly 'Christian' of the Gnostics" (Jonas 2001, p. 137)[3] and his teachings were a heretical misreading of the Gospel, he, indeed, greatly influenced Benjamin's early speculations on Jewish messianism. The core of his antithetical doctrine was a thesis of two Gods: the malicious demiurge responsible for our entrapment in this fallen world and the unknown Redeemer who will combat the world-god and liberate humans from

---

[1] Benjamin's piece, dated 1920 or 1921, is clearly inspired by the reading of Ernst Bloch's *Geist der Utopie* [The Spirit of Utopia] (first published in German in 1918), where the thesis of the unbridgeable gap between the historical and the messianic appears (Bloch 1980). Although Benjamin never mentioned reading Karl Barth, the Fragment also seems highly influenced by his "dialectical theology," especially the argument of the absolute otherness of God (Barth 2010, pp. 111–59).

[2] Taubes's essay is not so much a polemic with the Fragment but with its "Judaic" interpretation pushed forward by Gershom Scholem (Scholem 1975, pp. 276–78).

[3] Marcion's misreading of the Gospel was, admittedly, very selective: of the New Testament, he only accepted the Gospel according to Luke along with the ten Paul's Epistles, although with considerable amendments.

the condition of imprisonment.[4] Inspired by the lecture of the Pauline Epistles, Marcion associated this demiurge with the Old Testament God of fierce justice and the Redeemer with the New Testament God of mercy, whose son and messenger is Jesus Christ. Needless to say, this anti-Jewish dualism was a radical oversimplification and distortion of Paul's message but its apocalyptic lure is hard to deny. That is probably why it inspired the early works of Benjamin, aptly diagnosed by Taubes as pricked with a Gnostic sting.

Adolf von Harnack (Von Harnack 1924, pp. 106–17), perhaps the greatest investigator of Marcion's heresy, accentuates yet another property of his doctrine which every apocalyptic spirit might find alluring: the role of law. If the god of creation is a punisher, law must be conceived of as the form in which he reveals his nature. It means that any legal system is an instrument of the world-god's sovereign power over people and, as such, needs to be repudiated. This "retributive and vindictive" (Jonas 2001, p. 142) understanding of law results in the association of redemption with the state of liberating lawlessness, necessary to overcome the earthly principle of sovereignty. In his recent book, *The Faith of the Faithless*, Simon Critchley (Critchley 2013) argues that today precisely this feature of Marcionism exerts a strong influence on the philosophy of Giorgio Agamben who follows Benjamin's early intuitions and assimilates the apocalyptic-messianic discourse to his critical theory. For Critchley, Agamben's messianism is a disavowal of the juridical apparatus, based on Marcion's radical opposition of law and redemption. Although he never quotes Marcion and rather appoints Paul as a patron of his messianic enterprise, "the way in which a certain ultra-Paulinism assets itself in Agamben (. . .) might lead one to conclude that the contemporary return to Paul is really a return to Marcion" (Critchley 2013, p. 195). Critchley is highly critical of this renaissance of "crypto-Marcionism" which, as he claims, brings about revolutionary tendencies to suspend law, understood as a domain of subjection and never emancipation. At the same time, the messianic anti-legalism must be a philosophy of "radical novelty, of an absolute or pure beginning", which makes Critchley conclude that Agamben's utopia of lawlessness is "a purist and slightly puerile dream" (Critchley 2013, pp. 202–3).

Indeed, Critchley has a strong point in his critique of Marcionism, but I am going to argue that he wrongly positions Agamben as its follower. Whereas Marcion's doctrine was both antinomian and antithetical, Agamben's critique of law demonstrably breaks with dualistic thinking. Consequently, his messianic philosophy is not about a "new" world without law but about a structural transformation of the legal system so that this crucial apparatus is no longer an instrument of sovereign power.[5] I further argue against Critchley that—if we want to look for Gnostic inspirations in Agamben's work—his anti-dualism makes it much more accurate to call him a "modern Sabbatian," with reference to Sabbatai Zevi's (1626–76) kabbalistic doctrine. Although his catastrophic discourse bears a likeness to Marcionism, it also rejects antithetical remedies to propose instead an idiom of deactivation, clearly inspired by Sabbatai's teaching. Even more importantly, Agamben seems influenced not only by this kabbalistic ontology but also by the idea of Marranic messianism of which Sabbatai, the infamous apostate messiah, is a supreme figure. Agamben repeatedly "contaminates" his references to Jewish tradition with Christian ideas as if implying that betrayal is the necessary condition of redemption. At the same time, however, his Marranic disposition leads him to overemphasize antinomianism and problematically associate all Jewish messianism with a radical critique of law. I am going to argue that things are a bit more complicated: in Judaism, law has not infrequently been endued with an emancipatory potential, not only in Halakhic, but also in the apparently antinomian messianic tradition. To show this, I will conclude with a reference to Benjamin's fragment on Kafka, in which this

---

[4] *The Antitheses* is the title of Marcion's only known work, in which he expounded on the core of his doctrine. The work has unfortunately been lost and Marcion's gospel has mostly been reconstructed from Tertullian (1972) polemic treaty.

[5] The term "apparatus" (or "dispositive"), borrowed from Michel Foucault (Foucault 1980, pp. 194–96), refers in Agamben's philosophy to the social instruments which are supposed to produce human subjects but tend to transform into oppressive mechanisms of subjection. For Agamben (2009), the most important apparatuses are language and law—the dispositives which fundamentally determine human reference to the world.

greatest ally of Agamben's antinomian project surprisingly reveals himself as an astute advocate of Jewish law.

The Marranic and Sabbatian backgrounds of Agamben's critique of law have not yet been a subject of any systematic analyses. Also, the influence of Jewish messianism on his works has been relatively neglected as the literature is rather focused on Agamben's Pauline inspirations (Kaufman 2008; Kotsko 2013) and tends to disregard the role that kabbalistic conceptions play in his antinomian thinking. For instance, Colby Dickinson's *Agamben and Theology* (Dickinson 2011), being the most systematic analysis of the religious lineage of his works, is written from a Christian perspective while the only monograph fully devoted to Agamben's messianism, Vivian Liska's *Giorgio Agambens leerer Messianismus* (Liska 2008), fails to elaborate on the kabbalistic background of his critical theory. This background is elaborated throughout the essays contained in the edited collection *Benjamin-Agamben: Politik, Messianismus, Kabbala* (Borsò et al. 2010), but even they do not identify the Marranic and Sabbatian motives in Agamben's writings. The aim of my article is to fill this serious research gap and discuss Agamben's crypto-Sabbatianism in order to demonstrate its specific antinomian nature and use it against Critchley's "Marcionite hypothesis".

2. Against the Sovereign Law

Agamben's antinomian messianism stems from his diagnosis of law as a territory of sovereign power which he understands, after Carl Schmitt, as the "unlimited authority" (Schmitt 2004, p. 18) over life. He also follows the German jurist in claiming that the principle of sovereignty is inextricably linked to the state of exception [*Ausnahmezustand*] because "he who decides on exception" (Schmitt 2004, p. 13) and suspends the rule for an indefinite period of time is the only subject of sovereignty. Using Aristotelian terminology, one could say that the introduction of the state of exception is the moment when sovereign power moves from potentiality to actuality and establishes itself as independent of any norm. This "exceptional" structure of sovereignty makes Agamben argue that if there is an intimate relation of exception to the legal norm which establishes the institution of sovereign power, it is hard to maintain that the exception is inherently external to the rule (Agamben 2005a, pp. 17–19). Quite the opposite, exception reveals itself as the internal logic of any norm, necessary for its constitution as the opposite of abnormality. This paradox makes a framework for Agamben's radical thesis that the state of exception is not only the domain of sovereign power but also the structure which determines the validity of law as the supreme normative system (Agamben 2005a, p. 26).[6] Consequently, it is no longer possible to speak of the state of exception as anomaly or even widespread political practice but as the foundation on which juridical order—for Agamben, one of the most important apparatuses—is built.

To specify the fundamental structure of exception, Agamben proposes to call it the "inclusive exclusion" [*esclusione inclusiva*]. He argues that although exception is an individual case of exclusion from the scope of the general rule, it is still related to the rule by the relation of suspension. As we read in *Homo Sacer*, the work which investigates the nature of sovereign power, "*the rule applies to the exception in no longer applying, in withdrawing from it*" (Agamben 2005a, p. 18).[7] What is important, the withdrawal not only constitutes the exception but also asserts the rule and the territory where it is in force. As such, exception might be considered an instrument by means of which law excludes an element from the system only to subordinate it and make it subject to sovereign power. Consequently, although exception seems to escape the rule, it actually—just like the proverb says—proves it. This is not yet everything: another result of "inclusive exclusion" is the phenomenon which we might call topological indeterminacy. Agamben accentuates that once the difference between the rule and exception has been blurred, it is no longer possible to distinguish the inside of law from its outside,

---

6 For more on this topic, see (Zartaloudis 2010, pp. 95–144) and (Gulli 2007). A representative selection of texts on the role of law in Agamben's philosophy can be found in (Zartaloudis 2016).
7 Original emphasis.

the crucial opposition of *physis* and *nomos* is devalued and juridical order "coincides with reality itself" (Agamben 2005c, p. 105). At the same time, on the "threshold of indistinction" (Agamben 2005a, p. 18) between law and life, the latter is absorbed by the former, much more powerful and governed by the principle of sovereignty. What does it mean for living beings? According to Agamben (2005a, p. 53),[8] humans subjected to the power of omnipresent law are like inhabitants of the village at the foot of the Castle Hill in Franz Kafka's *Das Schloß* (Kafka 1997): they fall victim to the tyrannical apparatus whose indeterminacy thwarts any strategy of resistance.

While Critchley attributes the Marcionite background to Agamben's antinomianism, let us notice that Agamben's radical critique of law consistently escapes antithetical thinking. Above all, at no point do we find in his work any anarchistic longing or a call to repudiate the legal system. Despite all his harsh criticism, the author of *Homo Sacer* is well aware that law is a crucial subject-making apparatus whose abrogation makes it impossible for a human being to turn into a proper subject (Agamben 2009, pp. 15–17). That is why instead of overcoming law and putting forward the utopia of lawlessness, Agamben chooses to think it anew by dismantling the logic of exception which founds the legal systems we know: "What opens a passage toward justice is not the erasure of law, but its deactivation and inactivity [*inoperosità*]" (Agamben 2005b, p. 64). The idiom of deactivation repeatedly applied by Agamben to his messianic philosophy is yet another argument why Marcionite associations fail. Agamben argues that as a consequence of the "inclusive exclusion," there is no opposite of the state of exception which could be used as a stimulus for defiance. Rather, in the "zone of indistinction" generated by the state of exception, oppositions cannot help but be absorbed by sovereign power, which makes all antithetical strategies futile.[9] Any critical practice must thus be initiated inside the structure of exception in order to neutralize it "messianically," using the divisions it generates against itself. Reminiscent as this strategy might be of Baron von Münchhausen pulling himself out of a mire by his hair, this is precisely how Agamben understands messianism, which makes him move away from Marcionism and brings him pretty close to the Sabbatian way of thinking.

What brings him even closer is the way in which Agamben conceives of the messianic law. Admittedly, at this point he is far from being precise and the elaborate strategies of deactivation[10] put forward in his writings are not counterbalanced by an in-depth analysis of their aftermath. However, even his scattered remarks make up an image equally distant from both the worlds of sovereign law and anarchistic utopia. Agamben directly addresses the problem in *The State of Exception* where he asks "what becomes of the law after its messianic fulfillment" (Agamben 2005b, p. 63) to enigmatically answer that "one day humanity will play with law just as children play with disused objects" (Agamben 2005b, p. 64).[11] Arguably, Agamben does not mean that in the messianic time law will become useless and thereby subject to abrogation; instead, it will be open to multiple uses which are nowadays hard to imagine. Figuratively speaking, humans will be like little kids who waste no time pondering the original function of documents found on the street but spontaneously make them into paper planes, thus initiating a completely new use of things. How to make it happen? The line of reasoning is like this: the legal apparatus as we know it is basically reduced to its normative aspect and, as such, cannot help but reinforce power over life. In order to think of a non-repressive law, there must be no instrumental attachment of the law to any goal because only the law which is not a means to an

---

8   "We see in the impossibility of distinguishing law from life—that is, in the life lived in the village at the foot of the castle—the essential character of the state of exception."

9   That is precisely why Agamben is highly critical of Theodor Adorno's negative dialectics, on which he comments in *The Time that Remains*. He follows there Jacob Taubes's argument that Adorno's theory is a "wishy-washy" aestheticization of messianic discourse which contemplates merely the pretense of redemption (Taubes 1993, p. 103). Agamben (2005c, p. 37) agrees with this objection and argues that once negativity is reinforced, it might prevent any messianic gesture of positivity from happening, which makes Adorno's dialectical messianism eventually ineffective.

10   Among the most significant, there are the strategies of profanation (Agamben 2007, pp. 73–92), pure means (Agamben 2000, p. 49–59) and the study of law (Agamben 2005b, p. 63–64).

11   More detailed considerations on play are to be found in Agamben's *Infancy and History*, in the chapter titled *In Playland: Reflections on History and Play* (Agamben 1993, pp. 65–87).

end can escape sovereign appropriation. To play with law thus means to "forget" its original function and celebrate its full potentiality, which Agamben makes pretty clear when he says that "what is found after law" is just "a new use" of the law (Agamben 2005b, p. 64).[12]

3. The Sabbatian Alternative

I believe Lorenzo Chiesa is right to claim that Agamben's antinomian project aims at transforming the sovereign state of exception into the messianic one (Chiesa 2009, p. 154), which Agamben calls, following Benjamin, the "real" state of exception.[13] Agamben argues that a redemptive potential is hidden in a principal paradox of the state of exception: as a result of the indistinction between the rule and exception, it is impossible to tell the difference between the execution of law and its transgression. That is why, figuratively speaking, "a person who goes for a walk during the curfew is not transgressing the law any more than the soldier who kills him is executing it" (Agamben 2005a, p. 57). Agamben maintains that a similar paradox marks the coming of the Messiah in kabbalistic tradition, especially in the Sabbatian doctrine of the two Torahs. Although the doctrine dates back to the thirteenth-century holy Book of Zohar, it is only the Sabbatians who made it into the very core of their messianic teaching four centuries later. According to this mystical idea, the present Torah, which the Sabbatians called the Torah of *beriah* ("in the state of creation"), is only relevant to the fallen, unredeemed world as we know it. Once the Messiah has come, this rigorous set of commandments that Judaism is associated with will be replaced by the Torah of *atzilut* ("in the state of emanation"), freed from the burden of Adam's original sin and thus liberating humans from the punitive function of law (Scholem 1995, pp. 287–324). Agamben argues that this messianic replacement bears a strong likeness to the logic of exception as it introduces the "threshold of indistinction" between law and lawlessness. What does it mean? At the moment when the Torah of *beriah* is consummated, its principles lose validity and give way to a totally new law which may violate the old principles but is also legitimized by the Messiah himself. Consequently, "the fulfillment of the Torah now coincides with its transgression" (Agamben 2005a, p. 57)—*bittulah shel torah zehu kiyyamah*, in Sabbatai Zevi's own words—which makes Agamben call this messianic moment the "real" state of exception that neutralizes mechanisms of "inclusive exclusion" and beats the paradigm of sovereign power with its own weapon.

Although such an operation, indeed, challenges the sovereign nature of law without falling into the utopia of lawlessness, it is not yet very distant from the Marcionite dualism that Critchley attributes to Agamben's thought. After all, if the messianic act limited itself to the simple replacement of one law with another, it would be a highly antithetical, and somehow naïve, way of thinking. However, what Agamben finds appealing in the Sabbatian doctrine of the two Torahs is that it is actually much more nuanced: it never undermines the authority of the pre-messianic Torah, neither does it question the Thirteen Principles of Faith formulated by Moses Maimonides (Maimonides 2012, pp. 151–172), according to which the Torah is one and indivisible. How is that possible? In one of his most important messianic texts, titled *The Messiah and the Sovereign* (Agamben 1999), Agamben accentuates that unlike that which the name of the doctrine suggests, it is not about two separate Torahs with different commands and prohibitions, but about two different aspects—or understandings—of the one essential Torah. This highly mystical idea assumes that the historical Torah as we know it is a defined text, but the spiritual Torah as it existed in the sight of God before the process of its materialization was rather "the totality of possible combinations of the Hebrew alphabet" (Agamben 1999, p. 164). It is only

---

[12] In the same fragment of *The State of Exception*, Agamben defines the messianic law as "a figure of law after its nexus with violence and power has been deposed" (Agamben 2005b, p. 63), which proves that what will be invalidated in the messianic world is not the whole apparatus of law but rather its coercive properties.

[13] The concept of the "real" state of exception appears in the eighth thesis in Benjamin's *Über den Begriff der Geschichte* [Theses on the Philosophy of History] where he writes: "The tradition of the oppressed teaches us that the 'state of exception' in which we live is the rule. We must arrive at a concept of history that corresponds to this fact. Then we will have the production of a *real* state of exception before us as a task" (Benjamin 1991e, p. 697), original emphasis.

due to the fall of the first man that this original totality was limited to concrete words and sentences, and the full potentiality of law reduced to its penalizing function.

Gershom Scholem, perhaps the greatest twentieth-century theorist of Jewish kabbalah, whose works Agamben has thoroughly studied, argues that the Sabbatians' doctrine was highly inspired by the thirteenth-century conception of the cosmic cycles, or *shemittoth*. According to this early kabbalistic teaching, the absolute Torah has the power to manifest itself in various ways so "in every *shemittah* men will read something entirely different in the Torah, because in each one the divine wisdom of the primordial Torah appears under a different aspect" (Scholem 1969, p. 78). Although the innermost essence of the holy text must stay the same and not a single letter may be added or taken away, the combination of the letters keeps changing so that they present a different appearance to the reader depending on the cycle. A very similar view was expressed by Rabbi Eliyahu Kohen Ittamary of Smyrna (d. 1729) whose theology, as Scholem accentuates, was "strangely shot through with ideas that originated in the heretical Kabbalism of the followers of Sabbatai Zevi" (Scholem 1969, p. 74). In one of his writings, not surprisingly quoted by Agamben (1999, p. 165), we read that the Torah "*originally formed a heap of unarranged letters*" (Scholem 1969, p. 74)[14] which only had to be ordered when God's word was transmitted to the lower spheres of being. When the Messiah finally comes, he will "annul the present combination of letters" (Scholem 1969, p. 74), restore the primordial plasticity, and liberate humans from their subjection to punitive law. In other words, he will materialize what Agamben terms the "new use": a figure of law no longer reduced to a collection of obligations and prohibitions, in which the full potentiality of law can be manifested.

That, precisely, was supposed to be the role of Sabbatai Zevi, who in the seventeenth-century Ottoman Empire declared himself the long-awaited Jewish redeemer and initiated the most widespread heretical movement in the modern history of Judaism. His unique position on the map of Jewish heresies comes from the fact that Sabbatai's messianic mission ended up in his infamous conversion to Islam and outward renunciation of Jewish faith. However, self-destructive as it appears, Sabbatai's apostasy did not put an end to the activity of the movement which flourished among European Jewry long after the death of this "apostate messiah." Scholem, who is the author of Sabbatai's monumental biography, points out that the faithfulness of the Sabbatians to their master even after he was discredited is not unrelated to the fact that a large portion of Sephardic Jews were at that time descendants of the Marranos: "Had it not been for the unique psychology of these reconverts to Judaism, the new theology would never have found the fertile ground to flourish in that it did" (Scholem 1974, p. 95).[15] Thanks to the Marranic mentality of his followers, argues Scholem, Sabbatai's conversion soon originated the doctrine of the necessary apostasy of the Messiah, according to which messianic acts shall not be committed publicly but only in concealment, under the guise of treachery.[16] In light of this, his conversion could no longer be interpreted in terms of betrayal but rather fulfilment of the Jewish messianic idea, or—to put it more dialectically—fulfilment by means of betrayal, strictly in accordance with the formula *bittulah shel torah zehu kiyyamah* ("the fulfilment of the Torah is its transgression").

---

[14] Original emphasis. Although the manuscript of Rabbi Eliyahu's book has been lost, his words are known thanks to the quotation in Hayyim Joseph David Azulai (Azulai 1986).

[15] Scholem quotes, e.g., Abraham Cardozo, one of Sabbatai's followers, who argued that "it is ordained that the King Messiah don the garments of a Marrano and so go unrecognized by his fellow Jews" (Scholem 1974, p. 95). It is worth noting that Scholem's argument has been criticized by his disciple Moshe Idel (Idel 1998, pp. 183–84) who claims that a reference to "Marranic mentality" bears the hallmarks of psychologization and is not a reliable explanation of the movement's expansion, whose reasons are much more complex.

[16] This doctrine is a reinterpretation of the Lurianic kabbalah, on which most of the Sabbatian cosmology was based. In the teachings of Isaac Luria and his disciples, the messianic mission involves collecting holy sparks which—due to the original cosmic catastrophe—have been entrapped by the forces of evil. According to the Sabbatian corrective, the imprisoned sparks can only be rescued if the Redeemer descends into the realm of impurity to destroy it from within; that means that the world is going to be redeemed through sinful and treacherous actions, no more, no less (Scholem 2016, pp. 801–2). For a recapitulation of the Lurianic cosmological doctrine, see (Fine 2003).

Let us notice that this Marranic nature of Sabbatianism perfectly corresponds to the messianic conception of the two aspects of the Torah. The supreme Torah of *atzilut*, which stayed in concealment for almost the whole existence of the material world, can only be actualized if the Torah of *beriah* is first "betrayed" by its violation. However, tampering with the commandments leads to the consummation of the pre-messianic Torah and prepares the ground for a new, liberating understanding of law, which makes one conclude that the apparent infidelity is actually necessary for the messianic mission to succeed. For someone like Agamben, whose messianic thinking is located on the borderline between Judaism, Christianity, and Islam, such a conclusion—although potentially nihilistic[17]—must sound philosophically fertile. I believe it is precisely his "crypto-Sabbatian" disposition which makes him repeatedly contaminate one religious tradition with another, as if intellectual purity could not help but degenerate into an instrument of oppression. Philosophical and theological crossovers, on the contrary, invigorate critical thinking and may serve as powerful allies of any emancipatory project, which is why Agamben persistently violates religious canons and explores their heterodox undercurrents.

4. The Marranic Abuse

Admittedly, Agamben has a strong point here, but the idea that a true messianic project lives on transgression and betrayal puts him in a convenient position to repel any philosophical attack and thus opens room for intellectual abuse. I would like to point now to at least one abusive consequence of such a Marranic position. As previously stated, all of Agamben's antinomian project is founded upon the thesis that "in Judaism as in Christianity and Shiite Islam, the messianic event above all signifies a crisis and radical transformation of the entire order of law" (Agamben 1999, pp. 162–63). In such a (mis)reading, the present law is firmly opposed to divine justice, and true redemption may only come about through deactivation of its repressive function. Although Agamben attributes antinomianism to the whole messianic tradition, his focus is constantly on Judaism as the religion most commonly associated with law. Even at times when he works on the Halakhic tradition, he reads it in a highly antinomian way, the holy day of Sabbath being a good example. In the essay *Hunger of an Ox*, Agamben pushes forward with a thesis that the Saturday suspension of works has a similar effect on daily activities as the coming of the Messiah has on the works of law: it nullifies them not through undoing but through making them inoperative, which in Hebrew is called *menuchah* (Agamben 2011, p. 104). What does that mean? When pious Jews refrain from work on the Sabbath, it is the scrupulous observance of *mitzvot* which strictly demand workweek labour and Saturday repose. At the same time, however, by respecting the Torah of *beriah*, Jews bring forward the arrival of the Messiah, who—as the Sabbatians believed—will render its commandments definitively inoperative (Agamben 2011, p. 110). Thereby, the fulfilment of the law is its transgression, which makes Agamben describe the logic of the Sabbath as parallel to the "real" state of exception.[18] No wonder, he adds, that in the antinomian tradition the Saturday rest is called the anticipation of *olam ha-ba*, the future world where legal orders will not just be temporarily suspended, but permanently invalidated.

This is precisely the abuse that I ascribe to Agamben: he reinforces the polarizing schema in which the law as we know it is reduced to its coercive and repressive properties in order to trade it against the messianic promise of liberation through "another use of the law." Such a crypto-Sabbatian position might escape the Marcionite utopia of anarchism, but it still denies the present juridical apparatus any emancipatory function. Jayne Svenungsson is right to contend in her recent article that although Agamben keeps distance from the dualism of law and lawlessness and is careful not to repeat anti-Jewish stereotypes, he nevertheless ends up making "a typical supersessionist gesture" of "counterposing law to liberation" (Svenungsson 2017, p. 69). Conspicuous as they are in their radicality,

---

[17] Nihilistic consequences of the doctrine of "redemption through sin" are especially visible in the activity of Jacob Frank (1726–91) and his followers; see (Maciejko 2011).
[18] For more on this topic, see (Kaufman 2008).

antinomian currents are hardly representative of the messianic idea in Judaism, where law has not infrequently been viewed as a progressive power and not an obstacle on the path to redemption. For instance, in Maimonides (and in most rational tendencies of Jewish philosophy) we find a highly affirmative view of law as a means of moral self-betterment which also has a significant role to play in the work of salvation. In *The Book of Judges*, his extensive codification of the Jewish law, we read that it is precisely the moral progress achieved through the observance of the law that will make it easier for the Messiah to arrive. That is why there is no need to transform the function of law in the messianic times, the only difference being the elimination of external constraints in its contemplation (Maimonides 1949, pp. 238–42). If we realize that this view is much more central to Judaism than antinomian critiques, the stress Agamben puts on the negative aspects of law to play it off against emancipation will seem a considerable distortion of the Jewish messianic tradition, which may be in accordance with his Marranic disposition but does not cease to be intellectually abusive.

Svenungsson speculates that this antinomian hyperbole is connected with Agamben's philosophical background, especially the establishment of Benjamin as a patron of his messianic project (Svenungsson 2017, p. 72). Indeed, a little glimpse into such works as *Zur Kritik der Gewalt* [Critique of Violence] (Benjamin 1991g) or *Schicksal und Charakter* [Fate and Character] (Benjamin 1991c) will suffice to conclude that Benjamin is equally uncompromising in exposing the sovereign, repressive nature of law. Striking similarities between the two authors become even more visible after the reading of Benjamin's essay *Franz Kafka: Zur zehnten Wiederkehr seines Todestages* [Franz Kafka: For the Tenth Anniversary of His Death] where he argues that the gloomy atmosphere of Kafka's novels stems not only from the tyranny of the legal apparatus, but also from the paradoxical coexistence of omnipresent law and absolute lawlessness (Benjamin 1991a, p. 412), which immediately brings to mind Agamben's notion of the state of exception.[19] However, despite these unquestionable parallels, things are a little more complex than Svenungsson suggests. In another piece on Kafka, a very short and elliptic fragment titled *Versuch eines Schemas zu Kafka* [Tentative Outline on Kafka], Benjamin powerfully describes Kafka's pre-historic "swamp world" [*Sumpfwelt*] only to conclude that some "defensive measures" [*Abwehrmaßnahmen*] against its sovereign powers are offered by the Halakhic tradition (Benjamin 1991f, p. 1192). This surprising statement makes it clear that Benjamin—at least at this point—is careful to distinguish between political and theological understanding of law, which is not to be found in any of Agamben's works. Rather, the author of *Homo Sacer* conflates secular legal systems of the modern state with the religious law of Judaism to counterpose them against the liberating promise of messianism. It is hard to deny that this operation boosts his antinomian argument, but at the same time makes him diverge from Benjamin who turns out a much greater advocate of Halakha than Agamben would like to admit.[20]

5. Conclusions

Having discussed Agamben's critique of law, let us now draw some final conclusions. Above all, Critchley's interpretation of his approach in terms of "crypto-Marcionism" seems mistaken. Unlike Marcion's heresy, what is at stake in Agamben's messianic enterprise is not the annihilation of the juridical order but its deep, structural transformation so that the authority of law is no longer founded on violence and subjection. What is more, he is clearly against the antithetical *modus* of thinking and puts forward the idea that due to its intricate mechanisms of "inclusive exclusion," the sovereign law can only be dismantled from within. That is why, as I tried to demonstrate, Agamben seeks inspiration in the Sabbatians' antinomianism, especially in their conception of the messianic deactivation of legal system, represented by the doctrine of the two Torahs. Although philosophically fruitful, I have argued that this "elective affinity" to the Marranic messianism has at least two problematic consequences:

---

19 See also (Benjamin 1991b).
20 For more on this topic, see (Liska 2017) and (Weiss 2014).

first, it allows Agamben to don the costume of a Marrano himself and repeatedly contaminate the Jewish tradition with Christian influences, e.g., hide his kabbalistic inspirations under the guise of Pauline Christianity;[21] second, and even more importantly, it leads to a serious distortion of the Jewish messianic idea which is in its essence much less antinomian than Agamben would like it to be. Irrelevant as it is to criticize Agamben for misreading the tradition he never claimed to represent, one should bear in mind that—at least at times—his Marranic position makes Agamben refer to it too carelessly. By no means does this carelessness discredit his use of the messianic discourse which should be read, however, in terms of an invigorating pastiche rather than a faithful continuation of the Jewish messianic idea. As such, it still makes a valuable contribution to untying the knot which links law and sovereign power; and if it involves the risk of intellectual abuse, may it not be the price that any Marranic enterprise eventually needs to pay?

Funding: This research was funded by the National Science Centre grant number 2017/27/N/HS1/01636.

Conflicts of Interest: The author declares no conflict of interest. The founding sponsors had no role in the design of the study; in the collection, analyses, or interpretation of data; in the writing of the manuscript, and in the decision to publish the results.

References

Agamben, Giorgio. 1993. In Playland: Reflections on History and Play. In *Infancy and History: The Destruction of Experience*. Translated by Liz Heron. London and New York: Verso, pp. 65–87.

Agamben, Giorgio. 1999. The Messiah and the Sovereign: The Problem of Law in Walter Benjamin. In *Potentialities: Collected Essays in Philosophy*. Daniel Heller-RoazenStanford: Stanford UP, pp. 160–74.

Agamben, Giorgio. 2000. Notes on Gesture. In *Means without End*. Translated by Vincenzo Binetti, and Cesare Casarino. Minneapolis and London: University of Minnesota Press, pp. 49–59.

Agamben, Giorgio. 2005a. *Homo Sacer: Sovereign Power and Bare Life*. Translated by Daniel Heller-Roazen. Stanford: Stanford UP.

Agamben, Giorgio. 2005b. *State of Exception*. Translated by Kevin Attell. Chicago and London: The University of Chicago Press.

Agamben, Giorgio. 2005c. *The Time that Remains: A Commentary on the Letter to the Romans*. Translated by Patricia Dailey. Stanford: Stanford UP.

Agamben, Giorgio. 2007. In Praise of Profanation. In *Profanations*. Translated by Jeff Fort. New York: Zone Books, pp. 73–92.

Agamben, Giorgio. 2009. What Is an Apparatus? In *"What Is an Apparatus?" and Other Essays*. Translated by David Kishik, and Stefan Pedatella. Stanford: Stanford UP, pp. 1–24.

Agamben, Giorgio. 2011. Hunger of an Ox. In *Nudities*. Translated by David Kishik, and Stefan Pedatella. Stanford: Stanford UP, pp. 104–12.

Azulai, Hayyim Joseph David. 1986. *Devash le-Fi*. Jerusalem: Yahadut.

Barth, Karl. 2010. *Der Römerbrief: Zweite Fassung 1922*. Edited by Cornelis van der Kooi and Katja Tolstaja. Zürich: Theologischer Verlag Zürich.

Benjamin, Walter. 1991a. Franz Kafka: Zur zehnten Wiederkehr seines Todestages. In *Gesammelte Schriften II*. Edited by Rolf Tiedemann and Hermann Schweppenhäuser. Frankfurt am Main: Suhrkamp, pp. 409–37.

Benjamin, Walter. 1991b. Franz Kafka: "Beim Bau der Chinesischen Mauer". In *Gesammelte Schriften II*. Edited by Rolf Tiedemann and Hermann Schweppenhäuser. Frankfurt am Main: Suhrkamp, pp. 676–83.

Benjamin, Walter. 1991c. Schicksal und Charakter. In *Gesammelte Schriften II*. Edited by Rolf Tiedemann and Hermann Schweppenhäuser. Frankfurt am Main: Suhrkamp, pp. 171–79.

Benjamin, Walter. 1991d. Theologisch-politisches Fragment. In *Gesammelte Schriften II*. Edited by Rolf Tiedemann and Hermann Schweppenhäuser. Frankfurt am Main: Suhrkamp, pp. 203–4.

---

[21] This Marranic tactic is best visible in *The Time that Remains*, where Agamben repeatedly applies the Lurianic conceptual apparatus ("contraction," "the void," "the remnant") to the analysis of Paul's Epistles, but never reveals its kabbalistic lineage; see (Sawczyński 2018).

Benjamin, Walter. 1991e. Über den Begriff der Geschichte. In *Gesammelte Schriften I*. Edited by Rolf Tiedemann and Hermann Schweppenhäuser. Frankfurt am Main: Suhrkamp, pp. 693–4.

Benjamin, Walter. 1991f. Versuch eines Schemas zu Kafka. In *Gesammelte Schriften II*. Edited by Rolf Tiedemann and Hermann Schweppenhäuser. Frankfurt am Main: Suhrkamp, p. 1192.

Benjamin, Walter. 1991g. Zur Kritik der Gewalt. In *Gesammelte Schriften II*. Edited by Rolf Tiedemann and Hermann Schweppenhäuser. Frankfurt am Main: Suhrkamp, pp. 179–203.

Bloch, Ernst. 1980. *Geist der Utopie*. Frankfurt am Main: Suhrkamp.

Borsò, Vittoria, Claas Morgenroth, Karl Solibakke, and Bernd Witte, eds. 2010. *Benjamin-Agamben: Politik, Messianismus, Kabbala*. Würzburg: Verlag Königshausen und Neumann.

Chiesa, Lorenzo. 2009. Giorgio Agamben's Franciscan Ontology. In *The Italian Difference: Between Nihilism and Biopolitics*. Edited by Lorenzo Chiesa and Alberto Toscano. Melbourne: Re.press, pp. 149–64.

Critchley, Simon. 2013. *The Faith of the Faithless: Experiments in Political Theology*. London and New York: Verso.

Dickinson, Colby. 2011. *Agamben and Theology*. New York and London: T&T Clark International.

Fine, Lawrence. 2003. *Physician of the Soul, Healer of the Cosmos: Isaac Luria and His Kabbalistic Fellowship*. Stanford: Stanford UP.

Foucault, Michel. 1980. The Confession of the Flesh. In *Power/Knowledge: Selected Interviews and Other Writings, 1972–1977*. Translated by Colin Gordon, Leo Marshall, John Mepham, and Kate Soper. Edited by Colin Gordon. New York: Pantheon Books, pp. 194–228.

Gulli, Bruno. 2007. The Ontology and Politics of Exception: Reflections on the Work of Giorgio Agamben. In *Giorgio Agamben: Sovereignty and Life*. Edited by Matthew Calarco and Steven DeCaroli. Stanford: Stanford UP, pp. 219–42.

Idel, Moshe. 1998. *Messianic Mystics*. New Haven and London: Yale UP.

Jonas, Hans. 2001. *The Gnostic Religion: The Message of the Alien God and the Beginnings of Christianity*. Boston: Beacon Press.

Kafka, Franz. 1997. Das Schloß. In *Die Romane*. Frankfurt am Main: Fischer, pp. 611–982.

Kaufman, Eleanor. 2008. The Saturday of Messianic Time: Agamben and Badiou on the Apostle Paul. *South Atlantic Quarterly* 107: 37–54. [CrossRef]

Kotsko, Adam. 2013. The Curse of the Law and the Coming Politics: On Agamben, Paul and the Jewish Alternative. In *Giorgio Agamben: Legal, Political, and Philosophical Perspectives*. Edited by Tom Frost. New York and London: Routledge, pp. 13–30.

Liska, Vivian. 2008. *Giorgio Agambens leerer Messianismus*. Berlin: Schlebrügge.

Liska, Vivian. 2017. Kafka, Narrative and the Law. In *German-Jewish Thought and Its Afterlife: A Tenuous Legacy*. Bloomington: Indiana UP, pp. 54–63.

Maciejko, Pawel. 2011. *The Mixed Multitude: Jacob Frank and the Frankist Movement*. Philadelphia: University of Pennsylvania Press.

Maimonides. 1949. *The Code of Maimonides: Book Fourteen: The Book of Judges*. Translated by Abraham M. Hershman. New Haven: Yale UP.

Maimonides. 2012. Thirteen Principles of Faith. In *Essential Teachings on Jewish Faith and Ethics: The Book of Knowledge and the Thirteen Principles of Faith Annotated and Explained*. Translated by Rabbi Marc D. Angel. Woodstock: Jewish Lights Publishing, pp. 151–72.

Sawczyński, Piotr. 2018. The Significant Nothing: Agamben, Theology, and Political Subjectivity. In *Subjectivity and the Political: Contemporary Perspectives*. Edited by Gavin Rae and Emma Ingala. New York and London: Routledge, pp. 75–89.

Schmitt, Carl. 2004. *Politische Theologie: Vier Kapitel zur Lehre von der Souveränität*. Berlin: Duncker und Humblot.

Scholem, Gershom. 1969. *On the Kabbalah and Its Symbolism*. Translated by Ralph Manheim. New York: Schocken Books.

Scholem, Gershom. 1974. Redemption through Sin. In *The Messianic Idea in Judaism: And Other Essays on Jewish Spirituality*. Translated by Hillel Halkin. New York: Schocken Books, pp. 78–141.

Scholem, Gershom. 1975. *Walter Benjamin: Geschichte Einer Freundschaft*. Frankfurt am Main: Suhrkamp.

Scholem, Gershom. 1995. *Major Trends in Jewish Mysticism*. New York: Schocken Books.

Scholem, Gershom. 2016. *Sabbatai Sevi: The Mystical Messiah, 1626–1676*. Translated by R. J. Zwi Werblowsky. Princeton: Princeton UP.

Svenungsson, Jayne. 2017. Law and Liberation: Critical Notes on Agamben's Political Messianism. *European Judaism* 50: 68–77. [CrossRef]

Taubes, Jacob. 1986. Walter Benjamin—Ein moderner Marcionit? Scholems Benjamin-Interpretation religionsgeschichtlich überprüft. In *Antike und Moderne: Zu Walter Benjamins "Passage"*. Edited by Norbert W. Bolz and Richard Faber. Würzburg: Königshausen und Neumann, pp. 138–47.

Taubes, Jacob. 1993. *Die politische Theologie des Paulus*. Edited by Aleida Assmann and Jan Assmann. München: Wilhelm Fink.

Von Harnack, Adolf. 1924. *Marcion: Das Evangelium vom fremden Gott*. Leipzig: J. C. Hinrichs'sche Buchhandlung.

Weiss, Daniel H. 2014. Walter Benjamin and the Antinomianism of Classical Rabbinic Law. *Bamidbar* 4: 56–78.

Zartaloudis, Thanos. 2010. *Giorgio Agamben: Power, Law and the Uses of Criticism*. London and New York: Routledge.

Zartaloudis, Thanos, ed. 2016. *Agamben and Law*. London and New York: Routledge.

Tertullian. 1972. *Adversus Marcionem*. Translated by Ernst Evans. Oxford: Oxford UP.

religions

MDPI

Article

Solovyov's Metaphysics between Gnosis and Theurgy

Aleksandr Gaisin

The Graduate School for Social Research, IFiS PAN, 00-330 Warsaw, Poland; gyssin@gmail.com;
Tel.: +7953-154-6247

Received: 29 September 2018; Accepted: 8 November 2018; Published: 13 November 2018

check for
updates

Abstract: This article provides a reading of Vladimir Solovyov's philosophy as expressed in his 'Lectures on Divine Humanity' and 'The Meaning of Love'. It seeks to unpack his eclectic thought in order to answer the question of whether there is a Jewish Kabbalistic influence on the Russian thinker amidst his usual platonic, gnostic, and Schellengian tropes. Interested as a young man in Jewish Mysticism, Solovyov fluctuates in his 'Lectures on Divine Humanity' between a platonic reading of Schellengian Gnosticism and some elements of Kabbalistic origin. In 'The Meaning of Love', he develops a notion of love that puts him very close to what Moshe Idel calls 'theosophic-theurgical Kabbalah'. Showing how 'The Meaning of Love' completes the narrative of 'Lectures', we can affirm that there is a certain Christian Kabbalistic line in Solovyov's thought that culminates in his theurgical understanding of love. In this sense, Solovyov might be called a philosophical Marrano as he is certainly a heterodox theosopher that fluctuates between Christian Gnosis and Christian Kabbalah, never assuming a solid identity.

Keywords: philosophical theology; heterodoxy; Judeo-Christianity; Russian religious renaissance; Christian Kabbalah; Vladimir Solovyov

---

The enigmatic and eclectic nature of Solovyov's thought is unveiled if we simply look at the early readings of his philosophy. Already, the Silver Age's thinker and poet Dmitry Merezhkovsky deemed Solovyov as a Gnostic writer, immersed in Christian heresy (Merezhkovsky 1991, p. 117)[1], whereas only several years later, Evgenii Trubetskoy, in his fully-fledged study of Solovyov read him as a staunch follower of Schelling (Trubetskoy 1913)[2]. However, more interesting for us is the assessment of Solovyov given by father Vasily Zenkovskiy—one of the first historians of Russian thought —who criticized Solovyov, while never elaborating on his claims, for introducing Jewish 'Magism' into his philosophy (Zenkovsky 1991)[3]. In this essay, I would like to both challenge and affirm Zenkovsky's reading. Based on Solovyov's 'Lectures on Divine Humanity' (1878–81)[4] and a later essay, 'The Meaning of Love' (1894), I will sketch Solovyov's metaphysics and show that there is

---

[1]   Says Merezhkovsky in my translation: 'Solovyov is gnostic, perhaps, the last great gnostic of all Christianity. Of course, he too suggests religious agency, pragmatism, which is, however, unavoidable for any Christian philosophy. Yet it is contemplation that is for him the first action. Theurgy (bogodelanie) stems for Solovyov from theology (bogopoznanie) and not vice versa, as for pragmatics. For him the essence of dogma opens up not firstly to will and only then to reason, but on the contrary it reveals itself firstly to reason and only then to will. He is rationalist just as any gnostic. Not God's will but God's knowledge is for him primarily religion' (Merezhkovsky 1991, p. 117).

[2]   For a more recent reading that emphasizes Solovyov's indebtedness to Schelling and Gnosticism see Gaidenko's study of Solovyov (Gaidenko 2001, pp. 69–83). One should also mention Aleksei Kozyrev's historical study of Solovyov's possible gnostic influences (Kozyrev 2007).

[3]   Zenkovsky says that Jewish Kabbalah is the most important mystic influence on Solovyov. Yet he only points out, that in Solovyov's anthropology one can clearly see Kabbalistic and Romantic influences, especially, in his notion of transforming love, which, according to Russian theologian, is purely magical. In general, Zenkovsky follows Trubetskoy's reading of Solovyov's philosophy (Zenkovsky 1991, p. 55).

[4]   I used a recent edition of the Russian original. Yet the 'Lectures' are available in English as well (Solovyov 1995).

indeed a possibility to read him as someone definitely influenced by and interested in Jewish Kabbalah. I will go on to say that what prompted Zenkovsky to misread Solovyov as suggesting some sort of magic is, in fact, Solovyov's closeness to, in Moshe Idel's words, theosophical-theurgical Kabbalah (Idel 2005, pp. 214–17). In my sketch of Solovyov's thought, I will show that he indeed fluctuates between Gnostic suspicion towards creation and more theurgical and erotic affirmation of the finite. In my reading, it is precisely the semi-hidden eroticism of his metaphysics that urges Solovyov to make a step from Christian gnosis to Christian Kabbalah. It is exactly this fluctuation between gnostic, Christian, and kabbalistic tropes that allows us to call, in a sense, Solovyov, a philosophical Marrano[5] whose oeuvre might look prima facie as Orthodox Christian theology but in a more attenuated contemplation, as my article points out, his work contains crypto-Jewish and hidden Gnostic elements that raise the question whether Solovyov assumes any solid theological identity.

Solovyov was not only a philosopher, but also a visionary. In the autobiographical piece 'Three Meetings' (1898) he sets to poetry his three encounters with Sophia. One happened in his early childhood, followed by a second vision years later in London, which called him to go to Egypt and meet Sophia, literally, in the desert. Surprisingly, Solovyov undertook a voyage to Kairo and there happened the final rendezvous with the eternal feminine. The 'Lectures on Divine Humanity' were delivered in Moscow months after the last vision. If the language of the poem sometimes references Goethe's 'Ewig-weibliche', it still has more influences than just that of German literary tradition. In fact, if Solovyov's work is to be defined as 'eclectic', then the story leading to lectures on Divine Humanity truly highlights intellectual influences Solovyov experienced throughout his early life. Well versed in Spinoza from his adolescence, he studied natural sciences in Saint Petersburg for three years, after which he switched to academic philosophy, only to change again shortly after to theology this time at the Moscow Theological Academy. Biographers say that, initially, Solovyov indeed wanted to study 'proper' theology but it was Christian mysticism, mainly the likes of Jacob Boehme, that took his attention in Moscow. While at the academy, Solovyov asked for a study trip to England and went to London, where he read at the British Museum for about a year. His interest there was to study Kabbalistic literature[6]. In Solovyov's words at the library in London, 'Mysterious forces chose my every book; and I read only of Her'[7].

In the "Lectures on the Divine Humanity', for the first time, Solovyov presents a rare systematic overview of his metaphysics. The starting point for Solovyov's discourse, as he draws openly on both Schelling and Boehme, is the relationship, the interconnection between God and the world. As in the preceding theosophical tradition, to give an account of this relationship, Solovyov's thought postulates and seeks to explain both creation and theogony as intertwined processes (Sholem 1954)[8]. That is, at the beginning the absolute or God exists, encompassing all single things inside itself. In this primordial existence there is no difference between things within the absolute. Solovyov calls this stage of God's being 'substance' and says that its mode of existence is will. In other words, at the dawn of everything, God existed as all-encompassing entity that found, in itself, a will to express itself. So at the next stage, the willing absolute starts positing or emanating (although Solovyov himself avoids this word) ideal platonic forms that constituted Absolute's content. This first creation/emanation is Logos of God, his word, or the second person of the Trinity. Solovyov calls it 'subject' and its mode of existing is ideas or concepts. The last theogonic step is when the posited Logos returns to the absolute as perception.

---

[5]   Agata Bielik-Robson defines the term 'philosophical Marrano' as 'a type of thinker< ... >who will never break through the Joycean "Jew-Greek, Greek-Jew" confusion, but nonetheless will try to turn it into his advantage' (Bielik-Robson 2014, p. 4). Despite not being a Jew himself Solovyov might be called a thinker of such productive confusion.

[6]   I take this short intellectual biography of Solovyov from Zenkovky (Zenkovsky 1991, pp. 11–14). In his more up to date study Aleksei Kozyrev points out that the official goal of Solovyov's trip to London was to prepare a monograph on gnosticism. However, he probably divided his time between reading gnostic tractates such as Pistis Sophia and investigating kabbalistic literature in form of Rosenroth's 'Kabbala Denudata'. Solovyov's library cards were lost, so we can only make educated guesses of what exactly he read in the British Museum (Kozyrev 2007, pp. 10–11, 30–33).

[7]   Translated by Ivan M. Granger. There is a newly published translation of 'Three Meetings' (Solovyov 2008).

[8]   I base this reading of theosophy on Gershom Sholem's understanding of it (Sholem 1954, pp. 12–14).

In other words, God, the substance, perceives the emanated ideas or Logos, and this way of being—as a perception of something—constitutes the third stage of process in God and is, accordingly, the third person of the Trinity (Solovyov 2006, p. 141). Solovyov defines it as 'feeling' and its mode of existence as beauty. Solovyov calls such a God 'the living God' (Solovyov 2006, p. 97), which means that he exists as an everlasting process that is present in every single piece of his creation as the positing of more platonic forms continues. It is remarkable that the creation ex nihilo is not even mentioned, and, moreover, is not even possible in such a strict system, in which, at least at this moment, there is no separate place outside Godhead. God emanates forms, which, in turn, open themselves up and posit lesser forms. In this sense, Solovyov regards platonic forms as having their own subjectivity and will (Solovyov 2006, pp. 89–90), that enables them to continue the process of creation and emanate things that existed within them without difference before that, thus, externalizing further the content of the primordial absolute. Another important point of his scheme is that it establishes and promotes a very rigid and strict hierarchy. There are highly consequent and sequenced relations within the personae of God and since the emanated platonic forms, essentially, take part in this process as well, it means that they are also subjects of this hierarchy. Solovyov extends it to the degree that, for him, all problems of the social world might be summarized as coming from the false hierarchies we build. In other words, instead of taking part in the divine order of things, that is oriented on the eternal harmony of an ideal world, we choose to pursue finite and singled goals, putting them above the infinite and divine. To put it differently, metaphysics as knowledge of the hierarchy of being always comes before any scientific disciplines or ethical reasoning. This line of thought is the foundation of his later theocratic utopia: to know the hierarchy of divine forms is to know the right social order in the world below[9].

Clearly, the backbone of Solovyov's system is a platonic reading of Schelling from whom he borrows some of his terminology—Absolute, Logos as the first emanation—being the most obvious examples[10]. However, there are nuances in Solovyov's thought that might indeed be explained by his early interest in Jewish Kabbalah. One of such details is that the posited forms in Solovyov's system have similarities with the Zoharic tradition of Sephirot, which, in Sholem words, are not intermediary stages between the phenomenal world and Godhead, as neo-platonic emanations are, but rather different phases of God's manifestation (Sholem 1954, pp. 208–10). So are Solovyov's forms: they exist in their own right, not as the spheres revolving around of the unum but rather as the growing tree that continuously externalizes the content of the Absolute bringing about its different attributes. The forms, Solovyov insists, also have their own free will, and, therefore, are in relations to each other[11]. Given that they produce even more forms, their relationship might be, if not overtly sexual, then still erotic. In fact, Solovyov's own claims in his late essay 'The Meaning of Love' are rather supporting such reading: the true love in its real sense, says he, is only possible in the ideal world of forms but not in our fallen phenomenal world, in which we might only learn to see our beloved ones as if they were glimpses of their true ideal selves. In other words, it is exactly Solovyov who says that love exists precisely in the ideal world of forms, and together with it, we might conclude, comes at least erotic desire and longing. Although the cosmoerotic relationship between God's emanations arguably has its roots in the neo-platonic renaissance, there might be a Jewish influence on Solovyov in how he differentiates between love in the human world and true love in the metaphysical realm of forms. The Italian kabbalist David da Vidas, writes Moshe Idel, 'distinguishes between two different modes

---

9   This insistence on knowledge also provokes Merezhkovsky to call Solovyov gnostic as shown above. In his 'Heterodox Hegel', Cyril O'Reagan argues that Hegel's preference for Eckhart is based on the fact that, for this medieval thinker, God's revelation has a concrete result, is summed up in words, in knowledge and not in some form of loose imagining (O'Reagan 1994, pp. 29–30). Solovyov here displays the same preference: as much as mystic way of knowing is superior to reason, it is so only when it might be summarized in concrete, commanding knowledge.

10   Here I agree with Trubetskoy's reading (Trubetskoy 1913, p. 277).

11   It is not unknown to German Idealism to postulate that God creates through his attributes. Franz von Baader believed that creation happens not directly from God, but from his revealed attributes (Mirror, Wisdom, Being, Idea). He too called these attributes Sephirot (Baader 1987, pp. 205–6).

of love. One is metaphysical, constituted by processes of attraction and unification between sefirotic elements within the supernal realm, and has nothing to do with human love'. That is, in the realm of God's emanations 'love serves as a virtus unitiva', that attracts and holds the emanations together, whereas the 'personal love is … ontologically derived from supernal love' (Idel 2005, p. 193). I will return to and analyze Solovyov's conception of love later in the text discussing Sophia.

As is shown in the exposition above, Solovyov's thought so far might be prone to pantheism: the chain of emanations from the absolute is never severed from its source at it were. In fact, he seems to be rather aware of that, and given his indebtedness to Schelling, Solovyov also wants to find ways to protect his own philosophy from being too Schellingian, i.e. pantheistic. Apparently, Solovyov read critiques of Schelling that disapproved his thought as pantheistic (e.g., Franz von Baader). That is, for Schelling in the dialectical process of theogonical world creation, the Absolute posits before itself matter light etc. (Schelling 1994, pp. 118–19). In this respect, as Baader claimed, there is a direct unmediated transition from ideal into material, which ultimately presents a pantheistic world view: certain stages of the Absolute's self-opening happen in the material world and, therefore, God is nature, and, vice versa, nature is God. Solovyov is aware of this problematic and insists that the initial creation consisted exclusively of platonic forms that had nothing to do with the corrupted materiality of the natural world. To defend his own philosophy from pantheistic readings, Solovyov offers several arguments. Firstly, like the persons of the Trinity are defined by their relation to one other, so are the ideal forms defined by their relation to God and to one another. This means, for Solovyov that, strictly speaking, absolutely separated existence would not be possible because it is precisely the shared ground of God and previous creations that binds everything together (Solovyov 2006, pp. 116–18, 130). Although Solovyov does not mention it openly, there are Boehmian[12] and Schellingian[13] concepts of unground at play here. Before God awakened and became self-cognizant, everything existed in a state of primordial abyss or unground, just as Solovyov thought, but after his awakening, God is source for every subsequent creation; yet all of what came after this, still shared with God, this first pre-created existence within unground. This doctrine is supposed to give a certain amount of autonomy to the created; Solovyov seems to be counting on it when he later introduces another argument against pantheism by saying that the Absolute exists as both plurality and singleness, otherwise, he insists, it could not be called Absolute after all (Solovyov 2006, p. 160). In this sense, platonic forms are part of God, but they are also subjects that through participating in primordial abyss have the roots of their existence and will within it, and are, therefore, if not equal in their autonomous will and existence, at least analogous to God. This allows Solovyov to say that God is, indeed, all, but all or nature is not God (Solovyov 2006, p. 116). Interestingly enough, in this phrase, Solovyov paraphrases Schelling himself, who defines Spinoza's philosophy saying that God is all that exists but not all that exists is God[14]. Even more intriguing is that both Schelling and Solovyov are to a degree paraphrasing Moses Cordovero who, as Scholem writes, 'a century before Spinoza and Malebranche', wrote 'that God is all reality, but not all reality is God. En-Sof, according to him (to Cordovero)', continues Sholem, 'can also be called thought (i.e., thought of the world) insofar as everything that exists is contained in His substance. He encompasses all existence, but not in the mode of its isolated existence below, but rather in the existence of the substance, for He and existing things are [in this mode] one, and neither separate nor multifarious, nor externally visible, but rather His substance is present in His Sefhirot, and He Himself is everything, and nothing exists outside Him' (Sholem 1954, p. 253). The Cordoverian argument is not exactly the defence Solovyov presented, but they both stress that because God as En-sof/Absolute had as its content everything that came to be before the emanation took place, there is no true separation afterwards, and the emanated carries God's presence in it, not physically or the way

---

12 I reference here Nicolas Berdyaev's essay on Jacob Boehme (Berdyaev 1970, pp. vi–xi).
13 Schelling's reading of Unground can be found in his Freiheitsschrift (Schelling 2011).
14 Sholem makes this observation in his 'Major Trends in Jewish Mysticism'. Schelling's phrase can be found in his *Muenchener Vorlesungen zur Geschichte der neuren Philosophie* (Schelling 1902, p. 44).

in which ideas/sefhiroth exist, but because everything ever emanated existed before its manifestation within Godhead.

For Solovyov, the initial good creation is constituted fully of ideal platonic forms that exist in eternal harmony with God, expressing and externalizing the Absolute. At this point, there is no material, as opposed to ideal, beings in the Russian thinker's universe. To explain the origin of the finite, real world Solovyov resorts to a very Gnostic[15] thematic: the world of matter came to being as a result of cosmic catastrophe, and is, therefore, damaged in its essence. It is striking how throughout his Lectures on Divine Humanity, Solovyov repeatedly calls the finite world 'abnormal' as something that should not be in the first place. As much as Solovyov is gnostic while diminishing the value of material world, he does not introduce an evil Gnostic demiurge. He rather again gives a very Neoplatonic reading of Schelling's Abfall[16], extending and developing it. In his Religion and Philosophy' (1804) the German philosopher argues that the material world splits away from the ideal in a catastrophic event (Schelling 2010, p. 26). Thus, according to Solovyov, the initial ideal creation finds its last stage in what or whom he calls Sophia, 'soul of the world' (Solovyov 2006, p. 173). She is the 'wisdom of God'—the pinnacle of creation—and the platonic form of humanity. As other forms in Solovyov's schematic, Sophia has her own subjectivity and will, i.e. she is free to do whatever she wants. In Solovyov's narrative, although he does not go into pointing out her exact motives, she uses her free will to commit the first crime in the ideal universe of God's emanations: she, instead of following the will of God the substance, wants to be separated, wants to exist on her own without God and outside Him (Solovyov 2006, pp. 192–94). One should look at this motive a bit more closely. Although Solovyov does not use the baroque rhetoric of Boehme, this trope seems to be coming precisely from him. For it is Boehme who describes God the Father as burning fire, righteous anger, and desire, to sin against whom is to deny His will and to put one's own separately[17]. In other words, the sinners rebel against God as they cease to follow His will and be freely subjugated under it. Solovyov, although lacking extravagant images of the shoemaker from Görlitz, still repeats the same argument: the only moral choice in his universe is between accepting the will of the Father or denying it. If one follows the will of God, one accepts his or her place in the harmonic hierarchy of eternal platonic forms. If one denies it, then one must undergo the separation from the pure world of ideas and attempt existence on one's own. Solovyov does not state the reasons or temptations that prompted Sophia to fall and to want herself more than she wanted to fulfil the will of God. However, the fall—in itself—still did not create the material universe as we know it but established the space in which separation between entities was possible. In this space, in the Russian thinker's narrative, everything existed in the state of utter chaos and disarray (Solovyov 2006, p. 196).

At this point, Solovyov's creation story begins, which eclectically mixes Gnostic, Christian, and Kabbalistic tropes. The catastrophe caused by Sophia, in Solovyov's narrative, cannot be overcome at the drop of a hat, which essentially makes both natural and human history a story of reconciliation. Although Schelling remains the ground of this schematic, Solovyov adds some nuances that make it different from the German's idealist perspective. After the fall, says Solovyov, Sophia immediately regrets and wants to restore her unity with God, and in a dramatic gesture, God the Logos plunges into the material space to save Sophia. In other words, God chooses to diminish himself as he enters the material space, so that the fallen creation could be returned to harmony (Solovyov 2006, p. 200).

---

[15] I should clarify my usage of the term 'gnostic' at this point. 'Gnostic' presupposes a stark differentiation or even alienation between true God and the phenomenal world; often a differentiation within Godhead as well would precede the creation of the material world. Gnostic alienation renders the finite, the creation as worthless or damaged and either introduces an evil demiurge, who knowingly or unknowingly rules the finite, or a cosmic catastrophe that creates the lacking finite universe. Either only the souls trapped in the finite universe or the whole world must be saved from its lacking existence, so the gnostic narrative sets up a soteriological view of history.

[16] Here, I disagree with Kozyrev's view that Solovyov simply took the notion of split from Valentinian Gnosticism and subsequently transformed its mythology into a philosophical narrative of creation (Kozyrev 2007, p. 76). After all, Schelling is one of the most crucial influences on Solovyov, so one can expect he read 'Philosophy and Religion'.

[17] I summarise here again Nikolai Berdyaev's essay on Jacob Boehme (Berdyaev 1970, pp. xi–xviii).

What is also interesting in Solovyov's kenotic narrative is the fact that the result of God diving into the material world is an erotic, although Solovyov avoids this word, union between Sophia and Logos, that seems to have Kabbalistic overtones. In this union, Sophia, according to Solovyov, is a rather passive, feminine side that receives and apprehends the Logos of God, which is active and carries the ideas that are incarnated in the material universe (Solovyov 2006, p. 201). Together, in their union, Sophia and Logos transform the chaos of the fallen world and co-create the material universe as we know it, first in the process of natural history and then in the moral history of the human race.

This kenotic motive here diminishes Gnostic suspicion towards the material world in Solovyov: the immediate result of the fall is the separation, the empty space between creations, but the phenomenal world is still co-created from this catastrophe in the good will by God and Sophia. In this sense, the finite is not a place where souls are tortured and await salvation that would bring them back to the true world of God, but the finitude has its own merit. In the phenomenal world, in Solovyov's view, we still encounter beauty that mirrors the true grandeur of the ideal realm.

It would help us to understand Solovyov's erotic story of creation if we look again at his later text 'The Meaning of Love', in which he describes a differentiation within God, that establishes his other as the feminine entity: 'God, as one, distinguishing from Himself His other, i.e., all that is not He, unites this all with Himself, presenting it to Himself, all together and all at once, in an absolutely perfect form, and, consequently, as a unity. This other unity, distinct though not separable from the primordial Divine unity, is, relative to God, a passive, feminine unity, seeing that here the eternal emptiness (pure potentiality) receives the fulness of the Divine existence. But if at the basis of this eternal femininity lies pure nothing, then for God this nothing is eternally hidden by the image of the absolute perfection which is being received from the Divinity' (Solovyov 1985, p. 91). One should note that 'pure nothing' in this passage is rather referring to the primordial existence of the Absolute, i.e., things later created had existed beforehand, in Schelling's words, as nothing. In this sense, Sophia existed there in nothingness as an 'inept image' and the creation manifests the concealed potentialities. Says Solovyov, 'For God, His other (i.e., the universe) possesses from all eternity the image of perfect femininity, but He desires that this image should exist not merely for Him, but that it should be realised and incarnated in each individual being capable of union with it. Such a realisation and incarnation is also the aspiration of the eternal femininity itself, which is not merely an inert image in the Divine mind, but a living spiritual being possessed of all the fullness of powers and activities. The whole process of the cosmos and of history is the process of its realisation and incarnation in a great manifold of forms and degrees' (Solovyov 1985, p. 92).

So, God differentiates from Himself His other, which is feminine, and the continuous creation of the world is a task that requires both God and Sophia, which is presented in a state of becoming. The narrative of "The Meaning of Love" does not repeat exactly the story of Sophia's fall that Solovyov tells in Lectures on Divine Humanity, but there is a single core: the differentiation within God is the process of the first creation, and the fullness of the first creation is a feminine entity, together with her God creates later the phenomenal material world. Yet, the split between God and the world, that Solovyov tells us about in Lectures on Divine Humanity, remains open. The finite world is not fully reconciled by actions of God and Sophia with the infinite. In fact, Solovyov says in both his 'Lectures' and in 'The Meaning of Love', it is up to the human race to restore the world in its connection to the eternal. Says Solovyov, 'The power of love, passing into the world, transforming and spiritualising the form of external phenomena, reveals to us its objective might, and after that it is up to us. We ourselves must understand this revelation and take advantage of it, so that it may not remain a passing and enigmatic flash of some mystery. The psycho-physical process of the restoration of the Divine image in material humanity has no means to perfect itself by itself, apart from us' (Solovyov 1985, p. 61). Several pages later, he repeats this in what appears to be more Schellingian rhetoric: 'Our personal concern, so far as it is true, is a common concern of the whole world—the realisation and individualisation of the unity-of-the-all idea and the spiritualisation of matter. It is prepared by the cosmic process in the world of nature and is continued and completed by the historical process in humanity' (Solovyov 1985, p. 105). We see that, within this scheme, another Gnostic and Schellingian trope joins Solovyov's narrative: in the process of the creation, it is God who tries to enter to the material world and to make Himself manifest within it. So, says Solovyov in Lectures on Divine Humanity, repeating late Schelling's philosophy, God manifested Himself throughout history as an ideal God in Greek philosophy, as persona in Jewish religion, until finally and literally coming to the world as a new human—Jesus Christ (Solovyov 2006, p. 222).

So the reconciliation between the finite and the infinite is the work of man, and is there any specific path Solovyov might have in mind? In the 'Lectures on Divine Humanity' the answer would be rather in historic terms: the new coming 'complete worldview'[18], that combines the advances of Western thought together with the pureness of Eastern Orthodoxy will bring about immediate changes to the world. Here, Solovyov is, at first sight, only engaged in romantic messianism, in which the source of eschatological opening is rather not the unspoiled people, but the religious tradition that, in its simplicity, preserved the truth of the early church (Solovyov 2006, pp. 244–45). However, a closer look might argue that his narrative is at least partly Gnostic: it is the philosophy or theology, the knowledge of the eternal harmony of God's world that is to save the finite and reconcile it with the infinite realm of forms. In other words, salvation comes from us knowing and realizing that the phenomenal or 'abnormal'—as Solovyov repeatedly calls material existence—should be brought back into harmony with the ideal[19]. Years later, in 'The Meaning of Love' Solovyov would give another solution. Some of his arguments in this essay fluctuate around monastic or again Gnostic suspicion to anything material: true love is not possible within the phenomenal world and sexual relations are basically not integral to any discussion on love (Solovyov 1985, p. 20). Yet, there is a change in his view that helps humankind to overcome the split between God and the world. Love is what defines existence in the world of platonic forms, so to close the divide and 'spiritualize matter', we should do the same so that it would not be a divided and empty space that defines the existence of the phenomenal world, but the harmony and realization of God's image. Says Solovyov, 'The task of love consists in justifying in deed that meaning of love which at first is given only in feeling. It demands such a union of two given finite natures as would create out of them one absolute ideal personality' (Solovyov 1985, p. 55). That is to say, true love is not possible in this existence, but Solovyov believes that even in its limited scope, it helps to transcend finite reality and shows us glimpses of the real world of forms in our beloved ones. In the lingua of the Christian Church, Solovyov would say that to love would be to perform Christ's commandment from John's Gospel. This altered attitude might be well attributed as that of theurgy. That is, it is our actions in the finite realm that do have a certain effect on the world above and gradually are to undo the catastrophe that the finite world came from. The fact that the world of platonic forms is basically love makes it easy to misread Solovyov as introducing magic in his philosophy. Yet, it is hardly magical as there is no way the action of love commands the infinite or promises any gain or profit for those who perform it. Moreover, it is God's commandment.

In other words, it can be argued that here, Solovyov changes from Gnostic alienation to the creation to a rather theurgic[20] practical view, and what allows him to make this step is the hidden

---

18 'Complete worldview' as a description of what is to follow was coined by Sergius Bulgakov in his 'From Marxism to Idealism' (Bulgakov 1903) where he develops his own vision of the synthesis between modern philosophy and theology. He is clearly influenced by Solovyov at that stage.

19 Volens nolens I agree here with Merezhkovsky's verdict on Solovyov shown above.

20 The term originates in Neoplatonism. I use it here, however, more narrowly in the sense in which Moshe Idel calls some trends in Kabbalah as theosophical-theurgical. Says Idel, 'The impact of human performance of the commandments, or of transgressions against them, on the supernal beings, including the sexual union is central to theosophical-theurgical Kabbalah" (Idel 2005, p. 214). Idel further distinguishes what he calls the augmentation model of Kabbalah. In such theurgy, the performance of commandments causes the feminine manifestation to grow, i.e., change for the better. He illustrates this with a story from Zohar, which tells of a forsaken feminine figure who, while separated from her beloved one, becomes "smaller and darker". However, "the powerful men who were her hosts shouted out like 'like strong lions', and the supernal lover heard that she was in love like him. < . . . > He kissed her and embraced her, and she started to grow, regaining her size and beauty" (Idel 2005, p. 215). According to Idel, the Zoharic author associates 'powerful men' with kabbalists. That is, the growing or diminishing of the Shekhinah is dependent on man. My argument here is that Solovyov proposes a very

eroticism of his metaphysics. He is, in fact, not a pure Gnostic as he sees good in the finite just as well as his theurgic attitude is also somehow limited—he hides the erotic colors of his thought in the *'Lectures on Divine* Humanity' when he calls any descriptions of the relationship between God and Sophia metaphoric; he basically employs ascetic and monastic language[21] in 'The Meaning of Love'. Curiously, we can read in Alexander Etkind's study of Russian Flagellants influence on the cultural elite of the Empire's last decades, that Solovyov was mocked by Russian Silver Age poet Valery Bryusov, who painted the eschatological last day of the world as a fest gradually slipping into a sexual orgy (Etkind 1998, pp. 177–78)[22]. It is rather a great exaggeration of Solovyov's thought, but I would argue that it only works as a parody precisely because Solovyov thought is in its core erotic[23].

Of course, to a large degree, Solovyov takes his eroticism from the platonic or Neoplatonic thought. However, it seems that we might also talk about Jewish influence, knowing that he had interest to study Jewish Mysticism in London. First of all, the motive of intra/extra divine differentiation into the female and male that produces the world as the result of their coupling as we have seen it above has its own story in Kabbala. In Moshe Idel's 'Kabbalah and Eros' we read that for R. Yehuda ben Nassim ibn Malka—a 13th century Kabblist—'the Agent Intellect, which emanated directly from the unknown God, is a male entity, and it couples with the cosmic soul, conceived of as female, in order to generate the cosmic hyle' (Idel 2005, p. 183). Idel notes on the same page that, in this case, the influence of Greek philosophy is clearly present and the scheme is different from more theosophical Kabbalah as 'those syzygies are not intradivine powers but extra divine ones'. That is to say, here, the philosophy still outweighs the influence of more religious sources. It is important to argue that Solovyov clearly goes beyond ibn Malka's more simple introduction of theosophical motives into the great scheme of Greek thought. He is, in fact, much closer to the renaissance Jewish thinker Leon Ebreo, who wrote that 'the world was created as the son of the supernal beautiful the father, and the supernal wisdom the mother, or the supernal beauty' (Idel 2005, p. 189). It is here that, although Solovyov calls the finite world 'abnormal', the fact that the phenomenal world is a child of the God, the Logos, and the eternal feminine beauty of Sophia tells us that there is self-sufficient beauty even in the world as we see it. In other words, the love for finite is more than possible—maybe not so ethically correct for Solovyov—but in the finite we do not see and love Ficino's 'shadows of God' but rather the shards of him that are beautiful by themselves and that need to be returned to him[24]. In this respect, another non-platonic influence disturbs Platonism in Solovyov—the Eros in his thought takes place in history and not in the endless cycles of nature.

In this sense, the catastrophe that makes God the Logos 'plunge' into the physical space and together with Sophia create the phenomenal universe, is also a form of erotic disjointing between the world of platonic forms and the newly created finite universe. That is, the split away world, itself created as a result of Logos and Sophia coupling, is still cut off from God, and the reconciliation between them is the goal of the world process. In this way, Solovyov sets up a philosophy of history that focuses on describing and predicting various stages of this reconciliation.

The whole Solovyov narrative that views history as a story of curing the catastrophic cosmic event that defined creation, might be read as a development of a motive found in the Lurianic Kabbalah. There, the primordial entities—the 10 Sephiroth—which were to contain the light of God's manifestation and revelation, thus, enabling creation as it should have happened, broke down in

close narrative in "The Meaning of Love". Love, performed by human kind, affects the fallen world, which is the estranged feminine manifestation of God—Sophia—and leads her back to restored union with God.

21 Aleksei Kozyrev offers an analysis of probable gnostic background behind Solovyov's language in 'The Meaning of Love' (Kozyrev 2007, pp. 109–15).

22 The poem is called 'Last Day' and to my knowledge has not been yet translated into English.

23 Evgenii Trubetskoy calls Solovyov's concept of love an 'erotic utopia' (Trubetskoy 1913). Alexei Kozyrev too notices the eroticisation of the divine in Solovyov. For him this signifies a departure from Orthodox theology (Kozyrev 2007, pp. 134–35).

24 My argument is that for Platonic Ficino the mediation is always involved, The 'shadows of God' mediate the true world of divine Unum, whereas for Solovyov the fallen platonic forms are present in the finite world—albeit distorted and damaged—but still worthy of love as they are by themselves.

the process and as the result of this breaking, our finite world, the way we know it, came into being. This narrative, known as the Breaking of the Vessels, serves as a foundation for a historiosophic view called Tikkun, which renders history as a process in which these vessels are repaired[25]. Given that the imaginary of Kabbalah is often erotic, the Breaking of the Vessels is also a moment of erotic disjointing between the sephirot. It is up to people to repair the vessels and the way to do it is to perform the mitzvah—the religious commandments of Judaism.

As we have seen above, Solovyov's history is also a story of the reconciliation between the finite and infinite, which unfolds in its search for a cure for the cosmic catastrophe. Together with Luria, Solovyov shares the same Gnostic inclinations: the 'abnormality' of the material world; the absence of God in it. However, it seems, that, in Solovyov, his theurgic understanding of love is precisely what makes him less Gnostic. In Solovyov's idioma, seeing a finite loved one as if already reconciled with the eternal world of forms means after all that there is beauty and love, i.e., goodness in this finite realm. Moreover, the fact that it is possible to see and experience beauty and love in the self-enclosed material world that tries to exist on its own outside of God, renders finite as having its own worth. This worth, in Solovyov's view, has of course a relative value and still needs to re-join the Absolute, but it has albeit a limited capacity to stand its own ground. The theurgy, the action here is possible because in its alienation, the world is still affirmed as having been made from the same 'material' as the ideal world of platonic forms, which means that what defines the true world—namely love—is also possible in the finite. In other words, it comes to the fact that, despite Gnostic abnormality of the finite world, there is no absolutely strict distinction or even dichotomy between transcendence and immanence in Solovyov. If action is possible in the finite world, then the pure gnosis—knowledge—is of a less value: it is not enough to just know the laws according to which spirit unfolds in history and matter, but it is rather more important to afflict spirit and, thus, affect history.

In this short sketch of Solovyov's metaphysics, I wanted to show that as much as he is indeed to a large degree defined by Schelling's Gnosticism, there are other voices in his philosophy, and one of these voices is a Jewish one, most likely, thanks to Solovyov's early interest in Kabbalah. What Zenkovskiy rightly called 'Jewish', and wrongly 'Magism', is rather a theurgic attitude to the relationship between God and the world, which unexpectedly alters and fluctuates Solovyov's otherwise Schellingian narrative.

Author Contributions: For research articles with several authors, a short paragraph specifying their individual contributions must be provided.

Funding: This research received no external funding.

Conflicts of Interest: The author declares no conflict of interest.

References

Baader, Franz. 1987. Vorlesungen über religiöse Philosophie. I Heft. Vom Erkennen. In *Sämtliche Werke. Band 1*. Aalen: Scientia Verlag, pp. 205–6.

Berdyaev, Nicolas. 1970. Unground and Freedom. In *Six Theosophic Points by Jacob Boehme*. Translated by John R. Earle. Ann Arbor: The University of Michigan Press.

Bielik-Robson, Agata. 2014. *Jewish Cryptotheologies of Late Modernity: Philosophical Marranos*. London and New York: Routledge.

Bulgakov, Sergei. 1903. *Ot Marksizma k idealizmu: kolleczia esse*. Saint Petersburg: Publishing House "Public benefit".

Etkind, Alexander. 1998. *Hlysty (sekty, literatura i revoluzia)*. Moscow: Novoe literaturnoe obozrenie, pp. 177–78.

Gaidenko, Piama. 2001. *Vladimir Solovyov i Filosofia serebryannogo veka*. Moscow: Progress-Traditziya, pp. 69–83.

Idel, Moshe. 2005. *Kabbalah and Eros*. New Haven & London: Yale University Press.

Kozyrev, Aleksei. 2007. *Vladimir Solov'ov i gnostiki*. Moscow: Savin S.A Private Publishing House.

---

[25] My source here is Sholem's chapter on Luria in his 'Major Trends in Jewish Mysticism' (Sholem 1954, pp. 244–86).

Merezhkovsky, Dmitry. 1991. Nemoi prorok. In *V tihom omute. Statii i issledovaniya raznyh let*. Moscow: Sovetskie Pisatel, p. 117.

O'Reagan, Cyril. 1994. *Heterodox Hegel*. Albany: State University of New-York Press.

Schelling, Friedrich Wilhelm Joseph von. 1902. *Schellings Muenchener Vorlesungen zur Geschichte der neuren Philosophie*. Edited by Arthur Drews. Leipzig: Meiner Verlag, p. 44.

Schelling, Friedrich Wilhelm Joseph von. 1994. *On the History of Modern Philosophy*. Translated by Andrew Bowes. Cambridge: Cambridge University Press.

Schelling, Friedrich Wilhelm Joseph von. 2010. *Religion and Philosophy*. Translated by Klaus Ottoman. Putnam: Spring Publications, p. 26.

Schelling, Friedrich Wilhelm Joseph von. 2011. *Über das Wesen der menschlichen Freiheit*. Edited by Herausgegeben von Thomas Buchheim. Leipzig/Hamburg: Felix Meiner Verlag.

Sholem, Gershom. 1954. *Major Trends in Jewish Mysticism*. New York: Shocken Books.

Solovyov, Vladimir. 1985. *The Meaning of Love*. Translated by Thomas R. Beyer Jr.. London: Lindisfarne Books.

Solovyov, Vladimir. 1995. *Lectures on Divine Humanity*. Translated by Peter Zouboff. Revised and Edited by Boris Jakim. New York: Lindisfarne Press.

Solovyov, Vladimir. 2006. *Chtenia o bogochelovechestve*. Moscow: Publishing house AST Moscow.

Solovyov, Vladimir. 2008. *The Religious Poetry of Vladimir Solovyov*. Translated by Boris Jakim, and Laura Magnus. San Rafael: Semantron Press.

Trubetskoy, Evgenii. 1913. *Mirososerzanie Vl. S. Solovyova*. Moscow: Publishing house Put'.

Zenkovsky, Vasily. 1991. *Istoria Russkoi Filosofii. Tom 2*. Leningrad: EGO.

religions **MDPI**

Article

A Ruby and Triangled Sign upon the Forehead of Taurus: Modalities of Revelation in Megalithic Archaeoastronomy and James Joyce's Novels *Ulysses* and *Finnegans Wake*

Simon Crook

Independent Researcher, Southampton, UK; familycrook@btinternet.com

Received: 4 October 2018; Accepted: 13 November 2018; Published: 20 November 2018

check for updates

Abstract: This paper proceeds from the concurrent interpretation of two distinct, apparently unrelated disciplinary contexts, at the crossroads of the positivism of archaeology and the imaginary world of literature. The character of the reciprocal relationship between megalithism in Neolithic Portugal and the writings of the twentieth-century author, James Joyce, is transfigured through the introduction of a third element of interpretation, a deeply paradoxical current of Jewish thought, with messianic dimensions, antithetical to the forces of mythic reconciliation present in Joyce's fiction and in archaeological conceptions of 'symbolic systems' in antiquity, which tend to erase the innumerable singulars of experience. Applying a cryptotheologically-inflected exegesis immanent to the materials of text and archaeology in the light of their respective orientation to the same astral phenomenon, I seek to generate insights unanticipated within interpretations restricted to the disciplinary boundaries, theories and methodologies of archaeology and literary criticism as discrete entities. Within allegorised readings of archaeology and an archaeologicised reading of Joyce's texts I bring into play non-synchronous elements which both disrupt the idealised harmonies of social and religious conformity and illuminate hitherto unseen connections between diverse, seemingly incommensurable contexts, beyond the discursive conventions of detached objectivity, without relinquishing irreduceible remnants to a totalising synthesis.

Keywords: archaeoastronomy; megalithic; prehistory; Portugal; kabbalah; Marrano; James Joyce; *Ulysses*; *Finnegans Wake*

1. Introduction

In this paper I draw upon the 'deeply paradoxical religious sensibility' (Scholem 1971, p. 95) of the Marrano phenomenon to explore parallels between modalities of revelation at play in James Joyce's novels, *Ulysses* (Joyce 1922) and *Finnegans Wake* (Joyce 1939), and that *implicit* in an archaeoastronomical interpretation of a group of Neolithic dolmens dating to around 4000 BC in the Mondego valley of central Portugal (Silva 2013, 2015). With a strong resonance in the Iberian context, the 'hidden faith' of the Marranos, the Sephardic Jewry who were converted by force to Christianity (Scholem 1971, p. 95), is the ultimate source for antinomian perspectives introduced to the configuration central to this study. This is the constellation formed between an episode in *Ulysses* involving Leopold Bloom's epiphanic vision of Aldebaran, the brightest star of the constellation of Taurus, and the orientation of the Carregal do Sal cluster of Neolithic dolmens upon the same star. The serendipitous conjunction of the latter two contexts manifests a dialectical encounter first staged between *Finnegans Wake* and Neolithic archaeology in north-west Europe (Crook 2004). However, by activating an antinomian current of the Marranic tradition as a third element I aim to interrupt any synthesis between contexts often too easily integrated in the closed circuit of myth. Regarding revelation as 'the first enlightenment, disenchanting the world from the pagan cosmic gods' (Bielik-Robson 2014a, p. 9), means not stopping at the interpretation of aspects of Neolithic archaeology in Iberia through Joyce's 'usylessly unreadable' (*FW* 179.26)[1] texts, and interpreting his texts reciprocally through archaeology. Rather, beyond this I seek the spectral trace of revelation—where 'all Marrano characteristics apply to its secret works' (Bielik-Robson 2014a, p. 191)—on the astral paths of the corridors of the megalithic dolmens and the sombre ground of Joyce's writing.

The antinomian current, as reconfigured in a recent speculative intervention in modern philosophy (Bielik-Robson 2014a), is evident in the critical thought of writers such as Walter Benjamin, Gershom Scholem, Theodor Adorno and Ernst Bloch, identified as 'philosophical Marranos' who are convinced that the antinomian message constitutes the very essence of their own 'hidden faith' (ibid., p. 23). It is the thought of this milieu in particular that I employ to subject archaeology and Joyce's texts to a *cryptotheological misreading*. This means converting the context of archaeological enquiry to a field of allegory, a plane where the corridors of the Carregal do Sal dolmens are coterminous with the corridors of the Holles Street Maternity Hospital in *Ulysses*, where Leopold Bloom experiences his epiphany. By dislodging these megalithic structures from their exclusive association with either the discipline of archaeology or the harmonious cycles of antique and modern mythologies, I invoke the unquiet shekhinah-spirit—cognate with the character, ALP, in *Finnegans Wake*—who 'tries to breathe life into the stony cosmos of indifference' (Bielik-Robson 2014a, p. 12). This evinces a 'swerve of concern', out of the sources of Judaism, confronting a philosophical idiom 'that merely mirrors the neutral status quo of what is' (ibid., p. 14). Defined as an 'affective pathos that rebels against the submission to the rules of existence' (Bielik-Robson 2014a, p. 21), revelation is antithetical to the 'mythical consciousness' ascribed to people in prehistory in archaeological accounts which privilege an overarching 'symbolic system'.[2] In the effort to dismantle the mythic totality of prehistory projected from the alienated logic of the capitalist present,[3] consists a kind of redemptive criticism of 'the inner core of myth' (Habermas 1979, p. 44). This is conducted against both the instrumental reason of positivist 'deritualisation' with its concomitant undialectical destruction of the aura (ibid.), and the atavistic submission to 'mythical fatality' characteristic of romantic neopaganism. This strategy resonates with what Walter Benjamin in 1914 considered as the historical task to 'give absolute form in a genuine way to the immanent condition of fulfillment', redeeming 'elements of the end condition ... embedded in every present as endangered, condemned, and ridiculed creations and ideas' (quoted in Wolin 1994, p. 49). Such elements, 'not present as formless tendencies of progress' (ibid.), I locate in the allegorical field of Joyce's novels and megalithic architecture. The kabbalistic thought of Isaac Luria (1534–1572)—along with that of Abraham Abulafia, and the *Zohar*—assumes a level of prominence in this field of interpretation. According to Scholem, Luria's thought invested Jewish history, especially the expulsion from Iberia and the situation of exile, with profound messianic significance (Idel 1992, p. 128).

The messianic register of this reading lends an 'exodic thrust' to the capricious dialectical leaps generated in a structured conjunction, avoidant of and not directed towards a reconciliation of the kind realised either in the 'eternal return' of myth or in the teleology of the Hegelian progress of the spirit. Indeed, the Hegelian narrative may be considered as complicit with the triumphal procession

---

1 Quotations from *Finnegans Wake* are indicated by the initials, *FW*, followed by page and line number.

2 Some arguments in this article were advanced in my Ph.D., *The World's End: Rock Images, Altered Realities, and the Limits of Social Theory* (Crook 2004), directed partly against social constructionist models of subjectivity which posit a 'discursive structure' or 'symbolic system' into which the subject 'must insert itself ... in order to become a "self"' (Thomas 1996, p. 46).

3 The tendency to ascribe an economic rationale to people in prehistory, categorised as hunter-gatherers, pastoralists or agriculturalists, extends to the identification of *labour* as a transhistorical category, such that social activities of a qualitative character like the making of rock art are characterised as a form of 'symbolic labour' (Biesele 1983), a concept derived from the Marxist anthropology of Maurice Godelier. Georg Lukács remarks on the essential methodological difficulty of applying historical materialism beyond the classical terrain of its application in capitalist society, 'to earlier societies antedating capitalism' (Lukács 1971, p. 232). Conceived as a transhistorical state, such capitalist alienation would demand its own negation as 'an objective historical order in which the exile continued in full force' (Scholem 1971, p. 121).

of history's victors in Walter Benjamin's messianic understanding of history (Benjamin 1968, p. 248). His perception of history's 'chain of events' as 'one single catastrophe which keeps piling wreckage upon wreckage' (ibid., p. 249) chimes with Stephen Dedalus' complaint in *Ulysses*: 'History ... is a nightmare from which I am trying to awake' (*U* 2. 377).[4] The Latin *fin negans* in *Finnegans Wake* indicates that Joyce too 'negates any suggestion of teleology or ends in history' (Sidorsky 2001, p. 305). On the horizontal axis of historical time in Hegel's philosophy of history, observes Franz Rosenzweig, 'nothing radically new can occur, especially not that qualitative leap into an absolutely *other* reality implied by Redemption' (Mosès 2009, p. 51). As 'the privileged moment taken out of the temporal flow' (Bielik-Robson 2014a, p. 190)—whether the circularity of myth or the forward march of progress—revelation restores the singularity of individual experience which, in Bloom's epiphany, gives the title of this paper.

Part 2 of this paper is concerned with elucidating the elements of archaeology and kabbalah which constitute the textual architecture of *Finnegans Wake*, which revolves around the microcosm of the prehistoric mound in which the book's everyman figure, HCE, is interred. Formed of the shattered remnants of the Divine withdrawal, in Joyce's reworking of the Lurianic narrative of the contraction of the divine light, the mound is also the 'Golgotha of the Spirit' in Hegel's *Phenomenology*, itself a philosophical transformation of Lurianic motifs. Correlating this archetypal structure with Neolithic dolmens in Iberia, I contrive in part 3 the crucial encounter between the archaeoastronomy of the Portuguese dolmens, as presented by Fabio Silva, and Bloom's epiphany in *Ulysses*. Here the cosmological dimensions of the seasonal movement of herds to and from mountain pastures is configured as a metaphor for the movement of souls occurring in *Ulysses*. In part 4 I then consider the 'messianic geometry' of this encounter as represented in the ALP diagram that forms the kernel of *Finnegans Wake*, embodying womb symbolism consistent with both archaeological interpretations of the dolmen corridors and kabbalistic iconography. The architecture and decorative repertoire of the dolmens is then configured as the performative space for the conflict between the tragedic reenactment of astrological myth and the exodic thrust of an inchoate messianism, embodied in the person of Leopold Bloom, whose entanglement within the competing forces of myth and messianic redemption is explored in part 5 of this paper. This raises the ultimate—and unanswered—question of whether Joyce's characters, active in an allegorised archaeological context, can carry the burden of messianic hope invested in them or are doomed to be recurrently submerged in the mythic flux.

2. Archaeologies of Text

James Joyce's novels are said to explore a purportedly transcendent truth in the immanence of experience (Franke 2006, p. 157), drawing from an epic tradition that proposes 'the experience of the individual subject as a definitive revelation of the ultimate reality of human existence and thereby also of divinity' (ibid., p. 156). *Ulysses* (Joyce 1922), set on one day, records the interior monologues of different characters, particularly Leopold Bloom, Molly Bloom, and Stephen Dedalus, constituting a stream of consciousness, shot through with 'divinatory-intuitive' moments, epiphanies that reveal 'a wonder of being that is, for an instant only, taken out of the rules of the mythic cycle' (Bielik-Robson 2014a, p. 309). According to Richard Ellmann, Joyce conceived of *Ulysses* as 'a silent, unspoken portrayal of an archetypal man who would never appear and yet whose body would slowly materialize as the book progressed, linguafied as it were into life' (Ellmann 1972, p. 73), a figure 'later baptized Finnegan in Joyce's last work' (Manganiello 1987, p. 196). In *Finnegans Wake* this stream of consciousness is the 'moanalothe inturned' (*FW* 254.14) of the fallen Finn, also known as Humphrey Chimpden Earwicker (HCE). His collapsed state by the banks of the River Liffey, the riverine form taken by his spouse, Anna Livia Plurabelle (ALP), is homologous with other falls in Biblical narrative, myth and history, including the Fall from Eden, the fall of the Tower of Babel, the fall of Finnegan in

---

4   Quotations from *Ulysses* are indicated by the initial, *U*, followed by episode and line number.

the song, 'Finnegan's Wake', and the great fall of Humpty Dumpty. In the clangour of the Fall resounds the *shevirath ha-kelim*, the 'shattering of the vessels' in the Kabbalah of Isaac Luria, the 'scrambling' of the cosmic order ensuing from the *tsimtsum*—the contraction of the infinite light, *Ein Sof*.

In the *coincidentia oppositorum* structuring *Finnegans Wake*, this is a 'Happy Fault', the motif of *felix culpa* repeated throughout the book in various forms. This dialectic is legible in the turn of Joyce's avatar, Stephen Dedalus, from seeking the 'absolute satisfaction' of a transcendence, divorced from life, to a consciousness of 'the beauty of mortal conditions' (Price 1983, p. 312). Notwithstanding Stephen's implicit reconciliation with 'the circle of nature', a similar dialectic is mobilised in a reading of Luria seeking to confirm finite being as *finite* 'without inscribing it automatically into a divine tragedy' (Bielik-Robson 2017, p. 44). Repeating the Gnostic motif of the crisis in the Godhead—transfigured by Hegel into the 'death of God' philosophy (ibid., p. 42)—Luria 'paves the way to a new metaphysics of finite being' in which 'the time of the world becomes the time of God's reconstitution' (ibid., p. 43), where, since the primordial crisis, 'all being has been a being in exile, in need of being led back and redeemed' (Scholem 1965, p. 112). Joyce too transfigures this crisis in the way Finnegan/HCE 'fell from story to story like a sagasand to lie' (*FW* 374.36–375.1), 'lying high as he lay in all dimensions' (*FW* 498.28), like the cosmic archetype of Kabbalistic theosophy, Adam Kadmon, the anthropomorphic representation of the *sephiroth*, ten aspects of the divine that emanate from the *Ein Sof* (Fine 2003, p. 56). The 'cranic head' (*FW* 7.29) of this 'Headmound, king and martyr' (*FW* 135.9), condenses the entirety of *Finnegans Wake* as 'Omnitudes in a knutshedell' (*FW* 276.L2), introducing the motif of Hegel's 'Golgotha of Absolute Spirit', the *Schädelstätte*, the 'Place of the Skull' which concludes *The Phenomenology of Spirit*, written 'entiringly as he continues highly-fictional, tumulous under his chthonic exterior' (*FW* 261.17–18). Hegel's concept of recollection or interiorisation, *erinnerung*, is a recurrent motif in *Finnegans Wake*, most obviously in ALP's 'riverrun' (*FW* 3.1) commencing the book. Identified as a revelation of some structure transcending the merely fragmentary, repetition 'produces a sort of eternal time of the text, whose end is at the same time its beginning' (Franke 2006, p. 162). In the simultaneity of all elements (ibid.) of *Finnegans Wake*, 'the seeds of any part of history may be present in any "event"' (Hart 1962, p. 77), dispersed from 'the eversower of the seeds of light to the cowld owld sowls' (*FW* 593.20), and condensed in the nutshell, the microcosm of the 'moppamound' (*FW* 464.26–27) (Lat. *mappa mundi*—map of the world) in and around which, and *of which*, the novel is constructed: 'who in hallhagal wrote the durn thing anyhow?' (*FW* 107.36–108.1).

The fallen 'litterish fragments' (*FW* 66. 25–26) of 'Reverest Adam Foundlitter' (*FW* 420.35) configure the 'oxhousehumper' (*FW* 107.44), 'the Mound of a Word' (*FW* 175.12) comprised of letters of the Hebrew alphabet, including *aleph* (ox), *beth* (house) and *gimel* (camel), a 'hermeneutic archaeology' pregnant with the interpretive number and letter mysticism of the Kabbalah, and its theosophical transmutations: 'Can you rede ... its world?' (*FW* 18.18–19). Its motivated nature ensures that 'Every letter is a godsend' (*FW* 269.17), implying both God's gift and God's end. This re-situating of theological revelation in the existence and consciousness of an individual results in 'the shattering of revelation into an open set of reenactments or repetitions' (Franke 2006, p. 157), *shattering* evoking Luria's cataclysmic differentiation of the *Ein Sof* from the finite world, sexualised by Joyce as *Ainsolph, this upright one, with that noughty besighed him zeroine* (*FW* 261.23–24).

The 'zeroine', the sighing void from which God has withdrawn, is the last of the ten emanations, or *sephiroth*, the *Shekhinah* (Dwelling), or *Malkuth* (Foundation), the *sephira* in which the feminine potencies of God attain their fullest expression (Scholem 1965, p. 104). In his kenotic vision of God's self-contraction, as reconstructed by Scholem—'He exiled Himself from boundless infinity to a more concentrated infinity' (Scholem 1971, p. 44)—Luria 'pioneers the new modern religious sensibility of *Shekhinah*-Spirit which, as Hegel puts it in the preface to the *Phenomenology*, abides only in and through its externality' (Bielik-Robson 2017, p. 42). Here, in 'the immediacy of finitude' left by the departure of God, it is the task of the Spirit to 'storm through the dispersed and disoriented material realm in order to turn it into a free, conscious, and self-assertive mode of existence' (ibid.). In *Finnegans Wake* ALP flutters furiously as Shekhinah/Fairy Godmother, in her reconfiguration of the fragmented HCE/Humpty, *'getting umptyums gatherumed off the skattert'* (FW 345.18), evoking, simultaneously, the restorative activity of *tikkun* and the end of God: 'Well, this ought to weke him to make up. He'll want all his fury gutmurdherers to redress him' (FW 617.17–19). Her gathering/scattering of 'rhunerhinerstones' (FW 207.7), repeating the Hegelian *erinnerung* in 'hegelstomes' (FW 416.33) scattered like 'rainstones ringing' (FW 279.2) in her persona of a world-making giantess. In this, ALP accompanies otherworldly females seen as legendary builders of megaliths across Europe, 'a skittering kitty skattering hayels' (FW 243.17–18), falling in 'Countlessness of livestories' as 'litters from aloft' to be 'all tombed to the mound' (FW 17.26–29), just as, during her dark exile in the abyss, the Shekhinah gathers the 'sparks' that fell into the demonic realms after God's withdrawal (Halperin 2001, p. 36).

Joyce's writing is infused with the linguistic theories of Jewish kabbalah, particularly that of Abraham Abulafia (c1240–91), Leopold Bloom being himself accused of being 'the false Messiah! Abulafia!' (U 15.1907). Abulafia believed that human beings are unable to see the 'true stream of cosmic life' other than through *written language*, which is the absolute object of meditation capable of stimulating the soul's deeper life, freeing it from ordinary perceptions (Cormack 2008, pp. 78–79). The 'stream of cosmic life' flowing through *Finnegans Wake*, where 'the world, mind, is was and will be writing its own wrunes for ever' (FW 19.35–36), has an Abulafian tenor, in which creation is 'an act of divine writing' (Jacobson 2003, p. 148). The microlinguistic speculation of Abulafia's 'science of prophecy' (ibid., p. 13) is comparable to 'the modern attempt to split the atom into its integral parts' in that 'the words that formed God's message were to be split open to reveal their letters' (ibid., p. 141), tantamount to 'the abnihilisation of the etym' (FW 353.22) in *Finnegans Wake*'s 'sameold gamebold adomic structure' (FW 615.6). 'Building blocks of revelation', the letters themselves were to become the centre of speculation (Jacobson 2003, p. 141). As Joyce averred, the words of *Finnegans Wake* are 'not fragments but active elements and when they are more and a little older they will begin to fuse of themselves' (Joyce 1957, p. 205). Joyce's 'Dumlat' (FW 30.10)—to be read right to left, like the Talmud—is 'not about something, it is that something itself' (Beckett 1929).

A geographical correlate of the archetypal 'darkumound' (FW 386.20–21) of *Finnegans Wake*, written 'from his Inn the Byggning to whose Finishthere Punct' (FW 17.22–23), is Cape Finisterre (Fisterre) in Galicia, once considered the westernmost point of the known world. Ultimate exteriority here turns simultaneously to the darkest interiority of *erinnerung* in the obscure transit of the sleeping giant, Finn/HCE, 'transmaried' (FW 50.11) from 'his funster's latitat to its finsterest interrimost' (FW 50.17). The merging of interiority and interment bolsters the connection to Finisterre, dominated by Mount Facho, an eminence once crowned by a dolmen, built by the enchantress Orcavella, beneath which she entombed herself with a shepherd (Lindström 2014, p. 61), aligning with the sexual archaeology of the mound where ALP and HCE are buried, 'Humperfeldt and Anunska, wedded now evermore in annastomoses by a ground plan of the placehunter' (FW 585.23).

3. Porta Coelorum: Aligning the Dolmen Corridors and Bloom's Epiphany

'Any object, intensely regarded, may be a gate of access to the incorruptible eon of the gods' (U 14.1166–1167). In 1600, contemplating the gleam of light reflected on a pewter vessel, Jacob Boehme had a sudden revelation in which he felt himself able to peer into the inner essence of all things: 'For I saw and knew the Being of all beings; . . . also the birth or eternal generation of the Holy Trinity; the descent and origin of this world' (Magee 2001, p. 36). Boehme's vision anticipates Leopold Bloom's in the 'Oxen of the Sun' episode of *Ulysses*: 'The voices blend and fuse in clouded silence: silence that is the infinite of space: and swiftly, silently the soul is wafted over regions of cycles of generations that have lived' (U 14.1078–1080). Indeed, the object of Bloom's contemplation, is an emblematic allusion to 'the birth or eternal generation of the Holy Trinity' of Boehme's vision:

> *During the past four minutes or thereabouts he had been staring hard at a certain amount of number one Bass bottled by Messrs Bass and Co at Burton-on-Trent which happened to be situated amongst a lot of others right opposite to where he was and which was certainly calculated to attract anyone's remark on account of its scarlet appearance.* (U 14.1181–1184)

The red triangle of Bass and Co., as a symbol, has a pedigree in the alchemical-theosophical current of which Boehme was a part, drawn from the number and letter mysticism of Christian Cabbala, derived from Pythagoreanism and the Jewish kabbalah. An upward-pointing red triangle looms above a page of one of the most important books of theosophical alchemy (Forshaw 2006, p. 195), Khunrath's *Amphitheatre of Eternal Wisdom* (1609), its engravings displaying 'a sort of Dantean ascent to a magical passage' resembling 'Christian Rosencreutz's tomb in the Fama' (Umberto Eco 1989, p. 13, cited in Forshaw 2006, p. 196).

Leopold Bloom's portentous meeting with Stephen Dedalus is presaged by a thrice-repeated incantation that implicates a horned animal/star in the incarnation of new life: 'Send us bright one, light one, Horhorn, quickening and wombfruit' (*U* 14.2). Bloom has visited the Holles Street Maternity Hospital to ask after Mrs Purefoy, who is in the third day of a difficult labour. In the corridor he encounters Dr. Dixon—who had dressed his bee-sting weeks before—and he is invited to join carousing medical students in the common room. Detached from the raucous insensitivity of the drunken students, Bloom drifts into a reverie in which he seems to be in some sort of telepathic communication with Stephen about reincarnation:

> *Theosophos told me so, Stephen answered, whom in a previous existence Egyptian priests initiated into the mysteries of karmic law. The lords of the moon, Theosophos told me, an orangefiery shipload from planet Alpha of the lunar chain would not assume the etheric doubles and these were therefore incarnated by the rubycoloured egos from the second constellation.* (*U* 14.1168–1173)

The second constellation, source of the 'rubycoloured egos', is Taurus, as becomes clearer in Bloom's continuing astrological vision:

> *And, lo, wonder of metempsychosis, it is she, the everlasting bride, harbinger of the daystar, the bride, ever virgin. It is she, Martha, thou lost one, Millicent, the young, the dear, the radiant. How serene does she now arise, a queen among the Pleiades, in the penultimate antelucan hour, shod in sandals of bright gold, coifed with a veil of what do you call it gossamer! It floats, it flows about her starborn flesh and loose it streams emerald, sapphire, mauve and heliotrope, sustained on currents of cold interstellar wind, winding, coiling, simply swirling, writhing in the skies a mysterious writing till after a myriad metamorphoses of symbol, it blazes, Alpha, a ruby and triangled sign upon the forehead of Taurus.* (*U* 14.1099–1109)

Upon the forehead of Taurus, Alpha, is the star, Aldebaran, Alpha Tauri, forming a ruby and triangled sign with the cluster of stars known as the Hyades, together forming an unexpected constellation with a cluster of Neolithic dolmens in Portugal.

Part of a broader phenomenon of megalithism across Europe, megaliths dot the landscape of Iberia from the northern Atlantic coast of Galicia to the platform of the Mondego river of central Portugal (Silva 2015, p. 120). Dolmens (*antas* in Portuguese) have a central polygonal chamber, composed of megalithic orthostats. The chamber might then have an entrance with or without a corridor, also megalithic in nature. Both chamber and corridor were roofed with cover-stones, the whole structure being surrounded by a tumulus: a mound, typically of earth, but covered with stone (ibid., pp. 120–21). The raising of ovicaprids—sheep and goats—suggests that winters were spent on low grounds and the spring and summer on the high pastures of Serra da Estrela (Silva 2015, p. 122). Archaeoastronomical analyses of the orientation of entrances of dolmens in the Carregal do Sal area of the Mondego river basin in central Portugal bolsters this 'seasonal model', suggesting this megalithic cluster marked the winter territory for people who had 'a high seasonal mobility' (Silva 2015, p. 123).

The view of the reconstructed horizon from within the dolmens displays a single feature towards the east: Serra da Estrela (ibid., p. 127), the high pastures aimed for in the spring and summer, and the mountain range that contains the highest peak in continental Portugal (ibid., p. 121). Anta da Arquinha da Moura, discussed below, is typical of the cluster of dolmens in the Carregal do Sal district which shared this orientation of the entrance. This mountain range acted as a foresight for an astronomical event significant to these Neolithic communities, observed from the aperture formed by the dolmen entrance within a region of the sky corresponding to azimuth range 98–111°. At the time of dolmen construction, circa 4300–3700 BCE, Aldebaran, the brightest star of Taurus, would have risen exactly within the band of the horizon visible from within all corridor dolmens (Silva 2015, p. 131) after a period of invisibility from late February to late April. The dolmenic alignments suggest that Neolithic communities here observed the heliacal rise of Aldebaran as a signal for the seasonal movement of their flocks to the high pastures (ibid., p. 132). The restricted scope of the aperture capturing the 'orangefiery' star, Aldebaran, configures it as a form of 'revelation' reserved for that person or those privileged to be in the passage. Silva suggests that social memory of the importance of this star may survive today as toponymical folktales of Serra da Estrela, which means 'the mountain range of the star' (Silva 2015, p. 133).[5]

In *Ulysses* Joyce configures a topographical correspondence between the triangular island of Trinacria—isle of the sacred oxen in the *Odyssey*—the triangular Bass insignia upon which Bloom's 'astrological epiphany' has settled (Seidel 1976, p. 58), and the triangle formed by Aldebaran and the asterism known as the Hyades. The presence of the Hyades, is considered significant in the context of the Portuguese dolmens, as it gives Aldebaran a 'different shine' (Silva 2013). The heliacal rising and setting of the Hyades, 'the rainy ones', was believed by the Greeks to be always attended by rain (Anthon 1847, p. 648). They are sisters who mourned their elder brother, killed in a hunting accident, so vehemently they died of grief (ibid.). A constellation can be drawn between the grieving Hyades and the Blooms, mourning for their lost son, Rudy, who died nearly eleven years before at eleven days old. When Leopold envisions Rudy in 'Circe' he is perceived as if he has aged in the intervening years, wearing a suit with 'diamond and ruby buttons' (*U* 15.4965) with a white lambkin in his waistcoat pocket (*U* 15.4966), suggesting the sacrificial connotations of the lamb, recalled when Bloom reads 'Blood of the Lamb' (*U* 8.9) on a leaflet. In 'Oxen' Mrs Purefoy's labour cries put Bloom in mind of Molly, who 'had borne him an only manchild which on the eleventh day on live had died' (*U* 14.265–266). Griefstricken, she had knitted 'a fair corselet of lamb's wool, the flower of the flock' (*U* 14.268–269), in which Rudy was buried. Stephen Dedalus seems to possess some unconscious awareness of the connection between wool and the Blooms' lost son when he imagines a woman walking along the strand holding a bag is a midwife, the bag containing 'A misbirth with a trailing navelcord, hushed in ruddy wool' (*U* 3.36–37), the phrase evoking Rudy's name.

The tears of the Hyades would be apposite to the proposed connection between the dead and Aldebaran as the heavenly abode of the dead ancestors, or their escort towards the afterlife, established at the time of its heliacal rising with the enactment of funerary rites' (Silva 2015, p. 133). The dolmen's corridor and entrance could serve as a conduit for the dead soul to be transported to the horizon and henceforth to the sky with the assistance of Aldebaran (ibid.), 'an opening in the passage of time, in which the same ghostly image constantly reappears' (Benjamin 1998, p. 135). The seasonal movement between the winter territories marked by the dolmens and the summer pastures of Serra da Estrela (Silva 2015, p. 130) likely had cosmological dimensions, expressed in the Irish saying, 'this life is merely booleying (summer pastures) and heaven our old township (permanent dwelling) for eternal life' (Lucas 1989, p. 65).[6] In the life of 'booleying' the Milky Way is, in most parts of Ireland, 'the path

---

5   Walter Benjamin's comments on 'aura' seem apposite here: 'What is aura, in fact? A gossamer fabric woven of space and time: a unique manifestation of a remoteness, however close at hand. Lying back on a summer's afternoon, gazing at a mountain range on the horizon ... until the moment or the hour shares in the manifestation—that is called breathing in the aura of those mountains' (Benjamin 2009, p. 175). While 'breathing' means 'the original prehistorical situation of harmony and peace' cognate with Hölderlin's concept of the unity of antagonistic dispositions (van Reijen 2001), under the conditions of a capitalist economy, a society that can be defined as 'false', the 'shine' of unity and harmony represented by the aura has to be shattered by Benjamin's dialectical image, to reveal the hidden forces of antagonism (ibid.).

6   In a world where any radical change no longer seems possible, where any hope consists in denouncing the existing totality as an 'untrue' one (Martins 2016, p. 187), perceptible in the Mondego dolmens is the opportunity of transcendence that *overwinters*, hidden in profane critique, according to Adorno's postulate of profanisation, directed not against Kabbalah but derived from it (ibid.).

of the white cow', (Doniger O'Flaherty 1980, p. 241). In Lancashire the Milky Way was believed to be the path by which departed souls went to Heaven and was called 'Cow Lane' (Hardwick 1872, p. 182). According to Pindar, Hades drives the dead down the hollow road with the *rhabdos*, like cattle (Vermeule 1979, p. 243). Porphyry reports that Pythagoras believed souls were 'assembled in the Milky Way', the heavenly bovine from which souls emerged being none other than the celestial constellation of *Taurus* the bull (Rigoglioso 2009, p. 158), known in Germany as *der Stier*, evoked in Joyce's allusion to Hegel's ghost story, the *Phenomenology*: 'their joke was coming home to them, the steerage way for stabling, ghustorily spoeking' (*FW* 323.35).

Joyce once told the poet AE (George Russell) that he thought it possible an avatar might be born in Ireland (Ellmann 1982, p. 99). The anecdote reveals Joyce's fascination with the theme of *metempsychosis*, a word that 'reverberates through *Ulysses* like the *thunderclap* in *Finnegans Wake*' (Tymoczko 1994, p. 44), central to the novel's 'mythic architectonics' (ibid.). Tymoczko suggests metempsychosis in *Ulysses* is of an Irish rather than Greek character, emphasised by Joyce's attitude to the body, which is not considered an encumbrance by the reincarnated figures of *Ulysses*, in contrast to the moralism of the Pythagorean view that the souls of the just are not burdened with a body (ibid., pp. 45–46). Joyce repudiated the social purity discourse inherited from this view, typified in Theosophists' revulsion from sex, that 'degrading demand of nature' (Mullin 2003, p. 117). As he told Frank Budgen, 'my book is the epic of the human body' (Budgen 1972, p. 21), declaring, 'If they had no body they would have no mind ... It's all one.' (ibid.). This parallels a rabbinic understanding of the self, whereby 'soul and body form a whole rather than a polarity' (Goshen-Gottstein 1994, p. 177, cited in Lachter 2014, p. 70). From Theosophy, Joyce draws the idea that 'only the plasmic substance can be said to be immortal' (*U* 14.1281), the 'plasmic memory' being the total memory of the soul's journey through successive incarnations (Gifford and Seidman 1988, p. 430).[7]

Another source for the doctrine of metempsychosis is the kabbalah, the 'general rule' of reincarnation 'up to a thousand times' being mentioned for the first time in *Sefer Ha-Bahir* (Elior 1995, p. 259), exceeded in the multiple selves of HCE, for whom 'only the caul knows his thousand and first name, Hocus Crocus, Esquilocus' (*FW* 254.19–20). Ernst Bloch, in *The Spirit of Utopia* (1918) discusses the absurdity of the notion of absolute death, identifying in metempsychosis the doctrine that could unite the two metaphysical 'puzzles'—memory and hope—'to understand that motion and life exist not only in this world' (Boldyrev 2014, pp. 148–49). In *Finnegans Wake* ALP is the '*Amnium instar*' (*FW* 287.8), the 'Ensouling Female' who sustains HCE's 'Agonising Overman', prefigured in 'Our grandam, which we are linked up with by successive anastomosis of navelcords' (*U* 14.299–300), imagined by Stephen as a generational telephone cable (Ramsey 1998, p. 62): "Hello! Kinch here. Put me on to Edenville. Aleph, alpha: nought, nought, one" (*U* 3.39–40), which connects to Eve: 'Spouse and helpmate of Adam Kadmon: Heva, naked Eve. She had no navel. Gaze' (*U* 3.41–42). The patterning of the human soul, 'in the image of its divine ancestor whom Paracelsus calls "the star in us"' (Woodman 1983, p. 51) is suggested in *Ulysses* in the appearance of Dignam's ghost at a spiritualist séance:

> *In the darkness ... a faint but increasing luminosity of ruby light became gradually visible, the apparition of the etheric double being particularly lifelike owing to the discharge of jivic rays from the crown of the head and face. Communication was effected through the pituitary body and also by means of the orangefiery and scarlet rays emanating from the sacral region and solar plexus. Questioned by his earthname as to his whereabouts in the heavenworld he stated that he was now on the path of pralaya or return. (U 12.338–346)*

The discharge of light from the crown of Dignam's head and face conjures up representations of Adam Kadmon, anthropomorphic configuration of the ten *sephiroth*, the highest *sephira* being *Keter* (Crown). The emanation of orangefiery and scarlet rays and the luminosity of ruby light heralds the

---

[7] The phrase, 'plasmic memory', appears in Joyce's notes on embryological development, compiled while planning 'Oxen' and listening to his daughter, Lucia, inside Nora's womb (Herring 1972, p. 171).

return of Rudy with his 'ruby buttons' (*U* 15.4965–66), reflected too in the reddish glow of the orange giant, Aldebaran, the eye of Taurus, perhaps the 'ireglint's eye' (*FW* 6.35) doubling as the island called Ireland's Eye in *Finnegans Wake*.

4. Messianic Geometry

In 'cycloannalism' Joyce condenses the repetition of Viconian cycles that informs the structure of *Finnegans Wake* with *psychoanalysis*, a term first used by Sigmund Freud in *The Interpretation of Dreams*: 'and we are recurrently meeting em, par Mahun Mesme, in cycloannalism, from space to space, time after time, in various phases of scripture as in various poses of sepulture' (*FW* 254.25–28). On the map of Jewish thought, psychoanalysis is immersed in the tragic paradigm which closes the individual's life in the past-oriented, cyclical and fatalistic eternal return of the same and, as such, offers no future and no hope (Bielik-Robson 2014b, p. 86). In *Minima Moralia* Theodor Adorno accuses Freud of failing to see the messianic potential of his psychoanalytic theory, which could reach beyond the conformist 'disgrace of adaptation' (ibid.). Benjamin's concept of the *constellation* may afford some escape from this, in its consonance with Freud's method of free association in dream interpretation, which utilises the dreamer's free associations, insisting that 'by a circuitous route they guide him back to the hidden meaning of the dream' (Frieden 1993, p. 103). Both moving configurations are redolent of Abulafia's technique called *jumping*: jumping from one conception to another, using associations as a way of meditation, every 'jump' opening a new sphere (Scholem 1974, p. 136). The temporal indeterminacy of dreaming, 'at no spatial time processly which regards to concrude chronology' (*FW* 358.5–6), subverts archaeologists' custody of the past in a way consistent with Benjamin's 'not-yet-conscious knowledge of *what has been*', in which 'its advancement has the structure of awakening' (Benjamin 2002, p. 883). The messianic charge of this advancement Joyce formulates as the 'sleeper awakening, in the smalls of one's back presentiment . . . a flash from a future of maybe' (*FW* 597.26–28).

Finnegans Wake's 'Grandmère des Grammaires' (*FW* 256.20), 'uptenable from the orther, for to regul their reves by incubation' (*FW* 397.33–34) is the artist-prophet, Shem's 'traumscrapt' (*FW* 623.36), a dream narrative obtained from the ether, 'bespaking the wisherwife . . . A Laughable Party' (*FW* 66.15–17), written at the behest of his mother, ALP, the *aleph* of her name expressed as laughter. With her 111 children, ALP transliterates the system of gematria in kabbalah, whereby a numerical value is assigned to each letter of the word which is the name of the letter in the Hebrew alphabet (Ifrah 1998, p. 255): 'Anna Lynchya Pourable! One and eleven' (*FW* 325.4–5). Aleph, the name of the first letter, 'the spiritual root of all other letters' (Scholem 1965, p. 30), 'an allforabit' (*FW* 19.1–2), has the value $1 + 30 + 80 = 111$ (Ifrah *op. cit.*): 'Allaliefest, she who pities very pebbles, dare we not wish on her our thrice onsk?' (*FW* 562.7–8). As Shem writes for ALP, so the 'divine element in revelation, the immense *aleph*, was not in itself sufficient to express the divine message, and in itself it was more than the community could bear' (Scholem 1965, p. 31); only 'the prophet was empowered to communicate the meaning of this inarticulate voice to the community' (ibid.). Shem the Penman, Joyce's alter ego, residing at the 'house O'Shea or O'Shame . . . no number Brimstone Walk' (*FW* 182.30–31), inhabits 'the proper element of the created being' (Bielik-Robson 2017, p. 48), a finite realm separate from God, 'cloaked in the dark "Luciferic" colours of Fall, Sin and Evil' (ibid., p. 44), denigrated by the upstanding bourgeois, Shaun, as a 'Negoist Cabler . . . whom 'tis better ne'er to name, my said brother, the skipgod' (*FW* 488.21–22). Denied the dignity of a name, Shem, scapegoat escapee from God, and 'first till last alshemist' (*FW* 185.34–35), is the 'unseen blusher in an obscene coalhole' (*FW* 194.12), his 'rosy gnoses glow' sliding 'lucifericiously within an inch of its page' (*FW* 182.4–5). Embodying Agrippa's *humor melancholicus*, which 'attracts certain demons into our bodies, through whose presence . . . men fall into ecstasies and pronounce many wonderful things' (Yates 1979, p. 62), Shem the 'Shamman' (*FW* 192.23), 'driven by those numen daimons' (*FW* 142.23), falls into such ecstasies:

> the whirling dervish, Tumult, son of Thunder, self exiled in upon his ego a nightlong a shaking betwixtween white or reddr hawrors, noondayterrorised to skin and bone by an ineluctable phantom . . . writing the mystery of himsel in furniture. (*FW* 184.5–10)

Writing the 'untireties of livesliving being the one substrance of a streamsbecoming' (*FW* 597.7–8) Shem universalises the materiality of altered consciousness (*substrance*), in 'various phases of scripture as in various poses of sepulture' (*FW* 254.28) within the cranial architecture of the chambered tomb, Hegel's 'Golgotha of the Spirit'. The scriptural exegesis of archaeology's 'jetsam litterage of convolvuli of times lost or strayed' (*FW* 292.16) configures pastoralism—practiced in the Mondego valley and Serra da Estrela—as a metaphor of the transmigration of souls:

> *Yed he med leave to many a door beside of Oxmanswold for so witness his chambered cairns a cloudlelitter silent that are at browse up hill and down coombe . . . a testament of the rocks from all the dead unto some the living. Olivers lambs we do call them, skatterlings of a stone, and they shall be gathered unto him, their herd and paladin.* (*FW* 73.28–35)

In a paragraph imbued with number and letter mysticism, 'Olivers lambs' evokes *Aleph Lamed*, the first two letters of ALP's name, meaning ox and ox-goad, respectively, illustrative of the congruence of grazing animals, tombs and reading. The first word, 'Yed', evokes *Yod*, the tenth letter of the Hebrew alphabet, having also the numeric value of 10. It is the letter that symbolises God and the first letter in the Tetragrammaton (YHWH), often inscribed within an upward-pointing equilateral triangle with the *yod* at the apex, a symbol derived, via the kabbalists, from the Pythagorean tetraktys, a triangular figure consisting of ten points (Potts 1982, p. 74): 'the first praisonal Egoname Yod heard boissboissy in Moy Bog's domesday' (*FW* 485.5–6). Appropriately, in *Finnegans Wake*, ALP is identified by a triangular siglum: Δ. The *Ma'ayan ha-Chokhmah*, 'the fountain of wisdom', describes *yod* as the source of all linguistic motion, both infinitely extending but returning to its centre and origins in its 'unfolding' (Jacobson 2003, p. 142). A translation of Knorr von Rosenroth's *Kabbalah Denudata* (1677–1689) available to Joyce, emphasises the linguistic potency of ALP's triangle: '*Yod, at the end of the Tetragrammaton denotes the synthesis, the circular movement by which the end returns to the beginning . . . Yod is represented by three circles at the angles of an equilateral triangle with the apex uppermost*' (MacGregor Mathers 1926, p. 63). The 'creating motion' of *yod* Scholem reads as an attempt to split open the atomic core of the divine name, 'unleashing a "magical" power locked at the root of spoken, linguistic motion'(ibid.), a literal potency embodied in ALP in *Finnegans Wake*, whose 'birthright pang . . . would split an atam like the forty pins in her hood' (*FW* 333.24–25). Considered as *separate* from the divine world of transcendence, the world of immanence 'is destructively impregnated with the idea of infinity that explodes it from within' (Bielik-Robson 2014a, p.133), seen in the *Wake*'s 'Accusative ahnsire! Damadam to infinities' (*FW* 19.30).

The suggestion that the dolmen's chamber acted as a 'womb' where initiates would spend the night in a vision quest that would culminate in Aldebaran rising in 'the penultimate antelucan hour' (*U* 14.1102–3) before sunrise (Silva 2015, p. 135), accords with the 'Night Lessons' chapter of *Finnegans Wake*, additionally to the maternal context of Bloom's epiphany. Here ALP's son, Shem (as Dolph) initiates his brother, Shaun (as Kev), in the embodied mystery of their mother, observed by their sister, Issy. Dolph instructs Kev in the construction of 'an equoangular trilitter' (*FW* 286.21–22), the latter word suggesting the trilithic structure of two portal stones and a lintel which forms the opening of chambered tombs. In the left margin looms a verbal evocation of the 'ruby and triangled sign' and 'everlasting bride' of Bloom's vision, including portmanteau allusions to the stellar bovine, *bos*, and the proud/brewed/broad/bride of the Mullingar Inn: '*The boss's bess bass is the browd of Mullingar*' (*FW* 286.L). Joyce's sexualised adaptation of Euclid's first proposition, the 'elementator joyclid' (*FW* 302.12), 'first of all usquiluteral threeingles' (*FW* 297.27), is 'the whome of your eternal geomater' (*FW* 296.31–297.1), 'the maidsapron of our A.L.P.' (*FW* 297.11), 'Mother of us all!' (*FW* 299.3). The brothers' 'trancedone boyscript' (*FW* 374.3–4), chiasmically rendered with bovine connotations as 'Boston transcripped' (*FW* 617.23), radiates from 'ann aquilittoral dryankle Probe loom' (*FW* 286.19–20) which climaxes with the 'ALP diagram' (Figure 1) on page 293.[8]

---

[8] The *vesica piscis* formed by the overlapping circles of the ALP diagram has a striking parallel in the esoteric drawings of the Christian Kabbalist, Paul Yvon (Wilke 2017), particularly his *Mathematical Propositions* of 1638. A 'feminist turn' is noted in

The ovoid form known as the *vesica piscis*, signifying an 'unspeakable mystery' and 'a symbol of the womb' (Stirling 1897, pp. 12–13), means 'astronomically at the present day a starry conjunction' (ibid., p. 13), 'the strait gate through which the Messiah might enter' (Benjamin 1968, p. 255). In Babylonian mathematics it is the 'ox-eye' (Friberg 2007, p. 212), *īni alpi* (Horowitz 1998, p. 42), an iteration of Aldebaran, the eye of Taurus, and a further linguistic echo of ALP.

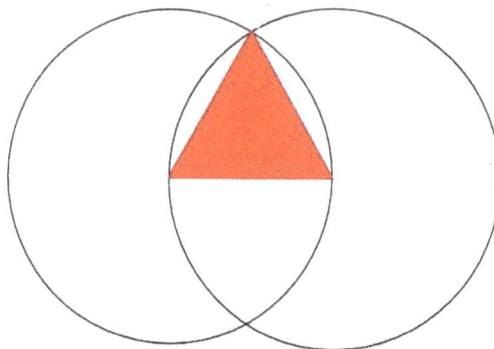

Figure 1. The First Proposition from Euclid's *Elements*, the inspiration for the ALP diagram in *Finnegans Wake*. The ovoid shape formed by the overlapping circles is the *vesica piscis*.

This geometry lesson correlates with the geometric construction of the Sabbath in the anonymous kabbalistic text, *Sefer ha-Mafteah*, in which she is described as 'a singular and glorious queen possessing six radii' (Lachter 2014, pp. 124–25). With an obscure reference to a 'Book of Euclid', the author demonstrates the elevated status of the Sabbath, who occupies an inner point at the intersection of six radii. Emanated from the *sephira*, Binah (the Supernal Mother), seven *sephiroth* are broken down into three pairs (forming three patterns like the paired circles of the ALP diagram), while the *Shekhinah*, as the seventh, has no partner (ibid., p. 125). The purpose for this emanation is to create the space for the Sabbath to dwell (ibid.): 'That she seventip toe her chrysming, that she spin blue to scarlad till her temple's veil, that the Mount of Whoam it open it her to shelterer!' (*FW* 562.9–11). In Moses de Leon's *Sodot*, the Sabbath, being called 'first', is accompanied by six radii (*kitzvot*), which are above, below, and the four directions, 'a perfected adornment' for 'a singular and perfected *sefirah*', for 'as it is said, "six wings for each one"' (Isa. 6:2)' (Lachter 2014, p. 125).

Kev objects furiously to Dolph's geometric revelation of the 'sixuous parts' (*FW* 297.22) of their mother, striking his brother so hard that he ends up 'seeing stars': 'I can't say if it's the way you strike me to the quick or that red mass I was looking at but at the present momentum, potential as I am, I'm seeing rayingbogeys rings round me' (*FW* 304.05–09). Painted in the polygonal chamber of Anta da Arquinha da Moura—'the Ark (treasury) of the Enchanted Moor'—is a circular configuration redolent of the 'red mass' of 'rings round' perceived by Dolph, with paintings of quadrupeds and anthropomorphs. When the chamber was excavated fragments of red ochre were found, of a colour similar to the paintings. Disarticulated human remains had been unusually grouped, with skulls on one side of the chamber and long bones on the other (Cunha 1995, p. 135). The tomb/womb dialectic, continually at play in the 'doubling bicirculars' (*FW* 295.31), the crossed Os (letters *and* bones) of *Finnegans Wake*, linked to the utterance of the inarticulate voice of *aleph*, is suggested by '*Uteralterance or the Interplay of Bones in the Womb*' (*FW* 293.L), the marginal phrase accompanying the ALP diagram.

---

the Hebrew inscription beneath one etching, *immenu El*, which translates as 'God is our Mother' (Wilke 2017, p. 200). This is followed by the genital imagery of a globe within which opens a vaginal vesica piscis, 'the merciful womb of the intelligible world' (ibid., p. 201). A 'mathematical drawing with some discourses' by Paul Yvon was found in the house of João Pinto Delgado when an entire community of Portuguese Marranos in Rouen was accused of apostasy by French authorities in January 1633 (ibid., p. 185). For 'unknown reasons', Yvon was held in some esteem by the secret Jews of Rouen (ibid., p. 186).

This interplay coincides with the words of that 'Hailfellow some wellmet boneshaker' (*FW* 447.30–31), Hegel, for whom the life of the Spirit:

> *is not the life that shrinks from death and keeps itself untouched by devastation, but rather the life that endures it and maintains itself in it. It wins its truth only when, in utter dismemberment, it finds itself.* (Hegel 1979, pp. 18–19)

In the 'ossuaric' context of the tomb, where 'Spirit is a bone,' according to Hegel in *The Phenomenology of Spirit* (Hegel 1979, p. 208), 'when you cannot fall any further, you can only begin to rise' (Bielik-Robson 2014a, p. 264). This message 'rests in the figure of aleph', which contains 'the dialectical identity of Spirit and bone,' being, on the one hand, the breath-word from which creation sprang, and on the other, 'an allegorical scheme of a creaturely form, reduced down to a bone-like structure, aiming in a gesture of desperate prayer to its creator' (ibid.). Indeed, the ALP diagram, its 'owlglassy bicycles' (*FW* 208.9), triangles and lozenge, resembles the bone idols found at Almizaraque in south-eastern Spain, tibiæ carved with paired-circular 'eye' motifs, lozenges and triangles, imagic forms incorporated to perceptions of goddess worship and a postulated Mediterranean 'owl goddess', the owl of Minerva that, in the preface to Hegel's *Philosophy of Right*, 'spreads its wings only with the falling of the dusk' (Honderich 1995, p. 638) (Figure 2). In Benjamin's 'melancholy immersion', the ultimate objects handed down to us by tradition, uncanny, undecipherable, turn into allegories that:

> *fill out and deny the void in which they are represented, just as, ultimately, the intention does not faithfully rest in the contemplation of bones, but faithlessly leaps forward to the idea of resurrection.* (Benjamin 1998, p. 233)

Figure 2. Carved tibiae with 'owlglassy bicycles' (*FW* 208.9) from Almizaraque in south-east Spain (Luquet 1911, p. 443, after Siret 1908).

Evidence for ceremonies at the dolmens in the forecourt outside the dolmen entrance, interpreted as a 'scenic space' (Silva 2015, pp. 134–35), reveals a dramaturgic dimension, 'stage to set by ritual rote for the grimm grimm tale' (*FW* 335.5), with closed, possibly reserved, spaces (the chamber and corridor) and open spaces for the general audience (the frontal atrium) (Silva 2015, p. 135) where 'the heavenly one with his constellatria and his emanations stood between' (*FW* 157.18–19). The 'impossible leap' to escape the fate determined by the circularity of astrological myth, implicit in the arrangement of the dolmens, can be explored through Benjamin's 'messianic misreading of the tragic genre' (Bielik-Robson 2014a, p. 87), illuminating both the Joycean epiphany in *Ulysses* and *Finnegans Wake* and the megalithic 'moment-place' of the dolmens.

As a word, the Greek τραγούδια (*tragoudia*) may recall the hypothesised ritual origins of the tragic genre, as the 'goat-song' accompanying the sacrifice of a goat (Burkert 1966, p. 115). The agon between Benjamin and Nietzsche is centred on Nietzsche's *aesthetization of tragedy*, which pushes tragedy back into the world of myth and away from the world of history, the tragic hero being turned into a mere appearance, *a priori* doomed to *untergehen* (going under) (Bielik-Robson 2014a, p. 87). Conversely, Benjamin perceives a sense of historical novelty hovering over every ancient tragic drama; a silent, spectral pregnancy of a yet unknown word, of a yet unknown God (ibid.). This difference is seen as primarily reflected in the opposition of two concepts: *birth* versus *origin* (Bielik-Robson 2014a, p. 113), whereby Benjamin responds to Nietzsche's ideas about the birth (*Geburt*) of tragedy by choosing the word *Ursprung* (origin), which is deciphered as 'an initially silent and inarticulate, predominantly bodily, action of the *first leap*' (ibid.). His attitude to tragedy is influenced by Christian Florens Rang, for whom 'Tragedy is the astrological break-through but also an escape from the fate determined by the stars' (Bielik-Robson 2014a, p. 113). In tragedy the circular movement of the cosmos, retraced by the circular movement of the sacrificial victim around the altar 'is transected by the diametrical, diagonal straight line, the willed path of the tragic subject who has found a means of breaking through out of the circle' (Asman 1992, p. 613, cited in Bielik-Robson 2014a, p. 113). Here one may detect an anticipation of Benjamin's dialectical leap 'in the open air of history' (Benjamin 1968, p. 253). Jumping to the Anta da Arquinha da Moura, its red-painted imagery depicts just such an *ursprung*, if 'read' vertically, from bottom to top. Initially, the apparent confinement of a caprid in an enclosed space; then, concentric rings surrounding a void; finally, at the apex, the leaping caprid in what may be described as its 'agonistic moment of escape from the iron cage of astrological myth' (Bielik-Robson 2014a, p. 113), the passage of the dolmen forming the 'willed path' to Serra da Estrella and Aldebaran (Figure 3). Translating the 'exodic thrust' of the Biblical escape from Egypt from the collective to the individual in Greek tragedy, Benjamin performs an allegorical move in which Greek tragedy offers a personalised version of the messianic exodus, 'planting it truly and traumatically in the "heart of man"' (Bielik-Robson 2014a, p. 111). Thus tragedy re-emerges as 'a recurrent pattern-*eidos* of an original anti-mythic struggle' (ibid.) in 'the cosmic tug of war between the antinomian forces of redemption and the mythic forces of reconciliation' (ibid., p. 95). Would humour offer an escape from or reconciliation with the circle of fate, as Bloom carries the sins of the people as part of the staging of the scapegoat ritual in 'Circe' and 'All the people cast soft pantomime stones at him' (*U* 15.1902)?

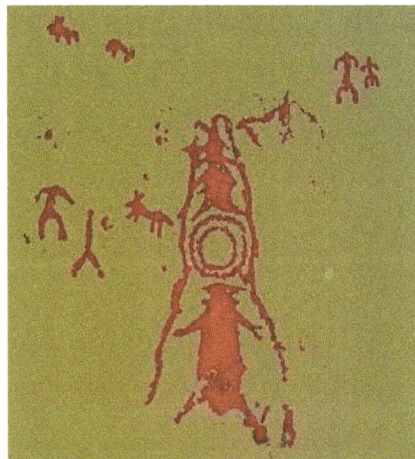

Figure 3. Representation of an ink drawing by the author of paintings within the chamber of Anta da Arquinha da Moura, showing the movement of caprids through a confined space.

5. The Ever-Renewing Birth of a Soul

An allusion in a Latin footnote written by ALP's daughter, Issy, in the Nightlessons episode of *Finnegans Wake*, offers a key to the epiphany central to the architectonic of this paper, Leopold Bloom's vision of 'a ruby and triangled sign upon the forehead of Taurus' (*U* 14.1109). It reads: 'Apis amat aram. Luna legit librum. Pulla petit pascua' (*FW* 262.F4). This translates as "The bee loves the altar. The moon reads a book. The foal seeks the pasture" (McHugh 1980, p. 262). Issy—'pretty Proserpronette' (*FW* 267.10–11)—is Persephone to ALP's Demeter. Porphyry states that priestesses of Demeter were named *Melissae* (bees), while Persephone bore the epithet, *Melitodes* (honeyed) (Ransome 1937, p.96). Issy is also Isis; the first *Apis* in her footnote implicating her in the mysteries of Apis, the 'mighty bull', guarantor of fertility and abundant harvests (Myśliwiec 2004, p. 76). Representations of Apis show him with a triangle upon his forehead (see Kater-Sibbes and Vermaseren 1975), sometimes being suckled by Isis (ibid., p. 79). Simultaneously, *Apis* is implicated in an epiphanic insight, implanted 'truly and traumatically in the heart' of Leopold Bloom. His trauma may be understood in the context of Rosenzweig's starry configuration of the move from creation to revelation, thence to redemption: the 'psychotheology of the soul' in which the shock of revelation is necessary before the self could become the beloved soul (Bielik-Robson 2014a, p. 138). Bloom is stung on the chest by a bee as he lay sleeping in the garden on Whit Monday, the day after Pentecost, the feast that commemorates the receiving of the Torah on Mt Sinai, and the day when the Holy Spirit descends upon Christ's disciples, inducing a speaking in tongues. Bloom's trauma, necessitating a hospital admission, aligns on a passage from Porphyry's *On the Cave of the Nymphs*, in Thomas Taylor's translation:

> The moon . . . who presides over generation, was called by them a bee, and also a bull. And Taurus
> is the exaltation of the moon. But bees are ox-begotten. And this application is also given to souls
> proceeding into generation. The God, likewise, who is occultly connected with generation, is a stealer
> of oxen. (Gilbert 1952, p. 256)

Stephen's nickname, *Bous Stephanoumenos*—'Garlanded Bull' (Gifford and Seidman 1988, p. 245)—suggests the constellation of the Bull and the mysteries of Apis, while its floral character attracts the bees, identified by Sophocles with the souls of the dead: 'The swarm of the dead hums and rises upwards' (Ransome 1937, p. 107).

The descent of a 'bee-soul' on the moon's day, implanted at a point corresponding to Bloom's heart, is explicable in the light of Boehme's twist to the orthodox typology of Whitsun (Ormsby-Lennon 1988, p. 319): at the descent of the Holy Spirit on the day of Pentecost, 'from the opened sensuall tongue', Peter 'spake *in one Language all Languages* . . . *Adams Language whence he gave Names to all creatures*' (ibid., pp. 319–20). Benjamin associates the Messianic era with the advent of this universal language, that everyone would understand 'as children on Sunday understand the language of the birds' (Löwy 1992, p. 233). This descent of holiness characterises shamanic possession among the Nilgiris in southern Karnataka (Smith 2006, p. 138) in the process of *jāya* (the invitation to a deity to descend and possess). The deity enters the heart of the person, which 'trembles' at an increased rate, 'changing' the possessed person's mind so that it can speak through him (Smith 2006, pp. 138–39). The possession trance is induced by drumming, swaying and singing a 'deity-inviting song' in which the deity is addressed as 'one who comes riding a black bee or dragonfly' (ibid., p. 139). Emanating as bee-souls from the stellar *bos* of Taurus, the alliterative buzz of 'The boss's bess bass' (*FW* 286 L), 'with his drums and bones and hums in drones' (*FW* 485.26–27), generates the tonal 'humminbass' (*FW* 295.1) of 'bierhiven' (*FW* 315.22)—combining Beethoven,[9] the pub's 'beer heaven', the funerary

---

9   Adorno's comments on the music of kabbalah 'reach their crescendo' (Wasserstrom 2007, p. 73) in his writing on Beethoven, emphasising the salvific connection between mysticism and music in his notes for his major Beethoven opus: 'Hope is always secret, because it is not "there"—it is the basic category of mysticism and the highest category of Beethoven's metaphysics . . . an image of hope without the lie of religion' (ibid.).

bier on which the-yet-to-be-revived Finnegan lies, and the beehive.[10] The seasonality of the bees correlates to the seasonality of Persephone Melitodes, absent for half the year, according also with the seasonal movement of the flocks between the Mondego valley and the starry summer pastures of Serra da Estrella, analogous to the circulation of souls, 'reberthing in remarrinent out of dead seekness to devine previdence' (*FW* 62.7–8) towards 'red resurrection' (*FW* 62.20).

A resurrection of messianic hope is staged in the pantomimetic inauguration of 'the Paradisiacal Era' (*U* 15.1630–31) in 'Circe', where Leopold Bloom is hailed by the 'Bloomite' Veiled Sibyl, but reviled by the evangelist, Dowie, as 'this stinking goat of Mendes' (*U* 15.1754) and 'the white bull mentioned in the Apocalypse. A worshipper of the Scarlet Woman' (*U* 15.1756). This white bull appears in the Animal Apocalypse of the Ethiopic *Book of Enoch*, 'a second Adam' emerging at the end of days as a messianic figure (Joseph 2014, p. 173). As 'worshipper of the Scarlet Woman' the messianic Bloom would surely qualify as an 'archetype of the paradox of the holy sinner' (Scholem 1974, p. 293), embodying the Sabbatian principle of 'redemption through sin' (Scholem 1971, p. 78), offering 'a starry glimpse of the bliss of the eternal Shabbat that knows no suffering and hardship' (Bielik-Robson 2014a, p. 292).

6. Conclusions

In the petrified unrest of this 'starchamber quiry' (*FW* 475.18–19), the chthonic goddess of myth, Bachofenian romanticism, and archaeological imagination is reconfigured in an unstable 'Shekhinic' formation with Joyce's female characters, Molly, ALP and Issy. However, as a 'chthonic solphia' (*FW* 450.18), is this configuration not ineluctably entangled, as an archetypal image, in 'the unconquerable dominion of myth' (Bielik-Robson 2014a, p. 28), or is it possible to dislodge such images from the mythic continuum? Through the deterministic cycles, generalities and repetitions of myth, the 'singular uniqueness' of the epiphany, realised in 'the starry image (*Sternbild*) momentarily detached from the oppressive totality' (Bielik-Robson 2014a, p. 310), glimmers as a 'phantastichal roseway anjerichol' (*FW* 470.18) of angelical ascent and Jericho's fall, illuminating individuated remnants of the 'Jericho' of the collapsed totality. The cryptotheological misreading of archaeology and literature, introduced as 'the astrologer, to the constellation of two stars' (Benjamin 1933, in Menke 2002, p. 357), defers the dialectical closure of a reconciliation that would either dissipate the antinomian charge of what remains unresolved, or shatter the ultimate coherence of irreconcilable elements. Hovering in this indeterminate space we may recognise the *messianic apprehension* crystallised in the hesitant ambivalence of 'the brideen Alannah . . . lost in her diamindwaiting' (*FW* 377.20), whose self-awareness, *contra* Gadamer, is infinitely more than 'a flickering in the closed circuits of historical life' (Gadamer 2013, p. 289), chiming with Ernst Bloch's anticipatory consciousness of a possible world, adequate to 'the soul' (Hudson 1982, p. 28). That the corridors of the Carregal do Sal dolmens no longer align on the heliacal rise of Aldebaran registers 'the spectral semi-presence of lost historical openings and chances' (Bielik-Robson 2014a, p. 176), Adorno's hopeless hope that 'overwinters' (Martins 2016, p. 187).

Funding: This research received no external funding. The APC was funded by institutions through the Knowledge Unlatched initiative.

Conflicts of Interest: The author declares no conflict of interest.

References

Anthon, Charles. 1847. *A Classical Dictionary*. New York: Harper.

Beckett, Samuel. 1929. Dante . . . Bruno. Vico . . . Joyce. In *Our Exagmination Round His Factification for Incamination of Work in Progress*. London: Faber & Faber.

---

[10] Rachel Murray's article, 'Beelines: Joyce's Apian Aesthetics' (Murray 2017) proved invaluable in uncovering this aspect of Joyce's writing.

Benjamin, Walter. 1968. Theses on the Philosophy of History. In *Illuminations*, 1999 ed. Translated by Harry Zorn. London: Pimlico.

Benjamin, Walter. 1998. *The Origin of German Tragic Drama*. Translated by John Osborne. London: Verso.

Benjamin, Walter. 2002. *The Arcades Project*. Translated by Howard Eiland, and Kevin McLaughlin. Cambridge: Harvard University Press.

Benjamin, Walter. 2009. A Brief History of Photography. In *One-way Street and Other Writings*. Translated by J. A. Underwood. London: Penguin, pp. 172–92.

Bielik-Robson, Agata. 2014a. *Jewish Cryptotheologies of Late Modernity: Philosophical Marranos*. London: Routledge.

Bielik-Robson, Agata. 2014b. From Therapy to Redemption: Notes Towards a Messianic Psychoanalysis. In *Judaism in Contemporary Thought: Traces and Influence*. Edited by Agata Bielik-Robson and Adam Lipszyc. London: Routledge, pp. 86–99.

Bielik-Robson, Agata. 2017. The God of Luria, Hegel and Schelling: The divine contraction and the modern metaphysics of finitude. In *Mystical Theology and Continental Philosophy: Interchange in the Wake of God*. Edited by David Lewin, Simon D. Podmore and Duane Williams. London: Routledge, pp. 39–58.

Biesele, Megan. 1983. Interpretation in Rock Art and Folklore: Communication Systems in Evolutionary Perspective. *Goodwin Series* 4: 54–60. [CrossRef]

Boldyrev, Ivan. 2014. *Ernst Bloch and His Contemporaries*. London: Bloomsbury.

Budgen, Frank. 1972. *James Joyce and the Making of Ulysses, and Other Writings*. Oxford: Oxford University Press.

Burkert, Walter. 1966. Greek Tragedy and Sacrificial Ritual. *Greek, Roman, and Byzantine Studies* 7: 87–121.

Cormack, Alistair. 2008. *Yeats and Joyce: Cyclical History and the Reprobate Tradition*. Aldershot: Ashgate.

Crook, Simon. 2004. The World's End: Rock Images, Altered Realities, and the Limits of Social Theory. Ph.D. Thesis, University of Manchester, Manchester, UK.

Cunha, Ana L. da. 1995. Anta da arquinha da Moura (Tondela). *Trabalhos de Antropologia e Etnologia* XXXV: 133–51.

Doniger O'Flaherty, Wendy. 1980. *Women, Androgynes, and Other Mythical Beasts*. Chicago: University of Chicago Press.

Elior, Rachel. 1995. The Doctrine of Transmigration in Galya Raza. In *Essential Papers on Kabbalah*. Edited by Lawrence Fine. New York: New York University Press, pp. 243–69.

Ellmann, Richard. 1972. *Ulysses on the Liffey*. New York: Oxford University Press.

Ellmann, Richard. 1982. *James Joyce*. New York: Oxford University Press.

Fine, Lawrence. 2003. *Physician of the Soul, Healer of the Cosmos: Isaac Luria and His Kabbalistic Fellowship*. Stanford: Stanford University Press.

Forshaw, Peter J. 2006. 'Alchemy in the Amphitheatre': Some consideration of the alchemical content of the engravings in Heinrich Khunrath's Amphitheatre of Eternal Wisdom (1609). In *Art and Alchemy*. Edited by Jacob Wamberg. Copenhagen: Museum Tusculanum Press, pp. 195–220.

Franke, William. 2006. Linguistic Repetition as Theological Revelation in Christian Epic Tradition: The Case of Joyce's *Finnegans Wake*. *Neophilologus* 90: 155–72. [CrossRef]

Friberg, Jöran. 2007. *A Remarkable Collection of Babylonian Mathematical Texts*. New York: Springer.

Frieden, Ken. 1993. Talmudic Dream Interpretation, Freudian Ambivalence, Deconstruction. In *The Dream and the Text*. Edited by Carol Schreier Rupprecht. Albany: State University of New York Press, pp. 103–11.

Gadamer, Hans-Georg. 2013. *Truth and Method*. Translated by Joel Weinsheimer, and Donald G. Marshall. London: Bloomsbury.

Gifford, Don, and Robert J. Seidman. 1988. *Ulysses Annotated: Revised and Expanded Edition*. Berkeley: University of California Press.

Gilbert, Stuart. 1952. *James Joyce's Ulysses*. London: Faber & Faber.

Habermas, Jurgen. 1979. Consciousness Raising or Redemptive Criticism—The Contemporaneity of Walter Benjamin. Translated by Philip Brewster and Carl Howard Buchner. *New German Critique*, 30–59. [CrossRef]

Halperin, David J. 2001. *Abraham Miguel Cardozo: Selected Writings*. Mahwah: Paulist Press.

Hardwick, Charles. 1872. *Traditions, Superstitions, and Folklore, (Chiefly Lancashire and the North of England)*. London: Simpkin, Marshall and Co.

Hart, Clive. 1962. *Structure and Motif in Finnegans Wake*. Evanston: Northwestern University Press.

Hegel, Georg Wilhelm Friedrich. 1979. *The Phenomenology of Spirit*. Translated by Arnold V. Miller. Oxford: Oxford University Press.

Herring, Phillip F. 1972. *Joyce's Ulysses Notebooks in the British Museum*. Charlottesville: University of Virginia Press.

Honderich, Ted. 1995. *The Oxford Companion to Philosophy*. Oxford: Oxford University Press.

Horowitz, Wayne. 1998. *Mesopotamian Cosmic Geography*. Winona Lake: Eisenbrauns.

Hudson, Wayne. 1982. *The Marxist Philosophy of Ernst Bloch*. London: Macmillan.

Idel, Moshe. 1992. Religion, Thought and Attitudes: The Impact of the Expulsion of the Jews. In *Spain and the Jews: The Sephardi Experience 1492 and After*. Edited by Elie Kedourie. London: Thames and Hudson, pp. 123–39.

Ifrah, Georges. 1998. *The Universal History of Numbers*. Translated by David Bellos, E. F. Harding, Sophie Wood, and Ian Monk. London: Harvill.

Jacobson, Eric. 2003. *Metaphysics of the Profane: The Political Theology of Walter Benjamin and Gershom Scholem*. New York: Columbia University Press.

Joseph, Simon J. 2014. *The Nonviolent Messiah: Jesus, Q, and the Enochic Tradition*. Minneapolis: Fortress Press.

Joyce, James. 1922. *Ulysses*. Paris: Shakespeare & Co.

Joyce, James. 1939. *Finnegans Wake*. London: Faber & Faber.

Joyce, James. 1957. *Letters of James Joyce*. Edited by Stuart Gilbert. London: Faber & Faber.

Kater-Sibbes, G. J. F., and Maarten Joseph Vermaseren. 1975. *Apis: Monuments from outside Egypt*. Leiden: E. J. Brill, vol. 2.

Lachter, Hartley. 2014. *Kabbalistic Revolution: Reimagining Judaism in Medieval Spain*. New Brunswick: Rutgers University Press.

Lindström, Henna. 2014. Casas das Mouras Encantadas—A Study of Dolmens in Portuguese Archaeology and Folklore. Master's thesis, University of Helsinki, Helsinki, Finland. Available online: https://www.academia.edu/12656316/Casas_das_Mouras_Encantadas_A_Study_of_dolmens_in_Portuguese_archaeology_and_folklore._Masters_thesis_2014 (accessed on 22 June 2018).

Löwy, Michael. 1992. *Redemption and Utopia: Jewish Libertarian Thought in Central Europe*. Translated by Hope Heaney. London: The Athlone Press.

Lucas, Anthony T. 1989. *Cattle in Ancient Ireland*. Kilkenny: Boethius Press.

Lukács, Georg. 1971. *History and Class Consciousness*. Translated by Rodney Livingstone. London: Merlin Press.

Luquet, Georges-Henri. 1911. Les représentations humaines dans le néolithique ibérique. *Revue des Études Anciennes* Vol. 13: 437–452. [CrossRef]

MacGregor Mathers, Samuel Liddell. 1926. *The Kabbalah Unveiled*. London: Routledge & Kegan Paul.

Magee, Glenn Alexander. 2001. *Hegel and the Hermetic Tradition*. Ithaca: Cornell University Press.

Manganiello, Dominic. 1987. Vico's Ideal History and Joyce's Language. In *Vico and Joyce*. Edited by Donald Phillip Verene. Albany: State University of New York Press, pp. 196–206.

Martins, Ansgar. 2016. *Adorno und die Kabbala*. Potsdam: Universitätsverlag Potsdam.

McHugh, Roland. 1980. *Annotations to Finnegans Wake*. Baltimore: Johns Hopkins University Press.

Menke, Bettine. 2002. Ornament, Constellation, Flurries. In *Benjamin's Ghosts: Interventions in Contemporary Literary and Cultural Theory*. Edited by Gerhard Richter. Stanford: Stanford University Press, pp. 260–77.

Mosès, Stéphane. 2009. *The Angel of History: Rosenzweig, Benjamin, Scholem*. Stanford: Stanford University Press.

Mullin, Katherine. 2003. *James Joyce, Sexuality and Social Purity*. Cambridge: Cambridge University Press.

Murray, Rachel. 2017. Beelines: Joyce's Apian Aesthetics. *Humanities* 6: 42. [CrossRef]

Myśliwiec, Karol. 2004. *Eros on the Nile*. Translated by Geoffrey L. Packer. Ithaca: Cornell University Press.

Ormsby-Lennon, Hugh. 1988. Rosicrucian Linguistics: Twilight of a Renaissance Tradition. In *Hermeticism and the Renaissance*. Edited by Ingrid Merkel and Allen G. Debus. Washington, DC: The Folger Shakespeare Library, pp. 311–41.

Potts, Albert M. 1982. *The World's Eye*. Lexington: The University Press of Kentucky.

Price, Martin. 1983. *Forms of Life: Character and Moral Imagination in the Novel*. New Haven: Yale University Press.

Ramsey, Harly. 1998. Mourning, Melancholia and the Maternal Body: Cultural Constructions of Bereavement in *Ulysses*. In *Joycean Cultures/Culturing Joyces*. Edited by Vincent J. Cheng, Kimberly J. Devlin and Margot Norris. Newark: University of Delaware Press, pp. 59–77.

Ransome, Hilda M. 1937. *The Sacred Bee in Ancient Times and Folklore*. London: George Allen & Unwin.

Rigoglioso, Marguerite. 2009. *The Cult of Divine Birth in Ancient Greece*. New York: Palgrave Macmillan.

Scholem, Gershom. 1965. *On the Kabbalah and its Symbolism*. New York: Schocken Books.

Scholem, Gershom. 1971. *The Messianic Idea in Judaism*. New York: Schocken Books.

Scholem, Gershom. 1974. *Major Trends in Jewish Mysticism*. New York: Schocken Books.

Seidel, Michael A. 1976. *Epic Geography: James Joyce's "Ulysses"*. Princeton: Princeton University Press.

Sidorsky, David. 2001. The Historical Novel as the Denial of History: From 'Nestor' via the 'Vico Road' to the Commodius Vicus of Recirculation. *New Literary History* 32: 301–26. [CrossRef]

Silva, Fabio. 2013. Landscape and Astronomy in Megalithic Portugal: the Carregal do Sal Nucleus and Star Mountain Range. *Papers from the Institute of Archaeology* 22: 99–114. [CrossRef]

Silva, Fabio. 2015. The View from Within: A 'Time-Space-Action' Approach to Megalithism in Central Portugal. In *Skyscapes: The Role and Importance of the Sky in Archaeology*. Edited by Fabio P. Silva and Nicholas Campion. Oxford: Oxbow Books, pp. 120–39.

Smith, Frederick M. 2006. *The Self Possessed: Deity and Spirit Possession in South Asian Literature and Civilization*. New York: Columbia University Press.

Stirling, William. 1897. *The Canon: An Exposition of the Pagan Mystery Perpetuated in the Cabala as the Rule of all the Arts*. London: Elkin Mathews.

Thomas, Julian. 1996. *Time, Culture and Identity*. London: Routledge.

Tymoczko, Maria. 1994. *The Irish Ulysses*. Berkeley: University of California Press.

van Reijen, Willem. 2001. Breathing the Aura—The Holy, the Sober Breath. *Theory, Culture & Society* 18: 31–50.

Vermeule, Emily. 1979. *Aspects of Death in Early Greek Art and Poetry*. Berkeley: University of California Press.

Wasserstrom, Steven M. 2007. Adorno's Kabbalah: Some Preliminary Observations. In *Polemical Encounters: Esoteric Discourse and its Others*. Edited by Olav Hammer and Kocku von Stuckrad. Leiden: Brill, pp. 55–80.

Wilke, Carsten L. 2017. Where Geometry Meets Kabbalah: Paul Yvon's Esoteric Engravings. In *Lux in Tenebris: The Visual and the Symbolic in Western Esotericism*. Edited by Peter J. Forshaw. Leiden: Brill, pp. 179–205.

Wolin, Richard. 1994. *Walter Benjamin: An Aesthetic of Redemption*. Berkeley: University of California Press.

Woodman, Leonora. 1983. *Stanza My Stone: Wallace Stevens and the Hermetic Tradition*. West Lafayette: Purdue University Press.

Yates, Frances A. 1979. *The Occult Philosophy in the Elizabethan Age*. London: Routledge and Kegan Paul.

![religions logo]

religions

MDPI

Essay

Invisible Concealment of Invisibility Crypto-Judaism as a Theological Paradigm of Racial Anti-Semitism

Elad Lapidot

Institute of Philosophy, Freie Universität Berlin, Habelschwerdter Allee 30, 14195 Berlin, Germany;
elapidot@gmail.com

Received: 1 October 2018; Accepted: 30 October 2018; Published: 1 November 2018

check for
updates

Abstract: The motif of secret, crypto-Judaism has a history that reaches further back into the theological tradition. It no doubt structurally arises from or closely related to the epistemo-political challenges posed by the unworldliness and absolutely inner being of faith, which in the political or inter-subjective dimension immediately raises the question of evidence. The question of evidence, i.e., for the invisible faith, becomes acute in the case of conversion, where the basic premise is the initial absence of faith. Paradoxically, conversion is consequently the establishment of the convert's fundamental faithlessness, of her originally non-Christian element, which the convert, in the very same act of conversion, claims no longer exists. It is easy to see the conceptual constellation that would present the convert as structural deception. At the Iberian threshold of modernity, in the face of mass Jewish conversion and assimilation, this paradox appeared in the image of the "new Christians", the marranos, structurally suspected to be crypto-Jews, to the effect that the ultimate evidence of faith was a certificate of limpieza de sangre, "purity of blood". This paper will follow the historian Yosef Hayim Yerushalmi in tracing the conceptual link between the Inquisition's notion of crypto-Jews and the racialized figure of the Jew in modern anti-Semitism.

Keywords: crypto-Judaism; Judaism; anti-Semitism; epistemology; politics; religion; theology; Christianity; race

---

The notion of secret, crypto-Judaism has a history that reaches back into the Christian theological tradition. It arises structurally from or closely related to the epistemo-political challenges posed by conceptions concerning the unworldliness and absolutely inner being of *faith*. Such notions of inner being, posited in the realm of politics, society or inter-subjectivity, immediately raise the question of *evidence*. The question of evidence, i.e., for the inner and thus externally, inter-subjectively *invisible* faith, becomes acute in the case of conversion, where the basic premise is the initial *absence* of faith. Paradoxically, conversion is consequently the establishment of the convert's fundamental faithlessness, of her originally non-Christian element, which the convert, in the very same act of conversion, claims no longer exists. It is easy to see the conceptual constellation that would lead to presenting the convert as a structural deception.

At the Iberian threshold of modernity, in the face of mass Jewish conversion and assimilation, this paradox appeared in the image of the "new Christians", the *marranos*, structurally suspected to be crypto-Jews, to the effect that the ultimate evidence of faith (for eligibility to high office) was a certificate of *limpieza de sangre*, "purity of blood". According to historian Yosef Hayim Yerushalmi, the *limpieza de sangre* statutes obtained the highest level of official recognition, by both pope and king, in 1555, "as the last vestiges of active crypto-Judaism seemed to be disappearing and there was no basis for doubting the attachment of most of the New Christians to the Catholic religion".[1] In other words, *blood*, socially invisible element of life, emerges as a political marker with the complete disappearance of its supposed socially and culturally visible manifestations.[2] This could be described as the political emergence of race in the Jewish body.

Indeed, the logic of *limpieza de sangre*—invisible blood as evidence for invisible faith—is pushed to greater extremes on the other side of modernity's threshold, as the transformation of Jewish being is no longer carried out as *conversion*, i.e., as change of inner essence, as transubstantiation, but as *assimilation*, i.e., as change of appearance, as a phenomenal change, whereby Jews remain Jews—ever more so in view of the disappearance of all socio-cultural manifestations of Jewishness. The ensuing structural deception was clearly invoked in 1843 by the first theologian of the Jewish Question, Bruno Bauer: "Only by way of sophistry, of seeming, would the Jew be able to remain in state life; if he wishes to remain Jew, the mere seeming would prevail and become the essence."[3] Essence as *seeming*, so I wish to claim in this essay, will indeed become in anti-Semitism[4] the very operative definition of the Jewish race, of the Jewish as race, the paradigmatic political performance of which would be the "secret society".

The idea that the Iberian figure of the crypto-Jew is a precursor of the anti-Semitic figure of the racial Jew was already voiced by Yosef HayimYerushalmi, in fact this was the main suggestion of his afore-mentioned essay, subtitled "From the Spanish *Limpieza de Sangre* to Nazism". Pointing at "common traits" and "morphological affinities"[5], Yerushalmicalled into question the scholarly maxim of "radical rupture" (id., 25) between premodern religious anti-Judaism and modern racial anti-Semitism, and more specifically "the never questioned postulate of incompatibility in principle between Christianism and racial conceptions" (id., 27). He spoke instead of "latent *racial* anti-Semitism in premodern Christian Europe" (id.), "actualized" in Spain and Portugal. The difference to modern "organized forms of political anti-Semitism" arises according to Yerushalmi mainly from "the totalizing pretentions of modern ideologies" (id., 29), i.e., not from any fundamental conceptual difference.

In what follows, I wish to develop Yerushalmi's observation, by looking more closely at basic epistemo-political elements in the properly speaking anti-Semitic discourse, from Wilhelm Marr to Adolph Hitler. My analysis will show how anti-Semitic political epistemology could in fact be described as arising from and giving radical expression to the conceptual paradoxes already contained in the theo-political figure of the crypto-Jew.[6]

1. Anti-Semitic Discourse

My analysis focuses on the historical discourse that can be most properly referred to as "anti-Semitism". The propriety of this designation arises partly from the fact that at important moments and in considerable circles this discourse has referred to itself explicitly, declaratively, as anti-Semitism; and partly because this is how it has been and still is referred to without exception from the perspective of historical reflection, mostly critical, largely anti-anti-Semitic. It should be reminded however that "anti-Semitism" has in no way been the sole or even dominant or most

---

[1] On the question of the relation between premodern Iberian *limpieza de sangre* and modern racial anti-Semitism, see Yerushalmi and Carnaud (1993, p. 18).

[2] See Anidjar (2014), asserting "blood is the *element* of Christianity", such that "a consideration of what blood reflects, produces, and sustains, what it engenders, must take—as one adopts—the form of a critique of Christianity" (ix).

[3] Bauer (1843, pp. 176–78).

[4] Current academic discourse employs "antisemitism". One of the goals of this essay, however, is to recall attention to the *epistemic* nature of the modern anti-Jewish ideology designated by that name, i.e., its existence as a form of knowledge, a negative knowledge, "anti-", which refers to some object, "Semitism". It is my claim that the epistemic nature of anti-Semitism has been more or less explicitly suppressed by current academic discourse, an anti-anti-Semitic discourse, not the least through the orthography "antisemitism". My deviation from common usage is therefore intentional and purposeful.

[5] Yerushalmi and Carnaud (1993, p. 8).

[6] For an analysis of the marrano as a paradigm of modern *Jewish* philosophy, focusing on the question of language, see Bielik-Robson (2014).

characteristic self-designation of this discourse. In its most crucial moments this term is absent or, as in Nazi Germany after 1935, even explicitly rejected.[7] Referring to this discourse as "anti-Semitism", and thus positing this name and concept as the assembling center around which the perception and comprehension of this discourse are delineated and organized—this operation is a central feature of what I propose to call the discourse of contemporary "anti-anti-Semitism", the central tendency of which is to dissociate anti-Semitism from the Jews. Accordingly, a basic effort of my own so to speak anti-anti-anti-Semitic analysis of anti-Semitism will be to *suspend* the very designation "anti-Semitism", at least as a defining term for the conceptual unity of this discourse, i.e., for what constitutes it as *one*, as *this specific* discourse. Instead, as an initial and tentative attempt, I will indicate a few elements that, so it seems to me, constitute the specificity of so-called anti-Semitism as a reaction to and reformulation of the Jewish Question, and thus, fundamentally, as a modern perception and, most broadly speaking, *knowledge* of Jewish being.

It may sound trivial, but is not: anti-Semitism's central concern has indeed been the Question of the Jews. The Question of the Jews, or Jewish Question, is not an abstract question, but a concrete historical discourse. The Jewish Question has arisen from and concerns what is known as the emancipation of the Jews, the event in which Jews were to become part of the modern European polity.[8] A central, perhaps the central motif of anti-Semitism is the notion or image of Jewish emancipation and assimilation as a *defining* event of modernity, and thus of the Jewish Question as the decisive question of modern politics. This radical *significance* given to Jews by anti-Semitism, in manifold expressions, from early programmatic manifestos to the global politics of the Third Reich, in which the Jews feature as a corner stone for the entire structure of worldview and agenda, this radical significance is without doubt one of the greatest mysteries posed by anti-Semitism to anti-anti-Semitism.

More specifically, however, anti-Semitic discourse is defined by a fundamental *skepsis* regarding the precise nature and significance of the Jewish event of modernity. In this discourse, the emancipation and assimilation of the Jews, rather than signifying the ultimate triumph of human progress and civilization, signifies its ultimate downfall. At work here is something like a critical phenomenology: the disappearance of the Jews by the effect of assimilation would not arise from the non-existence of the Jews, but rather from their omnipresence, what Marx, in his famous response to Bruno Bauer, called "the Judaism of bourgeois society"[9]. It is this basic observation, in its specific anti-Semitic interpretation, which has no doubt guided the thought of Wilhelm Marr, "the Patriarch of anti-Semitism", who was greatly influenced by Marx.[10] Marr's most well-known work, published in 1879, was indeed called *The Triumph of Judaism over Germanism. Considered from a Non-Confessional Standpoint*[11]. This text is deemed as one of the first anti-Semitic manifests, though it makes no mention of the term "anti-Semitism" (it does occasionally use "Semitic"). In it, Marr writes: "I hereby loudly proclaim, with no ironic intention, the triumph of Judaism in world history" (*TJ*, 4). The same self-conscious spirit of paradox and social critique ("with no ironic intention") seems to characterize all proclamations on the *Verjudung*, the "Jewification" of modern society, such as another of Marr's sources of inspiration, Richard Wagner[12], and one of the louder voices of French anti-Semitism, Edouard Droumond, who a few years after Marr exposed "The Jewish France".[13]

---

7   Nipperdy and Rürup (1972, p. 151). See also Zimmermann (1986).
8   On the semantic history of the "Jewish Question", see Toury (1966). Toury's general conclusion was that "[t]he catchword *Judenfrage* emerged at the crossroads between old and new Jewry and between traditional Jew-hatred and new extreme antisemitism. In its anti-Jewish context it denied the feasibility of emancipation, or—where emancipation had been granted—its capability of solving the problem of Jewish integration" (p. 106).
9   Marx (1981, p. 374).
10 "The Patriarch of anti-Semitism" is how Marr reportedly called himself, see Zimmermann (1986, p. vii). For Marx's influence on Marr, see Marx (1981, p. 73).
11 Marr (1879).
12 Wagner (Wagner 1869, p. 12), writing on the *Verjudung* of modern art.
13 (Drumont 1886).

The title of Marr's book reveals, however, another basic feature of anti-Semitic discourse. The alleged "Triumph of Judaism" is over *Germanentum*, "Germanism". In other words, the paradigmatic rivalry and difference of Judaism, the paradigmatic difference that *constitutes* "Judaism", is not understood to be a difference vis-à-vis Christianity. Indeed, as Marr's subtitle asserts, anti-Semitism is the formulation and deployment of the Jewish Question "from a non-confessional standpoint". This is a crucial point. Anti-Semitism seems to fully subscribe to Marx's critique of Bauer, namely his critique of the religious-theological, the basically Christian framing of the Jewish Question. Indeed, one of the central solidarities between anti-Semitism and its anti-anti-Semitic critique is, as Yerushalmi pointed out, the assertion of a fundamental break and rupture, a decisive difference, between "modern" non-religious anti-Semitism and "traditional" religious anti-Judaism. Marr in fact sounds almost like quoting Marx when he declares that the Question of the Jews is not confessional but rather "a social-political question" (id., 41). That the phenomenon of Judaism is not primarily religious, and thus should not be primarily interpreted and not even thematized in "confessional" categories, is also what Adolph Hitler will later describe as a formative realization, namely that the Jews are "not German of a special confession, but a different people".[14] This proclaimed non-Christian perception of Judaism will manifest itself in the Nazis refusal to recognize Jewish converts to Christianity as non-Jews. In fact, anti-Semitism may be said to have gone even beyond Marx in de-Christianizing Judaism. Seemingly, anti-Semitic discourse departs from Christian theology so radically, that, unlike Marx, it no longer even *names* the object of its antagonism by the Christian category of "the Jews", but rather reverts to the scientifically sounding term "Semitism".

It is important to indicate the significance and potential fruitfulness of critiquing the dominance of Christian theological perception of the Jews, down to the very category "Jew". Indeed, as is often the case in the dynamics and history of discourse and thought, anti-Semitic discourse too, even in its worst, contains elements of enhanced clarity, in this case concerning the question of the Jews. Accordingly, be that in distorted forms and to sinister effects, it may strangely allow the appearance of a non-Christian image of the Jews, which would be closer to a Jewish self-understanding. Thus, the afore-mentioned Nazi non-recognition of Jews' conversion to Christianity as expunging their Jewishness, which, as I will immediately discuss, was motivated racially, and has been justly condemned as such, nonetheless has been de facto the dismissal of a Christian principle, i.e., faith, as defining Jewish being, which in this sense is consistent with historically dominant inner Jewish perspectives. Obviously, *not* believing in Christ has not been the foundational principle of historical Jewish self-understanding.

And yet, on a closer look, the contrast between anti-Semitism and theological anti-Judaism is less radical than both anti-Semitism and anti-anti-Semitism have it seem. On the level of naming, as already mentioned, the "Semitic" terminology has scarcely ever replaced the "Jewish". Interestingly, as Moshe Zimmermann showed, Marr's partner in founding the *Anti-Semiten-Liga*, the "League of Anti-Semites", in the same year that Marr's book was published, 1879, understood "Semitism" to designate a specifically Jewish mindset, expressed in Jewish *religion*, to the exclusion of non religious "Jewish Germans".[15] In this sense, the term "anti-Semitism", with its "appearance of scientificity", served to designate the spirit of Judaism, in contrast to Jewish being merely in the flesh. In other words, the term "anti-Semitism" may be even said to have had an *anti-racist* intention. The continuity with Christian anti-Judaism manifests itself, however, most clearly in the fact that anti-Semites, in contrast to Marx, never ceased from speaking of Jews. Whereas Marx, after the polemic with Bauer "On the Jewish Question", will scarcely ever again write about "Jews", will indeed replace the theological categories of Christians and Jews with socio-economico-political categories such as Bourgeois and Proletariats, Jews—and not "Semites"—are the constant center of anti-Semitism. Long before the Nazis

---

[14]   (Hitler 1943).
[15]   Zimmermann (1986, p. 91).

prohibited the use of the term "anti-Semitism" for describing their anti-Jewish politics, already in 1907, one of the most canonic anti-Semitic texts of the time, the title of which tellingly asserting its canonicity in theological terms, *Anti-Semiten-Katechismus*, "the Catechism of the Anti-Semites", changed its title to *Handbuch der Judenfrage*, the "Handbook of the Jewish Question". The "Catechism" had been published by Theodor Fritsch since 1887, and from the very beginning defined "anti-Semites" as "anti-Jewish" (*Judengegner*).[16] 8 years earlier, the League of Anti-Semites, in its bylaws, defines its objective as "saving our German fatherland from the complete *Verjudung*".[17]

In fact, considered from the point of view of political epistemology, as Yerushalmi noted, "modern" anti-Semitism is intimately connected to "religious" anti-Judaism. In epistemo-political terms, so I wish to argue, its "anti-confessional" standpoint does not as radically break with theology as Marx did. Rather, it remains within the *same* discourse and only *performs* it from a different standpoint. This standpoint, so my basic claim, the standpoint or perspective of "political" anti-Semitism within the Christian theological discourse, has as its organizing concept the category of "race". Epistemo-politically, "race" stands in a fundamentally different kind of opposition to "faith" as "class". The anti-theological force of Marx's notion of "class" is the attempted localization of political being and agency within social history, in explicit polemics with the utopian unworldliness—the "illusion"—of Christian spirit as consummated in the bourgeois state. In contrast to this, the force of the notion of "race" is the attempted scientific *grounding* of the spirit's consummation in modern enlightenment. Race is the *negative* of Spirit: it is the negative a-historical ground of history, which is nothing but the history of race's negation in the gradual "progress of spiritualism".[18]

2. Racial Epistemology of the Invisible

It is indeed the concept and idea of "race" that shapes anti-Semitic politics, from Marr to Hitler. My claim is that "political" anti-Semitism draws the most fundamental consequences from this category. I already noted how for the anti-Semites the emancipation and assimilation, i.e., the *disappearance* of the Jews in the modern polity, constitutes the critical political event of modernity. I also noted how the anti-Semites, like Marx's "On the Jewish Question", see in this disappearance "the triumph of Judaism". Both Marx and the anti-Semites thus indeed interpret the disappearance of the Jews not as the dissolution but on the contrary as the full realization of Jewish being. This, however, in two fundamentally different ways. For Marx, "Judaism" is a socio-political form that "disappeared" only insofar as it has become all too visible, in the omnipresent form of the "moneymen". For the anti-Semites, in contrast, the disappearance of the Jews means literally that the Jews have become invisible, imperceptible in any social and cultural phenomena, and it is this very invisibility which constitutes the consummation of Jewish being, namely as a "Semitic race"[19]. Indeed, in contrast to Ernest Renan, for instance, who identifies the contemporary paradigm of Semitic race-spirit in Muslim Turkey, the most *visible* Other of Christian Europe,[20] for the anti-Semites, the paradigmatic phenomenon of the Semitism is the *invisibility* of the assimilated European Jews.

This fundamental anti-Semitic position could in fact be said to be more consistent with the category of "race" than Renan's. Race, as the negative of spirit and just like spirit, lies outside of history. It is the key to history inasmuch as history is the manifestation, expression and therefore phenomenon or trace of race. However, history remains mere phenomenon of race—it is not race itself. The force of the race category is precisely that it transcends history. Accordingly, inasmuch as historical, social, political, cultural phenomena can be traced back to race, race itself cannot be traced back to

---

[16] (Fritsch 1893).
[17] des Vereins (1879).
[18] Renan (1855): "[A] progress of spiritualism, because it is an effort to make men forget their earthly origin, and only keep the brotherhood resulting from their divine nature".
[19] Marr (1879, p. 23).
[20] Renan (1859).

such phenomena. It is rather its independence or difference from historical and cultural phenomena that constitutes the essence of race. It follows that inasmuch as history manifests race, race presents itself most purely in detachment from history, namely as non-manifest or *invisible* in the historical and cultural medium. It is in its historical invisibility that race is most present, as I indicated at the beginning in the *limpieza de sangre*.

There is here a conceptual dynamics at work, which is no doubt akin to the logic operative in certain (perhaps Gnostic) constellations of the theological relation between God and world, and in certain (perhaps Heideggerian) conceptions of the ontological relation between Being (*Seyn*) and beings (*Seiende*). Be that as it may, it is possible, based on the aforesaid fundamental conception of race outside of history, for which the crypto-Jew would be a premodern paradigm, to sketch a very general outline of something like anti-Semitic political epistemology. This epistemology, far from being naïve or unreflective, in fact possesses some central features of *critical* thought, namely—to recall Adorno and Horkheimer—of enlightenment, insofar as it is based on a profound doubt vis-à-vis phenomena and received knowledge. However, as its object, "race", presents itself in invisibility, anti-Semitic epistemology is not just suspicious in face of phenomena, it does not just look for better or more certain evidence, but looks beyond or before evidence—looks *against* evidence. Whereas, therefore, Renan posited race as the foundation of *science*—philology and ethnography—, anti-Semitic epistemology is pronouncedly *anti-scientific*.

In fact, the anti-phenomenal relation that anti-Semitism asserts to its object, Jewish being, as race, challenges the limits of what can be called "knowledge". A basic operation of anti-Semitic epistemology is indeed to discredit and consequently to deactivate all epistemic spaces, all *media*, in which its object may become visible, known. Anti-Semitism is anti-media. More specifically, it disqualifies the spaces of inter-subjective communication, where knowledge is generated as a collective process, as epistemo-polity, and within which the assimilation of Jews was to take place by way of *disappearance*. Anti-Semitism discredits the socio-political media in which Jews were to become invisible: intellectual discourse, literature, press, economy.[21] It does so by qualifying all these media as "Jewish", thus explaining the invisibility of the Jews by their omnipresence. In contrast to Marx, however, for whom the media—"society"—is ultimate reality, which means that bourgeois society *is* Jewish, for the anti-Semites "Jewish" media is a *lie*, which conceals reality, i.e., the real, unassimilated and unassimilable Jewish race.

I once again wish to underline the conceptual solidarity or at least commensurability that this anti-Semitic epistemology, in contrast to the Marxist one, entertains with religious discourse, insofar as it revolves around unworldly faith. There is a statement of Hitler that provides a radical formulation of this situation, when he writes about the Jews, that "their entire existence is already built on one big lie, namely that what they are is a religious congregation, while [in fact] it is a race"[22]. Thus, socio-political media provides the phenomenal space for the apparition of Jewish assimilation, which means the apparition of Jewish invisibility in the socio-political sphere, according to which Jewish being is a non-political existence, a "religious congregation" of faith. This religious invisibility, however, would be a lie, *the* lie: a false invisibility that conceals a true invisibility, namely that of race. Race is the invisible behind the invisible, a real invisible concealed by a fake invisible.

I will shortly discuss the political implications of this epistemology of double invisibility. However, first I wish to indicate, next to its negative, anti-medial aspect, also its positive aspect, whereby anti-Semitism *does* assert knowledge of Jews. This knowledge can only be of course *immediate* knowledge, a highly paradoxical notion, which contains all the epistemological tensions and ambivalences animating the relations between evidence and presence and in fact seems to abolish the fundamental condition of the knowledge relation. Be that as it may, anti-Semitic discourse articulates

---

21 See Fritsch (Fritsch 1893, pp. 17–18); Drumont (Drumont 1886, p. xv); Dühring (Dühring 1892, pp. 13, 55).
22 Hitler (Hitler 1943, p. 253).

itself in fact most frequently in an epistemically critical and reflective manner, its negation of media always entailing the invocation of immediate knowledge or presence, which is most frequently the "instinct". "Instinct" is the liminal epistemic faculty, the proto-cognitive dimension, in which "race" is epistemically operative. "Instinct" is accordingly the faculty by which anti-Semitism asserts immediate relation to and knowledge of Jewish racial being. It is noteworthy how the immediacy of instinct, which explicitly operates as subversive to socio-political media and establishment, and in fact can only possess racial generality, i.e., the generality of organic species, that can only operate in the *individual*, is nonetheless embodied in anti-Semitic discourse as a socio-political, collective figure: "the people".

In contrast to and as countermeasure against the press and literature that corrupt the intellectual, the educated, the cultivated, *gebildete* mind, the philosopher Eugen Dühring, for grounding his view on "The Jewish Question as a Question of Racial Detriment [*Racenschändlichkeit*] for the Existence, Morals and Culture of the Peoples" (1880), thus invoked the "natural instincts and feeling" and the "immediate impressions" of "the low people and the common citizen".[23] Similarly, the historian Heinrich von Treitschke, summoned "the instinct of the masses", the alleged generator of popular anti-Semitism, as the truth-sensor for his famous pronouncement of the same anti-Semitic year of 1879 that "the Jews are our misfortune!"[24] In France too, forremoving the veil of Jewish press and literature, and seeing *the Jewish* France, Drumond wrote, "*C'est dans la rue que je vous propose de regarder*", "I suggest that you look at the street", using "the patriot's common sense".[25] Another one of Marr's sources of inspiration, Richard Wagner, in his *Judentum in der Musik* (1850), already appealed to the "instinct-like", "natural" and "unconscious sensation, which emerges in the people as innermost repulsion against the Jewish essence".[26] Whereas Wagner went ahead to explore this "unconscious sensation" of repulsion in the auditory realm, "in music", it is rather olfactory sensation, "smell", that will reveal to young Hitler the essence of Jews: "I often grew sick to my stomach from the smell of these caftan wearers"[27].

It is illustrative to indicate how this radical anti-scientific epistemology of race related more specifically to the realm of *language*, which, based on the traditional and common conception of "language as expression of the soul", was for Renan the primary medium of race's "manifestation" and consequently the primary medium for his *philological* race science.[28] Language has in fact been one of the most important media of Jewish assimilation. It is as German, French writers that the specifically Jewish being of Jewish authors could disappear, concretely accomplishing Renan's "progress of spiritualism". It is thus that language has become one of the important fronts of anti-Semitism. It is of course a highly complex front, since, anti-Semitism itself operating in language, it could not so simply discredit this medium as "Jewish". Accordingly, discussion on language has given rise to radicalized expression of anti-Semitism's race epistemology, in which, as stated above, the expression or manifestation of race (language) is *eo ipso* the concealment of race.

It is against this concealment, this pseudo-assimilation that conceals crypto-difference, that Wagner wrote on "The Jews in Music". According to him, it is indeed not on the manifest or visible level of language, but rather on the latent, subliminal, "unconscious" level that the essence of language would lie. If language constitutes a "historical communality", nonetheless "only he who grew up unconsciously in this communality also takes part in its creation".[29] Against all appearance, therefore, the Jew, who has been "standing outside of this communality", necessarily speaks "modern European languages" always "as a foreigner" (id. 14), a radical foreignness that Wagner extends by the power of metaphor to "[o]ur entire European civilization and art", which "remained for the Jews

---

[23] Dühring (Dühring 1892, pp. 3, 55).
[24] von Treitschke (1879, pp. 572, 575).
[25] Drumont (Drumont 1886, p. xx).
[26] Wagner (Wagner 1869, pp. 9–11).
[27] Hitler (Hitler 1943, p. 51).
[28] Renan (1855, p. 101). For a broader discussion on the interplay between modern science of language and modern science of race, see Olender (1989); see also Hutton (1999).
[29] Wagner (Wagner 1869, p. 15).

a foreign language" (id. 15). Echoing native or mother tongue ideologies, such as Schleiermacher's ("one [produces originally] only in one's mother tongue"[30]), Wagner thus proclaims that the foreigner, the Jew, may only imitate or reproduce, never "really speak, make poems or create works of art" (id.). The evidence for this latent foreignness, which Wagner paradoxically still insists on providing, he thus locates not in the semantics of language, but, as already noted above, in language as sensation, as sound. It is in the *music* of language, in *singing* that Wagner identifies "the liveliest and irrefutably truest expression of the person's essential sensation" (id. 17). Jewish foreignness would manifest itself acoustically in the "Semitic pronunciation", i.e., "the hissing, shrilling, humming and flawed sound expression" (id. 15).

This last paradoxical piece of evidence for the invisible Jewish foreignness behind the invisible Jewish sameness in language is rendered unnecessary and in fact impossible by the ever radicalizing discourse of Hitler, who draws the last consequences from the understanding of language as "expression" of thought: "A person can simply change the language, i.e., he can use a different language; in the new language, however, he will express the old thoughts; his inner essence will not change".[31] Indeed, race, the "inner essence", is only expressed in and manifested by language, but *is* not language. Language still belongs to media, to society, to history—to exteriority, or in Lutheran terms, to "works". It is indeed at this point that the intimacy of race and spirit, race and *pistis*, becomes visible, as "race spirit" is embodied in one phenomenon of "inner essence"—the essence, the spirit, the liquid of life: "blood".[32] "Race does not lie in language, but only in blood, something that no one knows better than the Jew, who in fact places only very little value on preserving his language, and rather all value on keeping his blood pure". (id., 342).

3. The Secret Race State

I will shortly discuss this anti-Semitic motif of identifying the Jew as the paradigm of race, an identification that may seem contradictory in Hitler's race politics. Before that, however, I wish to point at the latter's politically crucial conclusion regarding language, which in fact stands in direct opposition to Renanian philology. If for Renan's science language manifests race, for Hitler—who on this point, as I indicated, is more consistent with the logic of race—language *conceals* race. "The language of the Jew", he writes, "is for him not the means to express his thoughts, but the means to conceal them. Speaking French, he thinks Jewish." (id., 337). This is the logic that will later guide the "12 Theses Against the Un-German Spirit", a flyer formulating the platform of the Nazi students' *Aktion* that culminated in the book burnings of May 1933, in demanding that "Jewish works shall be published in the Hebrew language. If they are published in German, they shall be designated as translations".[33]

In fact, the anti-epistemic epistemology of anti-Semitism, the epistemology of double invisibility, carries inherent political implications, is *eo ipso* political epistemology. It is after all for a certain *politics* that ant-Semitism has primarily become the name. I already indicated the formally similar assertions of both Marx and the anti-Semites about shifting the Jewish Question from religion to politics, and their formally similar underlying anti-religious or anti-Christian critique. For Marx, this initially meant re-interpreting Jewish particularity as the specificity of a certain socio-political practice, i.e., egoism, which subsequently meant abandoning "Jews" as a political category and politically significant historical agent altogether. Anti-Semitism, in contrast, turns the de-christianized Jews into a paradigm of politics—a paradigm of a people, a paradigm of a state. Indeed, one of the fundamental operations of anti-Semitic discourse has been to *assert* the political essence of Judaism

---

[30] "[J]eder [producireursprünglich] nur in seiner Muttersprache"; see ibid., 60. *Über die verschiedenenMethoden des Übersetzens* ("On the Various Methods of Translating"), written in 1813, Störig (1963).
[31] Hitler (Hitler 1943, p. 342)
[32] Anidjar (2014, p. viii).
[33] See Treß (2003, 2009).

against its religious interpretation. Wilhelm Marr's basic observation from his "non-confessional standpoint" was: "The Jewish 'confession' was nothing more than the statutes of a people".[34] Judaism is not a religion but "the particular Jewish state" (id., 9). I already mentioned Hitler's constitutive realization that Jews are "not German of a special confession, but a different people [*ein Volk fürsich*]".[35] In support for this claim he refers, among others, as Eichmann will too in Jerusalem, to Zionism[36], and to the "factual" nature of the Talmud: "In fact, the Talmud too is not a book of preparation for the hereafter, but only for practical and tolerable life in this world".[37]

Visible here is the assertion of "the people" *against* "confession": the Jews are not confession *but* a people; the Talmud is not about the hereafter *but* about this world. I already indicated how this allegedly anti-Christian position is in fact an anti-confessional position within the confessional discourse: it asserts the political as the non-confessional versus the confessional, "the people" versus faith. The political, "the people", thus draws its meaning from faith, from the "hereafter", i.e., as the *negative* thereof, which is, as I discussed above, "race". The Talmud is not about the hereafter, but about collective life in this world, namely, Hitler explains, it provides "instructions for ensuring the purity of blood of the Jewry [*Judentum*]". (id.) "Not . . . but". This is the structure of the formally critical quality of anti-Semitic discourse, *unveiling* truth behind seeming. For understanding the political implications of this epistemic claim it is crucial to recall the paradox of unveiling race behind confession, i.e., a true invisible behind a seeming invisible, which is the underlying paradox of crypto-Judaism. It is by virtue of this logic that anti-Semitism considers assimilated, i.e., invisible Jews as the most accomplished form of the Jewish polity, an invisible state that would constitute—rather than Renan's Turkey—the most accomplished form of race state.

The political significance of this conception becomes more visible in the—essentially paradoxical—anti-Semitic image or imagination of this invisible Jewish polity. Once again, the comparison with Marx is illustrative. Marx interprets the disappearance of the Jews, Bauer's particularistic "chosen people", in the process of emancipation as the universalization of Jewish "egoism", such that the new Jewish figure is bourgeois society or the common "moneymen". Anti-Semitic discourse, in contrast, interprets the disappearance of the Jews in the imagery of *conspiracy*. Jewish disappearance signifies Jewish triumph not because Jewish politics has become universally visible, but, on the contrary, because Jewish particularistic politics has become so powerful as to control all media, all "conditions of possible experience", and thus to make itself invisible, which is the consummation of race politics.

Herein lies the suggestive power of what will become the canonic document of 20th century anti-Semitism, *The Protocols of the Elders of Zion*, or as titled in the Marsden translation, *The Protocols of the Meetings of the Learned Elders of Zion*.[38] In the present context, where the theo-political figure of crypto-Judaism is posited as an epistemo-political paradigm for anti-Semitism, it is remarkable how the main motifs of the "Jewish conspiracy" theory are already present in 15th–16th century Iberia, as described by Yerushalmi. Yerushalmi describes the "historical irony"[39] in that precisely the fulfilling of the Christian hope of Jewish conversion (assimilation) generated the fear of the "inner enemy" (id.), which in some instances explicitly produced narratives concerning the "existence of an international Jewish plot that almost anticipates the modern *Protocols of the Sages of Zion*" (id., 15).

"The Protocols" are in fact a document and not a text. They are an artifact, a piece of evidence that *presents* the invisible. Their exact content is less significant than their material existence, which

---

[34] Marr (1879, p. 20).
[35] Hitler (Hitler 1943, p. 60).
[36] Id., pp. 60, 356. For Eichmann, see Arendt (Arendt 2006, pp. 40–41).
[37] Hitler (Hitler 1943, p. 336).
[38] *The Protocols of the Meetings of the Learned Elders of Zion*, with preface and explanatory notes, translated from the Russian text by Victor E. Marsden, formerly Russian Correspondent of "The Morning Post", 1934 (no place of publication and publisher specified).
[39] Yerushalmi and Carnaud (1993, p. 14).

attests to the existence and actual presence (the "meetings") of the invisible Jewish polity, and in fact not just attests to it, but re-presents it, reenacts the presence of the Jewish state, in the very clear and concentrated image of the "Elders of Zion", and so *embodies* the disappearing Jews. The Protocols speak in the first person plural of the "we"—they raise the claim to be read as a recording of the *authentic* Jewish voice.

This is why the main question raised by the Protocols concerns not their veracity, but their *authenticity*. This question redeploys the various paradoxes of evidenced invisibility: the authenticity of the Protocols means they make visible the invisible *as invisible*, whose thus evidenced invisibility would be the proof for its omnipotence and omnipresence. The connection of power and invisibility is a political precept confessed to by the Protocols "themselves", stating as their main principle: "Force and Make-Believe. Only force conquers in political affairs, especially if it be concealed in the talents essential to statesmen." (id., 147). Under these conditions, any positive evidence of Jewish conspiracy would *eo ipso* constitute evidence *against* its power. Thus, evidence is provided paradoxically rather by the manifest *opposition* to it, i.e., by anti-Semitism, to which in "the Protocols" the "Elders of Zion" virtually take credit: "Nowadays, if any States raise a protest against us it is only *pro forma*, at our discretion and by our discretion, for *their anti-Semitism is indispensable to us for the management of our lesser brethren*." (id., 169). Anti-Semitism itself would thus be the ultimate living evidence for the Jewish conspiracy, which is so powerful as to generate the appearance of anti-Jewish reality. Similarly, the authenticity of the Protocols is structurally proven by everything that *speaks against it*. Jewish authorship is evidenced by the lack of evidence of Jewish authorship, as Henry Ford's *The International Jew* (1920) argued: "If these documents were the forgeries which Jewish apologists claim them to be, the forgers would probably have taken pains to make Jewish authorship so clear that their anti-Semitic purpose could easily have been detected."[40] Indeed, Jewish authorship is proven by the very *denial* of Jewish authorship, as the argument goes: "The claim of the Jews that the Protocols are forgeries is in itself an admission of their genuineness."[41]

There is still much to be asked about the basic epistemo-political conception and presuppositions that underlie the effectiveness of the notion and image of Jewish politics as "world conspiracy". In the framework of this explicitly *epistemic* study of anti-Semitism, i.e., the study of anti-Semitism as a phenomenon or constellation of *knowledge*, namely of a certain reflective relation to an object, "Jews", it would be important to interrogate more closely how "the Protocols" and their anti-Semitic readings more or less explicitly refer to and represent, and thus constitute a certain *perception* of actual, *self*-affirming political and cultural performances of "the Jewish". One such obvious event was the First Zionist Congress of 1897, which the Marsden translation provides as the answer to the question, "When did the Meetings take place and by whom were the Protocols promulgated?".[42] There is much paradox in pointing at the Zionist Congress as the location of Jewish world conspiracy, of course, precisely due to the *patent* nature of the Zionist Congress: both its own constitutive visibility as a public event and the specific visibility it claimed for the Jews, i.e., a formally distinguished and separate state. In the logic of crypto- Judaism, however, the Zionist Congress, very much like *The Protocols* themselves, was not so much a text as a *document*, which demonstrated the existence, behind or beyond the visible event, of an invisible Jewish society, a secret, *international* Jewish polity, whose paradigm and *telos* is not really a nation-state, but a world-state, a *cosmo-polis*.

---

[40] Ford (1920). The publication states no author, place of publication and publisher specified, and has in its turn raised an authorship dispute resembling the one pertaining to the Protocols. See Woeste (2012); see also Wallace (2003).

[41] As stated in the introduction to Marsden's translation, *op. cit.* p. 137. The text nonetheless continues to explain the argument by criticizing the forgery allegations of evading answer to "the facts": "for they *never attempt to answer the facts* corresponding to the *threats* which the Protocols contain, and, indeed, the correspondence between the prophecy and the fulfillment is too glaring to be set aside or obscured." (*Id.*). Hitler, who radically asserts the epistemo-political power of paradox, typically uses the openly and intentionally paradoxical formulation: "[The Protocols] are based on a forgery, the 'Frankfurter Zeitung' moans every week to the world: the best proof that they are authentic". (*The Protocols*, 337).

[42] *The Protocols*, 137.

In this sense, *The Protocols* may be more cogently considered as an anti-Semitic perception or imagination *of* the Talmud. The Talmudic texts could indeed be described and read as minutes, transcripts or "protocols" of discussions between ancient Jewish scholars, "learned elders". These meetings, not only the ones of late antiquity and middle ages, but also in contemporary rabbinic academies, in contrast to Zionist Congresses, have in fact remained invisible for the European public. The only evidence for their existence is their protocols, the Talmud. From the perspective of my anti-anti-anti-Semitic investigation, it is noteworthy to what extent in fact the Talmud, rarely mentioned by anti-anti-Semitic authors, plays a significant role in anti-Semitic texts.[43] Much more than Zionist discourse, Talmudic discourse in fact contains innumerable elements of a *universal* vision, which may be very reasonably characterized as worldly-political rather than unworldly-religious. An unlikely designation for the Zionist nation-state paradigm, "world rule" could be used much more sensibly for describing the proclaimed Talmudic adhesion to the project of *ribonoshelolam*, "The Sovereign of the World".

In the anti-Semitic representation of the Talmud the universal is subjugated to the particular: the main point made by all anti-Semitic accounts is the Talmudic political and legal, i.e., *normative* distinction between Jews and non-Jews. It has been of course a traditional anti-Jewish trope, as visible in Kant for instance, to criticize Judaism for being basically a *nomos*—law, institution and culture—of particularism.[44] The unique feature of anti-Semitism seems to be the notion that this particularistic *nomos* is nothing but the expression of a particularistic *physis*, namely race. Jewish law would be the expression of the Semitic race spirit, which is so to speak the spiritual incarnation of race. The primary epistemological feature of this *nomos* is that it is—like race—hidden beneath the surface of historical phenomena: it is a secret racial law of an invisible race state that is most powerful when nowhere to be seen.

In these epistemo-political conditions, the Talmudic or Jewish universal claim can only be interpreted as a Jewish conspiracy for world domination, the basic principle of which is Jewish *exploitation* of non-Jews. Here lies the sense of acute menace arising from the anti-Semitic imagination of the invisible Jewish polity and the modern event or process of *Verjudung*. In political terminology, the Jews are imagined, in contrast to Muslims, the *external* enemy, as the *internal* enemy[45], which always means a secret, invisible and hidden enemy, an enemy that does not *look like* an enemy, but rather as a friend or better—that has no visible distinction at all. This internal political rivalry is paradigmatically described as "a state within the state", an inner state within the state that exploits the state and does so under the false pretense of being a religion. As Marr put it: "[t]he Jewish confession was nothing more than the statutes of a people, which constitutes a state within the state and this by-state or counter-state [*Nebenstaat, resp. Gegenstaat*] demanded very specific material advantages for its members".[46] Emancipation would consequently mean admitting the enemies of the state to be its citizens and potential *rulers*, "equal political participation in legislation and administration of the very state they theocratically negate" (Id., 21), which automatically evokes the image of political suicide.

The more extreme anti-Semitic language, asserting more explicitly and radically the logos of race, does not describe the invisible Jewish state in political terms but in biological terms. The internal

---

[43] There is in fact a motif of "exposing" the Talmud as the secret, anti-Christian and later anti-non-Jews book of the Jews, which operates as a constitutive act of modern anti-Judaism and later anti-Semitism. The history and development of this motif can be traced, in German literature, from Johann Andreas Eisenmenger's *Entdecktes Judentum* ("Judaism Revealed") of 1700, exposing Jews' contempt of Christianity as stated in their "own books", "so far completely or partly unknown among the Christians", to the 1893 edition (Dresden, Otto Brander), which present itself as "literal translation of the most important passages of the Talmud and other Hebrew-rabbinic literature, to a large extent still completely unknown to the Christians", passing through Rohling (1871), and featuring in works such as Fritsch's *Anti-Semiten-Katechismus* (12ff.) and Hitler's *Mein Kampf* (336).

[44] (Kant 2003): "Jewish faith, in its original setting, is a compendium (Inbegriff) of mere (bloß) statutory laws, on which a state constitution was founded".

[45] Cf. Anidjar (2003).

[46] Marr (1879, p. 20).

malignant Jewish agent is not a state nor *enemy* but "a foreign element"[47] or "a parasite"[48], namely an agent whose harmfulness immediately arises from its foreignness to the organic system, something for which Hitler had many names, such as "poison", "spiritual pestilence", "germ carriers".[49] The inner destruction that they signify is not death by suicide, but death by disease. It is noteworthy that the biological semantics detaches its object—and thus itself—from any moral or more generally from any *normative* aspects. The phenomena it describes are not in the order of the political but in the order of the natural. The death and destruction associated with Jewish emancipation arise in a process that involves no real guilt or responsibility, but is moved by organic necessity. In this sense, the Jews are not even real agents or causes, but an epiphenomenon of the inner downfall, parasites not of life, but of death: "like maggot in the rotting flesh".[50]

The powerfulness of these strong images, namely what makes them strong *images*, what constitutes and intensifies their specific operation of making visible, lies no doubt in their insistence not only on the death of the body, but on the body of death, on the body as death. The flesh appears there not as the matter or substrate of spirit and form, not quite as *body*, but as the formless, decaying biomass, which above all provokes disgust and horror. Disgust is the basic relation to the invisible not as the unseen visible, such as the Platonic ideas, which, invisible to the sensual eye, are nonetheless the very intellectual *forms* of all visibility, and so shine forth in beauty.[51] Disgust, nausea, repulsion, is the relation to the invisible in the mode of formlessness, or the invisible as de-formed, monstrous, *ugly*—it not only evades but repulses the eye, it repulses the *will* to see. Jews, the racial being, embody the ugliness of the invisible real, the appalling flesh and blood beneath the skin of appearance. The horror of their image arises from their essential concealedness. The less they are seen the more horrific their image gets. Like Baudelaire's devil, their finest trick was to convince the world, by "the progress of enlightenment", that they did not exist.[52] Or as Hitler put it: "It is one of the most ingenious tricks that were ever devised, to make [the Jewish racial] State sail under the flag of 'religion'."[53] Jewish politics of race is at its peak when the Jew—together with the Marxists—*denies* race: "While he seems to overflow of 'enlightenment', 'progress', 'freedom', 'humanity' etc., he himself exercises the strongest locking-up of his race [...]. To mask his activity and lull his victims; however, he talks more and more of the equality of all men without regard to race and color." (id., 346; 69).

4. Kampf

The anti-Semitic *struggle* against the Jews, an agenda that immediately arises from the anti-Semitic representation of the Jews and that becomes ever more urgent as Jews continue to assimilate and disappear, thus consists initially and importantly in a multifaceted operation of *discerning* and rendering the Jews *visible*. The Jews must be displayed as the invisible being that is concealed by the invisible being they claim and seem to be: race and not confession. Against Jewish denial of race, anti-Semitism proclaims and *asserts* race, is in this sense *racist*. This seems to go completely against something like Renan's "progress of spiritualization", in which, for the sake of the nation, race is to be *forgotten*.[54] In this Christianist modern logic, race is posited as the sacrifice demanded by spirit, which is seemingly

---

47 Wagner (Wagner 1869, p. 31).
48 Dühring (Dühring 1892, p. 8); Hitler (Hitler 1943, p. 334).
49 Hitler (Hitler 1943, p. 62).
50 Fritsch (Fritsch 1893, p. 155); Hitler (Hitler 1943, p. 61); see already Wagner: "the flesh dissolves in the swarming multiplicity of worms" (idem, *Juden*, 31).
51 Plato, *Phaedrus* 250d, as discussed by (Heidegger 1996).
52 Baudelaire (1869), where the devil tells that the only moment whenhewasconcerned about his power waswhenheheard a preachershouting: "Mes chers frères, n'oubliez jamais, quand vous entendrez vanter le progrès des lumières, que la plus belle des ruses du diable est de vous persuader qu'il n'existe pas!".
53 Hitler (Hitler 1943, p. 165). For a discussion of affinities between Baudlaire and Hitler on the question of "evil", see Hill (2006).
54 Renan (1882).

the opposite of racist politics, i.e., the justification of political power on the basis of race, a fundamental feature of all *political* anti-Semitism and a basic law of Nazism.

This is not the place for a thorough analysis of Hitler's race theory, but *Mein Kampf* no doubt asserts race, i.e., the "drive of self-preservation of the race", as the basic principle of politics. "The drive of preservation of the species is the first cause for the formation of human communities" (id., 165); "all events of world history are only the manifestation of the self-preservation drive of the race" (id., 324). Like Marx's "class", Hitler's "race" is the collective agent of history; Marxist history is animated by class struggle, Hitler's by race struggle. However, whereas the *telos* of Marx's history, the end of class struggle, is to end class, like Renan's history works to end race, Hitler's race struggle does not work to end race, but rather to *preserve* race. Race struggle is the "means for promoting the health and force of resistance of the species" (id., 315). Indeed, forgetting race, which for Renan is the condition for the rise and very event of the modern nation, is proclaimed by Hitler to be the cause for the downfall of all great cultures in history (id., 316). It is in properly theological terms that he preaches the principle of race: "The sin against blood and race is the original sin of this world and the end of humanity that commits it" (id., 272).

This terminology, however, simultaneously asserts and undermines the anti-religiosity of the race principle. The proximity to theology is in fact greater than it first seems. It shows itself most clearly in Hitler's and general anti-Semitic narrative of the actual history of race struggle, as articulated most fundamentally and radically by the struggle between Aryans and Semites. As is the case in all race theory, its theology manifests itself in its teleology and eschatology. Indeed, Aryans and Semites are not just two competing races, like all races. Rather, they represent different moments or stages in the principle of race, and thus provide the basic articulation of the logic and *telos* of race as the principle of human history. The Aryan race stands for the end of this history as culture and civilization, is thus the *superior* race, the actual paradigm of humanity. According to Hitler, human culture is "almost exclusively the creative product of the Aryan", such that "he alone was the founder of superior humanity in general, and is thus the paradigm of what we understand by the word 'man'" (id., 317). What precise quality does the Aryan race posses, which qualifies it for culture? The foundation of superior humanity, of "culture", is "the capacity to form a broader commonwealth [*Gemeinwesen*]", namely beyond the natural family, which requires "the readiness to put back purely personal interests" (id., 325). Culture demands, so Hitler, a "will to sacrifice" (id.), a sense of "duty", or "idealism" (id. 327), which means the will to transcend self-preservation and therewith to transcend race. The Aryan, superior race of culture, would be the race that transcends race, the idealistic, spiritual race.

Now, "the most radical opposition to the Aryan is the Jew" (id. 329). In contrast to the spiritual Aryan race-spirit stands the racial Semitic race-spirit, which for Hitler was embodied by the Jews. The Jews therefore paradoxically appear as the paradigm of race politics, the politics based on "self-preservation drive": "Hardly any people in the world have a more developed self-preservation drive than the so-called chosen ones. The best evidence for this should be already provided by the simple fact of the mere existence of this race." (id.) "What an infinitely tenacious will to life, to preserve the species arises from these facts!" (id.), Hitler wrote in admiration. The problem of the Jews is that they are too much race, namely lack "the most essential condition for a people of culture, the idealistic mentality", the "will to sacrifice" (id., 330).

Accordingly, in *Mein Kampf*, Hitler can describe his "struggle" in the name of and for the Aryan race not just as a mere biological, natural necessity, but as a historical event of a religious mission: "What we have to fight for is securing the existence and multiplication of our race and our people, nurturing our children and maintaining the purity of blood, the freedom and independence of our fatherland, so that our people may grow to fulfill the mission that it too was allotted by the creator of the universe." (id., 234). The casual "too", *auch*, is dramatic here. It shows how easily and conveniently, in what familiar and obvious way, the bluntest race discourse draws on the tradition of theology. The theological notion of a collective "mission", a collective chosenness, election and calling, a collective historical pre-destination and destiny, provides the epistemo-political meaning of the category "race". The spirit of race, race-spirit, is a divine calling. The "too" invokes of course the other, more well-known, *exemplary* chosen people, the Jews, Israel in the flesh, the race of Israel. The chosen race of Israel serves as the paradigm for the chosen German race—but not only as paradigm: both as a proto-type and as adversary, namely as an inferior version of itself. Aryan Israel is chosen precisely to fight Jewish Israel: "And so I believe today to act as intended by the almighty creator: by fending off the Jews, I fight for the work of the Lord." (id., 70). Anti-Semitism thus shows itself to be a modern operation of supersession and *Aufhebung*—of the race of Israel in flesh by the race of Israel in spirit.

5. Final Conversion

It is in accordance with this political epistemology that the anti-Semitic *agenda*, its plan of action, its operative *anti*, namely its anti-Jewish war, has taken its shape, eventually amounting to what will be called the "Final Solution" of the Jewish Question, and later the Destruction of the Jews, the Holocaust or the Shoah. I am aware of the temptation and risk of reading history from Auschwitz backward—but there is also a risk in avoiding such a reading, which is the risk of avoiding history, namely as a dimension where ideas become real and reality visible, i.e., history as a dimension of positive political epistemology. Of course, it is only to a very limited extent that Hitler's text can be considered as *theory*: not only due to the strong anti-scientific, anti-epistemic intentionality of anti-Semitism, and not only due to the ensuing powerfully operative, militant and *sermonic* nature of anti-Semitic discourse, pushed to extremes in Hitler's text and speeches. Hitler's text is of course more than that: it is one of the closest things to a universally accessible blueprint and conceptual matrix for the actual politics carried out by both Nazi German state and society. It is thus a manifest epistemo-political location, a strong link between a certain, central and even constitutive modern political epistemology, as I tried to present it in the basic paradox of crypto-Judaism, and a paradigmatic catastrophe of modern politics.

What was conceived, planned, organized, coordinated and carried out on a world scale as "The Final Solution of the Jewish Question" was directly conditioned through the interrelated conceptions and perceptions that were named "The Jewish Question" or "The Question of the Jews", the conception and perception of the Jews as the Question. A fundamental anti-anti-Semitic tendency endeavors to neutralize the epistemic nature of anti-Semitism by denying its Jewish Question any epistemic relation to the Jews—anti-Semitism would constitute no knowledge, neither bad nor good knowledge, *of* Jews. The Jewish Question would have nothing to do with the Jews. This tendency is at least one significant motivation for the very current use of the term "anti-Semitism", a modern phenomenon, which would be essentially separated from traditional, religious "anti-Judaism", which, presumably, *would* know about Jews. Against this anti-anti-Semitic tendency, my analysis shows that the anti-Semitic Jewish Question discourse: first, constitutes a reaction to, and thus a perspective on and a *perception* of the defining modern Jewish event, i.e., the so-called "emancipation"; and second, *conceptually* draws, through race discourse, from the theological tradition. Looking closer at this perceptual and conceptual anti-Semitic knowledge of Jews, I do however concede to anti-anti-Semitism that anti-Semitic knowledge of Jews is epistemologically *negative*, which *eo ipso* also invokes its similarity to anti-anti-Semitic knowledge of Jews. Whereas the paradigmatic anti-anti-Semitic perception of Jews is the negative perception of the Jew "flesh and blood", a Jew without any concept, form and figure, a Jew behind the "Jew", the anti-Semitic perception of the Jews is the double negative of the invisible race behind the invisible confession, the crypto-Jew.

The Final Solution of the anti-Semitic Jewish Question, namely the question, problem or issue posed by the Jews to the modern polity as a different political entity or a different political being, could have been neither conversion nor assimilation. Conversion and assimilation were rather the problem, since it is precisely by disappearance that the invisible comes into being. The less Jewish Jews seemed, the Jewisher they were. The race state, a human base state, prehistorical origin of history, re-emerged from beneath the cover of all its historical manifestations, purely present in its invisible glory. Transcending this origin, this root and race, progressing from race to spirit, to nation, to culture, namely consummating modernity by solving once and for all the question of the Jews, can no longer take place in the dimension of socio-historical phenomena, but must proceed at the root itself, in the dimension of real being, of the individual "flesh and blood". The ultimate conversion from race to spirit is not the disappearance but the extinction of race, the termination of its racial being, its organic life. The final conversion of the Jews into modernity, as the ultimate moment in the European "progress of spiritualization", was to be their conversion from life to death, their physical, bodily, individual extermination. It is through a striking fidelity to this theo-political epistemology that the official post-WII memory of Auschwitz, i.e., its existence as anti-anti-Semitic state knowledge, will in fact conceive and make sense of it by the category of ultimate sacrifice, will name and know it to be *The Holocaust*.

Funding: This research received no external funding.

Conflicts of Interest: The author declares no conflict of interest.

References

Anidjar, Gil. 2003. *The Jew, The Arab. A History of the Enemy.* Stanford: Stanford University Press.

Anidjar, Gil. 2014. *Blood. A Critique of Christianity.* New York: Columbia University Press.

Arendt, Hannah. 2006. *Eichmann in Jerusalem. A Report on the Banality of Evil.* London: Penguin Books. First published 1963.

Baudelaire, Charles. 1869. IV. Petits Poèmes en prose, Les Paradis artificiels. In *Petits Poèmes en prose. Œuvres complètes de Charles Baudelaire.* Paris: Michel Lévy frères, p. 90.

Bauer, Bruno. 1843. Die Fähigkeit der heutigenJuden und Christen, freizuwerden. In *Einundzwanzig Bogenaus der Schweiz.* Zürich und Winterthur: Herausgegeben von Georg Herwegh, pp. 56–71.

Bielik-Robson, Agata. 2014. *Jewish Crtyptologies of Late Modernity. Philosophical Marranos.* London and New York: Routledge.

des Vereins, Statuten. 1879. *Anti-Semiten-Liga.* Berlin: The Saxon State Library—State and University Library.

Drumont, Edouard. 1886. *La France Juive. Essai d'Histoire Contemporaine.* Paris: C. Marpon et E. Flammarion. First published 1883. p. 43.

Dühring, Eugen. 1892. *Die Judenfrage als Frage der Racenschädlichkeite für Existenz, Sitte und Cultur der Völker. Mit einer weltgeschichtlichen, religionsbezüglich, social und politisch freiheitlichen Antwort.* Berlin: H. Reuther's Verlagsbuchhandlung. First published 1880.

Ford, Henry. 1920. *The International Jew. The World's Foremost Problem. Being a Reprint of a Series of Articles Appearing in the Dearborn Independent from May 22 to October 2, 1920.* La Crosse: Dearborn Publishing Company, November, p. 110.

Fritsch, Theodor. 1893. *Anti-Semiten-Katechismus. Eine Zusammenfassung des wichtigsten Materials zum Verständnis der Judenfrage.* Leipzig: Verlag von Herm Beher. First published 1887. p. 25.

Heidegger, Martin. 1996. *Nietzsche I.* Frankfurt am Main: Vittorio Klostermann. First published 1961. pp. 190–202.

Hill, Claire Ortiz. 2006. *The Roots and Flowers of Evil in Baudelaire, Nietzsche, and Hitler.* Chicago: Open Court. Chicago: Open Court.

Hitler, Adolf. 1943. *Mein Kampf.* München: Zentralverlag der NSDAP. First published 1925. p. 60.

Hutton, Christopher M. 1999. *Linguistics and the Third Reich. Mother-Tongue Fascism, Race and the Science of Language.* London: Routledge.

Kant, Emmanuel. 2003. *Die Religion innerhalb der Grenzen der bloßen Vernunft. Miteiner Einleitung und Anmerkungenherausgegeben von Bettina Stangneth.* Hamburg: Meiner. First published 1793. p. 125.

Marr, Wilhelm. 1879. *Der Sieg des Judentumsüber das Germanentum. Vom nichtkonfessionellen Standpunkt aus betrachtet.* Bern: Rudolph Costenoble.

Marx, Karl. 1981. Zur Judenfrage. In *Werke.* Edited by Karl Marx and Friedrich Engels. Berlin: Dietz Verlag, Band I, pp. 347–77.

Nipperdy, Thomas, and Reinhard Rürup. 1972. Anti-Semitismus. In *Geschichtliche Grundbegriffe. Historisches Lexikon zur politisch-sozialen Sprache in Deutschland.* Edited by Otto Brunner, Werner Conze and Reinhart Koselleck. Stuttgart: Klett Verlag, Bd. 1, pp. 129–53.

Olender, Maurice. 1989. *Les langues du Paradis.* Paris: Editions du Seuil.

Renan, Ernest. 1855. *Histoiregénérale et systèmecomparé des languessémitiques*. Paris: Michel Lévy Frères, p. 102.

Renan, Ernest. 1859. *Nouvelles considérations sur le caractère général des peuples sémitiques, et en particulier sur leur tendance du monothéisme*. Paris: Michel Lévy Frères, p. 93.

Renan, Ernest. 1882. *Qu'est-ce qu'une nation? Conférence faite en Sorbonne, Le 11 Mars 1882*. Paris: Calmann Lévy, pp. 4–5.

Rohling, August. 1871. *Der Talmudjude*. Münster: Adolph Russells Verlag.

Störig, Hans Joachim, ed. 1963. *Das Problem des Übersetzens*. Darmstadt: Wissenschaftliche Buchgesellschaft, pp. 38–70.

Toury, Jacob. 1966. 'The Jewish Question'. A Semantic Approach. *The Leo Baeck Institute Year Book* 11: 85–106. [CrossRef]

Treß, Werner. 2003. *Wider den undeutschen Geist. Bücherverbrennung 1933*. Berlin: Parthas.

Treß, Werner. 2009. *Verbrannte Bücher 1933. Mit Feuer gegen die Freiheit des Geistes. Eine Anthologie*. Bonn: Bundeszentrale für politische Bildung.

von Treitschke, Heinrich. 1879. *Unsere Ansichten*. Berlin: Preußische Jahrbücher. Band 44, pp. 559–76.

Wagner, Richard. 1869. *Das Judentum in der Musik*. Leipzig: Weber. First published 1850.

Wallace, Max. 2003. *The American Axis: Henry Ford, Charles Lindbergh, and the Rise of the Third Reich*. New York: St. Martin's Griffin.

Woeste, Victoria Saker. 2012. *Henry Ford's War on Jews and the Legal Battle against Hate Speech*. Stanford: Stanford University Press.

Yerushalmi, Yosef Hayim, and Jacqueline Carnaud. 1993. L'antisémitisme racial est-ilapparu au XXe siècle? De la limpieza de sangre espagnol au nazisme: Continuités et ruptures. *Esprit* 190: 5–35.

Zimmermann, Moshe. 1986. *Wilhelm Marr, the Patriarch of Anti-Semitism*. New York and Oxford: Oxford University Press, p. 114.

MDPI

St. Alban-Anlage 66

4052 Basel

Switzerland

Tel. +41 61 683 77 34

Fax +41 61 302 89 18

www.mdpi.com

Religions Editorial Office

E-mail: religions@mdpi.com

www.mdpi.com/journal/religions

www.ingramcontent.com/pod-product-compliance
Lightning Source LLC
Chambersburg PA
CBHW051313020426
42333CB00028B/3326